The United States

in Central America,

1860–1911

The United States in Central America,

1860–1911   *Episodes of Social Imperialism*

and Imperial Rivalry in the World System

Thomas D. Schoonover

Duke University Press   Durham and London   1991

© 1991 Duke University Press
All rights reserved
Printed in the United States of America
on acid-free paper ∞
Library of Congress Cataloging-in-Publication Data
appear on the last printed page of this book.

Dedicated to the memories of
Harriet Rislove Schoonover, Robert (Bush) Schoonover,
and Werner Biehlig

and to the encouragements in my life
Ebba, Paco, Erna, Klaus, Elisabeth, Dieter, Sandra, Mike,
Crystal, Shane, Cindy, Kevin, and Keith

Contents

Tables

Preface

This collection of essays traces its lineage back to my doctoral and postdoctoral research. I pursued my study of the relationship of ideology and social change by working on the liberal revolutions of Central America. My interest in U.S. relations with Central America was an outgrowth of my fascination with the transnational aspects of the U.S. Civil War, the Mexican *reforma*, and the war of the French intervention in Mexico, all of which occurred in the 1860s. I was attracted to the relationship between liberalism and imperialism and the world aspect of the French intervention; Maximilian and Napoleon III were interested in acquiring influence in the isthmian area as a consequence of their Mexican empire.

After a decade of work in the archives and libraries of Central America, Europe, and the United States, I had ample material for three book-length manuscripts on the 1823–1929 period. I have drafted three "research syntheses," to borrow a phrase from Michael Hunt, on imperialism in Central America, 1821–1929. One will treat U.S. relations with Central America, a second will describe German relations with Central America, and a third will focus upon French relations with Central America. I decided not to undertake a fourth study of British relations with the isthmus because much work had been done on the British in Central America. The initial drafts of the manuscripts describing French and German involvement in Central America were of reasonable length. After considerable cutting and compressing, the 2,800-page manuscript on U.S.–Central American relations was reduced to about 1,400 pages. To shorten this manuscript further, I created a fourth book—this one—out of nine episodes which were related by theoretical and methodological considerations.

These essays will introduce traditional historians to the breadth of research design and explanatory power of U.S. international history when done within a theoretical framework and convince theory-oriented students of international history of the value of archival research, narrative, and the historical method. I expect this approach to challenge scholars, teachers, and policymakers to broaden their view of U.S. relations with the world. I also hope these essays introduce college students, concerned lay-readers, and nonspecialists to the capacity for enlightenment, the explanatory potential, and the social value of a non-nationalistic history which is sensitive to theoretical matters. These essays should also bridge the gap between "nationalist," "realist," "conservative," and "post-revisionist" historians who see the source of U.S. foreign relations as a response—usually altruistic or defensive (moralist-idealistic for the realists)—to foreign initiatives and the "revisionists," or "radicals," or "corporatists" who see the motor of U.S. foreign relations in the dynamic of a U.S. expansive political economy.

In the past fifteen years I have acquired personal and institutional debts on a scale commensurate with the world system theory. Four people are well aware of my debt to them, because I plagued them for all kinds of help over the years—Ebba Schoonover, Walter LaFeber, Ralph Lee Woodward, and Robin Winks. Woodward and Winks guided NEH Summer Seminars which I attended, supported my grant requests, responded to my research and conceptual problems, and encouraged me to continue an endless task. LeFeber read a number of the individual chapters as well as other related writings. He supplied valuable critique and never tired of encouraging me, often when I felt like postponing the project for a century or two (one gets a different perspective on time from reading Fernand Braudel!). My wife helped me with research, editorial and secretarial support. Her professional career as an instructor of languages has reduced the time she can give me but it has not dampened her enthusiasm for my projects.

Many colleagues have stimulated my thinking and helped me improve my work. Hoping I have not forgotten anyone who critiqued some part of this manuscript, I gratefully and warmly again thank Judy Gentry, James Dormon, Matt Schott, David Pletcher, Richard Salisbury, Steve Webre, Brenda Gayle Plummer, Richard Immerman, Frank Merli, John Chasteen, Robert May, Glen Jeansonne, Thomas Leonard, Amos Simpson, Vaughn Baker Simpson, Robert Kirkpatrick, Herman Hattaway, and Brad Pollock. Peter Agree offered counsel and support. Gene Tanke helped me search for a better organized and more explicit presentation of my research. Student aides Mayra Rodríguez, Barbara Drummer, and EkJuana Fruge helped with the word processing through several revisions. Lawrence Malley and Duke University Press have been an author's dream of support and assistance.

A number of foundations supported the research for these essays, which are rooted in my conviction that international history must be multicultural and multilingual to have much lasting value. I have tried to develop a broad cosmopolitan perspective in these essays. Without the aid of the National Endowment for the Humanities, the German Academic Exchange Service (DAAD), the Fritz Thyssen Foundation (Germany), the American Philosophical Society, the Southern Regional Education Board, Tulane University's Mellon travel grants, the American Historical Association's Albert Beveridge Fund, and USL Summer Research grants, I could not have completed the research and writing necessary for these essays (and the three books in manuscript).

During a summer as visiting professor at Cornell University and a year as a Fulbright Senior Lecturer at the University of Bielefeld I encountered colleagues, departments, and universities which strove to aid scholarship in a most impressive manner. I am grateful for those experiences. When the French magazine *L'information* polled European historians, it discovered that they considered the history department at Bielefeld University one of the five best in Europe. *The Chronicle of Higher Education* placed Cornell's history department at the top of those in the United States. I concur with both evaluations.

The United States

in Central America,

1860–1911

Introduction

John Quincy Adams once wrote that "a historian must have neither religion nor country." Unfortunately, many historians of United States foreign relations have not followed this sage advice; U.S. diplomatic history is commonly written from a narrow nationalistic perspective, dominated by assumptions of U.S. exceptionalism and uniqueness. This perspective encompasses two chief qualities. First, it is presumed that foreign historians or leaders cannot share any common historical experiences with the United States, and hence are presumably unable to understand, let alone evaluate, the unique exception. Second, U.S. diplomatic historians have avoided theory as unnecessary and irrelevant precisely because the United States is an exception. These qualities explain why U.S. diplomatic history is often written in an unguided narrative that ignores the abundant materials available in foreign languages.

This volume adopts a different approach. I assume that U.S. historical experiences fall within a wide range of common social phenomena that are shared with other societies. I also assume that there is a necessary and close relationship between a nation's foreign and domestic histories. Because of these shared experiences both internal and external, U.S. foreign relations can be studied most profitably as part of international history. Further, this approach yields the best results when guided by theoretical considerations. The search to find well-being and security for the U.S. political economy can best be understood within a world systems approach. The essays in this book use a theoretical framework and research in various foreign countries to explore imperial rivalry in Central America during the late nineteenth and early twentieth centuries.

Any historical study of U.S. foreign relations, U.S. foreign policy, or U.S. diplomacy can fruitfully be conceptualized and studied as part of international history, for even apparently simple bilateral relations encompass a wide variety of transnational elements that have an impact upon far more than two or three nations. The industrial powers used liberal capitalist tools in the world system in order to cope with domestic problems. These problems—large and persistent unemployment, maldistribution of goods and services, the weakening of national prestige and patriotism, uncertainty about preserving elite and class privileges, desire for a more rapid accumulation of wealth and power, the unreliability of progress under laissez-faire, the restricted national markets, and a lack of safe and productive investment opportunities—all suggested to them the need to expand their spheres of activity. Their fears drove domestic businesses into combinations, larger corporations, and holding companies on the national and international level. The U.S. government, distrustful of foreign penetration of the New World, staked its claim to a privileged position through the Monroe Doctrine and panamericanism. It recognized clearly that foreign competition would undermine the capacity of the United States to use Latin America to ease its own social and economic crises.[1]

The essays in this book point to the broad, multistate dimension of international affairs. The research encompassed public, business, organizational, and individual records from fourteen countries; it was organized according to a world systems approach and on the assumption that social imperialism and dependency theory are useful tools for analyzing the international history of Central America in the nineteenth and twentieth centuries. This approach has a sound pedigree. The French historian Fernand Braudel and the American sociologist Immanuel Wallerstein, to name two of its best-known proponents, have described the theoretical underpinnings and the structural transformations that have defined the world economy since the tenth century. The world systems theory describes the relationships of classes and groups from metropole (core), semi-peripheral, and peripheral states within the world economy. A metropole state, which the United States had become by the end of the nineteenth century, not only controlled the factors of domestic production and distribution but also acquired the political power and technology to control foreign factors of production and distribution in peripheral and semi-peripheral areas. A semi-peripheral state functioned both as exploited and exploiter in the world economy. Metropole and semi-peripheral states exploited peripheral areas (such as Central America, the five states that formed the Central American Federation—Guatemala, El Salvador, Honduras, Nicaragua, and Costa Rica)—societies that lacked most factors of production or were unable to control them.

The world economy has not been a static structure but a dynamic, changing system. Since ancient times, some producers and distributors have recognized that exchange of commodities over large distances generates a large accumulation of value. The variety of products received from distant interchange, by raising the expectations of material prosperity, became the motor for future economic growth. When the European maritime nations realized that only a narrow land band separated the Atlantic and Pacific oceans at the Panama isthmus, Middle America (Central America plus the Tehuantepec and Panama isthmuses) engaged the minds of statesmen, entrepreneurs, and military leaders, who began to contemplate a distribution system encompassing the whole world. (The Suez region, of course, offered a similar hope.)[2]

Social imperialism defined a link between metropole and periphery in which the preservation of well-being and security in the metropole rested on its ability to ameliorate domestic social woes through its ties to the periphery. In the mid-nineteenth century, the United States was a semi-peripheral society. It exercised only limited control over the factors of production—land, labor, capital, and distribution—and was therefore dependent to some degree upon others for its well-being. By the late nineteenth and early twentieth centuries, however, the United States had transformed itself into a metropole state, in large part by using social imperialist policies to exploit the transit, market, and investment opportunities of the Central American–Caribbean region. This process cast many of that region's peripheral states into dependent relationships with the United States. Bernard Semmel, Hans-Ulrich Wehler, and Thomas McCormick have described social imperialism as a policy that aims to resolve internal social problems through a resort to external programs. McCormick, for example, in speaking of the desire "to export the social problem" and "to export the unemployment," succinctly suggests the consequences of this policy. Social imperialism allowed the problems, the burdens, and the injustices of a metropole's political economy to be exported or obscured. Policymakers in the United States openly discussed the expected benefits that social imperialism would confer on the domestic U.S. economy; only rarely, however, did they consider the consequences it would have for the host societies, the peripheral and semi-peripheral states.[3]

The social imperial relationship frequently established the dependent status of the peripheral societies. The definition and description of *dependencia* has been best expressed in the work of Fernando H. Cardoso, Enzo Faletto, André Gunder Frank, and Samir Amin. Dependency scholars point out that metropole development in the competitive world economy required the underdevelopment of the periphery: if the periphery ever became developed, the option to exploit and extract accumulation from it would dissipate. Dependency theory focuses upon the international ties of the metropole-periphery relationship. I use social imperialism to shed light on the impulses operating within the metropole states and dependency theory to illuminate the consequences of metropole intrusions into the peripheral states on the isthmus.[4]

Social imperialism was used in an era of intense competition to transfer internal social tensions abroad to states less able (materially) to respond to the increased burden. The small Central American nations possessed limited resource bases, smaller and less educated populations, and less capital, communications, and technological development, yet they were supposed to bear some of the burden of metropole unemployment and social disorder in addition to their own. Much of the internal disorder in the Central American societies was related to their ties with the metropole states.

The metropole states and the multinational corporations established comprador relations with individuals and groups on the isthmus. The Central American compradors had two chief functions. They facilitated the entrance of U.S. corporations and political influence; and they managed the domestic order in the peripheral society, because disorder reduced business opportunities and increased the likelihood that foreign powers (other than the United States) would become involved on the isthmus. Collaborators in the host society stifled the disorder that arose from nationalist disgust over the loss of sovereignty and from worker protest against imperial exploitation. Often disorder was most efficiently and quickly removed by political repression, but repression generated violent resistance, and the ensuing spectacle alienated supporters of democratic and human rights in the metropole state. When this occurred, metropole leaders—under siege in their own political castles—sought rescue in the quick restoration of order, at times through military intervention to remove former collaborators. The home society—the United States—had been educated to define its well-being, prosperity, and security in terms of events in the Central American (or other peripheral) host societies. Disorder in the isthmus posed a threat to the home.[5]

Central America's relationship to the colonial and imperial powers of the North Atlantic had been loose and unhurried throughout the Spanish colonial era and the first half-century of independence. These relationships would become more intense and disruptive, as well as intrusive, in the last quarter of the nineteenth century and throughout the twentieth century. From the colonial period to about the 1850s, Central America had played a marginal role even in the political economy of Spain; it exported some cocoa, tobacco, gold, silver, hides and skins, indigo, cochineal, and hardwoods, but the total value of these was almost always modest even by Spanish trading standards with the New World. The gold and hardwoods were frequently removed from Central America by illegal British operations on the Atlantic coast of the isthmus—an area that Spain never controlled very well during the more than three hundred years of its colonial rule.[6]

Early contact with European or North American governments during the Spanish colonial years and the era of the Central American Federation (1823 to 1847) had been quite limited because Central America had few products for the world market, and the metropole states had not begun determined competition for the transit. The expanding metropole economies in the 1840s initiated the competitive imperial grasping for land, opportunities, and authority that blossomed into acquisition and intervention in the early decades of the twentieth century. Some of the foreign penetration was welcome, some was not.[7]

In the 1850s, Central America was experiencing its first real opening to the liberal, industrializing states of the North Atlantic. The first sign that Central America was assuming an important role in the world economy occurred with the development of coffee in Costa Rica around 1840. By 1850 Costa Rican coffee was a major export crop. The second sign of foreign interest in the isthmus consisted of two transit concessions granted by Nicaragua: a concession to Cornelius Vanderbilt's Accessory Transit Company which would provide river, lake, and carriage transit along the San Juan River and over Lake Nicaragua to the Pacific; and a concession to a New York group to build a railroad across the Panama isthmus. Both projects reflected an interest in worldwide Pacific trade. Mexico, Central America, and New Granada had negotiated about a dozen unfulfilled contracts in the years from 1820 to 1846. The projects undertaken between 1847 and 1854, the Panama Railroad and Vanderbilt's Accessory Transit, did not, however, satisfy the transit needs of the metropole economies, but merely whetted their appetite for more. The appeals for a canal, a railroad, or an all-weather carriage road increased in the next half-century. The French initiated a canal project in 1879, and U.S.-British interests undertook two trans-isthmian railroad projects in 1869 and 1871 in Honduras and Costa Rica. The first railroad failed in the mid 1870s, but the second, under the guidance of Minor Cooper Keith, was a success, although Keith decided not to extend it to the Pacific because he feared that Costa Rican officials would take a livelier interest in his business activity if they were more efficiently connected to his empire on the Atlantic coast. Keith's activity corresponded with the worldwide surge of metropole activity, not only in the division of Africa and the threatened division of Asia but in intensified commercial and investment activity in Latin America. The United States was particularly concerned that the increased economic activity in and around the Caribbean–Central American region might threaten its national well-being and security.[8]

Several new capital-intensive, export-oriented activities developed in the 1880s, including banana plantations linked to the Costa Rican railroad project and mining operations such as the New York–Honduras Rosario Mining Company which began in 1880. After bananas had built a solid foundation out of the more or less ad hoc fruit-growing activity in the 1880s and early 1890s, United Fruit was formed in 1899 from the combination of about twenty existing fruit and steamship companies. These three products—coffee, bananas, and minerals—formed the heart of Central American export activity until after World War II. The other export products—cotton, meat, hides, live cattle, and sugar—proved transitory and distinctly secondary in producing exchange or attracting foreign capital.[9]

By the 1880s, the Germans were well established in Guatemala, and the British were established on the Mesa Central (the central tableland) of Costa Rica. The British controlled the bulk of Costa Rican coffee exports (with the Germans generally in second place) and supplied most of the capital to modernize and expand Costa Rica's coffee production. The United States and Britain shared use of the Atlantic coast of Costa Rica initially (the railroad was built with U.S. and British engineers and mostly British capital) until Keith transferred the management and headquarters to the United States with the formation of United Fruit in 1899. The British remained influential on the Mosquito Coast of Nicaragua until U.S. interests replaced them, commercially and politically, in the 1890s. Honduras had been largely ignored except for the British extraction of hardwoods on the Atlantic until the 1880s, when U.S. mining, fruit, and lumber interests began investing significant capital in mining gold, harvesting bananas, and extracting hardwoods there. El Salvador did not excite much attention from U.S. interests until the United States began work on the Panama Canal in 1904, at which time the U.S. military and commercial interests recognized the value of Salvadoran harbors—especially Fonseca Bay, which lies between El Salvador, Honduras, and Nicaragua and offers the best harbor facilities south of Mazatlán. By this time, British and French interests had already acquired the coffee trade and conducted much of the trade of El Salvador, although some German shipping and merchant interests were playing large roles.[10]

The small Central American states tried to play the metropole powers off against each other and thus create breathing space for themselves. In the early nineteenth century, when Britain was dynamic and aggressive, they periodically sought U.S. aid. Later, when the United States assumed the more aggressive role, they called upon France, Austria, Prussia, Italy, Mexico, Japan, and even Britain. Seduced by the competitive world system and the preponderant power of the industrializing states, they replaced subsistence agriculture with a plantation cash crop system.[11] Only after being fully incorporated into the world economy did they discover the severe limitations this placed upon their sovereignty and capacity for self-government.

The period from 1865 to 1898 has been seriously slighted in studies of U.S. foreign relations. Most textbooks have devoted little space to it; it has been interpreted as a time when the U.S. government was concerned mainly with Reconstruction and the development of its western states, or as a period in which its leaders were confused and unable to agree upon the proper course to pursue internationally. The essays in this book are intended to support several very different conclusions: that domestic politics worked to promote a program of social imperialism; that the expansion abroad was not separate from the liberal program of the 1860s and domestic western expansion, but was part of the idea of "material progress" so dear to liberals; and that U.S. leaders moved toward imperial policies as soon as they recognized the inability of the domestic economic order to produce and distribute regularly within the domestic market. Within two decades of the 1873 depression, most leaders recognized the need to pursue social imperialism.

In the nineteenth century the major liberal states used power and diplomacy to assure themselves of unfettered access to the linkage between the Atlantic and Pacific half-worlds. The North Atlantic metropole nations—Great Britain, France, Belgium, the United States, Germany, Holland, and Italy—were motivated by the desire to alleviate internal crises or by apprehension over the alternatives of competition—growth or death—that liberal intellectuals and theorists, from Thomas Robert Malthus to Brooks Adams and Otto Spengler, found so threatening and ominous. The metropole powers all competed at the Central American isthmus.[12]

The inhabitants of North America had long recognized a relationship between their well-being and security and the Caribbean–Central American region. In the 1790s the U.S. government proclaimed the "no transfer" principle (the idea that no New World possession of an Old World power could be transferred to another Old World state), and in the 1820s the Monroe Doctrine was promulgated to protect its security and economic interests. The origins of U.S. interest in this region were not only external, however. For many years, a bitter contest raged in the U.S. political economy between the remnants of a paternalistic and mercantilistic agrarian order and the blooming laissez-faire system of industrial capitalism. Both northern and southern leaders responded to internal social problems through external activity. Interests in both sections supported colonization schemes and filibustering to acquire control over Caribbean territory, actions which clearly illustrated the social imperialist presumption that Central America should serve to relieve internal U.S. disorder.[13]

The traditional surpluses in agricultural goods and the slowly growing surpluses in some types of manufactured goods prompted the more far-sighted geopoliticians and Manifest Destiny people to urge securing the Pacific-Asian trade basin. Admittedly, the U.S. economy had little capital to export in the mid-nineteenth century. What capital there was, however, went into communications in the Caribbean–Central American region— the Panama railroad, the Nicaragua transit route over the San Juan River, and steamship lines. Overseas activity spread to Oceania and Asia with Edmund Roberts's diplomatic mission to Asia (1831–1832), Lieutenant Charles Wilkes's naval expedition in the Pacific (1838–1842), the treaty of Wanghia (1842–1844), and Commodore Matthew C. Perry's mission to Japan (1853–1854). These efforts coincided with the signing of transit treaties, the establishment of steamship lines, and vigorous diplomatic representation in Central America to underscore the link between U.S. conduct in Latin America and in Asia.[14] The well-being and progress of U.S. society was bound to visions that connected the industrial and commercial centers of the northeast and mid-Atlantic states with the Pacific basin.

In the 1860s U.S. liberals implemented a national development program which included a national currency, a national banking system, a protective tariff, and aid for communications, transportation, immigration, and agricultural and mining education. By the late 1870s the political economy spurted into a period of rapid growth, punctuated with grave crises that produced widespread social unrest, violence, misery, and political corruption. Because the domestic economy developed unevenly, certain sectors of production filled the domestic market more quickly than others. When a variety of public and private steps proved unsuccessful in halting the recurring depression, cheaper raw materials and expanding foreign markets were touted as panaceas that would produce full employment and thus lessen social strife. Liberalism's focus on growth sharpened both internal and external competition.[15]

Both liberal, free-market rhetoric and collective bodies of capitalists (domestic holding companies and multinational corporations) spearheaded the drive to enter foreign areas. The ideology praised individualism and free market values, but the actual agencies of penetration were collectivized planning organizations. U.S. businessmen and politicians looked first to Latin America for markets because that region had long been expected to become a closer economic partner. But U.S. officials conducted little study of the Latin American economic situation and entered into no systematic consultation with Latin American leaders because the U.S. vision expressed in the doctrines of Manifest Destiny, panamericanism, and the Open Door was restricted to resolving U.S. domestic problems, not meeting Latin American needs.[16]

The panamericanism initiated in the 1880s, which was expected to create the market conditions necessary to assure U.S. commercial expansion, also exposed fundamental differences between the U.S. and Latin American visions. While the United States proposed mainly commercial programs, the Latin American delegates often struggled to include political, social, and cultural affairs on the agenda of panamerican meetings. Selling U.S. "overproduction" (which was in fact underconsumption, since millions of U.S. citizens lacked adequate food, clothing, shelter, education, and medical care) meant keeping domestic employment and production high while increasing the unemployment and subsequent social and political problems in peripheral areas that accepted the exports. Some U.S. leaders recognized this, and a few of them warned that pursuing the Open Door policy would involve the United States in wars and revolutions around the world.[17]

The United States was not the only metropole state that tried to enlarge its marketplace by expanding its power into other regions. From 1870 to 1930, the shock waves of the world economic crisis contributed significantly toward persuading political, business, and military leaders in all metropole nations to expand through formal colonialism and informal imperialism. Despite their free trade rhetoric, U.S. businessmen and government officials did not welcome foreign competition in the Caribbean–Central American region.[18]

In the late nineteenth and early twentieth centuries, the land of much of the world fell under the control of multinational corporations or metropole states (through colonialism). Metropole firms frequently controlled the land, labor, capital, and distribution systems that drove the political economies in peripheral societies. By the mid-nineteenth century, large transnational firms dominated world shipping, transoceanic telegraph cables, maritime services, and marketing operations that serviced the Central American isthmus. Central America, though not a prime example of these larger forces, was by no means exempt from them—a fact that most Central American leaders recognized.

Throughout the world, as well as in Central America, large transnational institutions, other than business firms, were the instruments of metropole domination of political, judicial, social, cultural, labor, and professional organizations. They were of many types: political (the Hague organizations, the Panamerican Union); judicial (the World Court, the Central American Court); social (the Central American Educational Bureau, the YMCA); cultural (the International Conference of Americanists); labor-oriented (the First and Second Internationals, the Latin American labor committee of the AFL, the International Workers of the World); and professional (international organizations of lawyers, historians, doctors). In the late nineteenth and early twentieth centuries, such organizations swelled to international size as various interest groups sought to develop the capacity to interact with the gigantic firms of the world economy on an approximately equal level of organization.[19]

The episodes described in this book may appear familiar to some historians, but they are analyzed here within the context of the world economy in order to suggest their broader and theoretical meaning. Chapter 1 reexamines the common ground tilled by Civil War historians—sectional resistance to a centralized national authority, Southern nationalism, and the European orientation of Civil War diplomatic affairs—by interpreting Confederate activity as a response to the world economy. Chapters 2 through 5 treat the supposed "quiet period" of U.S. foreign relations, by examining specific aspects of the broader world system's intrusion upon regional activity. Thus Chapter 2 investigates the scheming of a typical promoter, John C. Frémont, to describe the uncertain expansion and competition of two states—the United States and Germany—which were passing from semi-peripheral to metropole status. Chapter 3 describes the appointment of a Grant supporter, George M. Williamson, to a diplomatic post as more than a response to domestic issues. As a former sectional leader, Williamson was uncertain whether the United States should pursue a state-oriented, national, regional (panamerican), or world policy. Chapter 4 suggests how two great powers—Germany and the United States (still in the metamorphosis to metropole states)—tested their limits of cooperation and competition, and how the United States was forced to examine the relative merits of regional versus world policies. Chapter 5 discusses the revival of panamericanism as a device to promote social imperialism and U.S. hegemony in the New World. In the late 1880s U.S. officials proposed a regional plan to use the New World to aid in alleviating domestic disorder. A decade later, the United States formally adopted a world policy—the Open Door—yet did not surrender its regional policy.

While Chapters 1 through 5 describe some of the international and domestic problems faced by the United States when it was a semi-peripheral society in transformation to a metropole, Chapters 6 through 9 discuss problems of a metropole power. Chapter 6 discusses President Theodore Roosevelt's role in Panamanian independence. The president used information management to veil the conflict between the imperial need to expand power and authority and the ideological need to maintain democratic and morally just images for the domestic political system. Chapter 7 examines U.S. exports—in both capital and labor—to Guatemala in the early twentieth century; also the racial and anti-American reaction in Guatemala, which was actually a specific form of anti-imperialism. Chapter 8 discusses U.S. intervention in Nicaragua in the early twentieth century. It highlights the manipulation of regional ideas (the Monroe Doctrine and panamericanism) to conform to U.S. domestic expectations. Chapter 9 discusses the efforts of various U.S. officials to obtain long-sought commercial ties with El Salvador. The U.S. government hoped to adjust the Salvadoran political economy to suit the U.S. political economy.

It is not possible with these few episodes to present a complete history of social imperialism in Central America, nor a thorough analysis of how the world system affected all the metropole powers, but they do illustrate how the theories can be used to analyze what have traditionally been small, bilateral episodes within a world system. (Three studies which are near completion on the French in Central America, the Germans in Central America, and the U.S. competition with other industrial powers on the isthmus will combine evidence and theory on a much grander scale.) These essays will encourage historians to reconsider the value of such concepts as ethnocentrism, nationalism, and paternalism not only in U.S. history but in U.S. historiography, and prompt them to reassess the need for transcultural approaches to research. This is not simply the familiar professional call for "multiarchival" research. It is an appeal for greater openness to the theory and methodology necessary to comprehend the cultural values of all the other societies with which the United States must deal on a regular basis. We can profit from a move toward international history in which the U.S. government and U.S. corporate bodies are understood as only a few of many actors in the world system.

The Confederates in Central America:

Coming to Grips with the World System

_____

American scholars writing on international relations during the Civil War have tended to focus rather narrowly on the actions of the Confederacy: its efforts to gain diplomatic recognition, to break the Union blockade and deal with the cotton embargo, to develop its own trading partners, and to attract foreign loans. They have treated these efforts as crucial in determining Confederate successes and failures. (A historiographical discussion of Confederate international history is included in the Appendix.) But this approach, which implicitly assigns decisive authority to the Confederate government and treats Confederate programs as separate from their roots in the prewar Southern political economy, cannot capture the larger reality. So long as the South relied upon a discontented and potentially rebellious labor force, exhausted land, and borrowed capital to produce cotton for export—despite the fact that cotton was not an irreplaceable material in foreign textile production—it would remain on the periphery of the world system.[1]

Although the political leaders and economic elite of the Confederate States of America inherited what historian Robert May has nicely called "dreams of a Caribbean empire," in fact it was the dictates of geography, the requirements of geopolitics, and the realities of the world economic system that led them into efforts to exploit Middle America and its surrounding seas. The demands of a paternalistic plantation economy that quickly exhausted its soil forced them to seek new lands to restore productivity and to maintain their existing class structure. When their westward expansion was blocked by Northern free-soilers and when the war came, this elite turned its attention southward to the Caribbean–Central American region.[2]

Considered from a world systems point of view, the American Civil War demonstrates the limits of nationalism in the increasingly dynamic and inclusive world economic system of the mid-nineteenth century. In that era, any nation aspiring to some international power would have sought to project itself into the world economy by assuring access to the isthmian transit and trade in the Caribbean rimlands. The Confederacy had received a legacy of political involvement in Central America from filibusterers William Walker in Nicaragua and Narciso López in Cuba, and the southward thrust they represented had been intensified by links to overseas trade from ports in Texas and in the Mississippi delta. The world views and expansionist desires of men like Matthew Fontaine Maury and John A. Quitman prescribed a southward course of empire that Confederate wartime leaders could not entirely ignore. Some Yankee entrepreneurs and Southern planters and politicians saw Middle America as fertile ground for territorial expansion and future economic security. Others saw it as offering opportunities to weaken the Union's war-making ability—particularly through privateering raids, which could extract booty from Union shipments of wealth from the Pacific coasts of North and Central America.[3]

The West Indian islands and Mexico could serve as way stations for Confederate blockade runners, and the isthmus was of strategic importance because it contained the only transcontinental railroad in the world (in Panama) and a second transit route in the waterways of Nicaragua. So, while the expansionist efforts of the prewar years helped turn Southern eyes toward the Caribbean, it was the imperatives of the world economic system that made that region a prime target of Confederate activity during the Civil War. As in the glorious days of the Spanish Main, over three hundred years earlier, the narrow neck of Panama served as a conduit of gold from west to east; for many in the Confederate elite, the lure of treasure ships was as strong as it had been in the days of Sir Francis Drake and the buccaneers.

In this century, however, most historians have neglected the story of Confederate interest in the Caribbean and therefore failed to give a satisfactory assessment of its impact on the course of the Civil War. Scholars have for example frequently noted that the Confederacy appointed about half of its foreign agents to posts in the Caribbean–Central American area, but they have said little about what those agents actually did there. The topic has enormous potential for illuminating many aspects of mid-nineteenth century international history: it draws attention to an area of Confederate naval activity that has not yet been properly evaluated; it points up new dimensions in the troubled relations of Latin America with the United States; and it provides the opportunity to examine a neglected phase of Confederate diplomatic history that deserves study.[4]

The Civil War involved conflicting world views. The commercial agrarianism of the South differed from the commercial industrialization of the North in matters of investment, communications, and financial policy, but not in the fact that for well-being and security both societies had to expand their links to the world economy. Many leaders on both sides of the Mason-Dixon line were captives of a European metropole outlook that dominated the finance, insurance, shipping, production, and distribution systems of the world economy. Europe, in turn, sought either control of or assured access to the transit routes (Suez and Middle America) to the Pacific basin, a region not yet fully incorporated into the world's economic structure. If the leaders of the Union or the Confederacy were to obtain a stronger voice in the future of their societies, they needed greater control over the factors of production and distribution.[5]

Both sections struggled for greater control of their destinies, the North as a semi-peripheral state, the South as a peripheral one. A semi-peripheral state, serving as both exploiter and exploited in the world system, had a measure of autonomy in one or more vital areas of economic activity, but not in all. In the United States, by the early nineteenth century the North had achieved semi-peripheral status because it possessed ample land and a sophisticated distribution system rooted in its large, experienced merchant and shipping classes; yet it lacked technology, could not produce many things the economy needed (especially machine tools, which provide the capacity to reproduce industrial machinery), and it could not finance its growth. Peripheral areas, such as the South, rely upon simple economic structures bound to the world economy by the slender threads of several basic products. Alternative sources of the product, substitute products, or altered consumption patterns undermine the impact of peripheral states upon the exchange mechanisms of the world economy. The core areas that dominated technology and the sophisticated financial system were in oligopolistic situations that reduced competition and partially shielded them from the competition of the world economy. The capital accumulation required for the North to achieve metropole status or for the South to achieve semi-periphery status would have to come from domestic accumulation and from exploitation of the world system. Given the core's hold on the processes of accumulation, such a transformation would be difficult, but not impossible.[6]

Confederate leaders acted in ways that suggested they were not immune to the pull of the world system. Their traditions and predilection directed them toward Europe, but reality persuaded some of them of the value of expanding westward to the Pacific, either through California or northern Mexico, or southward to the Caribbean and Middle America. Thomas Jefferson had recognized that the Caribbean could play a vital role in the expansion of the Southern plantation system long before the Civil War. John Calhoun, Jefferson Davis, and other leaders of the Southern political economy had struggled for a railroad to the Pacific. Many historians have concerned themselves with Confederate policy in the Caribbean–Central American area because it was linked to wartime trade; they have focused attention on specific acts rather than on the Braudelian *longue durée*, the long-term, cyclical rhythms that the French *Annales* school has seen as the best indicators of social changes. This focus, though valid in itself, is too narrow. It had been important for a South which relied upon a plantation economy, coerced labor, and external technology, capital, industry, and educational and cultural centers.[7]

In the 1820s and 1830s, when the United States had begun to exploit Central America, it sought trade and transit treaties to facilitate its access to the Pacific basin. In the 1850s, the governments of the isthmian area viewed the impending crisis of the Federal Union with apprehension and a hint of opportunism. When war came, Central American conservative leaders condemned Southern territorial expansionism, but sympathized with the South's aristocratic ("cavalier") ideals and its claim to the political right of secession (a claim that had been essential in their own struggles against the centralized rule of the Central American Federation in the 1830s and 1840s).[8]

The gathering storm in the United States affected Central American affairs in various ways and called for a variety of regional responses. For example, in November 1860, Guatemalan Minister to the United States Antonio José de Irisarri foresaw several major problems as a consequence of "the forthcoming" disintegration of the Union. The Southern confederation, he suggested, would require careful watching because the states participating in it had exhibited the spirit of filibustering. Guatemala should avoid taking sides in the conflict, he argued, because it would have to maintain good relations with the new political units that would emerge from the Civil War. Central American leaders were not shocked when both sides in the U.S. Civil War presumed that Central America should play some role in their well-being and security. They knew that U.S. leaders often saw Central American aspects of their problems.[9]

The Confederate leadership recognized that certain opportunities for promoting its own independence were linked to previous North American policies in the Caribbean–Central American region. The Confederacy had to overcome its expansionist image in order to compete with U.S. diplomats for public support in the area. Southerners operating in Central America had to combat residual distrust of "Yankee" annexationism (Southerners were "Yankees" to most Latin Americans). Nevertheless, the conservative leaders of that region often shared class values with Southern planters, and the Central American conservative elite exploited large landholdings that relied upon coerced Indian labor (which differed, however, from slave labor in that it left the laborers a certain measure of legal and constitutional freedom). Both elites dominated education, politics, and the church, and enjoyed a prestigious status.[10]

The Central American cotton industry inadvertently undermined the Confederate agrarian elite. British and North American merchants had brought the opportunities in cotton cultivation to the attention of Central American agriculturalists. (The Central American area, in fact, was only one small target of the worldwide British campaign to develop alternative cotton supplies.) Using promotional techniques, financial incentives and punishments, subsidies, technological advances, and a host of other devices, Britain induced entrepreneurs and landowners to experiment with cotton production. And when cotton prices rose dramatically after 1861, Central American producers could compete in the world market. As the ex-diplomat and Honduran railroad promoter Ephraim George Squier observed in January 1861, "The Southern troubles are directing the attention of Northern capital & enterprising men to Central America & the W. Indies as a source whence to draw future tropical staples. Secession will be good for sugar and cotton production." In fact, Guatemala, Nicaragua, El Salvador, and Mexico increased their cotton exports during the Civil War. The South's crisis thus brought some economic benefits to Middle America.[11]

After the war, cotton exports declined sharply. Guatemala's political economy, experiencing the decline of world cochineal prices in the 1850s and 1860s, used cotton exports as a cushion for the elite until the liberal revolution of 1871 laid the groundwork for a coffee boom which readjusted wealth and power in that society. Having contributed to the demise of the Southern cotton elite by participating in the process of replacing Southern cotton production, various Middle American governments made clear, when it appeared that the Confederacy would be defeated, that they would welcome white, agrarian immigrants who were without a government's protection. The Central American elites, however, sorely misread the goal of the defeated planters, who were unlikely to migrate to Central America to perform field work.[12]

Central American leaders were suspicious of projects in the early 1860s to colonize Central America with free blacks or former slaves under U.S. protection. The Union's announced objectives were to sustain free institutions and stable governments in Central America and to deny Southern expansionists access to the isthmus, since they had the reputation of seeking to reintroduce slavery there. Northern leaders and organizers of the colonization projects had two goals in mind: the black colonists could conduct agriculture that would benefit Northern industry (by the exchange of raw materials for manufactured goods), and their presence would offer the justification for intervention to protect the transit route if such a step were deemed necessary. But the Central American leaders—victims of past filibustering expeditions which planned to transport slaves into Central America—refused to accept large colonies of blacks under U.S. supervision, properly fearing for their independence.[13]

Several projects after the Confederacy's birth indicated that an independent South, in the quest for empire, might develop closer ties to the world system. To begin with, there were two unsuccessful projects in the west. The first was Texan Hugh McLeod's effort, involving the Confederate State Department, to secure a railroad route over northern Mexico to Mazatlán or some other suitable west coast port, giving the Confederate states an access to the great Pacific trading basin. The second, part of the New Mexico campaign of 1861–62, sought to secure land for a railroad route between the independent Confederacy and California and the Pacific basin. Without fanfare, some Southerners urged the need for a link to the Pacific for future well-being.[14]

Southern expansionism in the 1860s was not only pointed west. In April 1861 Confederate Secretary of State Robert Toombs recommended sending agents to Mexico and Latin America with instructions to establish commercial ties. Southern leaders recognized the opportunity to capture ships and booty by disrupting Atlantic-Pacific interchange at the isthmus. The leaders expected to benefit from the use of ports as privateering havens and for improving trade at Southern Gulf coast ports. Confederate leaders realized that successful activity in Central America, the Caribbean, and in the Pacific would extract some advantages for the South and deny some benefits to the Union.[15]

Later in the war, Confederate strategists attacked U.S. operations in the Pacific and near the Central American isthmus. Some leaders wanted to injure U.S. trade while others argued for seizing gold shipments and capturing ships and cargoes. Though they had only a small navy, the Confederate leaders realized that they could take advantage of the exposed nature of Union maritime activity between California and Panama. The weak Union naval force in the Pacific presented them with intriguing opportunities for privateering and boarding-party operations (to seize private passenger steamers) that could lead to a broad attack on Union shipping throughout the Pacific basin. Too often Southern leaders expressed interest in policies that could hinder Union participation in the world economy, but then opted instead for raids to collect gold and booty, or for the seizure of vessels that could be used as merchant raiders.[16]

A Southern presence in Middle America in the early Civil War months meant that U.S. diplomats had to exercise caution. Union representatives saw Southern sympathizers everywhere and viewed them as part of a grand design to revive prewar visions of empire. U.S. Minister to Nicaragua Andrew B. Dickinson sought to close one consulate and open another in Nicaragua in order to circumvent a suspected secessionist sympathizer who might have been tampering with the mails. Dickinson and the minister to Costa Rica, Charles N. Riotte, wanted to use oaths of allegiance, the power to deny passports, and their role in protecting Americans in order to handicap citizens suspected of giving aid and comfort to the enemy.[17]

Initially, U.S. diplomats expected Guatemala to be the focal point of U.S.-Confederate competition for influence on the isthmus because that state was the largest, the wealthiest, and traditionally the leader of Central American society. U.S. Minister to Guatemala Elisha Oscar Crosby believed that official Guatemalan friendship toward North America increased during the secession crisis. Thus he believed that the efforts of a New York-based company to build water communications from Santo Tomás to the Motagua River would redirect Guatemalan, Honduran, and Salvadoran trade from Europe to the United States. He considered the U.S. steamship lines on the Pacific an important "Americanizing influence" in developing trade between San Francisco and Guatemala. He acknowledged the residual distrust of the United States created by the Walker episodes, and said that Central Americans had united to oppose Walker's filibustering because they feared the extension of slavery into the region. He regretted that during the previous decade the ministers in Guatemala had been Southerners sympathetic to slavery. But he considered his efforts to distinguish between Northern and Southern societies successful and claimed that he had reversed Central American hostility toward the United States. With U.S. influence at an all-time high, he said, the positive feelings toward the United States would undermine Confederate efforts to obtain advantages in Central America.[18]

In reality, however, the conservative governments of Costa Rica and Guatemala remained skeptical of U.S. objectives. Secretary of State William H. Seward complained that Guatemalan Minister Irisarri publicly sympathized with the Confederacy. Irisarri assured his government that he was innocent of any expressions of such sympathy, but he admitted opposing the Monroe Doctrine because it placed "all Hispanic-American states in the sad position of minors submitted to the tutelage of a foreign tutor who governs us as he best sees fit." He insisted that no European monarchy had treated the Hispanic American states as poorly as the United States had, robbing them of their territory, sovereignty, and independence. He hoped El Salvador and Guatemala would receive Seward's complaints in silence, just as the United States had received his complaints about its applications of the Monroe Doctrine.[19]

Irisarri rejected the Union objective of forced unification and supported the Southern position on secession. He insisted that secession coincided with Guatemala's stance during the 1840s. The Southern states were independent when they joined the Union, just as the five Central American states had been independent when they formed the Central American Federation. If the Southern states were sovereign at joining, he argued, they retained the right to leave the union. He urged caution in conversation about the rupture in the Union in the presence of Crosby, however, because President Lincoln had threatened to dismiss the diplomatic agent of any government that recognized the secessionists. Irisarri acknowledged that the Central American states should sympathize with the Federal Union because they had suffered from Southern filibustering. He recalled, however, that New York capitalists and North American journalists had aided the filibusterers.[20] In short, Irisarri recognized kindred conservative values in Southern society, but he mistrusted its expansionism. Yet he also distrusted the materialistic, commercially expansive North.

Central American governments often presumed that Southerners were responsible for filibustering and therefore expected better conduct from the U.S. government with the Southern element withdrawn. The president of the Panama Railroad steamship service contended that Walker had virtually ruined Nicaragua and retarded progress in the rest of Central America. To counter such sentiments, Dickinson cultivated the friendship of Nicaragua and labored hard to alter Nicaraguan anti-Americanism. Nicaraguans, he thought, were "assuming something like the old affection . . . for the United States, [which] is no less encouraging because of its slow and difficult growth through deep rooted prejudice, hatred, and distrust, the seeds of which have been thickly sown by perfidious and abandoned Americans, who have long infested this Country, with the hope of some day making it their own." Annexationism produced a psychological burden: "The dread of their conquest by Filibusters and the consequent enslavement of the mixed population . . . weighed like a nightmare upon the people of Nicaragua. They are breathing more freely of late, under the fervent hope that the great Enemy, which they have so long feared, is now writhing in his last death struggle." The Central American states expected that the federal government's opposition to secession would put an end to Southern expansion. U.S. leaders presented the earlier Walker expeditions as Southern phenomena by disguising the supporting role of North American shipping and financial circles. Central American leaders, well aware that American disputes worked themselves out in nearby areas, such as the Caribbean, studied North American society in order to respond better to North American policies affecting their fate.[21]

During the war, expanding commercial activity on the isthmus attracted U.S.-Confederate competitive interests. The Panama Railroad's steamer line had opened up Central America in the 1850s and the Civil War and the disorders in Central America had not halted the growing trade. Between 1861 and 1865 customs revenues doubled in Guatemala and Costa Rica, quadrupled in El Salvador, and increased greatly in Nicaragua. The dynamic growth of the U.S. Pacific coast had multiplied opportunities to exchange Central American products at San Francisco for products from the United States, Europe, China, and India.[22] The struggle to influence or control the Central American region was an integral part of assuring access to the storied Asian wealth.

Three European powers—Britain, France, and Spain—pursued a more influential role in the Caribbean area during the Civil War. Together, they undertook an invasion of Mexico in late 1861. U.S. protests and the exposure of the aggressive design of the French quickly persuaded the British to withdraw. The Spanish paused, unwilling either to withdraw or to expand their involvement. Only the French sought to pursue the intervention despite U.S. protests. The French government developed an extraordinary interest in U.S.–Latin American relations in the 1860s. It did not see the U.S. expansion to the south before 1861 as merely an expression of planter interests; it believed that the projects to colonize freed blacks and to acquire land in Central America confirmed that U.S. expansionism was independent of Southern forces, and was aimed at gaining domination of Latin America and control of the route linking Europe and Asia. The Civil War offered Napoleon III the option of playing on the fears of Central Americans. As a counterweight, the French proposed a Franco-Austrian empire in Mexico and a reorganization of the old Belgian colonization company at Santo Tomás, Guatemala. A Franco-Belgian company at Santo Tomás could protect French nationals and establish an auxiliary French military base in the Gulf of Mexico. Napoleon III thought that a new Mexican empire, a victorious Confederacy, and a friendly Central America (essentially unified under Guatemalan President Rafael Carrera) would unite under French tutelage to limit North American expansion. He expected to gain support from Carrera and other Central American leaders for his effort to substitute a shared Latin culture (under French direction) for U.S. hegemony in the Caribbean–Central American region.[23]

Early in the war, Southern vessels tried to use Central American ports for privateering and to exchange cotton for war materials. Later, Confederate leaders contemplated using these ports and the Panama transit route as jumping off points for attacks upon U.S. shipping in the Pacific. Various Mexican, Caribbean, and Central American ports served to transship European cargoes to smaller vessels able to run the Union blockade. The blockade runners carried cotton and sometimes other Southern products on the return voyage. The chief Central American port used for Confederate trade was Belize. Belize received Southern cotton, which it exchanged in New York for dry goods, shoes, powder, ball, and shot. The movement of cotton was appreciable. In 1863 Belize imported 768,000 pounds of cotton and exported 2,300 bales (about 350,000 pounds) to the United States and Britain. The U.S. consul noted in 1863 that Belize's "trade and commerce has been principally with the Confederate states," and observed that recruits headed for the Confederacy passed through Belize. In early 1864, when the war turned sharply against the South, he reported that Southerners were arriving to work cotton lands in the interior of Belize. Belize's governor hoped that the United States would permit thousands of disgruntled Southerners to benefit Belize's growth and prosperity. Thus, Belize functioned as a commercial entrepot for exchange, a stop-off station for migrating Southern manpower, and toward the end of the war as a safety valve for defeated Southerners.[24]

Confederate leaders, hoping to achieve maritime objectives in Middle America that would strengthen their war effort, settled for the short-term tactics of raiding commerce. They attempted to persuade the Central American republics to open their ports to Confederate privateers. Each of the Central American states, though interested in reaching common agreement on how to treat privateers, reacted differently. For example, in November 1861 Nicaragua issued a decree authorizing privateers to stay a maximum of twenty-four hours in its ports and to take on "very necessary" articles. U.S. Minister to Nicaragua Dickinson believed that secessionist influence was responsible for this objectionable decree. He thought that Nicaragua's recent history should have taught "her that nothing but harm can result . . . from any intercourse with adventurers who roam the high seas against the laws of Nations and their own Government." He believed that Nicaragua would gladly adopt any corrective which would not wound "Spanish pride." In June of 1862, in response to Dickinson's insistence, a second Nicaraguan decree permitted entry of privateers only in cases of overriding necessity and, even then, did not allow for provisioning. The Guatemalan government, without a navy or good ports, considered it presumptuous to issue a decree on privateering. U.S. Minister to Guatemala Crosby inquired whether he should try to influence the Guatemalan government to issue such a decree. Minister in Honduras James R. Partridge obtained an order preventing privateers from using Honduran ports. He suspected he could obtain a declaration of neutrality if it were considered important.[25] Union diplomats had moved alertly to deny Confederate privateers use of these Caribbean ports, many of which were near the Panamanian isthmus.

From the beginning of the war, some Confederate leaders and sympathizers considered raiding the Federal gold shipments from California, for this rupture of gold would play havoc on Federal financial and trade relations with Europe. Early in the war, Union Secretary of the Navy Gideon Welles had extended special protection to the gold routes. The sparsely inhabited coast of Baja California and the isthmus of Panama were danger points of special concern. In December 1862 the Confederate ship *Alabama* seized the *Ariel*, a Panama steamer headed from New York to Colón; according to one naval historian, this ended any Confederate hope of capturing a gold shipment on the Atlantic side of the isthmus, because it led the United States to initiate an armed escort service after this incident. Nevertheless, rumors continued to surface about Confederate schemes to attack the gold vessels.[26]

Confederate schemes to seize the Pacific coast California gold vessels particularly alarmed U.S. diplomats, and Seward suspected that Confederate operations sought to cut off U.S. ties with the Pacific basin. The vulnerable point was the Panama isthmus. Dickinson thought the consuls at Panama and Aspinwall on the isthmus were reliable and discreet men who would vigilantly search for secessionists trying to operate against the Pacific trade.[27] And the U.S. government believed that its competent consular agents were supported by naval officers and diplomatic and consular officials in Central America and the Caribbean.

Confederate schemes to stymie U.S. use of the isthmus became more frequent and sophisticated as the war progressed. In mid-1862, Kentuckian Asbury Harpending and Englishman Alfred Rubery, both residing in California, obtained a letter of marque from the Confederate government to allow them to seize a California gold steamer. This plot was foiled in early 1863, when the U.S. war vessel *Cyane* seized the *J. M. Chapman* and arrested and imprisoned Harpending and Rubery as they prepared to launch their raid.[28]

The Harpending-Rubery venture was quickly followed by another scheme. In mid-1863 James M. Tindel suggested that a Confederate force of about 125 men could pass from Texas to Matamoros and then split into two parties, with one moving through the Caribbean toward Aspinwall and the other going overland to San Francisco; each party would then try to seize a steamer plying trade with the Panama isthmus. While not adopted, Tindel's scheme refocused Confederate attention on the vulnerability of the isthmian segment of the Atlantic-Pacific trade route.[29]

In August of 1863, Louisianan A. J. Grayson wrote to the Confederate government from Mazatlán, Mexico, that he could find the men, equipment, and vessels to attack Union shipping in the Pacific. He thought he could disrupt Federal commerce in the Pacific "before a sufficient fleet of vessels of war could be sent to protect it." Confederate Secretary of State Judah Benjamin favored Grayson's project if the bonding (a form of insurance for government officials who will be responsible for considerable wealth, especially cash and other forms of liquid assets) prescribed by Confederate law on privateering could be arranged. Grayson assured President Jefferson Davis that with several letters of marque, the original vessel would obtain wealth to aid the Confederate cause from the prizes seized and from additional vessels which it would convert into privateers.[30] For various reasons this scheme withered on the vine.

The largest, most sophisticated, and most threatening Confederate plan for a naval raid was organized in 1864 under the leadership of Thomas E. Hogg. Hogg, born in Baltimore, but a resident in the South during the war, had already failed in a private effort to gain a fortune by capturing Union vessels. In late 1863 he and five associates had boarded the schooner *Joseph L. Gerrity* carrying cotton from Matamoros to New York. They seized the vessel without bloodshed and sold its cargo in Belize, but British officials arrested them for piracy. In the *Gerrity* affair, Hogg and associates had acted as pirates because they seized the vessel as private citizens for personal gain. Privateers, the equivalent of mercenaries on land, acted under letters of marque issued by a belligerent government and within international law. While disclaiming any official role in the *Gerrity* incident, the Confederate government had appreciated the zeal of Hogg's misadventure and aided several of the Hogg party when they were tried in Great Britain.[31]

Although the Confederate government disapproved of Hogg's first escapade, it appreciated his energy and activity, and in 1864 Confederate authorities selected him to head a small group to disrupt activity between Panama and California. Confederate Secretary of the Navy Stephen Mallory ordered Hogg to seize either the *Guatemala* or the *San Salvador*, Pacific Mail Steamship Company vessels making scheduled runs between San Francisco and Panama, and to use the captured vessel to attack the California trade, the Pacific whaling fleet, and the bullion ships.[32] Mallory wanted Hogg to disrupt the shipping that tied California to the U.S. east coast, and he hoped that when suitable vessels were seized they could be converted into auxiliary cruisers for the Confederacy.

After learning of the Hogg project, U.S. officials at Havana and Panama alerted military and commercial personnel. In mid-1864 the U.S. consul at Omoa, Honduras, spotted Hogg and several of his men, but they escaped before he could have them arrested. In early November of 1864, as the result of cooperation between several consuls, an admiral, and a Pacific Mail agent, Hogg and six armed associates were captured aboard the Pacific Mail vessel *San Salvador*. Documents seized with the conspirators revealed that sixteen members of the Hogg party remained at large and that the party had intended to operate against U.S. vessels in Chinese waters after successful operations on the Pacific coast. Since the Pacific Mail steamers carried several guns each, and often transported weapons and military supplies, the seizure of any one of them could have seriously threatened U.S. shipping in the Pacific.[33]

On several occasions after Hogg's capture, U.S. Consul Charles Leas observed small parties moving through Belize and he guessed that they might be linked to the Confederate goal of raiding Pacific coast vessels. In fact, to avoid suspicion Hogg's men planned to board the *Guatemala*, commanded by Captain John M. Dow, as individuals at three different ports— Acajutla, La Libertad, and La Unión in El Salvador. Dow saw two of them come aboard at Acajutla but they returned to shore to await the next ship— probably, he thought, because they had not found the expected members of their party on board. Later, at La Unión, the Panama Railroad agent reported suspicious characters on shore, men who he claimed had left Havana and crossed the isthmus in order to board the Pacific steamer. Originally, Dow considered allowing the suspects to board and then trying to seize them. But with only a few old weapons and a crew he did not trust completely, he decided to refuse them entry to the vessel. He cast off while the would-be pirates cried out from shore, shouting their desire to travel on the *Guatemala*. Partridge later ascertained that they were Confederate agents.[34]

After the incident at Panama and the conspiracy to seize Dow's vessel, California shippers presumed to see numerous threats to their commercial interests. In December 1864 and January 1865, Allan McLane, president of the Pacific Mail Steamship Company, warned of dangers to his vessels from Confederate privateers at Acapulco and Panama. In response, the Navy Department assured the shippers of protection.[35]

Since the Confederate government refused to acknowledge its lost cause when the Army of North Virginia surrendered in early April of 1865, Confederate personnel continued to devise maritime schemes until mid-1865. Confederate Secretary of State Benjamin argued in early 1864 that the U.S. political system was about to be disrupted as a consequence of Confederate action and of further separations in the West and Far West. Under this assumption, he instructed Confederate diplomat William Preston to establish friendly relations with the various Caribbean political authorities in order to establish a more favorable balance of power. Benjamin observed that the postwar Confederate economy would need an outlet for the mining output of Texas, New Mexico, and Arizona, and that a secure passage across Sonora and Chihuahua to the Pacific would furnish it.[36]

In March of 1865 the U.S. consul general at Havana uncovered another Confederate plot to seize a Pacific steamer. The implicated parties—Captain Prince, Captain Charles Austin, Hank Jones, David Johnston, and a Mr. Richard—reportedly left Havana for Truxillo, Honduras, to cross the isthmus and seize a west coast steamer. The Navy Department dispatched a vessel to patrol the west coast of Central America on the lookout for a Confederate pirate vessel.[37]

The Union government did not extract heavy penalties from the participants in the privateering, although Northern merchants paid a price for the Confederate commerce raiding in the postwar decades through higher freight rates and fewer U.S. merchant vessels because so many U.S. ships had changed their national registry to avoid Confederate raiders. Ultimately, San Francisco courts sentenced Hogg and his six companions to hang for piracy. Major General Irwin McDowell reduced the sentence to imprisonment. President Andrew Johnson released all seven at the end of the war. After the war, State Department officials conceded that Southern expansionism in the 1850s and 1860s had diverted Central American commerce to Europe.[38]

The Confederacy exaggerated the power of cotton in the world system and misunderstood its own subordinate role in it. Cotton was not king, and it never had been. Without understanding the ways in which their political economy was structurally integrated into the world system, the Confederate leadership could only stumble toward policies intended to effect a separation from the Northern states and to allow the South to develop its version of the political economy. Without considering the broadest consequences of its position, it protected a labor system that the world economy had already rejected. Instead of following a grand strategy, it pursued ad hoc policies in responding to specific situations. Some Confederates did recognize the tactical importance of Middle America and the isthmus for waging commercial war on the Union, and some even saw transit as a means for expanding the distribution of raw cotton (to Asia) and finding an outlet for a new raw material, the ores of the Southwest. The sparse record on this hints that a few of them even perceived the significance of transcontinental communications for their future as an independent state. They did not understand, however, that protecting their society's role as a raw material producer, by gaining independence, would not be sufficient to lift them out of peripheral status; for that, they would need access to the production, finance, and distribution facilities of the world economy. During the war,

Confederate leaders frequently acknowledged the importance of international trade, only to be distracted by schemes for acquiring gold and booty, or more vessels to pursue gold and booty.

While Confederate nationalism may have been insufficient to sustain a victorious war effort, there is no reason to believe that anything the Confederate leadership could have said or done in the early 1860s would have created the intense commitment necessary to build a resolute national movement. The most frequently cited example of a determined nationalism that succeeded—the Vietnamese movement led by Ho Chi Minh—involved an entire colonial population which had been brutally exploited and mistreated for over a century. In the American South, the only victims of such exploitation were the blacks. White Southerners were not trying to overthrow an authority that had historically exploited them excessively. They merely disagreed with the northern and western sections of the nation regarding what would be acceptable alterations of their shared constitution and political economy; they wanted the U.S. political economy with a Southern accent. Not remarkably, then, there were limits to the sacrifices they would accept to obtain that objective.

2

Speculators and Schemers: John C. Frémont,

Otto von Bismarck, and the Costa Rican Railroad

Since gaining its independence in the 1820s, tiny Costa Rica, with 120,000 inhabitants in the 1860s, had plotted and struggled to obtain a convenient, cheaper communications link with the North Atlantic metropole states. In 1866, it granted an Atlantic coast railroad contract to the explorer, politician, Civil War general, and promoter John Charles Frémont. The Frémont concession quickly drew Costa Rica into the expansionist competition and security consciousness of two newly unified, market-oriented, industrializing nations—Germany and the United States.

Frémont was one of countless promoters who tried to reap benefits from liberal governments in peripheral countries, which frequently expected Western capitalists to encourage development and "progress." Promoters often sought foreign outlets for the developmental energy that found insufficient opportunity in the United States. Costa Rica was bombarded with schemes, mostly foreign in origin, for colonization and development of agriculture or infrastructure. Coffee, the strongest magnet for foreign entrepreneurs, was essentially foreign to Costa Rican society. It had not arrived there until around 1800 and contributed little to the internal economy, but its export potential supplied most of the motivation to develop ports and internal transportation links to them. While Costa Ricans often owned the coffee land, foreign interests controlled the investment capital and distribution system for coffee.

Like all states on the isthmus, however, Costa Rica attracted foreign interest for more than the value or potential of its chief export item. The ability to exploit the world system required the facility to distribute material goods, which in the nineteenth century was normally accomplished by shipping lines, railroads, canals, export firms, and insurance companies. In the 1860s, the expanding political economies of the United States and Germany competed intensely as the world economy became crowded with entrepreneurs seeking to exploit peripheral and semi-peripheral land, labor, and raw materials for profit and to remove the surplus value for the home country. The fact that during the late 1860s a U.S. promoter and a German chancellor were mutually attracted to the site of a Caribbean–Central American naval station and a transoceanic isthmian railroad reflected the competitive yet cooperative aspects of metropole penetration of Costa Rica.[1]

The Civil War, America's liberal revolution, instituted expansive laissez-faire capitalistic programs, including a national currency, a program for incorporating a national market with a national transportation and communication system (the transcontinental railroad and telegraph), land distribution through the Homestead Act, and an immigration bureau to encourage foreign settlers. The liberal objectives of promoting "progress" and increasing the national wealth hastened the development of the American west. The Republicans created the Bureau of Agriculture to increase production from farming and endorsed the Morrill land grant college act to foster advances in agriculture and mining. This liberal program encouraged forces of speculation, self-interest, and acquisitiveness which would create railroads, giant firms, corrupt political machines, robber barons, and a myriad of bright and blighted accomplishments. Liberals intended to unleash energy, and they hoped that the invisible hand would guide it into desirable channels.

As the United States, Germany, northern Italy, and Sweden joined England, Belgium, Holland, and France in the race for progress and prosperity, the competition increased. Many competitors, seeking great wealth at minimum cost, combined entrepreneurship with speculation and cunning. Central America, only marginally valued as a market for products or capital, or as a supplier of raw materials or exotic products, was important to any nation that wanted to enter the Pacific basin. Since all industrial, free market powers eyed at least some part of that basin, Central America attracted increasing attention.

Germans had long been present in Central America. German-speaking craftsmen and technicians had participated in the Hapsburg and Bourbon colonial exploitation of the New World, but their numbers had declined during the years of the French Revolution and the Latin American wars of independence. These German inroads, as well as activities by Britain, France, Belgium, Holland, and Austria, confronted the antipathy of the United States toward European expansion in the New World just as the territorial expansion of the United States, long before the 1860s, had once confronted the authority and power of the European states in the New World. U.S. expansionism had been manifested in filibustering, threats of war, and diplomatic and military rivalries in Central America. Historians have tended to see competition between the United States and Germany developing about 1880, yet the tension had often surfaced earlier, whenever Germans had penetrated an area where the United States was particularly sensitive. Prussia had sent a special mission to Central America from 1850 to 1861. This mission sustained Prussia's claim to primacy in the internal German struggle for unification by obtaining the commercial concessions it considered essential to gain the support of the Hansa cities of Hamburg and Bremen and the manufacturing areas of Germany. In the 1860s, the Prussian leadership sought to demonstrate its capabilities abroad in order to enhance its prestige in Europe and to justify its decision to form a North German Confederation without Austria. These leaders saw the vital role the isthmus could play in the expanding trade into the Pacific and Asia.[2]

Germanic entrepreneurs sought to use the local economies in the Caribbean area as a sponge for small but growing surpluses of German textiles and iron wares and as a supplier of additional raw materials and new products to improve the German standard of living. The Central American–Caribbean region presented opportunities in mining, commerce, plantation systems, raw material production, and land speculation. It offered sites for colonization by the frustrated segments of the German population, and for building market areas and increasing German cultural and political influence in key strategic areas. Some of these "advances" had long been pushed by merchants, manufacturers, and exporters in the Hansa cities and the Rhine and Ruhr areas. Elements of the traditional aristocratic, military, and bureaucratic classes joined the merchants and manufacturers in viewing expansion as a useful tool for alleviating some of the internal problems of an industrializing economy. This policy of social imperialism generated support to pay for the army (and later the navy), to satisfy merchant and liberal groups, and to reduce the threat of liberalization of German politics by exporting individuals who tended to be discontented and reform-oriented. A host of other social problems—the breakdown of guilds, the migration from rural to urban areas, chronic high unemployment, the growth of socialist labor groups, and rising crime rates—lent themselves to amelioration by social imperialism.[3] In addition, the security of German communications over the isthmus would require a naval presence.

In mid-1866, the veteran consular agent Carl Bernhard argued that Prussian victories in the Danish and Austrian wars made it necessary for Prussia to obtain a naval station on the west coast of America to protect "German trade" and "the interests of German subjects," or alternatively, for Prussian ships to visit that coast at least once a year. In 1867, the Prussian commerce minister indicated the increased importance of Central America by filling the vacant consular post in Costa Rica quickly with R. Friedrich Lahmann, a German merchant.[4]

The increasing German presence in Central America produced various proposals for a naval station. About 1866 the German businessman and promoter Edward Delius thought of a way to exploit a contract he had acquired about 1850 from the defunct Berlin Colonization Society. Delius had entered Central America with a Bremen merchant firm about 1850, but had soon turned to other projects in his haste to acquire a fortune. He claimed to hold a contract with Costa Rica which offered large land grants as compensation for the transportation of settlers. By selecting land at potential harbor sites, Delius argued, Prussia could obtain control over the best harbors in the Darien area of the isthmus. The contract did not conflict with the Monroe Doctrine, he stressed, because Costa Rica would retain sovereignty over the land even though ownership would pass to Germany. Adding a mail service to a naval station and the best harbor would, in his opinion, give Prussia a premier position in Central America. He offered to turn the contract over for whatever the Prussian government considered it worth and then accompany the expedition to Costa Rica to negotiate a contract extension.[5] Although Prussia did not adopt Delius's specific proposal, his and Bernhard's suggestions were consistent with Prussian goals that were persistently visible in the 1850s and 1860s.

Costa Rica's search for a serviceable communications route to the Atlantic coast intensified as the coffee production in the *mesa central* (central plateau) grew sharply. Since the 1830s, the coffee trade had fueled the development of the mesa central and the growth of the Pacific port of Puntarenas as an international harbor. The coffee left the mesa for Puntarenas, where foreign merchants normally acquired ownership or agency control over it. Sailing vessels carried the coffee either to Chile for reshipment or directly to Europe via Cape Horn. In the 1850s, talk focused on the possibility of a railroad. Between 1854 and 1857, an Englishman, Richard Farrer, built a nine-mile tramway from Puntarenas to Barranca.[6]

A railroad was of special interest to North American and European speculators because the principal existing transportation route directed Costa Rican coffee to Europe, especially England. The North Americans wanted to redirect the coffee to New York, while the British promoters hoped to retain control of the coffee but profit from the reduced freight costs of the Atlantic route to Europe. U.S. Consul Addison M. Bailey reported that because "of the great cost of transportation over the Panama-Railroad, Costa Rican coffee reached Europe by cheap sail vessels until the last quarter of the nineteenth century." The Panama railroad was feasible only for expensive or compact goods or for freight that could be given a through rate. Since Costa Rica's products did not meet these criteria, producers and merchants in that country sought alternative transportation to Europe.[7]

In 1861 Belgian Army Captain Edmund Pougin proposed to build a road to the Atlantic side of the isthmus in conjunction with attracting up to six thousand immigrants per year to a site in Costa Rica. He argued that a permanent road would benefit the colonists along such a route and would generate return freight for the vessels bringing the immigrants. He advocated a through transportation system to compete with the Panama route, and his fledgling company published a tonnage freight rate below that of Panama. David Hoadley, president of the Panama Railroad Company, suspected that Pougin's project would probably not be undertaken, almost certainly not completed, and if finished, be of no value.[8]

The U.S. minister to Costa Rica, Charles N. Riotte, expected the Pougin road to undermine the high rates charged by the Panama line and thus to facilitate the entrance of U.S. goods into Costa Rica. He was surprised to find scarcely any American goods in the Costa Rican stores. He attributed this to four main factors: "the dislike of and distrust in Americans generally"; the exorbitant prices of shipping U.S. goods via the isthmian route; the fact that Europe, and England in particular, consumed almost all of Costa Rica's coffee; and "the more than wretched condition of the mail-connection from and to the United States." Riotte quickly obtained agreement in principle on improving mail matters. Amazed to learn that the French paid for Costa Rican coffee with flour, the great American surplus product, he argued that significant economic benefits would flow from a commercial treaty that allowed the United States to pay for Costa Rican products with its export goods.[9] Trade expansion, of course, would require improved Costa Rican transportation and external communication facilities.

Around 1860 public and private groups in the United States began to show interest in developing railroad projects and naval stations in the Caribbean area. One such project was the Ambrose Thompson railroad and coaling station scheme in Costa Rica and Panama. In 1860 Thomas Francis Meagher, acting for Thompson, received a concession to build a railroad linking San José with the Atlantic. In 1861, Thompson publicly charged the Panama Railroad with unfair efforts to have his concession annulled, and then claimed victory over it when both Costa Rica and Colombia gave him permission to build a railroad. But because the Civil War made it difficult to unite the necessary technological skills, manpower, and capital, the Thompson-Meagher project collapsed.[10]

In the postwar years, Costa Rican officials inquired whether public interests in the United States wished to acquire a naval station, or whether private U.S. parties wanted to build an interoceanic railroad across Costa Rica. Presuming (correctly) that Secretary of State William H. Seward's "holiday trip" through the West Indies in 1866 was in fact a search for a naval station, the Costa Rican government offered Puerto Limón for consideration and hinted at an interoceanic railroad concession. Observing the difficulties facing the Central American Transit Company on the Atlantic coast because the shallow waters of the San Juan River required offshore loading of goods, Minister Riotte recommended accepting Costa Rica's inducements for a railroad from Puerto Limón to the Gulf of Nicoya. He assured Seward that Costa Rica would concede land, timber, and other privileges in the area around the naval station. Secretary of the Navy Gideon Welles, however, exhibited little interest in Puerto Limón as a naval station, for by the mid-1860s negotiations for sites at St. Thomas in the Virgin Islands and Samaná Bay on Santo Domingo were well advanced. Riotte was not swayed. He claimed that the United States would acquire the best port in the Caribbean and a foothold in a country with industrious, productive inhabitants who were "the only ones of all the peoples of Central America able by and by to understand our institutions and to assimilate with our people." He advised Washington officials that Costa Rica's director general of public works, Franz Kurtze, was traveling to New York in 1866 to raise capital for a railroad project.[11] Interested parties in both Costa Rica and the United States were examining the possibilities for improved communication between the two countries.

One ambitious speculator who became interested in Costa Rican communications was the "pathfinder" John C. Frémont. His venture in Costa Rica encompassed domestic and foreign issues, security factors (military installations and political power), and financial and communications projects. It also reveals the competition that speculative international schemes attracted when other actors sensed that power and large sums of money were at stake.

Frémont has not been well served by historians, if by well served we mean depicted as he was. In two biographies, both recording essentially the same image, Allan Nevins describes Frémont as moral and upright, though sometimes naive and careless. For example, after describing how false statements and misleading advertising led one Frémont scheme to destructive legal judgment, Nevins insists that Frémont's fault "was of omission, not commission," and concludes: "We cannot believe that a man of his sense of honor consented to an improper act, but he did not sufficiently guard against such acts by others."[12] If Frémont's conduct toward weak foreign powers was any sign of his moral and ethical fiber, this assessment is far too kind.

In mid-1866, he tried to negotiate a contract with the Costa Rican government to build a railroad from Puerto Limón to the central plateau and then on to the Pacific. Since he lacked both capital and know-how, or access to either, this was clearly a speculative venture. Simultaneously he pursued a railroad concession from Mexico. In fact, his proposals typified the style of metropole expansion in the nineteenth and early twentieth centuries. The liberal dream of the age, so ardently advertised, was that expansionist projects promised something of benefit to all, but the reality was that the benefits usually came immediately and tangibly only to the promoters, leaving all others to await their reward from the supposedly beneficient natural law of economics. Frémont, like all conartists, pursued this dream. He expected his reward up front; other people or nations would get theirs later, somehow. He sought formal written commitments from Mexico and Costa Rica to provide enormous cash advances, large subsidies, and other benefits in return for his own oral promises to fulfill his obligations. Both countries were fortunate that, although he duped their preliminary negotiating agents, he could not obtain approval for proposed contract terms from Mexican Minister Matías Romero nor from Costa Rican Minister Esquivel Gutiérrez—two cautious, intelligent, and level-headed men. Romero and Gutiérrez managed to deflect Frémont's schemes with a minimum of retaliatory political damage from Frémont and his associates.[13]

Despite its highly speculative character, Frémont's project attracted the services of several technically competent naturalized Costa Ricans, notably Franz Kurtze and Henry F. W. (Guillermo) Nanne, native Germans who had come to Costa Rica about 1850 and built reputations as engineers. Kurtze surveyed the line and Nanne, who worked as a contractor under Frémont until the first $6,000 in drafts returned protested, believed he was responsible for Frémont's adopting Puerto Limón as a terminal. Their talents and labors were appreciated later by the entrepreneurs who ultimately built the railroad in the 1870s.[14]

Riotte hoped that U.S. capital would control Costa Rica's Atlantic coast railroad, despite British, German, and French competition. He suspected that the Costa Rican president, José María Castro Madriz, who was unsympathetic toward the United States and predisposed toward the French, might sabotage Kurtze's mission to the United States. Although Castro had approved the Kurtze mission, he remained apprehensive about entering into contracts with citizens of powerful states. Costa Rica still smarted from the injuries of filibusterers. Riotte suspected that the British minister, George Matthews, was behind Foreign Minister Julio Volio's efforts in mid-1866 to remove the Costa Rican minister to the United States, Luis Molina, and to recall Kurtze. Matthews expected that Kurtze's recall would facilitate a British project for a Costa Rican transcontinental railroad.[15]

As the Costa Rican government contemplated the Frémont contract, it developed doubts. Frémont awoke Delius's interest in his scheme and then authorized Delius to spend "unlimited" funds in promoting the Costa Rican railroad. Volio instructed Gutiérrez to investigate Frémont's financial reputation and the financial strength of his group. Gutiérrez reported a mixture of judgments, mostly negative: D. G. W. Rigges, one of Washington's wealthiest and most respected bankers, said Frémont was "poor and considered as a visionary speculator, with not very strict moral principles": the New York bankers Duncan and Sherman considered Frémont "worth a million dollars, but did not wish to conduct business with him"; the New York firm of Allen and Garrison evaluated him as "poor, visionary and of questionable honesty"; the Nicaraguan Consul Juan J. Barril judged him worth "a half-million dollars and of sufficient integrity to merit the epithet honest"; General Gustave Paul Cluseret, the editor of the *New Nation*, having shared quarters with Frémont, considered him "poor, of poor reputation, undeserving to inspire confidence and easy to conceive bold plans but lacking the tact to carry them to completion"; the financial editor of the *New York Herald* claimed that Frémont had suffered recent commercial and political losses, hence his name inspired no confidence, and he was viewed as poor with the vanity of a rich person. A rare positive assessment came from the Farlee and Piper firm which conceded him dedication, integrity, managerial skill, expansionist views, a fortune worth $3,000,000, and the capability of assembling $10,000,000. Gutiérrez's contacts judged Frémont's business associates—Motlings, Leonidas Haskell, Senator James Warren Nye of Nevada, and Eldridge Pearl—to be poor, speculators, or nonentities.[16] The consensus was that Frémont was a poor businessman of questionable values and that his group lacked capitalists and entrepreneurs.

Alerted by this assessment of Frémont's group, the Costa Rican government insisted upon, and Frémont and his associates accepted, three contract modifications and a compromise on a fourth one. These modifications reduced Costa Rica's financial obligations and required more performance by Frémont before subsidies would be paid. The Frémont group also accepted five minor changes that Gutiérrez inserted to preserve the guarantees and to augment Costa Rican rights. One change denied the group the right to register in the United States, thereby keeping it within the jurisdiction of Costa Rican law. After these modifications were made in February, both Frémont's company and Costa Rica expressed satisfaction with the ratified contract. Many Costa Ricans treated the approval of the contract as a national holiday.[17]

British officials questioned the capacity of the Frémont group to fulfill its obligations. The British consul, Allan Wallis, who had attended the Costa Rican cabinet meeting which had received Frémont's proposal to build a railroad, had expressed reservations immediately. He speculated that the Costa Rican government had accepted Frémont's project not because it expected a railroad to be built, but "to create an excuse to abandon completely the cart road which the last administration began to the Atlantic at a very great cost." At Wallis's suggestion, Costa Rica informed its agents in Paris and London to look for European capital. The Costa Rican government, according to Wallis, "would prefer treating with an European to an American company." U.S. officials inquired about Costa Rica's good faith after the U.S. minister to Great Britain had reported that the Costa Rican consul general was seeking a loan to complete the wagon road to the Atlantic.[18] Gutiérrez denied this, claiming that the activities of the consul general in London had apparently been misunderstood. But it is clear that when Costa Rican officials realized Frémont might lack the capacity to complete the railroad, they revived dormant projects and turned to British capital as an alternative.

Immediately after closing the contract, signs of the speculative nature of the venture began to appear. James B. Hodgskin addressed the Costa Rican minister with a claim that Kurtze had promised him $5,000 in gold to obtain approval of the railroad contract. Gutiérrez denied authorization to make such a payment and referred the matter to San José. His sources in the United States had warned him that "the contract might have been no more than a farce to permit Hodgskin to obtain the $5,000 offered him by Kurtze," and that "conceivably Frémont had lent his name for a share of the $5,000 gold."[19] Gutiérrez's informants advised treating Frémont's project with caution.

Several months later, Gutiérrez's suspicions were deepened when Frémont's Costa Rican Railroad Company deliberately altered its procedures to reduce the participation of Costa Rican agents in its activities. Gutiérrez and Thiesen, the Costa Rican consul in New York, served as the Costa Rican directors of the Costa Rican Railroad Company. After a brief honeymoon period, the company and Gutiérrez moved rapidly toward a divorce when the Costa Rican minister expressed reservations regarding various initiatives proposed to the board. The company assured Gutiérrez that it had the contractually required $50,000 to invest in Costa Rica and that various small work parties were on their way to Costa Rica. However,

Gustave Wagner, one of Frémont's engineers headed for Costa Rica, had to borrow $100 from Consul B. Squier Cotrell in Nicaragua to complete his journey, which suggested the shoestring nature of the project. Although a second small party of Frémont's railroad people left the United States on schedule, Gutiérrez remained skeptical. Riotte concluded that the company was proceeding in bad faith, wishing only to appear to spend the required minimum of $50,000 to avoid cancellation of the contract.[20]

Unable to raise funds in the United States, Frémont's agents sought additional concessions that would enhance the firm's value in the eyes of foreign capitalists. William Aufermann, a director of Frémont's firm, announced that a steamer line was scheduled to run from Bremen over the Antilles to Central America's Caribbean coast. He asked Gutiérrez to inquire whether Costa Rica would allow the establishment of a Prussian naval base on its territory because such a base would supply large advantages to the railroad. Ominously, even before beginning work, the company also requested a reduction of its obligations. It found little hope in Gutiérrez's answer: it was unlikely, he said, that his government would consider reducing the company's obligations until the project was done or nearly done, and presumably that the Prussian and Costa Rican governments, rather than the company directors, would settle the question of a naval station; further, although his government wanted to increase commerce, it would doubtless refuse to sell or transfer any of its territory. The directors of Frémont's company, finding Washington meetings inconvenient and unhappy with Gutiérrez's responses, created an executive committee to meet in New York. Since Gutiérrez could not, and Thiesen would not, participate in the New York meetings, Costa Rica became isolated from company activity.[21] Even after the Costa Rican directors were effectively excluded, the company made no progress with the railroad.

As financial difficulties prevented Frémont from pursuing the project, if that is what he had intended, some Costa Ricans began to examine other options for building the much needed railroad. A court judgment precipitated a sharp fall in the stock of the Atlantic and Pacific Railroad, of which Frémont was the president and major stockholder. As Frémont became poorer, Gutiérrez suspected that Costa Rica's only compensation for this venture might be the company's explorations and plans which would suggest where a railroad could be built at a later date. Seeking a way out of his financial crisis, Frémont asked for guarantee of a section-by-section payment for construction, which would facilitate raising funds in the United States. He also proposed changing the $15,000 monthly subsidy from the Costa Rican government to $15,000 for each mile completed and accepted. Gutiérrez recommended caution. His informants insisted that "the commercial world views [Frémont's group] with much disconfidence and considers them personally of little or no responsibility, to the point where some businessmen refuse to take into consideration any affair in which they intervene." John Meiggs Keith, a materials supplier for Frémont's project who enjoyed the confidence of U.S. businessmen, confidentially confirmed Gutiérrez's views of the Costa Rican Railroad group. In late 1867 Gutiérrez enclosed a railroad proposal from Henry Meiggs, a relative of John Meiggs Keith and a railroad builder in Chile and Peru who associated with some of the richest men in the United States. Until the Costa Rican government finished its business with Frémont, the Meiggs' proposal was meant only for the eyes of Foreign Minister Julio Volio and Castro Madriz.[22]

Frémont's company hustled about in an effort to save the contract for resale. In late August 1867 Frémont's contractors and engineers arrived at Puerto Limón to declare the port open to commerce. A U.S. consular official optimistically proclaimed that the Atlantic terminus work was being energetically carried forward: "Although doubts exist in the minds of many as to the prosecution of the enterprise beyond the point requisite for certain speculative purposes, the [Costa Rican] government . . . shows a praiseworthy disposition to render the company every facility possible for carrying on the work." He said he hoped the project would be speedily concluded, but four months later he reported that it was at a standstill.[23]

By early 1868 Frémont's financial position and economic prospects were collapsing. In early January, Frémont, Senator Nye, and Aufermann complained bitterly that Keith and his associates had not completed their contract to deliver supplies to Frémont's company (Keith responded that he had not been paid for previous deliveries) and that Kurtze had submitted enormous expense vouchers without accomplishing anything for the company. In January 1868, Gutiérrez noted, they "confessed slowly that they had not invested [the required] $50,000 in Costa Rica," when they requested a ninety-day extension to meet this contract stipulation. Gutiérrez recommended that Costa Rica should be fair, but not generous, and should hold the Frémont company to the letter and spirit of the contract. Gutiérrez expected the company to lose the contract for nonfulfillment.[24]

The Frémont group urgently tried to salvage something from the endeavor. Undaunted, the speculator offered to sell his "rights" to either the Prussian or U.S. governments for a quick profit. The company contacted the Prussian government and various U.S. capitalists and entrepreneurs. In January 1868 Frémont and associates negotiated a sale of the Costa Rican Railroad Company to a group composed of Edmund C. Pechin, Albert A. Núñez, and LuRe Tiernau Brien. The new entrepreneurs claimed that the successor railroad company was entirely reorganized and that only finalization of the papers was needed to perfect the sale.[25] The sale hinged, however, upon Costa Rica's granting the new company a time extension to complete the project. When the government refused the extension, the sale fell through. The U.S. consul in Costa Rica decided that some people looked upon the project with "jealousy and distrust." He believed that the Costa Rican government remained friendly toward Americans, despite the poor record of the Frémont group. Frémont's contract was cancelled.[26]

In July 1868 Aufermann lodged a formal complaint against the "unjust and pretended cancellation of the contract." He asked the U.S. government to "protect its citizens" and to bring the matter before the House Committee on Foreign Relations. Frémont complained to Seward about the conduct of Gutiérrez and the Costa Rican government toward the company. Since Seward did not mention the complaint to Gutiérrez, the Costa Rican diplomat ignored the charges in order not to lend them unmerited credence. Hoping to restore friendly relations with the Costa Rican government, Aufermann suggested replacing Gutiérrez as a director on the board of the company. He charged that Gutiérrez lacked the experience and judgment necessary to aid in the management of such an enterprise, and that he harbored animosity toward the company. Gutiérrez replied to his superiors that the complaints against him were no better founded than those against the Costa Rican government.[27]

Frémont's plan to resell his interoceanic railroad concession found the warmest response in Germany. Although occupied with German unification and European affairs in the years from 1866 to 1868, Chancellor Otto von Bismarck of Prussia became interested in the Frémont-Delius schemes. Frémont solicited Prussian funds and participation in building his railroad: he expressed a desire to use German laborers and said that in exchange for German capital to build his railroad he could offer the Puerto Limón naval station and bonds in his company. Bismarck's government was intrigued by the possibilities of a naval station and interoceanic transit. A German engineer who had worked near Puerto Limón for some years claimed that the impregnable port was suited to handle all of Costa Rica's foreign trade and considerable interoceanic trade besides. During early 1868 a Prussian naval squadron conducted a naval survey along the Caribbean coast of Central America. In April the steam sloop *Augusta* arrived at Puerto Limón. The squadron's commander, Captain Friedrich Wilhelm Franz Kinderling, then undertook a confidential mission linked to the Frémont project.[28]

Captain Kinderling and a small party made the difficult overland trip from Puerto Limón to San José. Kinderling's primary interest was in finding a naval base for Prussia's West Indies squadron. He encountered strong resistance in San José to his inquiry about a possible treaty or contractual transfer of rights over Puerto Limón to Prussia. Since Kinderling lacked authority to negotiate an agreement with Costa Rica, he requested that the Costa Rican government allow the Prussian government time to respond. Avoiding any exclusive promise, Volio emphasized Costa Rica's preference for a private company to manage Prussian interests near Puerto Limón.[29]

This Prussian initiative rang alarm bells in other diplomatic circles. The U.S. consul, Arthur Morrell, thought Prussia was considering the formation of a colonization and road construction company. British agent E. Corbett thought Kinderling's visit signified interest in an interoceanic railroad terminus as well as a naval station. Kinderling's report to the Imperial Navy recommended Puerto Limón as a site for a naval base and explained the Costa Rican desire for an agreement with private groups. When a mysterious leak revealed Kinderling's proposal to the government in San José, Berlin denied that Prussia was negotiating with Costa Rica about a naval station at Puerto Limón.[30]

Kinderling's activity unsettled U.S.-Prussian relations. In Washington, German Minister von Gerolt acted quickly to repair the damage. He declared that the North German Confederation disapproved of Kinderling's conduct and would not protect Costa Rica's interoceanic railroad. Seward and von Gerolt agreed that Prussia should abstain from affairs on this continent to avoid disrupting friendly mutual relations. Charles Riotte warned von Gerolt that Frémont's railroad scheme was a fantasy that could bring large losses to German investors. Carl Schurz, politician, ex-general, and the most prominent German-American, suggested that Germany ought to find U.S. friendship more valuable than a naval station in the Caribbean. He suggested, however, that it might be consistent with the Monroe Doctrine for the United States and Germany to trade some kind of naval facilities in Europe and the New World.[31] Despite Schurz's speculation, the U.S. government feared the strategic and economic leverage that Germany might acquire from a naval station and railroad in Costa Rica.

In the 1940s two historians disagreed about the purpose and official status of the Kinderling mission. Helmuth Polakowsky accepted Bismarck's explanation of Kinderling's mission as an overambitious personal initiative and the chancellor's disclaimer of any intention to acquire a naval station. In contrast, Tulio von Bülow has argued that Kinderling was undoubtedly Bismarck's confidential agent, instructed to send up a trial balloon. After the leak prematurely exposed Kinderling's objectives in San José, the Prussian government immediately explained that the mission of officers on the *Augusta* was only to seek protection of North German Confederation commerce and other related interests; in fact, Kinderling was reprimanded and treated as if he had acted upon his own. Von Bülow pointed out that one could expect Bismarck to deny his government's plans, especially in response to criticism from abroad.[32]

Kinderling's confidential reports to the Prussian naval high command sustain von Bülow's interpretation. In response to instructions, Kinderling reported on a wide variety of commercial, consular, diplomatic, and naval-strategic matters regarding Costa Rica. Delius claimed that Bismarck suppressed the publication of Kinderling's final report because it undermined the Prussian government's assertion that Prussia had nothing to do with Kinderling's proposal regarding Puerto Limón.[33]

Von Gerolt's correspondence reveals another dimension of the Prussian–Puerto Limón affair of 1868. He described how the struggle among German officials and businessmen to replace Lahmann, the North German consul in Costa Rica, was related to the Frémont railroad and Puerto Limón naval station projects. Although Costa Rica welcomed the prospect of German rather than North American immigration—because it feared that the United States ultimately sought annexation—Lahmann's reports failed to support Berlin's hope that German capital and German colonists would find a warm welcome in Costa Rica. Dr. Friedrich L. Streber, one of Frémont's associates, conspired to replace Lahmann as North German Confederation consul in Costa Rica. Riotte endorsed Lahmann and warned against Streber. Whereas Lahmann had advised Berlin to be cautious about the Frémont railroad scheme and the acquisition of a naval station at Puerto Limón, Streber had encouraged North German Confederation interests in them. Kinderling, also, recommended Lahmann's removal, which would have facilitated elevating Streber to the consular post and the sale of the Frémont concession to Prussia. Despite von Gerolt's denial that the North German Confederation had any plan to acquire a naval station in Costa Rica or Central America, it is difficult to accept Bismarck's claim that Kinderling's activity did not represent official aims. The North German Confederation was seeking naval stations in Asia and elsewhere and German governments had shown interest in a Caribbean area naval base both before and after the 1868 incident. Using personal contacts in the Costa Rican government, U.S. Consul Morrell had forwarded copies of correspondence which revealed that Prussia expected to acquire a base for its West Indies squadron. Finally, Kinderling's promotions in 1871 and 1878 hint that he was serving rather than undermining German government objectives and policies.[34] In sum, the evidence supports a presumption that Kinderling was acting within his instructions.

Despite the disappointment of the Frémont project, the Costa Rican minister of public works insisted that the "prompt and expedient" development of communication was "the most efficient means to increase Costa Rica's wealth." After the Frémont project collapsed, the Costa Rican government entertained railroad proposals from several U.S. business groups. After discussions with various parties, Volio concluded that all these proposals were speculative and not made in good faith. Their central concern, he lamented, was "to assure the facility to issue stock and easily sell it under the Government's guarantee." These speculators wanted to win U.S. government support to enhance the value of any concession. Reputable, wealthy individuals refused to support the projects, suspecting that the opening of a Panama canal in the near future and the competition of the transcontinental and Panama railroads would prevent a reasonable return on the investment. Suspecting that negotiations in the United States would lead to serious dangers, Volio favored securing a loan in Europe to construct the railroad. Although the Costa Rican government had continued to work on the roads to Puntarenas and Puerto Limón, it considered the railroad from Puerto Limón to the Gulf of Nicoya the best way to develop the country.[35]

Despite the preeminent place of British capital and entrepreneurs in Costa Rica's coffee and communications business, some U.S. promoters remained interested in Costa Rican projects. The U.S. minister Jacob B. Blair reported in early 1869 that Costa Rica had signed a contract for a railroad from Puerto Limón to the Gulf of Nicoya with a group of North Americans, including Edward Reilly, Alexander Hay, William H. McCartney, and David Vickers. Other investors and businessmen looked for opportunities in a gas factory and telegraph line to accompany the railroad. The French chargé Julien O. de Cabarrus said that the Reilly railroad project held great potential for European trade with the west coast of America and the Pacific. In general, English opinion strongly condemned the Reilly contract. The British groups delayed approval of the Reilly concession but were unable to prepare a convincing alternative. President Jiménez resigned when the Costa Rican congress seemed inclined to reject the Reilly contract, but the legislature refused to accept his resignation. The Reilly contract was eventually ratified, and the grading and construction of the railroad began on August 25, 1869. Six months later, the Costa Rican government nullified the contract for nonfulfillment of the terms. De Cabarrus remarked that this failure proved the futility of Costa Rica's sacrifices to obtain a railroad. But hope lingered on with Costa Rican officials. In 1871, at Costa Rica's request, the United States named two engineers to survey a route for a wagon-road or railroad between San José and the Atlantic. Unable to locate funding, the Costa Rican government postponed the survey.[36] Despite Costa Rican and metropole interest in an Atlantic transit route, various projects had failed to link the coffee area to the Caribbean coast in the 1860s.

Delius's fascination with Puerto Limón, coffee, and a transcontinental railroad did not dissipate because of failure, and he continued to pursue Prussian officials. In 1876 the undaunted remains of Frémont's company again offered Puerto Limón to Germany. At this point, with the unification crisis behind it, Bismarck's foreign office launched inquiries about Frémont and the New York firm. They learned, as the Costa Rican officials had earlier, that neither Frémont nor his Costa Rican Railroad Company represented a substantial economic force. Aware that Frémont's concession rights were dubious at best, the German government dropped the matter. Delius rejected de Lesseps's canal as "folly" and argued that Minor Cooper Keith's Costa Rican railroad would not go interoceanic. In 1881 he wrote to former president Ulysses S. Grant about support for reviving his concession as a colonization project and as the best site for an isthmian interoceanic railroad route. He contended that Germany would not interfere because of internal problems and a lack of a desire to contest U.S. power in the isthmus. There is no indication that Grant replied.[37] The Frémont-Delius scheme had vanished for everyone but Delius.

Costa Rica finally obtained an Atlantic coast railroad when Henry Meiggs and his nephew Minor Cooper Keith organized the project. In July 1871 Meiggs contracted to build a railroad from the Atlantic coast to Costa Rica's coffee-rich mesa central. Minister Blair presumed that his railroad would shift the coffee trade from London to New York. J. R. Gill, a longtime resident of Panama, wrote a friend: "If the Costa Rica R.R. should go through, the country will become one of great importance as it is very valuable in products, and mines, and only requires Anglo-Saxon brains to make order out of chaos." Jiménez's successor as Costa Rican president, Tomás Guardia, expected the railroad to encourage commercial enterprise, to induce a large immigration, and to develop the fertile territory on the Atlantic periphery, previously of little value. Meiggs transferred the contract to a relative, John Meiggs Keith, who turned the contract over to Minor Keith. Minor Keith not only built the railroad but used subsidiary concessions to create the United Fruit empire, which was to dominate Central American societies for four generations.[38]

Part of a later conflict between Costa Rica and Keith over whether the Costa Rican railroad should serve Keith's Puerto Limón coast-fruit objectives or Costa Rica's national objectives was related to the "purpose" of the developmental projects initiated with metropole capital. Keith knew that a transisthmian railroad traversing the populated, coffee-producing mesa central would strengthen major political and economic interests of the native coffee elite, which in turn might endanger his enclave. For this reason he decided not to complete the transcontinental route originally planned. The Costa Rican railroad route was also one battleground between the Panama Railroad and its steamship line and the Pacific Mail Steamship Company. Pacific Mail wanted an alternative isthmian transit to free itself from dependence on the Panama railroad monopoly for transshipment of its Pacific-generated business to the Caribbean-Atlantic side. The Panama Railroad discouraged converting the Costa Rican railroad into a transcontinental line.[39] Pacific Mail sought to subordinate Costa Rican development to its own specific vision of metropole trade interests. The objectives of these two firms were not noticeably different from those of Frémont and Delius or Meiggs and Keith. All the projects inevitably supported the personal profit motive or metropole developmental objectives better than they met the needs of the host society. Recognizing this, the Costa Rican government independently completed the interoceanic rail line in the twentieth century.

The triumph of a liberal political economy in the United States after the Civil War stimulated the pursuit of material objectives. Mexico, Central America, the Caribbean, Hawaii, Alaska, Samoa, China, and Japan received attention from U.S. entrepreneurs and speculators in the mid-nineteenth century. The distinction between entrepreneurs (who sought wealth through producing something) and speculators (who sought wealth through trading the right to produce something) deserves attention. Frémont, like most other promoters of Costa Rican railroads, viewed his project chiefly as a means to create negotiable paper that would make him rich. Even Henry Meiggs's concession was transferred through family members before arriving in the hands of Minor Keith, an entrepreneur who used the opportunity to build a railroad, a fruit company, and a personal fortune. But Frémont's projects in Costa Rica—a railroad, port construction, and the development of Costa Rica's east coast—were presented as grand designs for serving national objectives. And unquestionably, implementing Frémont's concession would have benefited U.S. exploitation of Central America and the Pacific basin.

The same combination of personal and national objectives, with a different mix of motivations, encouraged Bismarck and the German government to investigate the possibilities of German development of a potentially important transit link between the two great oceans of the world. The German interests in Costa Rica and Puerto Limón reflected that country's desire to acquire foreign naval bases, communication links, and business sites to improve outlets for its expanding industrial economy. Like Germany, most metropole states in the nineteenth century pursued social imperialism—external policies and activities that would ameliorate internal socioeconomic disorders and decrease domestic opportunities.

The German attraction to Central American transit produced tension with the rival U.S. political economy in an area which the United States defined as central to its security. In the late 1860s neither state faced such severe internal problems that it considered this particular skirmish in Costa Rica vital. Yet both viewed their access to the isthmian region a matter of great concern. U.S. diplomats and political leaders had responded quickly to stymie German inquiries about the possibility of a naval station at Puerto Limón, colonization sites, and transit rights in Costa Rica. When Bismarck learned that the United States would jealously guard its special sphere, Germany withdrew its exploratory operations and denied any official involvement. The withdrawal was only that, not a surrender. In the 1880s and 1890s, German merchants and investors captured the dominant position in Guatemala's economy, a major place in Nicaragua's development, and significant roles elsewhere in Central America. In the late 1860s a laissez-faire speculative scheme involving a potentially valuable Caribbean naval station and transcontinental railroad had brought Germany and the United States to the brink of a confrontation that neither power sought. This confrontation was relatively easy to avoid. A generation or so later, both powers might have reacted differently.

3

George McWillie Williamson and Postbellum

Southern Expansionism

In the 1860s, after the Republican party came to power, the United States began to pursue material progress within the general framework of an individualistic, free-market capitalism of the sort advocated by Adam Smith. The adoption of a laissez-faire order created many internal opportunities for profit, which increasingly attracted the attention of entrepreneurs and speculators and led to massive production increases and rapid capital accumulation. Within a decade, the depression of 1873 shocked many observers and analysts of the U.S. political economy, and some of them argued that market disturbances resulting from overproduction were the chief cause of the factory closings, unemployment, strikes, and social disorder that plagued the nation. Republican leaders agreed, and called for resolving the economic crisis by expanding the market for U.S. products abroad. The administration of General Ulysses S. Grant complied by seeking consular and diplomatic agents who were energetic, inventive, and expansionist. It also welcomed the support of southern politicians in its plan for expansion.[1]

The South had barely begun to recover from the destruction of the Civil War when the depression of 1873 hit, with devastating long-term effects. In Louisiana, for example, agricultural output did not regain its 1873 level until 1900. Grant's choice for U.S. minister to Central America, the Louisianan George McWillie Williamson, was naturally interested in creating opportunities for Louisiana and the South, but he also recognized that the socioeconomic problems of the mid-1870s were national in nature, and he believed it essential for the U.S. government to assume a more active role in promoting economic expansion. Believing that overproduction was a key factor in the depression and that Central America was a promising market and the transit key to many other markets (China and the rest of Asia), he argued for policies that would tie Central America more closely to the U.S. political economy.[2] The importance he assigned to the isthmus made him suspicious of foreign activity in Central America. In order to expand U.S.

markets in that region and to facilitate access to Central American products, he advocated improving internal communications on the Caribbean coast of Central America and establishing shipping links from Louisiana and the U.S. Gulf ports to Central America.

Williamson was by no means alone in hoping that trade and economic expansion would facilitate recovery from the war and its ensuing economic depression. In fact, southern business and political leaders had been promoting southern expansion into the Caribbean since the 1840s. Prominent among them were Jane and William Cazneau, who had encouraged southern filibustering to acquire new territory for slave-produced cotton in the era of William Walker, but had become promoters of commercial and communications ventures since the war; and U.S. Senator John T. Morgan of Alabama, a member of the antebellum elite and a Confederate general, whose ideas were similar to those of Williamson. Thus, mid-nineteenth century southern expansionism continued after the war in part for social reasons: the reconstruction leadership shared personnel, ideology, and policies with the antebellum planter class and its associates.[3]

This expansionist tendency also reflected longstanding links between southern society and the European economic system. Cotton grown in the South was sold largely to Britain, France, and Belgium, and in return the southern wealthy consumed large quantities of goods from Europe, especially Great Britain. After the Civil War, although the cotton trade remained essential to the southern economy, its relative importance declined. Historians James C. Cobb and Gavin Wright have called attention to the problems that arise from examining and critiquing the southern economy from a too narrow, parochial perspective. They agreed that one can only understand postbellum southern economic activity within a perspective of national and world market forces.[4] What remained constant was its infrastructure: a communications system pointed at ports, oceans, and rivers rather than at roads and railroads—a system, in other words, built to serve oceanic trade rather than local or regional economic integration. So long as the South looked to its ports for trade, commercial links with the nearby Caribbean and Central American areas would be extremely valuable. Recognition of this fact led southern leaders like John T. Morgan and George Williamson to dream of an interoceanic canal across the isthmus.

If the United States were to compete successfully with other industrialized powers for trade, transit, and investment opportunities in Central America, it would have to find agents of character and ability to serve that cause. Williamson apparently filled the bill, for U.S.–Central American commercial relations changed dramatically during his six-year term of service. Historians have said little about Williamson's precise role in this

transformation. This is surprising, since his career, which began in the antebellum period, included important professional, political, military, business, and diplomatic activity.

Biographical information on Williamson's life is sparse. The son of
Thomas Taylor Williamson, a prominent Mississippi River steamboat captain involved in the founding of Shreveport and Bossier City in Louisiana,
and Tirzah Ann McWillie, he was born in Fairfax, South Carolina, on
September 29, 1829. After graduating from the University of South Car-
olina in 1850, Williamson practiced law in Mansfield and Shreveport. He
served as the corporation (city) attorney in Shreveport in 1852 and 1853.
Two marriages produced eleven children. In 1861 he represented Caddo
Parish in the Louisiana Secession convention. He served in the Confederate
army as a staff officer for generals Leonidas Polk, John Magruder, and
E. Kirby Smith, rising to the rank of colonel. He was wounded at Shiloh and
Murfreesboro. After the war, he practiced law in Shreveport. Although
elected to the U.S. Senate in 1867, that body refused to seat him. In mid-
1872, the Reform party, a faction organized in opposition to Governor
Henry Clay Warmoth, nominated Williamson for governor of Louisiana.
Later, when the Democratic, Reform, and Liberal Republican tickets combined into a Fusion ticket, Williamson lost his place on the ballot. But as a
prominent figure who had helped Grant's party defeat Warmoth in 1872,
Williamson was in line for a political reward. His service as U.S. minister
resident in Central America from May 17, 1873, until January 31, 1879,
revealed his views on Louisianan and U.S. trade expansion. After his tour as
minister, he returned to conduct business and practice law in north Louisiana. In the 1880s he acted as general counsel for the Texas and Pacific
Railroad.[5] The date of his death is unknown.

Williamson's support for market expansion was energetic and inventive. He had the advantage of being from the South, a region that had
traditionally promoted contact with Central America. He saw the potential
value for New Orleans, Louisiana, the South, and the nation to invest in the
progress of Central America. In Central America, he lobbied for improvements in communications networks (both internal and external), for conditions to encourage a flow of mining and agricultural capital and skill from
the United States, and for alterations of Central American laws and regulations on colonization, capital investment, and marketing. He also advocated improved postal links and an expanded consular service. He was
convinced that U.S. entrepreneurs and the Central American societies
would benefit as transit routes and laws regulating business and market
opportunities were molded to accommodate material progress in those
countries.[6]

The United States had ample reason to be interested. The depression of 1873–1877, which had worldwide scope and was the severest economic collapse the United States had experienced in its hundred-year history, prompted various contemporary analysts to develop an overproduction perspective, which went as follows. Overproduction produced a market glut and compelled layoffs, which brought labor unrest and violence. The resolution to the socioeconomic disorder appeared to lie in market expansion, but the domestic market was saturated from overproduction. If overseas markets could absorb the surplus production, adequate employment levels and social tranquillity could be restored. Williamson valued Central America in two ways: directly, as a market and a source of cheap raw materials (which could reduce the production costs and therefore expand the domestic market because the lower prices would create new customers); and indirectly, because it could provide cheap and convenient transit for U.S. goods into other areas. He expected Central America to contribute significantly to relieving U.S. overproduction.[7]

In 1873 the Central America that was projected as a source of relief for a faltering U.S. political economy was itself in turmoil. In the early 1870s Costa Rica and Guatemala experienced liberal revolutions. In the mid-1870s, in order to secure their country's southern border, Guatemalan liberals encouraged successful liberal revolutions in Honduras and El Salvador. Only Nicaragua's conservative government avoided a liberal revolution in the 1870s.[8] Williamson thus arrived in a Central America rocked by the world economic crisis and in the midst of responding to major revolutions which transformed the ideology, constitutions, and economic outlook of four societies. Central American positivists (followers of a particular branch of liberalism associated with Auguste Comte) acknowledged the need for foreign capital, immigrants, and technology to achieve the desired material progress in their country.

Despite the political and economic disorder in North and South America, U.S. trade with the isthmus increased rapidly. Between 1872, the year prior to Williamson's appointment, and 1879, the year he resigned as minister, U.S. trade with Central America increased 50 percent in dollars and 65 percent in terms of its share of total U.S. trade (see Table 3.1).

Trends rather than yearly anomalies best describe social change, and Table 3.1 indicates that the impact of the Williamson era upon Central American long-term trade marked a trend. For the two five-year periods before Williamson became minister, U.S. imports from Central America averaged $560,000 and $1,100,000 annually, which represented 0.16 and 0.23 percent shares of total U.S. imports for those periods. In the two five-year periods after he left office, these imports averaged $3,700,000 and

Table 3.1   U.S. Imports from and Exports to Central America,
1848–1908, in Five-Year Averages

Year	Total U.S. imports from Cent. Amer.	Cent. Amer. as % total U.S. imports	Total U.S. exports to Cent. Amer.	Cent. Amer. as % total U.S. exports
1848–52	121,239	0.06	190,583	0.10
1853–57	166,556	0.05	280,719	0.10
1858–62	247,332	0.08	131,266	0.04
1863–67	558,736	0.16	365,954	0.12
1868	1,128,735	0.30	244,437	0.09
1869	730,714	0.17	455,129	0.13
1870	734,565	0.16	232,478	0.05
1871	1,481,016	0.28	521,822	0.12
1872	1,590,011	0.25	937,025	0.21
1873	1,974,968	0.31	961,810	0.18
1874	2,855,093	0.50	828,960	0.14
1875	2,435,151	0.46	784,232	0.15
1876	1,597,515	0.35	929,841	0.17
1877	2,678,672	0.59	960,730	0.16
1878	2,968,996	0.68	1,254,757	0.18
1879	2,251,589	0.51	1,155,776	0.16
1880	3,313,469	0.50	1,784,855	0.21
1881	3,159,786	0.49	1,625,738	0.18
1882	4,735,398	0.65	1,644,013	0.22
1883	5,121,315	0.71	2,003,467	0.24
1884–88	6,749,337	1.02	3,131,032	0.44
1889–93	8,958,064	1.10	5,616,070	0.64
1894–98	9,253,694	1.29	6,593,259	0.70
1899–1903	9,771,199	1.15	6,004,876	0.43
1904–08	11,941,190	1.01	9,379,072	0.55

Sources: U.S. Bureau of Foreign and Domestic Commerce, Foreign Commerce and Navigation of the United States (annual); U.S. Bureau of the Census, Statistical Abstract of the United States (annual).

$6,750,000 annually, and their share of total U.S. imports rose to 0.57 and 1.02 percent. An examination of U.S.–Central American trade data shows that U.S. imports for the decade after he served rose over 500 percent in dollar amount and their share of U.S. total imports increased 300 percent in comparison with the decade before he served. U.S. exports to Central America for the same decades increased 470 percent in dollar value, and their share of total U.S. export trade increased 120 percent. Clearly, Williamson's tour of duty served as a pivot point for a stagnant U.S. trade with Central

America, which increased markedly in the postbellum years and then accelerated upward in the 1880s and 1890s.

It is not easy to determine how much of the expanding U.S.–Central American trade entered or left southern ports for Central America. Not even the role of New Orleans in the exchange with Central America can be determined adequately. Its fruit trade grew in the middle and late 1880s, and by the mid-1890s New Orleans was the leading import center for Latin American fruits. The trade data does indicate that New Orleans's exports recovered strongly in the postbellum years, but it is not known whether the Central American states played a major role in that revival.[9] Still, the fact that New Orleans shared in the rapid trade expansion of the last quarter of the nineteenth century suggests that Central America was not ignored in the rush to relieve domestic social disorder through trade expansion.

Secretary of State Hamilton Fish outlined a set of policy objectives—continental security, Central American union, increasing trade, and the construction of a canal—for Williamson to pursue. He wanted Williamson "cautiously and discreetly" to implement steps toward union, ostensibly to promote the prosperity and happiness of the five states. But while the U.S. government often mentioned Central American union, in reality it continuously shifted its commitment to the idea. When the government felt confident that it could exercise hegemony in Central America, it actually promoted union because it would be easier to control one state than five. When it suspected that some other power might be preparing to challenge its dominance in the region, it cautiously avoided insisting upon the urgency of union. Around 1870, residual British power (especially in Costa Rica and Honduras) and a growing German presence (especially in Guatemala) may perhaps explain the discrepancies between Williamson's instructions to work for union and the low priority that Williamson and the State Department actually assigned to that task. Despite the rising tension from liberal revolutions and metropole competition, Fish contended that increasing U.S. trade with the Central American states would facilitate peace and prosperity in the region and also benefit U.S. manufacturing and commercial interests. He considered political stability and economic progress interdependent.[10]

In late 1873 Williamson offered some preliminary thoughts about why U.S.–Central American trade was conducted in only a modest volume. He noted that an unreasonable anti-Spanish prejudice common to North Americans produced a reciprocal hostility that hindered the growth of business relations. He added that freight and insurance rates were higher to the United States than to Europe and that European merchants offered longer-term credit and lower interest rates than U.S. merchants. The commonly used trade route led from Central America's Pacific ports to Europe. Trade to and from the United States was transshipped in European ports, which added appreciably to the freight charges. Williamson believed that as long as Central American trade used the Pacific outlet, Europe would compete successfully with the United States. To undermine Europe's preeminence, he encouraged new internal communications lines to redirect Central American trade to the Caribbean and then to U.S. Gulf coast ports, particularly New Orleans. The U.S. consul at Belize seconded Williamson's judgment.[11] They believed that advantageous European maritime services and poor communication links to the United States underlay the low level of commercial activity.

Williamson believed that the United States and the Central American republics had to revise tariffs, negotiate new trade treaties, and facilitate improved communications if they hoped to encourage increased commercial interchange. He argued that if the United States were to obtain "its proportionate share of the trade of Central America," it would be necessary to promote communications development in those countries which brought their trade to the Caribbean coast. He secured Guatemala's permission to explore three reputedly navigable rivers that emptied into the Gulf of Mexico. He requested the Grant administration to select an exploration party to tie these "very valuable commercial outlets for the trade and products of Guatemala ... [to U.S.] cities on the Gulf coast." He was pleased when Guatemalan President Justo Rufino Barrios announced plans for a road from the capital to Izabal on the Gulf of Mexico. If this road were properly completed, Williamson said, one could expect that "a large portion of the trade of Guatemala, some from El Salvador, and a great deal from the Departments of Gracias and Santa Barbara in Honduras, will seek markets in the United States instead of, as now, in Europe."[12]

The persistent spoiler for Guatemalan efforts to fulfill Atlantic coast communications projects was insufficient capital resources. Williamson recommended establishing a U.S. consulate at Cobán, a small town along the projected railroad route. He assumed that a consular presence there might attract more economic activity to the route and thus make the project more attractive to capitalists. In fact, an Atlantic coast railroad concession was granted in the 1870s, but, largely for lack of capital, it was not completed until the first decade of the twentieth century.[13] In order to increase commercial activity throughout the region, Williamson also sought to establish regular steamship service between Central America and New Orleans and the Gulf ports.

Williamson recognized that more than trade treaties and communications were necessary to facilitate trade. To this end, he recommended steps to create greater efficiency and economy in the consular service in Central America. He thought that creating a consul general to supervise the gathering of Central American commercial information would be a good start. He advised granting consuls small salaries, denying them the right to trade, but permitting them to serve as agents for U.S. commercial, manufacturing, or insurance firms. Agency income would supplement their salaries "and at the same time would stimulate them to take a larger interest in promoting trade with our country. Such a system would make private interest and official duty cooperate for the same end." If the administration appoints consuls "who take an interest in the subject of extending our commerce with these states," he wrote to Fish, "there will be a marked increase in the volume of trade with our country."[14]

In proposing this large role for U.S. officials, Williamson was offering an alternative to the policy that Secretary of State William Henry Seward had announced in the 1860s. Seward had ordered U.S. diplomats and naval commanders to protect U.S. citizens only at the coast, not inland. Seward extended extraordinary protection only to transient U.S. citizens, arguing that U.S. citizens who chose to reside in foreign countries should expect to live under the conditions they had chosen. Williamson proposed redefining the consular function, "so that instead of consuls being appointed to protect our commerce and navigation, they should rather be appointed to promote those great interests."[15] As U.S. officials came to perceive U.S. commercial expansion as vital to domestic well-being and tranquillity, they altered their view of the purpose of U.S. consular and diplomatic service. Williamson was a leader in changing the purpose from passive protection to active, aggressive promotion. The State Department, commercial interests, and analysts of the U.S. political economy came to agree that active promotion was necessary for the desired expansion of U.S. commerce.

Williamson discovered that it was not easy to find competent Americans willing to serve as consuls. He protested that "too many consulates and agencies were held by foreigners," whose national sympathies had to be overcome before they could promote U.S. trade. The State Department accepted Williamson's contention that U.S. commercial interests would best be served when competent North American citizens served as consular agents, but this idea was not easy to implement. For example, Williamson requested the removal of the U.S. consul in Guatemala City, Henry Houben, a good man but a German citizen who merely had declared his intention of becoming an American and whose sympathies and friendships, according to Williamson, inclined him "to favor the large German interests in Guatemala." Houben protested, claiming that Williamson's Louisiana roots and southern sympathies were behind the request. He argued that because he had been a Union sympathizer, Williamson wanted to replace him with a former Confederate army comrade. He also maintained that his refusal to change a report and declare New Orleans a prime market for Guatemalan coffee and sugar had displeased Williamson; in his view, New Orleans might become a market for Guatemalan products only if a regular steamship service were available. Finally, the State Department agreed to Houben's removal.[16] Thus a foreign-born U.S. consul who discounted the value of New Orleans for Central American trade was replaced with a southern-born consul, John Graham, who saw possibilities for New Orleans trade with Central America.

The U.S. government did not prize the Central American region primarily for its trade, or even for its investment opportunities, however. It considered the isthmus the key to binding the Atlantic and Pacific half-worlds into a single large unit for economic activity. Both the Grant and Rutherford B. Hayes administrations considered the isthmian canal an "American project" of vital importance. The Hayes administration, for example, became upset in the late 1870s when a "foreign nation" (represented in the person of French engineer Ferdinand de Lesseps) sought to build the waterway, although Williamson had assured Grant and Hayes that no European power was actively pursuing a canal project.[17]

Williamson encouraged the hopes of Central American states—especially Nicaragua—for construction of a canal in the near future. During his ministerial reception in Nicaragua in 1873, he proclaimed a canal through Nicaragua the only practical route, one which the commercial world would soon consider indispensable. But in 1878, after Williamson explored the idea in several talks with leaders in Nicaragua and Costa Rica, the State Department rejected his request to pursue negotiations for a canal. Assistant Secretary of State Frederick W. Seward remarked that "the United States has much less direct interest in transit by that route than it had before the Panama and Union Pacific railways went into operation [in 1855 and 1869]." Nicaraguans were deluded, Williamson feared, in believing that the canal was indispensable for the United States; hence they drove too hard a bargain.[18] The world economic crisis of the 1870s and the initiation of de Lesseps's Panama canal project in the late 1870s made a Nicaraguan canal unlikely in the 1870s or 1880s. But the feeble U.S. private and public interest in a Nicaraguan canal emphatically did not mean that the U.S. government felt that European interests were free to undertake the project.

While the U.S. government perceived dangers if European powers controlled the Nicaraguan transit, it was willing to cooperate with European governments in other matters in Central America. In an effort to promote U.S. commercial opportunity, Williamson joined a German protest against the Nicaraguan government. In 1877, German Minister Werner von Bergen drew Williamson into a dispute between the Nicaraguan government and two German businessmen and consuls, Paul and Christian Moritz Eisenstück, regarding family matters which were elevated into a series of incidents involving gunshots and physical assaults on the streets of a Nicaraguan town. Initially, Williamson received State Department approval to offer strong support for the German position. German pressure on Nicaragua mounted. About mid-1878, six war vessels and the threat of a German landing force sharpened the German ultimatum for an admission of responsibility, a salute to the German flag, and an indemnity. In face of superior force, the Nicaraguan government admitted the injustice of the attacks upon the Eisenstücks and the delay in settling the matter. It agreed to pay a sizable indemnity and to salute the German flag.[19]

The German capacity to marshal such an impressive naval force prompted Williamson to reconsider his support for the Germans. While he still hoped the Eisenstück incident would teach Nicaragua to abate its mistreatment of foreigners, he suspected that his participation had been detrimental to long-term U.S. interests. He considered German commercial penetration of Central America the major roadblock to an increase in the U.S. commercial role in that region. He interpreted the six war vessels off Nicaragua's coast as an indication that the German government was "exhibiting an injudicious zeal or that the question has assumed an entirely new phase." Reflecting upon his role in the Eisenstück affair, he recommended that U.S. diplomats in Latin America should not exercise good offices on behalf of European powers because U.S. cooperation with Old World states "tended to create the belief . . . that we have abandoned the Monroe Doctrine," and thus generally weakened the U.S. position in Latin America. The Nicaraguan government circularized all Latin American states with a note which argued that U.S. support for Germany was contrary to the spirit and letter of the Monroe Doctrine.[20] Williamson acknowledged that the United States needed to restore its prestige if it hoped to create opportunities for its citizens in Central America.

Williamson was handicapped not only by his role in the Eisenstück affair but by his cultural and racial biases. He remarked derogatorily that although Central American governments might quarrel among themselves, they cooperated to resist foreign governments no matter how unjust the cause. He warned: "Although promises of doing much are freely and almost recklessly made . . . the habits of a people who do not work for results, and who have a certain mawkish pride . . . do not inspire much confidence that these countries will be well represented." Williamson considered Central Americans shrewd but unreliable and lazy, and he referred to Nicaragua's foreign minister as a "mendacious negro statesman."[21] These prejudices made negotiations with Central American leaders difficult and often fruitless.

Williamson's position was in fact typical. The biases of all the "superior" industrial civilizations competing for advantage in the region threatened the dignity and sovereignty of the Central American societies. In the mid-1870s the Guatemalan government denounced almost all of its existing treaties as unfair and announced that in all future treaties "the equality of Guatemala in all respects should be recognized." The Guatemalan foreign minister said he was "scandalized" by the ease with which powerful nations resolved misunderstandings with naval squadrons, a step that weak nations could not take. Williamson informed him that "so long as Guatemala kept herself in the right in her dealings with other nations, she had a protection as efficacious as she need desire against unprovoked acts of violence on the part of more powerful nations—that of public opinion of the civilized world." But the minister answered that he had "small faith in such a protector."[22] Guatemala's efforts to gain respect for its sovereignty implied that it would offer only grudging and limited cooperation with any U.S. plans for commercial penetration of the country.

The opinion that the United States had to promote trade to alleviate domestic surpluses lent an urgency to its expansionist efforts that made it difficult to deal with another country's sovereignty. An example involving Williamson may be instructive. In Guatemala in 1874, a U.S. merchant, A. Zadiks, was charged with smuggling alcohol, a state monopoly, but he proclaimed his innocence and protested the confiscation of the smuggled goods. Williamson told Guatemalan officials that he did not intend to interfere in Zadiks's claim against their government while the matter rested with Guatemalan courts. But he warned them that if the courts decided against Zadiks "without sufficient evidence and apparently under orders of the Government . . . I should consider it my duty to report the case [to the State Department] . . . for instruction." Personally, Williamson believed that the Jews were out of favor for not intermarrying with Guatemalans, for underselling competitors, and for introducing only American manufactures. He suspected that the key issue for Guatemalans was that Zadiks and his family, naturalized American Jews and merchants (who "like most of their race are shrewd and enterprising") did business only with San Francisco.[23] He never claimed Zadiks was innocent, but he threatened to challenge Guatemalan sovereignty because he wanted to establish special protection for U.S. merchants, especially those like Zadiks, who conducted business chiefly with U.S. products and U.S. ports and thus facilitated the export of U.S. overproduction.

Looking for foreign trade to lift U.S. society out of an economic quagmire, the State Department issued a circular dated July 13, 1877, which observed that "it would be wise for all the nations . . . to consider more carefully than heretofore how they may best enlarge their trade with each other." The circular continued: "A favorable opportunity for the development of such trade would seem to be now offered by the prevailing stagnation of business and depression of prices. It is desirable . . . that [the United States] should find markets for the export of their products and manufactures; and . . . it is advantageous to the people of those countries that they should be able to purchase at the present decreased valuation." The circular argued that "apart from questions of merely commercial or pecuniary advantage, the development of such trade would have also a beneficial influence upon the political condition of the republics of this continent. It is for the interest of both North and South America that all those republican governments should have stability, peace, law, and order." It admitted that whereas trade promotion could not be expected to be easily and rapidly accomplished, it was "the purpose of the Department that it should be continuous."[24] By 1877 the State Department had adopted a position Williamson had advocated in 1873, in the early stages of the depression: disposing of U.S. overproduction in Central and South America would promote political stability in both regions.

The State Department apparently told Williamson as early as 1874 that gathering commercial information might shed light on why the United States did not receive a fair share of Latin American trade. In response, Williamson wrote to Secretary Fish that neither the Central American governments nor their learned and scientific societies published statistical tables, which he believed would reveal "how unjustly [the Central American states] discriminate against the commerce of the United States." He said that in addition to statistical data, the United States needed a better knowledge of Central American tariff laws in order to negotiate future commercial treaties.[25]

To fill the gap in commercial information about Central America, Williamson responded to the circular of July 13, 1877, with a detailed, analytical report buttressed by a wealth of empirical data. The data revealed that the United States sold small amounts of its domestic production to Central America but imported large quantities of that region's production. Williamson recalled "the old rule . . . in political as well as private economy, that he who sells more of his produce to his neighbors than he buys of theirs makes more profit out of them than they out of him." He concluded that "the states south of us are deriving a much larger profit from the United States than the United States are deriving from them." Williamson's erroneous conclusion ignored many key commercial factors: the control of pricing and the currency exchange rate; the financial, marketing, shipping, and insurance mechanisms that distributed the profit from the exchanges; the ownership of the firms in Latin America that imported the U.S. products; and the comparative qualities of U.S. and European products. The United States, Williamson believed, with "superior civilization and more persistent energy ought to become the manufacturers for the peoples south of us."[26] He expected that intelligent, informed policies would create an isthmian market to absorb a larger volume of U.S. goods.

Williamson recognized, however, that it could be difficult to persuade U.S. manufacturers, who had a tariff-protected, growing, and profitable domestic market, to study the tastes and habits of Central American buyers. Overlooking his pronounced prejudices, he warned that looking down upon Central America as backward was a business error. "Socially and politically these populations may be nearly stagnant," he conceded, "but their increased volume of foreign commerce indicates that agriculturally and commercially they are moving onward." U.S. trade with Central America had grown fourfold between 1864 and 1874 "without apparently an effort upon the part of our countrymen, and in the face of some disadvantages." Williamson assigned the temporary decline after 1874 largely "to the enterprise of German and French merchants and manufacturers, and to the lack of interest" by U.S. traders.[27] He recognized that in order to increase trade and alleviate domestic overproduction, U.S. trade practices and policy with Central America had to undergo significant alterations.

Williamson recognized that efforts to increase the U.S. commercial role in Central America would encounter resistance from European metropole powers (states that controlled the production, distribution, and consumption of an extensive array of industrial products and had the capital accumulation needed to sustain continued industrial growth). U.S. commerce in Central America faced stiff competition from British and German business interests. In 1873, Consul Houben noted that Britain enjoyed the largest share of Guatemalan trade, with Germany in second place. A year later, John Graham, Houben's successor, noted that "unfortunately for our commerce most of the mercantile business of this country [is] transacted by Germans." Williamson asserted: "The Germans and not the British are our real competition for the trade of the whole of Spanish America." While Britain retained a modest statistical lead in trade volume over the Germans, German merchants were the most active, prosperous, and numerous traders. The dynamic German commerce and the established British economic power represented the chief competition for U.S. objectives in Central America.[28]

After years of trying to improve communications links between New Orleans and Central America and to promote his native state of Louisiana, in March of 1877 Williamson reluctantly confessed that "under existing conditions San Francisco enjoys advantages over any other city of the United States as a base from which trade relations with these States may be promoted." He conceded that Central America's population, its best harbors and ports, and its better inland communications were located on the Pacific coast. The Atlantic side lacked agricultural development, population, ports, and inland communications.[29]

Although he conceded the advantages of San Francisco in trading with Central America, Williamson did not want to accept that condition as permanent. In the late 1870s he cooperated with several immigration projects that would have alleviated Louisiana's unemployment problem and built support for developing Guatemala's Atlantic coast. In the 1870s the Mutual Aid Benevolent Association of New Orleans inquired through Williamson about inducements that Guatemala offered to immigrants in land grants, reduced liability for tax and military service, or the option of introducing articles duty free for personal use. The Guatemalan government offered liberal concessions. Yet even in the area of colonization, California had advantages over Louisiana. The Sociedad de Inmigración, a liberal developmentalist group, only appointed immigration agents in California.[30] While Williamson aided several groups of emigrants from his native Louisiana, a successful colonization project—one that would export some of the unemployed and thus reduce domestic tensions during the depression— escaped him.

Unable to establish a regular U.S.–Central American steamship service or a flow of Louisianans to Central America, and stymied in his efforts to persuade Guatemalan officials and U.S. capitalists to undertake an Atlantic coast railroad to facilitate trade with New Orleans, Williamson became disheartened. He looked to advance his personal fortune. In October 1878 he proposed moving the U.S. legation to Amapala, Honduras, where he had just entered a mining business. When the State Department refused, Williamson resigned effective February 1, 1879. He cited two grounds: first, the State Department's projects to protect people and property and to promote more beneficial commercial relations had not been effective; and second, the Department had not adequately responded to Nicaragua's complaint about his conduct during the Eisenstück affair. Secretary of State William Evarts believed that Williamson expected the United States to break relations with Nicaragua over what Williamson considered discourteous treatment. The British minister suspected that U.S. relations with Central America might improve with Williamson's resignation because he "certainly has not succeeded in gaining the confidence of any one of the Governments."[31] Disappointed with his modest success in building trade with New Orleans and Louisiana, dissatisfied with the business venture, Williamson returned to Louisiana shortly after resigning.

During the period of Williamson's government service, the United States began to exhibit the salient features of an economy in transition from semi-peripheral to metropole status. The most vital sign of this transition was the development of recurring crises (overproduction) and persistent conditions in the socioeconomic order (unemployment) for which the elite could not (or would not) find solutions within the confines of the national political economy. Thus, policies of social imperialism were pursued. External areas became necessary not just for generating profit but for absorbing some of the shock from a variety of internal disorders—surplus labor and production, strikes and violence, rising crime and corruption, and social instability. When Louisiana and the whole nation experienced economic collapse in the 1870s, Williamson believed that trade had to expand into the nearby Caribbean because the internal economy was plagued with overproduction and consequent stagnation, unemployment, and capital losses. Perhaps the key element in all his efforts was his conviction that U.S. foreign economic relations required active promotion, not merely protection.

While Williamson was by no means the initiator of a new trade program with Central America, his work was important. His constant contact with both the State Department and Guatemalan officials about increasing the U.S. participation in Guatemalan affairs reinforced existing supporters of a liberal, developmentalist approach to bringing Guatemala into the modern age. He emphasized commercial relations with Guatemala because its population and its wealth were large in comparison with the other Central American states. The logic of his analysis and his home state sentiments led him to make repeated calls for the development of internal Guatemalan and external U.S.–Central American communications. He also recognized the value of a canal for U.S. producers to dispose of their overproduction in the Pacific basin, but since the State Department kept canal negotiations in Washington, he played a small role in that matter. Initially, he supported the Germans in the Eisenstück affair, but later he admitted that his support was unwise because rising German competition for Central American opportunities jeopardized U.S. ability to reduce its "overproduction" problem in that region. He and his consuls offered a quick and reliable service to those businessmen who wrote inquiring about trade, investment, or agricultural opportunities in Central America. He educated or at least supplied the possibility for many to learn about opportunities to undertake roads, ports, steamship lines, mining and agricultural investment, and migration.

Although he was frustrated in his efforts to alleviate U.S. domestic problems by expanding the U.S. role in the trade, immigration, and investment in Central America, U.S.-Guatemalan relations did in fact develop in the directions he had outlined in 1873 and within twenty years after his tenure as minister, many of the projects he advocated were in progress. The average annual U.S.–Central American trade during the decade after he left office was about six times the average annual trade with Central America for the decade before he served as minister. From 1875 until 1909, U.S. capital built most Central American railroads, including one to Guatemala's Atlantic coast. U.S. and German capital helped to develop the Atlantic coast's agricultural and mining possibilities. Around 1900, regular shipping lines linked Guatemala and the other Central American countries to New Orleans and other Gulf ports. These developments, however, did not resolve the U.S. overproduction problem, nor did they usher in the era of economic prosperity that Williamson—and many of his contemporaries—had envisioned. And yet his pursuit of a larger U.S. role often acted to curtail Central American sovereignty and intensify distrust and conflict between North and Central Americans.

4

The Eisenstück Affair: German and

U.S. Rivalry in Central America, 1877–1890

The late 1870s conflict between the Nicaraguan government and the German merchant-consuls Paul and Christian Moritz Eisenstück sheds light on the limits of cooperation in Central America between Germany and the United States. Initially, the two states cooperated because they wanted security for their entrepreneurs and personnel in Middle America. Both governments agreed that foreign businessmen should have unhampered access to the development of Middle America's commerce, mining, and agriculture. Cooperation was limited, however, because each nation defined its well-being and survival as dependent upon its capacity to expand externally. In Nicaragua during the late 1870s, the cooperation ended when the United States suspected that Germany might obtain competitive advantages from further cooperation.[1]

Germany's status in the mid-nineteenth century derived from unification, industrialization, and the expansion of its ties to the world economy. A united Germany, expanding the benefits of the *Zollverein* (a customs union that combined many Germanic states economically under Prussian leadership), was expected to facilitate the economic growth that would satisfy the demands of state and society.[2] Merchants, manufacturers, and exporters from the Hansa, the Rhine, and the Ruhr areas had long pushed for external "advances," and after unification in 1871, elements of the traditional ruling class—landed aristocrats, the military, and the high bureaucracy—came to believe that external expansion could ameliorate many of the problems that were causing turmoil in its industrializing economy: the breakdown of guilds, the migration from rural to urban areas, the chronic high unemployment, the growth of socialist labor groups, and rising crime rates. External expansion through social imperialism could serve objectives that conservatives would welcome. It generated support to pay for the army (and later the navy), to satisfy merchant and liberal groups, and to reduce the threat of a liberalization of German politics. The expanding German economy required more raw materials, more external markets for producers who could find no profitable disposition of "overproduction" within the empire, more investment opportunities for excess capital, and exotic products to fill the expectations of a growing bourgeoisie.[3] Germany, like most industrial states confronting internal economic crises related to unstable distribution situations, believed that expanding the market area would promote recovery and growth.

Since approximately 1860, German naval and economic activity had indicated a long-term interest in Central America. German entrepreneurs invested large sums of capital, created regular freight and mail lines, and established lucrative merchant houses in Central America. The region presented German businessmen with opportunities in mining, commerce, plantation systems, raw material extraction, land speculation, and colonization sites. German merchants expected important trading opportunities; and since a protected access to the Pacific basin would require a naval presence, by the late 1860s the Prussians were searching for naval stations in Asia and the New World. Some German businessmen and politicians also assumed that the Caribbean–Central American region would absorb part of the frustrated and underemployed segments of the German population, while at the same time building market areas and fostering German cultural and political influence in a key strategic area.[4]

German aggressiveness disturbed U.S. officials sensitive to foreign power near the projected canal routes. Germany acted to enter the Caribbean-isthmian area, even though German Chancellor Bismarck was advised that President Grant would be more inclined "to direct his view to Central America and Mexico than towards Europe." Despite the warning, the German government had long recognized Middle America as the area for an inexpensive, efficient communications link to tie the developed North Atlantic region to the raw materials, luxury goods, and labor of the Pacific and Indian Oceans. Nicaragua, Panama, and Tehuantepec were the most promising interoceanic transit sites. While the United States could cooperate with other metropole states to establish the conditions under which foreigners could conduct business abroad, it was unwilling to share access to the chief isthmian transit sites with Old World powers.[5]

In a comparative light, the mid-1870s revealed a successful German penetration of Central America and a weak but very slowly improving U.S. commercial and investment position. Although U.S. officials proclaimed their support for the principle of free trade competition in Central and Latin America, U.S. diplomats regularly blamed commerce between Latin America and Europe (Great Britain and Germany in particular) for U.S. trade deficiencies in the Southern Hemisphere. In 1870, the U.S. minister to Central America, Charles N. Riotte, noted that Germany had many merchants in Nicaragua who "import[ed] heavily from the fatherland" and that "the number of German ships in Nicaraguan ports [was] second to that of Great Britain." He argued that the more a Latin American country freed itself from Spanish customs and culture, the more it traded with North America, whereas the more it remained "stationary or even retrograde (like Nicaragua, Guatemala, Venezuela, Ecuador) the more insignificant [its] commercial relations with our people." U.S. officials clearly viewed German economic success in Central America as threatening to U.S. security and well-being.[6]

Many aspects of the new German empire's role in Nicaragua and the world were revealed during the course of the Eisenstück affair in 1877 and 1878. The Eisenstück brothers, Paul and Christian, had successful careers in business and in the consular service.[7] The controversy began when the stepdaughter of Paul Eisenstück married into the prominent Leal family against her parents' wishes. A German report charged that Francisco Leal, a Nicaraguan official, so mistreated his wife that she had returned to her parents and initiated divorce proceedings. When Leal was unsuccessful in persuading the Eisenstücks to return his wife to him, he harassed and threatened them. Several incidents occurred. One involved a verbal exchange in the street. A second, which according to the German version involved gunshots, physical detainment, and other abuses, was allegedly directed against Paul Eisenstück but touched both brothers. After the second incident, Consul Christian Eisenstück called for an immediate Nicaraguan admission of responsibility. The German government sought U.S. and British diplomatic support, claiming that the affair involved the rights and security of foreigners in Nicaragua and, by implication, in the rest of Central America. German officials, determined to gain U.S. approval, misrepresented Britain's reaction to the Eisenstück affair. The German consul had asked the captain of a British vessel to adopt a posture indicating support for the German position. The captain investigated, refused to sustain the German position, and quietly criticized the diplomatic offensive.[8]

Once the Nicaraguan government recognized the dimensions the affair was assuming, it opted to ignore the event publicly while quietly appealing for British and U.S. support to resist German demands. Nicaragua's 1877 *Memoria* on foreign affairs ignored the Eisenstück affair; it merely noted the promotion of Werner von Bergen to minister and indicated that Costa Rica had produced the only serious problems for Nicaragua that year. The Nicaraguan government denied to the British government any inherent diplomatic character to the incident, claiming that it was a matter involving the sanctity of the family. In Nicaraguan diplomat José de Marcoleta's version, Leal's wife had been enticed to return to the Eisenstück home, and when she changed her mind, she was prevented from returning to her husband. In Marcoleta's version, during Leal's attempt to "liberate" her, someone had fired warning shots and Paul Eisenstück had been mistakenly wounded by his wife. When shooting occurred, the authorities intervened to prevent further disorder. Marcoleta denied that the authorities had used excessive force. Emphasizing that the British captain had discovered no grounds for Germany's charges against the Nicaraguan government, he argued that Germany was blowing a street incident into an international affair and then seeking U.S. and British support only because it lacked the military means to enforce its will.[9]

In contrast to Britain, the U.S. government supported German objectives. Germany appreciated U.S. support because Nicaragua was "unwilling and reluctant to comply with Germany's just demands." If Nicaragua did not respond speedily, the German government intended to demand a large indemnity and a formal salute to the German flag. If Nicaragua rejected its demands, the German government contemplated a joint proceeding of interested powers. In preparation for this possibility, von Bergen inquired about the state of prior U.S. claims against Nicaragua. Possibly, U.S. Minister George M. Williamson at first supported von Bergen because he judged the situation ideal to press old claims.[10] To allay any suspicions, Germany informed the Washington government prior to each step.

Nicaraguan officials were able to point out significant weaknesses in the German case. Marcoleta warned the British government of two major errors. First, von Bergen had called for the immediate arrest of Leal, reparations to the German flag, and an indemnification of $30,000, before any investigation had determined the facts. A second problem arose, Marcoleta noted, when the U.S. and German diplomats in Nicaragua demanded to be received under circumstances of their choosing. After Nicaraguan courts had acted indecisively about convicting those guilty of the assault upon the Eisenstücks and the government was lackadaisical about intervening to speed the process, the German government ordered its minister, Werner von Bergen, to Managua to expedite a resolution of the incident and punishment of the culprits. Williamson agreed to the German diplomat's request to accompany him. They arrived on June 28, 1877, and requested an immediate audience with the president. The Nicaraguan foreign minister informed them that the president could not receive them until one P.M. on June 30. Von Bergen refused to stay later than noon on that day, and the Nicaraguan government did not advance his appointment.[11] As British Minister Sidney Locock pointed out, von Bergen had demanded an audience on the Nicaraguan president's birthday (his saint's day), an important day in Catholic countries; and even if the president were using this celebration as an excuse, the custom was so old, important, and widespread that it was unwise to challenge it by refusing to accept a one-day postponement. Regardless, both diplomats viewed their treatment as disrespectful and insulting, and they left Nicaragua together.[12] Neither von Bergen nor Williamson conducted an investigation. They simply accepted the Eisenstück version of the incident.

Before going to Managua, Williamson had anticipated Nicaraguan ill will. After the visit, he described the "uncivil behavior of the Nicaraguan towards the American and German representatives" and the "unfriendly and, indeed, purposely impolite character" of this response. At von Bergen's urging, Williamson reported to Washington that the Nicaraguan conduct was a complete and deliberate denial of justice. He expected the German government to seize the opportunity to make an impression upon Nicaragua. He regretted the failure of the visit to Managua, but noted that Nicaragua had trouble with Britain, France, and the United States in addition to Germany.[13]

Germany's image was not the only one to be tarnished. The Nicaraguan foreign minister, Anselmo H. Rivas, lodged a complaint in Washington to the effect that Williamson's support of the Eisenstück claims undermined the mutual obligations of New World states under the Monroe Doctrine and that Williamson had shown no friendly consideration toward Nicaragua. Williamson countered that Rivas was a "mendacious negro statesman." The Nicaraguan government sent a long note on the affair to all Latin American governments protesting U.S. support for the claims of a European power against a New World state. It argued that the U.S. claim for $2,000,000 for alleged damages to the Nicaraguan Transit Company, presented during this affair, applied pressure on the government of Nicaragua in favor of Germany. In the summer of 1877, Williamson argued that if the Eisenstück affair taught Nicaragua to abate its prejudice against foreigners, the lesson would be worthwhile. But within a year he revised this view and recommended that in the future U.S. diplomats in Latin America should not exercise their good offices on behalf of European powers. Aid for a European state, he said, "tended to create the belief . . . that we have abandoned the Monroe Doctrine," and that this weakened the U.S. position in Latin America. The United States needed to restore its prestige in Latin America, if it wished to aid its citizens to expand successfully into that region.[14]

Williamson, under sharp personal attack from the Nicaraguan government, acknowledged an important inconsistency between his initial position and the Monroe Doctrine. In late 1877, the escalated German diplomacy prompted Williamson to reevaluate the incident. He observed that "this affair is likely to become more serious for Nicaragua than could have been supposed from its beginnings." Since both assaults upon the Germans had occurred in the street, he did not see how the Nicaraguan government could be held responsible, except for neglect in arresting the person charged with the attack. He developed more serious reservations, however, when six war vessels appeared off Nicaragua's coast. The squadron's size indicated that von Bergen was "exhibiting an injudicious zeal or that the question has assumed an entirely new phase," and he began to revise his views on Germany's role in Nicaragua and Central America.[15]

From the beginning of the affair, Britain adopted a neutral position. British diplomatic and naval officials discovered no significant misconduct on the part of the Nicaraguan government. Nicaragua tried to widen the breach between the British non-support for Germany and the U.S. decision to support von Bergen. Marcoleta reminded the British foreign office that the U.S. position defending the alleged grievances of Germany was not an unusual stand for the United States in Central America. In 1854, he recalled, U.S. officials had shelled the city of Greytown in the British protectorate of Mosquitia on Nicaragua's Atlantic coast, and the U.S. government had aided filibusters like William Walker. Whether stimulated by Nicaraguan recollections or not, Britain continued to seek a peaceful resolution of the differences between Germany and Nicaragua. The British foreign ministry offered its good offices for Nicaraguan-German negotiations, but refused to advise the Nicaraguan government.[16] Britain would not support its competitor Germany, but was reluctant to bolster the resistance of a peripheral state to great power authority.

Nicaragua, able to obtain no more than British neutrality and much in need of moral and material aid, turned to Guatemala, the largest and wealthiest state in Central America, for support. Williamson, conveniently overlooking his own support of von Bergen, remarked derogatorily that although Central American governments might quarrel among themselves, they cooperated to resist a foreign government no matter how unjust their cause. He exaggerated Central American cooperation. Guatemalan President Justo Rufino Barrios advised Nicaragua to settle the Eisenstück affair unconditionally. He feared that the appearance of German warships would stop the arrival of immigrants who were so necessary for Central America's development. Furthermore, he speculated that resistance would cost as much as a settlement. Despite strong misgivings about the justice of the German claims, he advised Nicaragua to submit to German demands.[17]

The French naval commander also found the German claims exaggerated. French officials discovered new German vessels in the area, apparently to support the German claims. Smarting from the 1870–71 war, the French naval ministry ordered its vessels to avoid direct contact with the German vessels; but although it wished to avoid taking sides in the dispute, the French government followed the affair closely.[18]

The German government chose to see the Eisenstück affair as one of a class of insults that small countries directed toward great powers. Foreign Minister Bernhard Ernst von Bülow, who Bismarck biographer Otto Pflanze claims "had become Bismarck's most trusted lieutenant even in domestic affairs," sought a general framework to guide future German responses to similar incidents caused by the expansionism of German foreign policy and business activity in the Mediterranean, Africa, Asia, and Latin America. A German foreign ministry official had been killed at Salonika, Greece, in 1876; other incidents had produced the death or injury of German merchants or government officials in Asia and Africa in 1875 and 1876. The German government had responded slowly and ineffectively with a navy that had only received modest increases since the early 1860s. Von Bülow insisted that the German cabinet establish rules to respond to similar situations in the future. He presumed that the policy adopted in the Eisenstück affair would establish a precedent for German response to inappropriate action by other governments around the globe.[19]

In response to von Bülow's efforts, the German government demanded complete respect for its agents and its empire. In the process, it would test the capacity of its new navy to respond to distant disturbances and to enforce respectful treatment of imperial officials or subjects. The German government gathered a squadron of six war vessels off the coasts of Nicaragua and a landing party in case its ultimatum—a twenty-four-hour period to pay $30,000 and to salute the German flag—was ignored. In order to protect the squadron, a German landing party actually seized weapons and munitions at San Juan del Norte. Von Bülow was convinced that a forceful response of this sort would undercut future affronts to imperial interests.[20]

The Eisenstück affair deeply scarred German-Nicaraguan relations. The Nicaraguan government, under threat of a landing force, paid the indemnity and arranged a symbolic salute to the German flag. In June 1878, the German government expressed its appreciation to the U.S. government for its support and proclaimed that the settlement would increase the security of all foreigners in Central America. Later, von Bergen solicited a medal from the imperial government to acknowledge the retiring Christian Eisenstück's service to German businessmen. Fifteen years later, however, Germany could not obtain Nicaraguan approval for the nomination of a consul from the successor firm to the Eisenstück company.[21]

U.S. and other foreign observers shared a respect for the hard work of German merchants, diplomats, and migrant entrepreneurs. In reevaluating the significance of the increased German activity in Central America, Williamson noted that U.S. merchants seemed to be losing interest in Guatemala just as German merchants were becoming enthusiastic. He observed that German merchants managed the chief commercial establishments, traded in goods from all countries, and profited more than merchants from other countries. He concluded: "The Germans and not the British are our real competition for the trade of the whole of Spanish America." U.S. Consul H. H. Leavitt noted that "Germany was becoming the great rival of the United States" in many manufactured articles. American commercial agents, too, considered Germany the prime competition throughout the isthmus.[22] It was unwise, Williamson decided, for the United States to support the diplomatic campaigns of its chief commercial competitor in Central America, especially when the German goals assumed geopolitical significance.

U.S. diplomats faced aggressive German diplomacy in Central America, spearheaded by the dynamic von Bergen. In mid-1880, Edward Lehnhoff, a German merchant and consul, was charged with fraud against the Guatemalan customs laws. When Guatemala withdrew Lehnhoff's exequatur, von Bergen solicited the good offices of U.S. Minister Cornelius A. Logan. He became incensed when Logan, having concluded from his own investigation that Lehnhoff was probably guilty, declined to support the German position. Short-tempered and impatient, von Bergen addressed the Guatemalan government disrespectfully. Logan suspected that in response to this raspy behavior, the Guatemalan government had led the other Central American governments in an unsuccessful request for von Bergen's recall.[23] Von Bergen's combative nature, strong language, and willingness to hint at the use of force earned him a hearing, but it did not earn him much respect from U.S. or Central American officials.

Von Bergen's personality may have been abrasive and his method of achieving goals unnecessarily confrontational, but his policies were consistent with German imperial decisions. Internal German economic disorder was directing attention to policies that would open up foreign markets. Foreign Minister von Bülow reminded von Bergen that "your chief task is to advance German trade interests in the area of your responsibility." Von Bülow awaited extensive reports relative to each Central American country, its products, transportation routes, commercial institutions, and trade connections in order to aid German businessmen. Von Bülow judged that Central America was awakening commercially. Blossoming economies frequently offered valuable concessions to the early comers before foreign competition was attracted to the awakening trade needs.[24] The German government hoped to obtain a strong position for its entrepreneurs in Cen-

Table 4.1   German Imports from Central America, 1880–1900
(data values in thousands of current marks;
three-, four-, or five-year averaging)

Year	Nicaragua	Central America	Total German Imports	C. A. imp. as % of Germ. imp.
1880–1884		1,692[b]	3,096,000	0.05
1885–1889		9,014[b]	3,324,000	0.26
1890–1892		16,894	4,302,000	0.39
1893–1896		34,550	4,306,000	0.80
1897–1900	2,629[a]	30,547	5,583,000	0.55

Sources: German Empire, Kaiserliches Statistisches Amt, Statistisches Jahrbuch für das Deutsche Reich (Berlin: [various publishers], 1881–   ).

[a]El Salvador, Nicaragua, Honduras combined.

[b]Mexico and Central America combined.

tral America before other metropole capitalists fully comprehended the opportunities.

Von Bergen was sensitive to the direction of the German foreign ministry in matters of foreign trade and investment. He had prepared an extensive foreign trade report even before von Bülow had requested such information. In addition to this report, which was of a magnitude seldom achieved by a consular representative, he was preparing a supplementary report based upon information gathered from all the German merchants in Central America. In this trade report, he warned the German foreign minister against believing misleading criticism of German commerce in Central America. For example, he said it was not true, as commonly charged, that German products lacked access to Central America because of poor steamship service. He referred to one of Williamson's public statements that German industrial products did not lack access to Central America (and the five most competent German merchants agreed), because local merchants gladly imported German goods. Von Bergen traced the lower share (than desired) of German imports in Central American trade to superior foreign products. He noted that the Hamburg-Amerika-Passagier-Aktiengesellschaft (HAPAG), the Hamburg–West Indies Mail Steamline, and various connecting lines supplied good service. He doubted whether better steamer service was available without government subvention. Since entering his post, he had viewed his task as one of preserving the existing communications. He recognized that the need to protect the rights of entrepreneurs was a precondition for healthy trade. Von Bergen argued that the Central American countries would experience real advancement and

Table 4.2   German Exports to Central America, 1880–1900

Year	Nicaragua	Central America	Total German Exports	Exp. to C. A. as % of Germ. exp.
1880–1884		3,007[b]	3,186,000	0.09
1885–1889		7,631[b]	3,152,000	0.24
1890–1892		7,378	3,300,000	0.22
1893–1896		8,450	3,369,000	0.25
1897–1900	1,935[a]	5,437	4,230,000	0.13

Sources: German Empire, Kaiserliches Statistisches Amt, Statistisches Jahrbuch für das Deutsche Reich (Berlin: [various publishers], 1881–   ).
[a]El Salvador, Nicaragua, Honduras combined.
[b]Mexico and Central America combined.

progress when the foreigner felt physically secure, when the merchant had legal recourse to recover loans, and when overdue debtors could be compelled legally to repay.[25] As laws and customs in Central America were shaped to accommodate foreign businessmen, von Bergen hoped, German entrepreneurs would take advantage of the opportunities.

In order to encourage German entrepreneurs to enter Central America, the German government distributed von Bergen's detailed report to chambers of commerce and businessmen's associations. Von Bergen told von Bülow that he would welcome suggestions regarding the shortcomings revealed in his report, admitting that many of the weaknesses affected all German export activity. Von Bülow responded that "he would be prepared to examine thoroughly well-founded proposals relative to the possibility and purposefulness of intervention on the part of the government."[26] German economic involvement in Central America, which had waned during the 1860s, increased at a marked rate in the mid-1870s, although the volume of German exports and imports remained small in the early 1880s (Tables 4.1 and 4.2). Both exports and imports grew rapidly from the mid-1880s through the 1890s, although imports of Central American products developed much more quickly. U.S. trade with Central America gained momentum in the 1860s and 1870s and surged ahead in the 1880s and 1890s (Table 4.3).

In evaluating metropole trade with Central America, it is necessary to keep in mind that Central America's population represented about 0.35 percent of the world population. Thus, if a metropole nation conducted between 0.3 and 0.4 percent of its trade with Central America, that region was absorbing a fair share of the metropole's trade when calculated on a per capita basis. Whereas U.S. trade figures revealed a rapidly expanding expor-

Table 4.3   U.S. Imports from and Exports to Central America, 1848–1898
(data values in 1,000 of dollars; five- or six-year averaging)

Year	Total U.S. imports from Central America	U.S. imports from C.A. as % total U.S. imports	Total U.S. exports to C.A.	U.S. exports to C.A. as % total U.S. exports
1848–1852	121	0.06	191	0.10
1853–1857	167	0.05	281	0.10
1858–1862	247	0.08	131	0.04
1863–1867	559	0.16	366	0.12
1868–1872	1,133	0.23	476	0.12
1873–1878	2,419	0.48	954	0.16
1879–1883	3,716	0.57	1,643	0.20
1884–1888	6,749	1.02	3,131	0.44
1889–1893	8,958	1.10	5,616	0.64
1894–1898	9,254	1.29	6,593	0.70

Sources: U.S. Congress, *Commerce and Navigation* (Washington, D.C.: GPO, 1851–   );
U.S. Secretary of the Treasury, Bureau of Statistics, *Statistical Abstract of the United States* (Washington, D.C.: GPO, 1878–   ).

tation of "overproduction," both Germany and the United States experienced explosive growth in the importation of Central American coffee and other products.

Revitalized German activity in Central America—indeed throughout much of Latin America—was not restricted to trade, shipping, and investment. A permanent German penetration of the New World would require social and cultural agencies to preserve the Germanic character of new settlers, long-time residents, and entrepreneurial establishments. Dissemination of German culture could acquaint host country leaders and their children with German civilization. This domestic leadership group would facilitate further German penetration of these peripheral political economies. To this end, the institutions of German culture needed the best assistance the German government could supply. In 1879, for example, the royal chartered Evangelic Society for Protestant Germans in North America wished to drop "North" from its name so that it could work throughout the New World, a sign of the increased presence of Protestant Germans there. The view of culture as a cohort to informal economic expansion was also evident in the formation of the Deutsches Auslands-Institut (German Foreign Institute) in the 1880s. Germans assumed more active roles in Central American society, yet they also organized to maintain the German language and culture.[27] German society marshaled cultural support for the nation's economic expansion.

Von Bergen welcomed cultural support for German economic objectives because he recognized that German and U.S. objectives in Central America were essentially competitive. The anti–North American attitude he began to develop in the late 1870s intensified in the course of the 1880s. In late 1880, during a dinner attended by the U.S. minister and many Central American officials to celebrate the opening of the Guatemalan Central railroad, von Bergen asked Salvadoran Foreign Minister Gallegos "how long he believed El Salvador could retain her freedom and autonomy." According to Gallegos, when he asked for an explanation, von Bergen replied that "the United States proposed to absorb the Central American states; that, if [Salvadorans] wished to avoid such a result, they should at once form an alliance with some power able to protect them; that the [Guatemalan Central] railroad . . . was the entering wave of a flood of Yankee immigration which would submerge the Central American States and drive out the natives." Gallegos verified that these incredible remarks were made at a public ceremony, and when von Bergen repeated similar sentiments on other public occasions, the U.S. minister in Central America was alarmed. Secretary of State William Evarts, assuming that the German government could not possibly approve of such inflammatory statements, expected to dispose of the matter easily. Although the German government offered satisfactory explanations, von Bergen probably expressed the thoughts of many German businessmen and officials in Central America.[28]

By 1880 even U.S. Minister Cornelius Logan, a long-time Anglophobe, agreed with his predecessor George Williamson that Germany, rather than Britain, represented the severest threat to U.S. security and transit objectives in the region. He categorized German competition as the gravest challenge to U.S. primacy in Central America. He concluded that "the nation which is now more directly and openly aspiring to supremacy in Central America is that of Germany." Most merchants and sailing vessels on the west coast, he reported, were German. The German penetration was so complete that German-born, naturalized Americans often headed American firms. This undesirable situation, Logan cautioned, contributed to the success of foreign imports, to the low volume of U.S. imports, and to the strong prejudice against U.S. citizens. He later reported to the State Department that the busiest diplomat opposing American policy was von Bergen: "His zeal in opposing the United States was remarkable. He constantly called private conferences of the European representatives, at which he revealed some new plan of our Government against the interests of their respective countries." Because he saw von Bergen trying to coordinate French, British, and German opposition to U.S. objectives, Logan viewed

German New World activities as the chief threat to the Monroe Doctrine and panamerican cooperation.[29]

Germany was not alone in challenging U.S. economic penetration of Central America. Other major European states retained interests there. Logan noted that Spain had also warned of American influence tied to the Guatemalan railroad. Logan observed widespread foreign influences being used "to prevent the entrance of Americans into this country"; England tried, for example, to obtain the second railroad concession in Guatemala. Logan believed, however, that U.S. resistance had blunted Britain's designs on Central America. Transit was vital to all trading nations. Since the European powers predominated commercially in Guatemala and along the Pacific coast of Middle America, Logan doubted whether these powers would allow the best routes to their trading areas to fall under the sole control of the United States. He suggested that the United States should meet the challenge from the European trading nations by unilaterally terminating the Clayton-Bulwer Treaty and establishing protectorates.[30]

Metropole expansion in the late nineteenth century raised pressing problems of cooperation and competition for the core states. Germany and the United States both viewed Central America with rising expectations and a growing sense of the usefulness of that region as a pathway into the world economy. The possibility for cooperation was reduced when both became acutely aware that Central America offered valuable opportunities that could not be conveniently shared. Transit and coffee were obvious values, but Central America offered more. Its land and labor could be shaped into profitable forms, if adequately understood. If treated correctly, for example, the region could absorb various types of technological products. In fact, in the 1880s Germany established markets in Central America for industrial firms like Krupp and Siemens, for pharmaceutical products, and for other advanced technologies. Germany achieved market and investment successes in the years between 1870 and 1914 only through strenuous competition with the United States, Great Britain, and other states. Tension increased as the U.S. and German political economies sought similar market, investment, and political-military objectives in Central America.[31]

Despite the legacy of the Eisenstück brothers and von Bergen's arrogance in the late 1870s and early 1880s, German merchants and entrepreneurs were numerous in Nicaragua by the 1890s. The fifteen persons reported for 1891 (Table 4.4) represented only the adult male residents living around Managua; many other German residents lived in the coffee and mining areas. The figure of four hundred German residents in 1905 (possibly also only adult males) revealed how extensive German settlement had become in Nicaragua.

Table 4.4   Foreign Settlers in Nicaragua, 1860–1906

	French	German	U.S.
1861	12–15a		
1876	40b		
1885	ca. 12c		
1891		15d	
1892/4	54e		
1899	100f		
1904	200a		
1905		400g	
1906			123h

aChristine Eusebe, "Les investissements français en Amérique centrale et dans l'aire des caraïbes" (Maîtrise, Université de Paris X [Nanterre], 1972), 12.

bAube du Seignlay to Perigot, June 24, 1876, BB4 1075, Archive de l'armée de la mer, hereafter Adam.

cIn Managua, Descamps to Admiral, March 2, 1885, BB4 1596, Adam.

dAdult males living around Managua only. Gustavo Lembke to Marshall Biederstein, Nov. 19, 1901, 09.01, Nr. 52608, Bundesarchiv, Potsdam.

eTwenty-four Men, lists in Commerce, F12 7414, Archives Nationales, Paris.

fR. Duval to Min. Marine, Feb. 11, 1899, BB4 1319, Adam.

gPaul Behneke to Emperor William, May 18, 1905, RM 5/v. 5402, Bundesarchiv, Militärarchiv, Freiburg.

hArthur Wallace to Robert Bacon, Jan. 6, 1906, CD, Managua: 5 (T 634/r 5). Only those registered at Managua.

José Santos Zelaya's assumption of power in the revolution of 1893 facilitated the reopening of Nicaragua for German interests. President Zelaya represented the liberal elite which eagerly sought the development of national resources, which meant increased opportunities for foreign capital, technology, and trade. Zelaya also represented a nationalist movement which, learning from Central America's historical experience with U.S. expansionism, intended to attract a variety of foreign capitalists to develop Nicaragua.[32]

In the 1870s and 1880s, Germany and the United States experienced several economic downturns. Increasingly, the leadership in both societies argued for external policies—concerning access to foreign markets and raw materials—to ameliorate the alleged overproduction problems which were creating domestic social and economic crises. Expansion led to conflicts like the Eisenstück incident. When the German foreign office interpreted the affair as an affront to all foreign residents (although especially to German honor and status), it sought support from Britain and the United States, the other chief metropole powers in Nicaragua (and Central America). British officials considered the matter unworthy of their participation. With some U.S. support, the German military gained a short-term victory. Williamson originally seconded German objectives but quickly altered his view. He (and his successor, Logan) realized that Germany was the chief challenger to U.S. objectives in Central America. He recognized that the United States had to act alone throughout Latin America because it risked undermining the Monroe Doctrine by dragging European powers into the affairs of the New World.

The German foreign office considered the guidelines it adopted to resolve the Eisenstück affair fundamental to its long-term policy for confronting resistance by peripheral and semi-peripheral states to the penetration of German agents, entrepreneurs, and officials. Germans were encountering difficulties in many areas where they sought commercial control over raw materials. Germany's reaction to the Eisenstück incident demonstrated that German power would protect its subjects, officials, and national honor and prestige with force if necessary. The Eisenstück affair awoke U.S. officials to the challenge of the newly unified German state to U.S. predominance in Central America. When von Bergen followed the Eisenstück affair with an acrimonious public complaint of U.S. railroad building as a threat to Central American sovereignty and then with a venomous rebuke of Logan for not sustaining his position in the Lehnhoff dispute, German-U.S. relations entered a phase in which mutual support would occur rarely in Central America.

In the late nineteenth century, Germany and the United States increasingly viewed each other more as threatening competitors than as useful partners. The mutual distrust between German and U.S. agents was evident not only in Central America but also in Europe (over pork as symbol for trade generally), the Caribbean, Samoa, the Philippines, the Congo, and Turkey. They engaged in an ever-sharpening competition to dominate regions that held out the promise of ameliorating their persistent economic problems at home.

5

Conflicting U.S. and Central American

Economic Priorities: From the Open Door to Exploitative

Panamericanism, 1881–1889

The late-nineteenth-century U.S. economy was crisis-prone. The recurring economic turmoil prompted the leadership to adopt policies to create outlets in foreign markets, and the United States looked first to Latin America because that region was long expected to become a closer economic partner. The depressions of the 1870s and 1880s persuaded some U.S. leaders to shape a formal panamerican policy to facilitate trade with Latin America. With little study of the Latin American economies and no formal consultation with Latin American leaders, the U.S. vision of panamericanism was restricted to resolving U.S. domestic problems, not meeting Latin American needs.

The United States first called for a panamerican conference in 1881 in the hope of persuading Latin American nations to join in building an economic system similar to the U.S. domestic economy. The initial conference was cancelled in 1882 because of Republican party politics. Several years later, in the midst of another depression, the U.S. Congress formed the Central and South American Trade Commission to discover means to increase trade with Latin America. U.S. politicians, faced with recurring economic dysfunction, supported a bipartisan call for a panamerican conference in 1889. The United States, however, was not the only metropole society looking to Latin America for assistance in the resolution of domestic problems rising from the world depression of 1873–1898. And despite liberal free-trade rhetoric, U.S. officials and businessmen did not welcome foreign competition in the Caribbean–Central American region.[1]

The panamericanism of the 1880s, associated with "good" ideas— arbitration, peace, national security, the Monroe Doctrine, and the Western Hemisphere idea—was expected to create the market conditions necessary for successful U.S. commercial expansion. This initial panamerican activity pointed out a fundamental distinction between U.S. and Latin American expectations. Whereas the United States proposed mainly economic arrangements, the Latin American delegates to panamerican conferences often struggled to include political and cultural affairs on the agenda. Even in the realm of economic panamericanism, Latin American states considered getting U.S. investment that would promote their own development as important as expanding commercial ties to the United States. But U.S. leaders took little interest in encouraging investment in Latin America so long as the U.S. political economy was absorbing large quantities of European capital.[2]

The same market expansion tools that were fundamental in the domestic version of mid-nineteenth-century liberalism—a national currency and banking law, a national communications system, economic development programs, and a protective tariff—found panamerican counterparts in the 1880s. In other words, policies that had failed to produce stable, ordered progress on the national level were tried out in the hemispheric arena. The banking and currency legislation of the 1860s found its counterpart in the call for a New World silver coinage and a panamerican bank with the same limited objective as the Civil War domestic banking law—to facilitate commercial exchange. The transcontinental railroad and telegraph lines had their counterparts in resolutions encouraging steamship and telegraph service and a panamerican railroad. The domestic development sought through the homestead laws, and the mining and agricultural provisions of the land grant college act had counterparts in weights, measures, and customs regulations and in proposals for scientific and educational exchanges and expeditions. The scientific expeditions to Latin America, like similar expeditions in the development of the U.S. West, searched for minerals, transit or communications routes, and agricultural opportunities. The domestic tariff had its counterpart in James G. Blaine's call for a New World *Zollverein* (customs union). Just as the domestic reforms built a tariff wall around a liberal market economy, the U.S. version of panamericanism proposed a priority zone for hemisphere commerce.[3]

Distrust of foreign penetration led the United States to reject the Open Door policy for Latin America in favor of the privileged position of the Monroe Doctrine and panamericanism. U.S. trade expansion never depended chiefly upon penetrating Central America, or even Latin America, but rather upon using the Central American isthmus to reach the markets of the Pacific basin (from the west coast of the New World to the Pacific islands and on to east and southeast Asia). From this perspective, Central America occupied a key place in U.S. expansionism. Panamericanism became a vital tool in efforts to ameliorate the cyclical crises of the industrial economy and to expand U.S. authority in Latin America while simultaneously undermining European competitors there.[4] The successful implementation of this two-edged policy would cost the competing European metropoles dearly.

The depressions of 1873–78 and 1882–85 convinced more business-men of the need for external markets. The depressions reinforced the argu-ments of the spokesmen for sectors of the economy that had saturated markets in good economic years by adding the voices of businessmen who faced saturated markets in bad years. The increased pressure to export surpluses entailed expanding distribution. The Panama Canal project of the French engineer Ferdinand de Lesseps, ostensibly a private undertaking begun in 1879, greatly disturbed many U.S. political, military, business, and intellectual figures. The elite resented the idea that a European metropole competitor might control the vital link between the Atlantic and Pacific. Reviving panamericanism seemed a natural way to undermine this Euro-pean threat to New World well-being and security. U.S. expansion inter-acted with concepts like panamericanism, Manifest Destiny, and the Open Door policy to justify the search for well-being and security in the world.[5]

The French historian Archille Viallate observed that the United States had ignored the half dozen prior panamerican conferences. He pointed out that the depression of the 1870s and overproduction in the internal econ-omy coincided with Secretary of State James G. Blaine's calls for confer-ences in 1881 and 1889. Modern historians have rediscovered that Blaine's call for an 1881 panamerican conference was a response to the 1873–1878 depression and to an early "glut" analysis of U.S. economic troubles. In the mid-1880s, U.S. society faced the second economic downswing within a decade.[6] The recurring disorders caught the attention of many politicians.

In the 1880s, the United States expanded its commercial facilities to reach the world market effectively. It established regular inspection of consular posts, redefined consular functions and duties, published more frequent consular reports, and improved steamship, telegraph, and postal service. Domestic economic growth and the de Lesseps project revived canal interest. In addition to external steamship communications links, U.S. promoters offered the Central American states cheap internal com-munications to encourage exchange with metropole economies. Treaties providing for extradition and civil liberties were procured to facilitate the expansion of U.S. agencies abroad. Firms discovered that competent em-ployees were unlikely to accept jobs abroad if they could not enjoy civil liberties approximating those available to North Americans. Extradition was essential because enterprises were reluctant to invest abroad if the home office could not punish agents who misused the firm's assets. Many of the infrastructure alternatives, however, were not reciprocal. Central American agents did not flock to the United States to invest and sell. Most changes benefited firms and capitalists from the metropole, not the Central American states. Later, the United States manipulated the Pan American

Union movement to facilitate its own market expansion rather than to promote Latin American development.[7]

Historian Russell H. Bastert and German and British diplomats have assigned political as well as economic factors to Blaine's role in the revival of panamericanism. They have argued that Blaine's call for a panamerican conference in 1881 was a last-minute effort calculated to save his diplomatic reputation and to bolster his presidential aspirations for 1884. "With the aid of the expandable Monroe Doctrine," the German legation suggested, Blaine had used his hectic last months in office in late 1881 "to strengthen the influence of the United States on the whole American continent and to make himself visible, in view of the next presidential elections, as the representative of the Monroe Doctrine." Various foreign observers believed that this political perspective explained Blaine's notes to Britain on the Clayton-Bulwer pact, his intervention in the Mexican-Guatemalan border dispute, his call for a Washington arbitration conference in late 1882, and other steps in regard to Latin America. Bastert argued that the rejection of the proposed 1882 conference by Blaine's successor, Secretary of State Frederick Frelinghuysen, became a turning point in the interamerican conference idea. With Blaine dissociated from the project, the idea was removed from the inner bickering in the Republican party.[8] While arguments based on the internal political forces behind Blaine's call for a panamerican conference are informative, they are not the best perspective available.

The more convincing analyses of Blaine's 1881 call have focused upon geopolitics and social imperialism. Historian Ricaurte Soler considered Blaine the first imperialist of a new U.S. school that referred to "our America" in the sense of the Americas. Blaine's commercial continentalism spread from north to south in place of the territorial continentalist's east to west course. Blaine repeatedly acknowledged the need to promote the sale of the swelling surplus of the American economy in Latin America. His panamerican project envisioned a New World customs union, a north-south railroad, commercial reciprocity, steamship lines, a New World currency, and arbitration to extend the free trade system effectively into Latin America.[9] Soler considered Blaine's vision a master plan for a large informal empire.

Historian Richard Winchester also discerned an organized plan in Blaine's geopolitics. He argued that Blaine divided the world into three parts—Europe, the Americas, and Asia—and that "Central America formed the vital artery in Blaine's conception of the American system." The isthmus, intertwining a north-south railroad with an east-west canal, would bind the Americas together and connect European and Asian areas. Blaine contended that if Britain could control numerous points along the route to India, then "the United States must demand an analogous advantage for itself on the American continents." Blaine's vision was free-trade oriented because the problem was clearly a glut of goods, not of capital. He showed no interest in exporting capital, because North America still imported capital. Thus, he was unenthusiastic when some delegates at the 1889 conference called for an interamerican bank. When the conference nevertheless passed a hemispheric banking resolution, he neither endorsed its resolution nor asked Congress to address the matter.[10]

The bank issue revealed fundamental differences in Central American and U.S. views of interamerican relations. The liberal governments of Central America, eager for development, needed capital which the right kind of bank could furnish. The United States, seeking to unload its surplus agricultural and industrial production in exchange for raw materials, wanted Central America to reduce tariffs, improve transportation ties, unify weights and measures, agree to extradition and reciprocity laws, and to pass other legislation to improve the flow of trade. To achieve these goals, the State Department proposed seven specific topics for consideration at the 1889 conference: (1) steps to promote the prosperity of the American states; (2) "formation of an American customs union for promoting inter-American trade"; (3) establishing "regular and frequent communications"; (4) uniform customs regulations, port dues and charges, classification and evaluation of merchandise, invoices, and regulation of sanitation of vessels and quarantine laws; (5) a "uniform system of weights and measures, and laws to protect patent-rights, copyrights, and trade-marks . . . and for the extradition of citizens"; (6) creation of a common silver coin as legal tender for New World commercial transactions; and (7) an arbitration plan to promote peaceful settlement of disputes.[11] Blaine focused almost exclusively upon U.S. desires for increased commercial exchange and ignored Latin American needs for capital. This flaw disturbed the Central and South American officials who were expected to welcome Blaine's vision.

Cultural barriers, not just different economic objectives, underlay the tension between U.S. and Central American officials. U.S. diplomats recognized the cultural difficulties connected with efforts to create panamericanism. The minister to Nicaragua, Charles N. Riotte, contended that U.S. trade would fare better in the Caribbean–Central American region once the Spanish American countries were freed from Spanish customs and culture. Assistant Secretary of State Francis Mairs Huntington Wilson maintained that "pan-Americanism, built upon any imaginary natural affinity between typical North Americans and the peoples who live between the Rio Grande and Cape Horn, must be doomed to failure." Cultural, racial, and ethnic factors marked the recurring Anglo-Latin misunderstandings on economic matters.[12]

Latin America was presumed to want and need the same things that the U.S. society wanted and needed. One idea that attracted considerable support was the proposal to construct an interamerican railroad from the United States to the tip of South America. Hinton Helper, whose book *The Impending Crisis* foretold in the 1850s of a civil war in North America, became fascinated with the project of an interamerican railroad in the 1860s. In the years prior to the panamerican conferences, Helper's lobbying attracted Central American support for such a railroad. The Honduran government offered to facilitate the project when it entered Honduras. The Costa Rican foreign minister, Cleto González Víquez, supported a conference to discuss a railroad to the tip of South America. He expected that a railroad running down the "spine of the continent" would become "the most efficient means of making firm and lasting the friendship . . . among the diverse American states and . . . would foment and advance in the highest degree their commercial and other relations."[13] The Central American leaders thought the interamerican railroad would expand communications with the world market, increase the sales of their products, and attract foreign capital and settlers. The U.S. government viewed the project as a means of securing a priority position in Latin America's trade.

The United States had traditionally neglected Latin America, and so the decision in 1881 to cancel the conference set for the next year did not surprise Latin American leaders. Frelinghuysen, however, regretted the anti–Latin American image created by canceling the conference. In 1884, he used the bipartisan call for a Central and South American Trade Commission to soothe Latin American sensibilities and to increase the modest trade between the Americas. The Central and South American Trade Commission reflected the developing consensus that getting out from under the economic downswings would require regular and cheaper shipping, more effective consular service, tariff adjustments, and uniform customs regulations, among other steps. An exchange of views had prepared treaties about postal affairs, traveling sales people, and civil rights. The trade commission attracted attention, but it lacked the prestige to assure a powerful position. Historian Joseph Smith has suggested that the commission did little to promote the U.S. image abroad. Conceivably, its chief function was to strengthen domestic awareness of Latin America and to marshal support for interamerican commercial goals.[14] The trade commission was the product of the rejection of the panamerican conference in 1882 and of the economic crisis of 1882–85.

The distribution problems of the U.S. economy played an important role in the formation of the trade commission. William E. Curtis, secretary to the commission, asserted that generally "the necessity of something being done by the Government to secure a market for the surplus products of the country seemed to be realized to a greater and more serious degree." Yet without satisfactory direct shipping lines, U.S. goods for South America had to be shipped via Liverpool or Hamburg, which reduced the volume of sales and the profit margin. The commission received numerous invitations to consult with business leaders, but time permitted formal visits only to New York, Boston, Philadelphia, Baltimore, San Francisco, and New Orleans. It learned that businessmen agreed on the need for commercial expansion abroad, but differed strongly on the specific policies necessary to achieve it. They agreed that reducing trade hindrances (chiefly tariff and customs matters) and distributing commercial information were desirable. Other proposals, like subsidized steamship lines, received only partial support. The commission learned that "manufacturers . . . are anxious that markets may somewhere be found for their surplus products, and favor . . . the encouragement of steamship communications by the granting of liberal subsidies." Manufacturers with secure markets in Latin America and established merchants in cities with regular trade connections, however, were not enthusiastic about reducing transportation costs, since this would encourage potential competitors. The businessmen also asked for more frequent publication of consular reports, which they complained were only obtainable by favor of a congressman.[15] The commission heard these views of the business community before it entered Central and South America.

The commission's work required the participation of U.S. diplomats and consuls. One of the most helpful was the U.S. consul in San José, John Schroeder. He supplied the commissioners with extensive information on Costa Rica's political economy and the actual and potential role of foreigners in business there. The issues he explored were vital to any group of foreigners who hoped to penetrate the isthmian political economies. His analysis of the other Central American states enhanced the value of his reports. In one report, Schroeder insisted that since "everyday politics in the Central American republics encroached upon the rights of their citizens to produce, export, and import the necessities of the country," he had to discuss domestic politics. The picture was not pretty. The countries had liberal constitutions, but their leaders were capricious. The armies that sustained the governments had little respect for treaties, constitutions, or the law. He cautioned that "neither politically nor commercially is . . . any friendly dealing with these republics possible, unless our Government at the same time is acting with unflinching authority." Because interoceanic transit was so vital, he preferred to acquire the Nicaraguan canal route. He recognized, however, that the options of annexation or colonization of the isthmian canal sites were unacceptable for cultural, ethnic, political, and legal reasons.[16] His view of the disordered nature of isthmian politics convinced him that relations with Central America had to be stabilized.

Schroeder observed that because Central American governments were more interested in patronage than in popular welfare, treaties would be upheld only if they offered personal advantages to Central American officials. He considered the "conditions [ripe] for enlarged and continued trade." He acknowledged the hierarchy of exploitation: "enlarged commercial activity in this country [must] . . . develop the purchasing power of the people at large, as the higher classes can enjoy the luxuries of life only by their income from the productivity of the actual laboring classes." He advised North Americans to export farm tools, machinery, hardware, utensils, and other goods needed by the agrarian population. The pitfalls and challenges for U.S. merchants were numerous, he said. Businessmen needed to become competitive with European merchants who warehoused goods, extended credit, and sent wholesale agents familiar with the language and customs of Central Americans. In particular, U.S. businesses had to avoid sending salesmen who belonged to "the well known greedy peddler tribe." Often peddlers, loaded with counterfeit goods, cheated the populace until they were robbed and then called for U.S. protection. Such incidents, he warned, left lasting negative impressions, for Costa Ricans believed "the master to be like his representatives." U.S. merchants needed a good reputation and a fair Costa Rican tariff. Schroeder conceded that "Costa Rica has managed to be the recipient of unjust profits out of the United States by sustaining an almost prohibitive tariff upon all goods imported, while almost all goods exported from Costa Rica to the United States are allowed free of duty." If U.S. shoes and boots could be imported duty free at Limón, Schroeder knew that they could compete against the high-priced domestic products. He hypothesized that a retributive U.S. tariff policy could ruin Costa Rican banana plantations, without considering who profited from them.[17] The largest profits in the banana trade belonged to U.S.-owned banana companies and railroads in Costa Rica and to U.S. shipping firms, wholesalers, and retailers.

Schroeder advised the commission that if Costa Rica was expected to develop the potential to supply U.S. markets with surplus agricultural goods and raw materials, it would need capital. He recommended establishing a hypothecary bank for farmers. Debt-burdened Costa Rica could not support a bank adequately, yet its rich land, unburdened by debt, desperately needed fertilizers and other improvements. A bank would allow borrowing to increase the land's value. Schroeder recognized that capital would not move into unstable foreign countries unless the United States did more than simply reaffirm the sanctity of treaties.[18]

Schroeder expected Costa Rica to use borrowed capital to modernize its agricultural sector, hoping that enhanced profitability would lead to purchases of U.S. products. He noted:

> This country is entirely void of [factories] and manufacturing establishments. It lacks consequently the strong patriotic class of citizens rightly surnamed 'the manufacturing nobility,' whose aim and pride it is . . . to drive out foreign imports. Costa Rica can consequently not defend itself against the press of foreign importations, and as our own manufacturing nobility . . . has produced goods in abundance for export, then it seems sensible for these goods to be made saleable first of all in those countries . . . situated so near the United States as the Central American republics.

He recommended a subsidized steamship connection to facilitate the exchange of Costa Rican primary products for U.S. manufactures. He argued that Costa Rica had to export in order to earn the funds needed to purchase U.S. goods. Costa Rica's "population needs an augmented purchasing power in order to support augmented trade. Neither treaties nor contracts alone will create trade. Money alone will buy goods, and where money lacks, there mercantile transactions are dead." He warned that U.S. commercial success in Costa Rica would require more than economic information; it would also require both countries to show a mutual respect for and willingness to meet each other's economic objectives. Schroeder suggested that capital was needed to build Central American infrastructure, to modernize and transform Central America's agricultural sector to fit metropole needs, to reform Central American politics, and to seduce Central American leaders into cooperation.[19] He foresaw the logic of the dependent enclave system.

Foreign Minister José Castro and Costa Rican businessmen asserted Costa Rica's desire to attract commerce, capital, and immigrants from the United States. There was, he noted, a growing dissatisfaction with the British economic role in his country. U.S. interests would have to compete with a powerful British influence, he observed, because "Costa Rica owes English capitalists an enormous debt, and . . . her public improvements are largely controlled by London Syndicates. This influence is prejudicial to American interests, and will undoubtedly be felt in whatever diplomatic negotiations the commission may have with the Government." Castro suggested that if Europe would not accept a reasonable gold to silver ratio, the New World nations should direct their products elsewhere, even if that meant confining American commerce to American waters. Costa Rica wished to exchange its natural products for North American manufactured goods, Castro claimed. He suspected that flour would not be allowed in duty free because falling coffee prices were turning some Costa Rican farmers to wheat production. He strongly endorsed a panamerican congress as one means to promote New World cooperation. Cooperation would be difficult because many Costa Ricans charged that U.S. canal diplomacy often ignored Costa Rican rights. He agreed that trade and shipping problems needed to be dealt with. His report concluded with a discourse on Costa Rica's need for favorable financial arrangements and investment capital.[20]

The Central and South American Commission's final report on Costa Rica underscored the basic North–South American divergence on mutual economic relations. The commission listed seven problem areas in which the United States could improve its modest but growing trade with Costa Rica. The problems were as follows: European coffee commissions that were more attractive than the one offered by the United States; European willingness to offer long-term credit at low interest; unreliable U.S. commission agents (a striking exception was the McKesson and Robbins drug firm which sent an "honest" agent who built up business from $5,000 to $250,000 in five years); the fact that German and British wholesale merchants residing in Costa Rica had links with Europe whereas the United States lacked a resident wholesale merchant; the ability of British and German merchants to make loans to coffee producers in advance of the crop harvest, which induced them to buy English and German goods; the 10 percent reduction in duties on goods entering Costa Rica on British Royal Mail packets (although this privilege was about to expire and apparently would not be renewed); and the fact that English, German, and French manufacturers and merchants had gained an advantage by thoroughly studying Costa Rican consumer tastes. The commission report claimed that "the exalted position of the United States in wealth, arts and civilization [was] a constant light drawing the attention of those who have modeled their political institutions on ours," and that "conditions existed for North Americans to secure the trade of this republic by the aid of a judicious reciprocity treaty and the practice of the same sagacity and fair dealing that characterizes their English and German competitors." It asserted that there was "a universal preference existing among importers to purchase merchandise in our markets," and then urged formation of a fraternal panamerican union to oppose European intervention.[21] It made no mention of establishing a device for transferring capital to Central America, apparently assuming that such a union would result from the satisfaction of U.S. objectives, not from the mutual fulfillment of North and South American needs.

The commission intended to hear from the leadership in all five Central American countries before submitting its final recommendations. Despite the rumors of regional hostility to his 1885 decree declaring the unification of Central America, Guatemalan President Justo Rufino Barrios received the Central and South American Commission warmly. Conceivably, concern about the political impact of panamericanism prompted him to try to unite Central America prior to a meeting of the New World states. He hoped the commission's work would help him "to secure immigration and the investment of capital" from the United States, and he expressed interest in treaties to further trade and to guarantee personal rights and property. He warmly supported the Nicaraguan canal, a north-south railroad, and a common New World silver coin. The U.S. commission praised Barrios's friendly disposition toward the United States and declared Guatemala to be the most progressive Central American state in education and internal development, citing a Protestant mission from the United States as one "evidence of progress." It said that the chief failures of U.S. firms seeking more trade were inattention to the needs of the Guatemalan market, improper packaging, and agents incompetent to study the needs of the Guatemalans.[22] The commission abbreviated its Central American stay because of the outbreak of hostilities when El Salvador resisted the Guatemalan Union decree with force and because it was content with its successful visits to Costa Rica and Guatemala.

The commission's "General Recommendations" to the U.S. government drew upon visits to Costa Rica and Guatemala, published information from the other three Central American states, and correspondence with U.S. consular agents. Its final report called for an effective navy and merchant marine, a speedy solution to the question of interoceanic communication, and an extension of the U.S. railway system to Central and South America. William Curtis insisted that Latin America could alleviate U.S. labor unrest and absorb commodity surpluses, especially if communication and transportation improvements were made, and suggested that U.S. tariff policy would have to accommodate Latin American needs.[23] The commission educated North Americans about Latin America and played a role in preparing the American political scene for the 1889 Pan American Conference.

The unrelenting world economic crisis of 1873–1898, and the U.S. "overproduction" crisis of those years nudged American businessmen, political leaders, and intellectuals toward social imperialism in the form of an Open Door hypothesis. The United States needed more trade, cheaper raw materials, security of communications, and even migration outlets so that businessmen, laborers, and investors of capital could seek short-term profit. Some of the more advanced sectors of the U.S. economy, such as the railroad

industry, even sought investment opportunities abroad. When U.S. entrepreneurs went abroad, however, they encountered sharpened competition
from the metropole states of Europe, which was frequently assumed to have
a political or national security dimension. Keener commercial competition
increased the fear among politicians and businessmen that the potential
canal routes might be lost to the United States. Blaine, motivated in part by
political and security concerns, regretted that Nicaragua had tried, unsuccessfully, to induce the European powers to grant protection for the canal
enterprise because Europe had not consulted American states during the
Suez negotiations. Whether the focus was economic, political, or strategic,
U.S. leaders, convinced that economic opportunities were essential to the
nation's well-being, were unwilling to accept foreign presence near the
isthmian transit routes.[24]

D. W. Herring, the U.S. consul in Tegucigalpa, argued that the isthmian
transit was of graver concern to the United States than to the European
powers because European commercial superiority could not last in the New
World. "When the United States becomes fully developed," he noted, "there
[will be] as much need for her to seek foreign markets for her surplus as the
need that now exists in these overdone countries" of Europe; for this reason,
the United States would have to root its policy in panamericanism. William
Curtis recognized the need to continue to expand hemispheric awareness of
the mutual benefit to be derived from closer commercial ties. He expected
that the "grand excursion" planned for the panamerican conference delegates in 1889—a forty-day tour of industrial and agricultural America—
would make the Latin Americans better aware of U.S. economic power and
also induce North Americans to become more energetic in pursuing Latin
American business. Curtis talked of mutuality, but he expected Latin
Americans to be awestruck with the U.S. economy. Both Herring and Curtis
chided U.S. leaders for slighting the strategic and economic value of the
Caribbean and Central American regions.[25]

Rising interest in the Pacific also focused attention on the canal areas.
Missionaries, U.S. naval officers, and merchants stressed the value of transit to a large audience in the United States. Since the French were at work
on a canal in Panama, Costa Rican officials emphasized the need for a canal
in Nicaragua. Nicaraguan diplomat Enrique Guzmán requested the 1889
conference to consider the advantages of panamericanizing a Nicaraguan
canal. When Nicaragua solicited a European guarantee for the neutrality of
the canal, Costa Rican diplomat Pérez Zeledón advised Blaine that his
government had to discuss the canal in Europe in order "not to remain
behind" Nicaragua. Costa Rica preferred to solicit U.S. advice on this
delicate matter before acting. Zeledón believed that "Blaine was absolutely

ignorant of Nicaragua's conduct" in negotiating with European powers about the canal. Blaine insisted that the United States "would never consent to the states of Europe injecting themselves . . . [into] an American canal in any form other than purely commercial, because . . . it would never suit the United States to be equal to those [powers] because of the importance of U.S. interests on the Atlantic and Pacific coasts." Blaine, anxious for all Latin American states to share his view, solicited Zeledón's concurrence. Zeledón, acting without instructions, had carefully avoided any compromise of Costa Rica's position. He had explored U.S. views, placed Nicaragua in a bad light, and gained "the sympathies of a man so important in this administration as Mr. Blaine."[26] Discussion of an isthmian canal resurrected U.S. distrust of European activity in the transit area.

The U.S. government frequently proposed panamericanism to counter European economic and transit incursions. It rejected regional Latin American cooperation as a satisfactory counter weapon to European incursions because regional agencies might also limit U.S. penetration. The Mexican minister to the United States, Matías Romero, discovered that Blaine retained his ideas on close interamerican relations and was unwilling to support Central American union. The U.S. opposition to union was understandable if disturbing. Any form of cooperation among the Central American states, Romero recognized, undermined Blaine's panamericanism and thus promoted Mexican interests in Central America.[27] The more effectively the Latin American states could deal with their own problems, individually or collectively, the less inclined they would be to join a panamerican movement headed by the northern colossus, the United States.

After the 1883–1885 depression, U.S. lobbying groups, firms, and individuals—including pressure groups like the St. Louis Exchange, the Los Angeles Board of Trade, and the San Francisco Chamber of Commerce—maneuvered persistently to link the U.S. economy to Asia and Latin America. The lure of the Asian market became more compelling as the world economic crisis deepened, but the poverty, distance, and cultural differences of the Asian market did not promise the cheap, quick opportunities the Latin American market appeared to offer. New Orleans's development of the fruit trade and U.S. domination of Central American railroads highlighted the profitability of Latin American opportunities, especially those in the Caribbean region. U.S. leaders, influenced by contemporary geopolitical thought, viewed Central America as a focal point for trade throughout the Pacific basin. In 1887, Democratic Secretary of State Thomas Bayard argued that the nation's increased interests in Central America elevated the concern of the government and society whenever disorder occurred in Central America.[28]

Central American affairs became intertwined with domestic U.S. politics in the 1888 election. The Republican platform accused President Grover Cleveland's administration of neglecting the Monroe Doctrine and permitting foreign influence and trade to obtain a firm footing in Central America. The Republicans criticized the Democrats for failing to give adequate support to the Nicaraguan canal project, which they said was indispensable for expanding trade relations with the west coast of the New World and with the whole Pacific Ocean area. The Cleveland administration's response was to have Secretary Bayard call for a panamerican congress to meet in 1889.[29]

The 1888 conference call quickly stimulated resistance from Guatemala and from the European diplomats in Central America. Guatemalan officials were upset because the United States, displeased with Guatemala's stance in a boundary dispute with Mexico, had not invited Guatemala to the congress. For a while, the Guatemalan foreign ministry threatened to maneuver to defeat the congress, but ultimately Guatemala was mollified and invited. The European diplomats were displeased for another reason. They considered the congress a step toward undermining European political, economic, and transit roles in the New World. "In order to oppose permanently the U.S. plans which threatened all European trade interests in Central America," German Minister Werner von Bergen found it "necessary to improve in every possible way the atmosphere among the five free states and to prepare them for union." The French minister in Central America believed that the projected panamerican customs union would injure all European commercial interests, and said he also expected the Latin American republics to recognize its disadvantages to them.[30] The European diplomats, however, were unable to convince their own governments that a major danger existed.

Prior to the 1889 Pan American Conference, many U.S. interest groups informed the State Department about the need for economic ties with Latin America. They suggested a variety of specific steps and general policies aimed at creating a panamericanism profitable for U.S. entrepreneurs. The Chicago and Richmond Chambers of Commerce and the American Short-Horn Breeders wanted better communications links so that U.S. wheat could penetrate Latin America and U.S. breeding steers could replace European ones. The Los Angeles Board of Trade insisted that liberal subsidies to establish first-class mail routes were vitally necessary for increasing trade. It argued that "all the Central and South American States, as well as Mexico and our own country, should share in the subsidies." Although it was the U.S. economy that desperately needed the steamship lines, the Los Angeles Board concluded that a Latin American state could be seduced to subsidize the lines by promise of growth and wealth, or by sufficient bribes.[31] U.S. interest groups commonly mentioned an improved steamship service as vital to trade expansion.

Other interest groups in the United States mentioned the need for a common currency, standardized commercial regulations, or facilities for commercial loans. The Los Angeles, National, and Omaha Boards of Trade encouraged a New World coinage based upon silver, a New World product. The New Haven Chamber of Commerce wanted commercial regulations, a standardization of port fees, invoices, sanitation, weights, measures, and trademarks. The Los Angeles Board of Trade also supported an American customs union. The Produce Exchange of Chicago asked Blaine, again secretary of state, to undertake the necessary steps to divert the huge flow of Latin American banking and office supplies from European sources to North American merchants.[32] Many interest groups alleged that adopting one or two key policies would greatly increase trade.

The Commercial Exchange of Philadelphia, a national lobbying agency, presented a whole program of changes to overhaul U.S.–Latin American commercial relations. It recommended that the 1889 Pan American Congress consider direct telegraphic communication with the export centers of South America, an interamerican commercial bank for exchange, uniform port duties, uniform classification and valuations of merchandise, commercial reciprocity, universal establishment of U.S. weights, measures, and patent law, free courts of admiralty in large ports, arbitration of difficulties without European interference, extradition for nonpolitical offenses, a Nicaraguan canal free of European interference, and "direct rapid communications" between the several countries. The Commercial Exchange condemned subsidies to shipping lines, but encouraged "proper and generous" compensation for mail lines and the removal of charges against vessels engaged in commerce. It encouraged a tariff policy aimed at establishing U.S. domination and rewarding U.S. capital that ventured into Latin America. The Commercial Exchange favored reciprocity, calling for the free admission into the United States of unmanufactured materials from Latin America in return for free entry into Latin America of U.S.-manufactured and processed goods. It was the only lobbying organization to call for a bank to facilitate the exchange of commercial paper, as a step necessary to increase trade (but not investment, as many Latin American leaders hoped).[33] In fact, all the lobbying groups placed a higher priority upon perceived U.S. needs for market expansion than on increased investment of capital in Latin America's infrastructure.

In mid-1889, the South Carolina politician and diplomat William Henry Trescott, a delegate to the Pan American Conference, counseled

Blaine that the State Department should plan carefully for the meeting. He observed that none of the seven major objectives listed in the State Department's circular for the meeting could be enacted at the conference itself, since all required legislation or treaties. The conference would only deliberate and formulate recommendations. Since the United States had initiated the conference, he assumed that the other nations would expect it to offer specific proposals. The first consideration, in Trescott's view, was whether the U.S. delegates would express their personal views or those of the U.S. government. He wondered whether the government had arrived at a definite position on the various questions. Even if the delegates were to exercise their own judgment, Trescott said, they should explore areas of agreement and distribute specific areas of responsibility prior to the conference. He recommended the creation of a special bureau to gather information, to serve as liaison with the delegation, and to offer coordination and translations to the delegation.[34]

Two items on the conference agenda, arbitration and an isthmian canal, struck Trescott as potentially explosive, because conference debate on them might produce unwanted recommendations. He doubted that the United States would submit questions of vital interest to "the decision of powers holding nothing like an equality of power and not impossibly subject to influences not friendly to our interests." Previous U.S. efforts at friendly intervention in Latin America had not produced the desired result, and arbitration seemed unlikely because there were pockets of hostility toward the United States in Latin America. A continental arbitration agreement would bring into question matters of the deepest importance to the United States, such as the interoceanic canal:

> Upon this subject we have declared with repeated emphasis our finest policy. Will any difference of opinion between us and any Central American or South American power induce us to change it? And even if we admitted the direct interest of these powers, could we admit the interference of this interest under the influence of those European powers with which their commercial relations are strongest? We ought not to conceal from ourselves that our relations with our Spanish American neighbors are not as close and friendly as they ought to be. They are suspicious.

Given the significant development of U.S. interests in the Pacific, Trescott said he "did not think a theoretical discussion advisable" on the interoceanic transit question. In the vital areas of arbitration and Central American transit, he recommended that the delegates "should be controlled and limited by the specific instructions of the government."[35]

A study of U.S. trade with Central America prepared by a Central American diplomat revealed a marked increase in the two decades before the 1889 conference, but U.S. exports to the area had actually declined (see Table 3.1). New regions of the United States, principally the Midwest, had begun to trade agricultural implements, tools, hardware, shoes, and furniture, but European goods in these classes were cheaper. The generally superior U.S. quality carried a higher price and logically would require a protected market. Among poorer consumers, not demanding superior intrinsic value in their purchases, "the competition offered by the same articles of English, French, and German make becomes irresistible." The study concluded, however, that "American genius and mechanical ingenuity overcomes in great part the cheaper labor and materials of the European competitor," so that ultimately U.S. goods will compete successfully in foreign markets.[36] The Pan American Conference was designed precisely to develop facilities to exchange U.S. surpluses of superior quality goods and processed foodstuffs for Latin American raw materials.

In addition to the conference calls and commissions of the 1880s, expositions in the United States allowed periodic State Department action to promote panamericanism. The State Department budgeted a small sum in the mid-1880s to subsidize the transportation of exhibit materials from Central and South America to the World's Industrial and Cotton Centennial Exposition at New Orleans in 1884. The State Department issued invitations to Atlanta's Cotton States and International Exposition (1891), informing its diplomatic and consular officials that "one of the principal objects of the Exposition will be to secure closer commercial relations between this country and those of Central and South America and Mexico and the West Indies." The State Department supplied funds and bureaucratic support to the various trade fairs held in the late nineteenth and early twentieth centuries for the purpose of promoting closer commercial links with Latin American states.[37]

In the immediate aftermath of the Pan American Conference, the Central American states pursued those proposals which they believed would encourage their growth and development. Between 1889 and 1898, there were interamerican conferences on monetary affairs, a railroad, and banking. U.S. Minister Lansing Bond Mizner discerned "a reluctance, or proverbial delay, on the part of these [Central American] countries to cooperate with us in the grand suggestions of the International [Monetary] Conference." Costa Rica, Honduras, and Nicaragua agreed to send delegations, but El Salvador expected to endorse "whatever action is taken by the majority of the conference" without sending delegates. Guatemala did not reply, probably because it resented U.S. pressure to resolve its border problems with Mexico. Although Manuel Aragón of Costa Rica's National Bureau of Statistics noted that financial and commercial activity would be facilitated with a panamerican currency, the U.S. government's desire for a panamerican monetary agreement received a cool reception in Central America.[38]

The 1889 conference's recommendation for an interamerican railroad met a warmer reception in Central America. The Inter-Continental Railroad Conference, which gathered in Washington in 1891, adopted the proposal for a railroad connecting North and South America. The State Department, fearing that speculators would gain control of the sale of land near the proposed route, warned each state that the final route surveyed should be free of encumbrances and should represent the "most direct, speedy and economical means of transportation by rail." The panamerican railroad project retained support until about 1905 when the U.S. automotive and highway construction businesses persuaded key domestic groups of the superior virtues of good automobile roads throughout the New World in an effort to expand the market for U.S. cars.[39]

In 1898, a meeting of Latin American countries approved the idea of founding an interamerican bank to facilitate trade. Costa Rican officials were enthusiastic: Costa Rican diplomat Joaquín Bernardo Calvo endorsed the idea of a bank, and the bureaucrat Manuel Aragón considered an interamerican bank an issue of "the most vital importance for the augmentation of commercial relations" between the American states. While granting that all American nations would benefit, they recognized that the major stimulus was "the necessity which the United States had to assure the largest markets for its overproduction"; they argued that a federally chartered bank would facilitate raising the capital, and Aragón said such a bank would benefit Costa Rica in matters of exchange and currency stabilization. The French consul in Costa Rica considered the bank proposal an effort to imitate the successful economic penetration technique of the Germans, and he warned his government that such a bank might drive the French out of Latin American markets unless France responded by creating a similar financial institution.[40] While Costa Rican officials expected a commercial bank to finance agricultural exports to both the U.S. and the European markets, a French official feared that it might redirect Costa Rican trade away from France and Europe and toward the United States.

After 1890, U.S. businessmen in Latin America enjoyed an institutional advantage not available to their European competitors. U.S. speculators and entrepreneurs benefited from the assistance of the International Bureau of American Republics, whose secretary, William Curtis, frequently assisted dubious business ventures (of North American origin) because he believed the purpose of the panamerican movement was to resolve U.S. internal problems by penetrating Latin America.[41] The committees established by the bureau inevitably bore titles that included the United States plus one Latin American state, never two Latin American states. The work of these committees served to weaken European economic ties to Latin America as well as ties between Latin American states.

Some European states responded to panamericanism with ethnic or culturally based programs of their own. Spain made efforts to resurrect its historical, cultural, and linguistic role. *La República* of Madrid claimed that the Latin American states were torn between the language and culture of the mother country and the modern civil and political system of the United States. France and Italy also emphasized the language and cultural heritage they shared with Latin America. The American promoter and publicist Francis A. Stout suspected that the Frenchman de Lesseps inspired the Hispanic revival in Spain to encourage a Latin union sympathetic to a French canal at Panama. One French writer argued that Hispanicism was a proper response to U.S. expansionism, provided Spain could assure its sister Latin states in Europe—France and Italy—that their interests were not endangered. French society, he said, expected to play a major commercial role in Latin America, and Italian society had sent a large number of emigrants to Latin America. The Hispanic movement did not fare well in Central America, however. The German chargé in Guatemala, for example, claimed that no Central American republic took a serious interest in the Madrid Hispano-American Congress. In his opinion, expressed to the German foreign minister, the Central American states wished the Hispanic movement well, but U.S. power lent panamericanism a prospect for material benefit that Spain's Hispanicism could not provide. Hispanicism could offer cultural revitalization in language, custom, and religion to Latin America's elite, but it offered much less to Indians, blacks, mulattoes, zambos, and mestizos.[42] In the 1890s, other Central American political leaders had similar reservations about both U.S.-sponsored panamericanism and Spanish-inspired Hispanicism.

The United States became a metropole state in the late nineteenth century when it developed the capability of incorporating other parts of the world into its network of accumulation. Latin America, and most immediately the Caribbean–Central America region, was an obvious and vital candidate for such incorporation, given the increased economic need to find profitable outlets for the agricultural surpluses of the Midwest and the industrial surpluses of the Northeast. As used by the U.S. government, panamericanism became a device for expanding the area encompassed in the distorted liberalism of the U.S. political economy, for solidifying the

U.S. position and preserving a priority relationship in Central America to the detriment of competitive European metropole powers. While other factors in addition to panamericanism played a role, three decades later the United States did dominate the export, import, and foreign capital markets of Latin America.

6

Morality and Political Purpose in

Theodore Roosevelt's Actions in Panama in 1903

Theodore Roosevelt's role in separating Panama from Colombia in order to obtain a favorable canal concession for the United States has attracted attention for almost ninety years. Since 1903, various historians and several contemporaries of Roosevelt have insisted that the United States was not officially involved in the Panamanian revolt of 1903, and is therefore immune to the charges of ethically unsavory conduct. Even recently, the historians Frederick Marks, James Vivian, and Richard H. Collin have sought to mitigate U.S. responsibility by presenting familiar arguments. Marks essentially adopts the position taken by Roosevelt in his autobiography, that his actions were morally justifiable because Colombian leaders acted improperly in rejecting the Hay-Herrán canal treaty. Vivian resurrects the old claim that although Roosevelt resorted to post facto braggadocio to strengthen his public image as a forceful leader, in reality, he had nothing to do with the Panamanian revolt.[1]

Most assessments of Roosevelt's role in Panama's revolution and the canal treaty of 1903 have been based on his own writings and on those of John Hay, William Howard Taft, Elihu Root, and other high-ranking associates. But there is still much to be learned from the papers of other associates of Roosevelt, particularly those of Francis B. Loomis, John B. Moore, and Frederick Jackson Turner. Yale political scientist Max Farrand, present in 1913 at a conversation about the Panama affair between Roosevelt and Harvard historian Archibald C. Coolidge, sent Turner a memorandum based upon his copious notes. Farrand's memorandum is lost, but Turner's extensive notes (about 1,200 words) and frequent quotations from it remain a major and hitherto untapped source for Roosevelt's version of his role in the affair. An examination of the Turner-Farrand notes, along with the Loomis and Moore materials, should enable us to clarify the moral and political responsibility of the Roosevelt administration in the Panama revolt. The question, simply put, is whether Colombia's alleged misconduct—in refusing to perfect a treaty granting the United States the right to build a canal at the isthmus—freed U.S. decision makers from moral responsibility for Colombia's loss of sovereignty over Panama and justified high-handed behavior on the part of U.S. officials. A reexamination of Roosevelt's role in the Panama revolution of 1903 is in order.

Since the 1820s, U.S. administrations and leaders of the political economy have frequently demanded control over any isthmian interoceanic transit site. In the 1850s, a U.S. firm built the Panama Railroad, the first transcontinental transit system and the first major U.S. investment in Latin America. In the 1870s, President Rutherford B. Hayes, concerned with the development of the United States, its security needs in the Caribbean area, and its future expansion in Asia, declared that the Panama isthmus had to be considered part of the U.S. shoreline. Admiral Alfred T. Mahan, among others, advocated a canal as a strategic necessity for the worldwide exercise of U.S. naval power. Roosevelt had long argued that a canal was essential to the security and well-being of U.S. society. Between 1897 and 1902, Republican administrations twice formed special committees under Admiral John G. Walker to investigate the transit options. For many years Nicaragua had been the favored site, but the Nicaraguan and Costa Rican governments remained unwilling to grant a canal treaty, balking at what they considered inadequate financial compensation and at the insistence that U.S. courts have jurisdiction in the canal zone. The second Walker committee decided that Panama, under the right conditions, offered the best interoceanic canal route. From the late 1890s through 1902, Colombia had negotiated several canal treaties with the United States, but each one had failed perfection and implementation. Until 1902, then, the U.S. government pursued various avenues in search of a satisfactory canal route.[2]

When Colombia rejected the canal treaty with the United States in 1901, however, Roosevelt badgered Colombia about unrelated U.S. claims, threatening that "if payment should not follow in the quickest time, the United States would find itself compelled, regretfully, to take armed action against Colombia." Roosevelt cited the need for isthmian transit to justify harsh actions against Colombia.[3]

Treaty-making involves a series of steps: negotiation, signing, legislative approval, executive ratification, and exchange of ratified treaties. Any sovereign state has the right to interrupt the process before the completion of the fifth and last step. Intriguingly, Roosevelt had led the movement in 1900 to persuade the Senate to defeat the first Hay-Pauncefote treaty (which would have allowed the United States to fortify the canal zone area) after it had been negotiated, signed, and submitted for Senate approval, precisely the kind of "jackrabbit" activity that he would condemn in Colombian leaders three years later. In both instances the rupture of the treaty process was legitimate.[4]

Whether it was wise for Colombia to exercise its sovereign right to terminate the treaty, however, is a different question. In June 1903 French promoter Philippe Bunau-Varilla cabled Colombian President José Marroquín that the rejection of the canal treaty left the United States with two options: to build a canal in Nicaragua, to the permanent loss of Colombia; or to construct a Panama canal "after secession and declaration of independence of the Isthmus of Panama under protection of the United States, as happened with Cuba."[5] Given Bunau-Varilla's close relationship to senior State Department officials and through these officials with Roosevelt, his warning to Colombian politicians deserved close attention.

As the tension in regard to the Panama canal mounted, both Roosevelt and Assistant Secretary of State Loomis stressed the moral, humanistic role of the United States in the Caribbean area. In July 1903 Loomis highlighted the values of liberty and education while downplaying the role of capitalism: "we may endeavor to Americanize the New World and perhaps the Old, not by the conquering power of the almighty dollar, not by manifestations of force, but rather by the dissemination of those lofty, civilizing agencies, those great principles, those fine ideals, those spiritual forces upon which our country was founded." In 1903 President Roosevelt argued that "our growth . . . is beneficial to humankind in general. We do not intend to assume any position which can give just offense to our neighbors. Our adherence to the rule of human rights is not merely profession. The history of our dealings with Cuba shows that we reduce it to performance." The U.S. performance in Cuba did not terminate massive poverty, 90 percent illiteracy, rampant disease, the short life span, or an underdeveloped, corrupt, and foreign-controlled and dominated political economy.[6] The U.S. leadership accepted its announced humanitarian objectives as evidence of the consequence of its action.

Roosevelt's administration, faced with the probability that Colombia would not bow to the needs of "higher civilizations," developed legal and political arguments that would justify more aggressive activity. After Colombia refused to ratify the proposed canal treaty, Roosevelt was given such arguments by Columbia University law professor and a sometime State Department consultant and official, John Bassett Moore. Assistant Secretary of State Loomis had discussed the Colombian situation with Moore in early August and requested him to submit his ideas in written form for the president's consideration. Moore argued that the United States could proceed to build the canal under a "license to dig" rather than a formal treaty. Abandoning the Panama site and concluding a treaty with Nicaragua and Costa Rica was, in his view, "a supposition that [might] serve the present purposes of diplomacy but certainly not those of permanent policy. If the Panama route is . . . the best and most practicable route . . . it is the one that we should have." He claimed that a hundred years of experience had demonstrated that private enterprise would not accomplish the project without a "responsible guarantee of a great government." His argument would excuse almost any course of action, since "the United States, in undertaking to build the canal, does a work not only for itself but for the world."[7] "Higher civilization" had issued Moore's "license to dig."

Moore unveiled various legal arguments to sustain a unilateral U.S. decision to build at Panama. He grounded his case, however, in distortions of fact and misrepresentations about U.S. relations with Colombia over the fifty-seven years between the 1846 U.S.–New Granada Treaty and the 1903 crisis. He argued that article 35 of the 1846 treaty, which granted the United States free transit over the isthmus in return for a guarantee of New Granadan sovereignty there, *created* a "partnership in sovereignty." The object of the treaty, in Moore's tortured logic, became a canal, although the treaty itself never mentioned a canal, because President James Polk's message accompanying the treaty to the Senate speculated that the route seemed "to be the most practicable for a railroad or canal." He even conceded that the word *canal* had not been mentioned in the 1846 treaty because "it is not probable that a dozen men would have been found in Congress who would have sanctioned" it, yet, he interpreted the very absence of the word as "proof" that the United States wanted the canal. He concluded that Colombia's right to request U.S. aid to keep the passage open, as provided for in the treaty, "approached the point of making [the United States] the responsible sovereign on the Isthmus." In an illogical bombshell, he argued that since "the United States has for more than fifty years secured to Colombia her sovereignty over the Isthmus, for the mutually avowed purpose of maintaining a free and open transit, the United States is in a position to demand that it shall be allowed to construct the great means of transit which the treaty was chiefly designed to assure."[8] Thus, the duty to protect Colombian sovereignty became the right to annex a canal site. Ultimately, then, Moore's case rested on mere force.

Moore boldly asserted that since Colombia had benefited from the guarantee of its sovereignty, "she is therefore not in a position to obstruct the building of the canal." He argued that a party which benefited from a contract could not prevent the second party from doing whatever it pleased, even outside the contractual agreement, to obtain a reciprocal benefit. He had discovered a right to build a canal under the 1846 treaty in the revelation that over the years U.S. views had undergone a change. Colombia's consent to the change was not required. The proper step was to enforce the new interpretation of the treaty. The U.S. government possessed a "right to require" Colombia to grant the United States permission to operate a canal.

Moore's final argument hinted at the ominous power of U.S. exceptionalism:

> The position of the United States is altogether different from that of private capitalists who . . . are altogether subject to the local jurisdiction and who . . . may be required to tread the paths of ordinary litigation and establish their rights before the tribunals of the governments against which they assert them. . . . The United States is not subject to such disabilities, and can take care of the future.

Exceptionalism placed the U.S. government beyond contract and international laws. This characteristic made the United States the ideal party to build the canal.[9] Similar ideas and phrasing which occurred in the publicity campaign in the summer and fall of 1903, which the French canal interests conducted to encourage the sale of their rights, underscored the shared vision and responsibility of the U.S. participants in the drama.

Moore's memorandum had a profound impact upon Roosevelt and others who read it. Moore recalled that shortly after composing the memorandum, he had been called to Roosevelt's Sagamore Hill residence. Roosevelt indicated his intention to abandon negotiations with Colombia and, if Panama should revolt and form an independent government, to recognize the new government. When Moore pointed out that Roosevelt's intention was contrary to normal U.S. diplomatic policy, Roosevelt added that he would grant recognition to Panama "under proper circumstances."[10]

The Moore memorandum was shared with people outside the administration whose objectives were considered friendly to U.S. goals. Bunau-Varilla and Loomis communicated frequently in the summer and fall of 1903 and met whenever Bunau-Varilla was in Washington. Loomis probably informed Bunau-Varilla of Moore's memorandum and even of specific arguments. Loomis may have allowed Bunau-Varilla to read the memo, for in September 1903 Bunau-Varilla used phrasing and ideas similar to Moore's in an article in *Le Matin* (Paris, circulation of about 350,000). Bunau-Varilla claimed his article had a significant impact because *Le Matin* reached sectors of France normally unfriendly to U.S. acquisition of the Panama Canal route. In Bunau-Varilla's view, Roosevelt's character prevented him from initiating construction of the canal at the "wrong place," or "against the antagonistic forces of nature," or in "an impossible way, of which the obligatory failure would be an everlasting reproach to his administration."[11] Bunau-Varilla echoed the views that Roosevelt, Moore, and Loomis shared regarding the desirability of building in Panama instead of Nicaragua.

If the canal could not be built in Nicaragua, Roosevelt had the options mentioned in the *Le Matin* article: to wait for a revolt in Panama, or, using Moore's logic, to "enforce the treaty of 1846." Bunau-Varilla presumed that Roosevelt would not wait long for a Panamanian revolt. He observed: "It is infinitely probable that the explosion of [Panamanian] sentiment will only take place if it should receive financial subsidy and a moral pledge that the new government will be recognized by America and protected from Colombia's soldiers immediately after the proclamation of independence." Bunau-Varilla, along with Panamanian politician and future president Manuel Amador Guerrero and Amador's associates, planned a revolt with only limited U.S. involvement. Bunau-Varilla proposed:

> There will be room for a Roosevelt doctrine . . . perfecting and completing the Monroe Doctrine. The right of protecting the South American interests against European interference . . . will have to be counterbalanced by . . . the right of protecting the European (and North American interests) against South-American interference. The superior right of free circulation is a universally recognized principle. . . . America cannot allow one of the nations she protects to [extort from the whole world by withholding its transit]. The right of protection involves the duty of policing.

Bunau-Varilla's language anticipated the Roosevelt corollary. Although Colombia had allowed road and railroad crossing of the isthmus, Bunau-Varilla borrowed Moore's reasoning to denounce that country for blocking "free circulation." Forcing acceptance of a canal had become a duty.[12]

Moore's papers refer to other documents that suggest improper conduct on the part of the United States. One of these was a cable from acting Secretary of the Navy Darling to the commander of the U.S.S. *Nashville*— sent several days before any uprising occurred—to proceed under sealed, secret orders to Colón (Colombia) and to prevent the "landing of any armed force with hostile intent, either Government or insurgent," and even to prevent the landing of government troops *before* an insurrection occurred, if the commander judged such a step might precipitate a conflict. "These instructions," Moore observed, "referred to an apprehended uprising on the Isthmus of Panama." Other vessels sailed under similar instructions to protect Panama City. On November 3, before any insurrection, Darling cabled the naval commanders of other ships at the isthmus: "In the interests of peace make every effort to prevent Government troops at Colón from proceeding to Panama. The transit of the isthmus must be kept open and maintained." One puzzled naval officer at Panama wanted to know by what authority he should keep Colombian troops from landing on Colombian soil (in peacetime and in the absence of a civil disturbance). On November 4, with the success of the revolt still in doubt, the U.S. navy was instructed to silence some Colombian artillery. When the United States became aware of possible danger to Colombian sovereignty on the isthmus, rather than warn that government, U.S. officials denied it the option of dealing with the threat on its own.[13]

The complicity went beyond the navy to State Department officials. Moore wrote that on November 3 the U.S. consul at Panama telegraphed the State Department several hours before the revolt: "No uprising yet reported. Will be in the night. Situation is critical." Less than a day after the revolt, he expressed alarm over the prospect that Colombian soldiers might attempt to restore order. A telegram from Amador to Secretary of State John Hay, sent within hours after the revolt started, began: "Isthmus independence proclaimed without bloodshed. Canal treaty saved." Apparently, Amador presumed that he and Hay were jointly in the business of saving the canal treaty.[14] In addition to the moral responsibility evident in these documents, and in the correspondence of the political advisers close to Roosevelt (notably Moore and Loomis), the archives of the State and Navy Departments bear abundant record of small acts that served U.S. objectives.

U.S. officials were hard pressed to find even an inferior argument in international law that would justify the U.S. action. The 1846 treaty justified U.S. troops entering the isthmus only in order to protect Colombian sovereignty or to keep the transit lane open. When U.S. officials decided that an appeal to the 1846 treaty was unconvincing as justification for destroying Colombian sovereignty, they resorted to arguments outside international law. They appealed to a higher law, the rights of a superior civilization, or world benefits. Hay stated: "The United States sought to keep the isthmus open for the benefit of world commerce. Landing of Colombian troops with hostile intent to protect their national soil, at this time would render our task more difficult." His words implied that the substitution of U.S. for Colombian troops would restore order and preserve authority on the isthmus. The U.S. forces, however, were not used to preserve Colombian sovereignty, but to help destroy it. The U.S. government expected the Panamanian revolutionaries to concede a canal treaty on advantageous terms. When they balked, U.S. officials and Bunau-Varilla warned the Amador government that if it did not sign the treaty, the United States would probably withdraw protection and negotiate a canal pact with Colombia.[15] U.S. officials were prepared to protect any government willing to sign a canal treaty advantageous to U.S. purposes.

After the Roosevelt administration had obtained the signed canal treaty, Latin American and U.S. observers widely condemned the U.S. role.

Roosevelt called upon Moore to aid in creating a post facto legal defense. To protect his reputation as an international lawyer, Moore recorded that "in regard to these sudden transactions [quick U.S. recognition and the canal treaty] I naturally was not consulted nor was any part of the President's ensuing annual message sent to me for consideration." He also distanced himself from the misreadings of his first memorandum which had inspired Roosevelt's action. Moore professed to discover, after the Panama revolt, that "the 'legalistic' views were inappropriate." A witticism credited to Attorney General Philander Knox epitomized the mentality in the cabinet: "Oh, Mr. President, do not let so great an achievement suffer from any taint of legality."[16]

A week after the revolt, Moore completed a second Panama Canal memorandum which aimed at justifying the seizure. He reconfirmed the tortured and specious arguments of the first memorandum. He repeated that "the prime object of this treaty was not only to secure a safe and unobstructed transit across the Isthmus of Panama," but "above all things else to assure the construction of an interoceanic canal." He admitted that in 1846 there was no intention to build a canal, but contended that because the U.S. government had assumed "an onerous protective relationship towards the Isthmus" in 1846, it was entitled to such an intention and could, without consulting Colombia, change the agreement and enforce its altered view. As for the hasty recognition of the Amador government, Moore simply claimed that diplomatic recognition of a foreign power was nothing more than acknowledging a de facto government, which was "not an uncommon thing." He did not mention the fact that the 1846 treaty restricted the U.S. right to recognize another sovereign power over the isthmus.[17]

Moore went even further. To assure a proper legal and moral stance, he asserted that "the present administration is entirely free from any connection with the recent revolutionary movement on the Isthmus of Panama." This was more than disingenuous. Navy and State Department correspondence, with which he was familiar, clearly demonstrated a U.S. connection. He was probably convinced that no one, at that time, could actually prove U.S. support of the Amador revolt. Moreover, his earlier memorandum had described forceful intervention as a viable alternative.[18]

Although historians have acknowledged the activity of Bunau-Varilla in Washington, they have usually focused on his lobbying work for the French New Panama Canal Company. Loomis, for example, often met with Bunau-Varilla. He arranged at least one meeting for Bunau-Varilla with Hay (October 16) and two with Theodore Roosevelt (on October 9 and 29). Historians have described the October 9 meeting between Roosevelt and Bunau-Varilla and the Loomis–Bunau-Varilla meetings in some detail, but the October 29 meeting has remained obscured until now. Since Bunau-Varilla, Roosevelt, and John Bigelow have all left traces of a meeting between Bunau-Varilla and Roosevelt in their memoirs, historians have assumed that Bunau-Varilla's October 9 conversation with Roosevelt and his frequent meetings with Loomis, including one on October 29, gave him the insight to wire Amador and the revolutionaries on October 30 to revolt as planned on November 3 because the United States was sending a ship to prevent Colombian interference. Although Loomis and Roosevelt denied instigating steps to aid the revolutionary forces, and Bunau-Varilla claimed that the hot tip came from Loomis, the Farrand-Turner notes reveal that at the October 29 meeting Roosevelt himself spoke in thinly veiled language to Bunau-Varilla about the fact that a warship could prevent Colombian reinforcements from interfering with the revolutionaries. With this apparent assurance ringing in his ears, Bunau-Varilla wired Amador's revolutionary group to act.[19] His intimate connections with the Roosevelt administration convinced him that the revolutionaries would be protected if they revolted on November 3, 1903.

On January 23, 1913, Theodore Roosevelt and Archibald C. Coolidge conversed at the Harvard Club in New York about the U.S. role in the Panama revolt of 1903 and in particular about Roosevelt's meeting with Bunau-Varilla on October 29, 1903. Max Farrand listened to and took notes of this exchange. Immediately afterward, he wrote a memorandum of the conversation, which he soon sent to Frederick Jackson Turner, adding that it was confidential and must be returned. Turner outlined the document and copied important passages before returning it to Farrand. Unfortunately, the memorandum has been lost; the Max Farrand Papers at the Huntington Library do not contain a copy. The only record of this conversation is Turner's notes of Farrand's typescript.[20]

According to the Farrand-Turner notes, Coolidge understood that Bunau-Varilla

> supplied [Manuel] Amador with $50,000 and A[mador] went to Panama to start the Rev[olution]. He had no direct intercourse or understanding with the U.S. government. What he wanted was to create a situation of which the U.S. w[oul]d not fail to take advantage. Colombia c[oul]d have crushed the Rev[olution] unless U.S. w[oul]d prevent the Col[ombian] soldiers from landing. Things went along for a while and Amador wired B[unau]-V[arilla] that everything was O.K. 'Send Yacht.'[21]

Bunau-Varilla was puzzled until he recalled that in South American revolutionary parlance, yacht meant man-of-war.

Coolidge recalled that Bunau-Varilla had convinced him during a conversation in Paris that the Panamanians would not have revolted

> unless they were assured of U.S. support. So Bunau-Varilla went to Washington. He talked to John Bassett Moore and one or two others who would be sure to report the matter to the president. [Note: Bunau-Varilla mentioned Moore who was not a U.S. government official but suppressed mention of meetings with Roosevelt and Loomis on October 29.] In his conversations with these men [Moore and the others] he confident[ially] predicted a revolution in Panama [and urged sending a war vessel].[22]

According to Coolidge, "when [Moore] asked how he [Bunau-Varilla] knew this, he replied that he had seen the same thing happen during Cleveland's administration, and [not wishing to reveal the sources of his information—possibly Loomis] never mind how he knew! He offered to bet any amount that his prediction would come true within a week." He then wired Amador: "Yacht has been sent." Coolidge continued his version as follows. The next day's papers noted that the *Nashville* had departed Jamaica under sealed orders. Then the United States prevented Colombian troops from suppressing the rebellion. Amador, not trusting Bunau-Varilla, wanted to negotiate and sign the treaty and delayed appointing Bunau-Varilla, who cabled "all is lost unless act[ion] taken immediately." Reluctantly, Amador authorized Bunau-Varilla to sign a preliminary agreement. Bunau-Varilla met Amador with a signed agreement that was acceptable to Hay.[23] This version of Roosevelt's role in the Panamanian revolt, put forth by Bunau-Varilla and accepted by Coolidge, suggested little official U.S. involvement.

After Coolidge finished, Roosevelt supplied "corrections," particularly to the latter part of Coolidge's story. According to the Farrand-Turner notes,

> [Roosevelt insisted he] had [been] kept accurately informed of cond[itio]ns in Pan[ama]. . . . Mr. R[oosevelt] accordingly knew that a rev[olution] was practically sure to break out in Panama. . . . Mr. R[oosevelt] wanted the Rev[olution] to come after the U.S. elections in November and before Congress met in December. It was a case for quick decisive action not for talk. He did not even want the members of his cabinet present [when meeting with Bunau-Varilla]. . . . Everything depended on the U[nited] S[tates] keeping out the Colombian troops. Mr. R[oosevelt] said it was not a case of his giving the signal but of raising his foot. . . . [At least three revolutions were in preparation: Bunau-Varilla's and Amador's, New York lawyer Nelson Cromwell's, and a filibustering expedition.] Mr. R[oosevelt] considered B[unau] V[arilla] the best of the lot. . . . It was pretty evident that he was

indirectly representing the French stockholders and he had money to use when needed. T[heodore] R[oosevelt] and Coolidge both thought he had been speculating on stocks.[24]

Roosevelt assured Coolidge that he was regularly informed of Loomis's talks with Bunau-Varilla and had met with the Frenchman. Roosevelt knew that U.S. forces had to prevent Colombian reinforcements from landing for the revolt to have a decent chance of success.

In the second meeting, according to Roosevelt's recollection, "B[unau] V[arilla] predicted a revolution in Panama and said he would like to know if the U.S. would prevent Colombian troops from landing." Roosevelt said he could not answer that. Then Bunau-Varilla asked, "will you protect Colombian interests?" To which Roosevelt replied: "I cannot say that. All I can say is that Colombia by her action has forfeited any claim upon the U.S. and I have no use for a government that would do what that government has done." Bunau-Varilla rose and departed at once. After he left, Roosevelt ordered troops sent, but the revolution succeeded before the troops actually landed. As in the case of the Mexican War, the U.S. government welcomed an excuse to do what it intended to do in any event. The Farrand-Turner notes summarized Roosevelt's version as follows:

> When Mr. R[oosevelt] was preparing his message to Congress a few days before, he had drafted a paragraph recommending the seizure of the Canal Zone if necessary. Mr. R[oosevelt] did not want the Revolution to come off in advance of the election for fear of the effect. It came off a few days before the election but he was able to delay the news of his [recognition] of Panama until it was too late to make any political capital of it. . . . [Later,] when the cabinet came back Mr. R[oosevelt] said to Hay and Root he was satisfied that ethically he was right, and that it was up to them to defend his action legally and constitutionally. When Hay and Root presented their report Mr. Roosevelt said he was surprised to find how constitutionally (legally) he had acted.[25]

When Roosevelt, defending his position in the cabinet, referred to the paragraph asking for the seizure of the canal route, Root made his famous remark: "Excellent, the defense is complete. To clear yourself of a charge of seduction, you confess to rape!"[26]

Although neither Roosevelt nor Bunau-Varilla were particularly reliable sources, there is no special reason to suspect that Roosevelt, in a private conversation after the 1912 presidential election, would construct an elaborate distortion of the second meeting with Bunau-Varilla and other related events. Moreover, there is corroborative evidence: Bunau-Varilla had some U.S. assurances behind his cable of October 30, 1903; Moore's first memorandum urged action to seize the canal route if necessary; and Roosevelt repeatedly made public condemnations of Colombian officials and their government. Roosevelt's story in the Farrand-Turner version may contain poetic license and faulty recollection, but it is consistent with the activities and viewpoints of the officials involved in the events of late October and early November 1903.

In the Farrand-Turner notes, Roosevelt admitted to extensive knowledge of revolutionary preparations in Panama. He also admitted to manipulating news of the Panamanian revolt so that it would not interfere with the fall elections. He obtained reliable information of revolutionary activity from Loomis's frequent meetings with Bunau-Varilla, and deliberately rejected the option of warning Colombia. Instead, his administration used the information about a likely revolt to conspire and plot with one revolutionary faction.

Despite his later claims, Roosevelt was not pursuing a humanistic and moral course to aid Panamanians and the world. His own account revealed little knowledge of precisely which group he was supporting or what objectives that group strove for. His indifference to the Amador group's goals undermined any claim for idealism as a motivating force behind his decision. He probably assumed that life would be better for Panamanians under U.S. protection, but that assumption derived more from nationalistic presumptions about U.S. culture than from an analysis of the forces at play in Panama.

Roosevelt's world view acknowledged a struggle for civilization among superior and backward peoples (Roosevelt shifted frequently between racial and ethnic definitions of "people"), with the superior ultimately winning by conquest, war, and bloodshed. The use of violence was acceptable because the superior peoples bore the civilizing mission. Social Darwinian theory was troubled with the internal contradiction of a static hierarchy of "superior" peoples involved in an ongoing struggle which implied change in the social order. Despite Roosevelt's denial of social Darwinian views, he advocated a world view rooted in a constant struggle among nations and a hierarchy of civilized states. His vision waivered between a persistent struggle and a static social order.[27]

Roosevelt's insistence upon the rights, even duty, of all superior societies to use force in assuming the "white man's burden" can be interpreted most meaningfully as a planned, conscious policy. Roosevelt (and Marks) accepted his actions as moral. Roosevelt's morality, however, was derived from an ahistorical application of social Darwinism which was independent of traditional morality. The rules, values, and prohibitions of a moral order could not apply if the exception (the United States) was the measure of man's value. Like many progressives, Roosevelt's assumptions of U.S. civilizing superiority were based on a self-evaluation of material and institutional success, yet the perceived superiority was transferred to areas of moral and social values.[28] There is no convincing evidence that U.S. society around 1900 was the measuring rod for human values.

In the heat of the turmoil surrounding the U.S. role in the Panama revolution, Loomis, Moore, and Hay created arguments that justified U.S. action as moral and wise. Loomis, conveniently overlooking the U.S. rejection of the first Hay-Pauncefote treaty two years earlier, declared that Colombia's rejection of the canal treaty was "in the nature of an unfriendly act." He leaned upon an "eminent international jurist" [Moore] who argued that the purpose of the 1846 treaty was interoceanic transit and "above all to secure the construction of an interoceanic canal." He borrowed Moore's argument that "Colombia could not . . . refuse to enter into a proper [canal] arrangement with the United States . . . without violating the spirit and substantially repudiating the obligations of a treaty, the full benefits of which she [Colombia] had enjoyed for over fifty years." The United States, however, had enjoyed free and unhindered transit over the isthmus railroad since the early 1850s. Both nations had gotten what the treaty offered until it was unilaterally discarded. And, of course, this treaty never mentioned a canal.[29]

In addition to interpreting the treaty advantageously, U.S. officials were concerned with the matter of secession. Moore tried to "remove from the minds of many people the idea that there is a parallel between the revolution in Colombia and the secession of the Confederate States . . . and that our recognition of Panama is an endorsement of the secession principle." Moore claimed that the United States refused to let Colombian troops land to defend their territory because they would precipitate "civil war and disturb for an indefinite period the free transit which we are pledged to protect." Yet Hay insisted that Panama had freely formed a government and received U.S. protection. Hay did not trust the leadership of the new Panamanian government, and proposed reaching a satisfactory treaty with Bunau-Varilla because he doubted that Amador would be as agreeable. Hay feared that Amador might "very likely mix things up, or at the least might delay them."[30]

Searching desperately for an argument to silence domestic criticism, Loomis raised the specter of impending foreign intervention to justify the U.S. role in Panama's revolt. Six weeks after the crisis, Loomis argued weakly at the Quill Club that the United States had landed the marines only to preserve order and quash a foreign threat in the form of a French landing party. In fact, the French government had repeatedly assured the

United States that it would not intervene on behalf of the canal company.[31] But for those who doubted that the United States had intervened to protect civilization or Colombian sovereignty, Loomis conjured up marines who stymied a French military intervention and saved the Monroe Doctrine.

U.S. intelligence regarding the isthmus never indicated, even confidentially, that it expected French interference in that region. U.S. officials were concerned only with the potential resistance of Colombian forces in Panama. Roosevelt's deepest concern, before and after the revolt, was finding a way to justify an aggressive role on the isthmus. He circulated Moore's memoranda among policymakers in the State Department and the White House. Moore's views influenced Roosevelt and Loomis and reached Bunau-Varilla, who used Moore's arguments and the euphemism "to enforce the treaty of 1846" in his publications in Paris. Roosevelt was regularly informed of the Loomis–Bunau-Varilla meetings which facilitated cooperation between the French canal company, people linked to the Panama insurgent forces, and the White House.

Roosevelt clearly had the information he needed to undertake covert intervention in the Panamanian revolt against Colombia. The Farrand-Turner notes described Roosevelt's significant role in the events of late 1903, and indicated that the Amador revolutionary faction communicated with the U.S. government through Bunau-Varilla. This collusion cannot surprise any student of turn-of-the-century U.S. foreign relations, latent with ideas and attitudes derived from social Darwinism, ethno-cultural superiority, and progressive haste to establish an ordered, efficient, and predictable world. It is necessary to keep in mind that Colombia's action did not endanger U.S. institutions, society, or existence. Moore, Loomis, Hay, and Roosevelt all had favored a pragmatic policy of expansion, widely shared in the progressive years, to extend and protect a superior society.[32] None of them revealed any fundamental moral concern or sensitivity to justice (as opposed to legality) in the quest for power, glory, and a narrowly conceived image of national well-being and security. The pay-off they sought was the U.S.-Panama canal treaty and a client state.

7

The World Economic Crisis, Racism, and

U.S. Relations with Central America, 1893–1910

The state of the world economy in the global depression of 1873–1898 posed serious problems for all industrial states. The "age of imperialism," the late nineteenth and early twentieth centuries, reflected the expansionism that most industrial states undertook to resolve the internal social disorders that accompanied the recurring crises. The expansionism, however, involved more than a search for markets for industrial goods, for raw materials, or for investment opportunities. The industrial states sought to bolster their domestic life style with exotic products, to control world communications, and to dominate larger portions of the world labor system. The isthmian-Caribbean region, an American Mediterranean, promised to facilitate U.S. socioeconomic stability by expanding the area of the free-market economic activity.[1] In the process of incorporating the Caribbean into the U.S. economy, entrepreneurs would establish new labor relations.

A fundamental characteristic of the imperialism associated with liberal, free-market expansion was the implementation of metropole control over peripheral labor. This control manifested itself in exploitation in colonial mines or plantations or the transfer of peripheral or metropole labor to areas of exploitation. From the mid-nineteenth century until the Great War, tens of millions of permanent or long-term Asian and European migrants traveled the world oceans. Territorial or financial expansionist schemes resulted in the Western industrial states acquiring control over scores of millions of laborers. Other millions made short-term or seasonal migrations.[2] Within the Caribbean area, the migration involved several hundred thousand people who were both permanent settlers and seasonal workers. A modest number of U.S. blacks participated in the migration. They moved into Central America, beginning in the depression of the 1890s, and worked on the construction of Guatemala's Atlantic coast railroad.

The changing role of the United States in Central America helped mold the approach of its diplomats to the incidents involving American blacks. The presence of the blacks was related to an expansive, imperial society that faced domestic problems related to altered accumulation processes, a sharpened division of labor, the mechanization of work, and unresolved internal social problems. In the late nineteenth or early twentieth centuries, many industrial states adopted social imperialism to transfer domestic problems abroad.[3]

Social imperialism, essentially the externalization of internal problems, worked for the metropole powers because they could more easily squeeze extra profits from alien labor forces than from domestic ones. An alien labor force was generally inferior to domestic labor in political capacity—the ability to use the family or other kinship group, the community, or some legal institution for legitimate protest. The alien workers were vulnerable. The United States and each Central American country used alien laborers extensively in the early twentieth century. In Guatemala, Jamaican and North American blacks formed an alien labor force scarcely able to protest unjust treatment.[4]

Some U.S. blacks in Guatemala became ensnared in incidents that assumed large proportions and which are instructive about the relationship of racism to imperialism. The blacks who fled the United States seeking work could normally count on little assistance from their government. Occasionally, however, diplomats or businessmen recognized that part of the future of U.S. society was interwoven with the fate of its black emigrants. In such cases, wisdom superseded "virtue" and dictated unusual courses of official action that offered some degree of protection to black residents abroad.[5] Thus some blacks tied to Guatemala's Atlantic coast railroad received the mixed blessing of State Department protection when a series of incidents between blacks and Guatemalan officials threatened to spread and thus injure U.S. white enterprises. The State Department acted within a general policy of bringing Central America into its sphere of influence during an era when expansion abroad was viewed as necessary to guarantee stability and prosperity at home.[6]

In the late nineteenth and early twentieth centuries, as the bankruptcy rate rose and signs of profitability sunk, U.S. capitalists maneuvered to assure their ability to accumulate wealth. They resorted to pools, trusts, holding companies, and government regulatory agencies in an effort to bring order and predictability to their business world. Entrepreneurs enticed European immigrants to the United States as a cheap labor force and used ethnocentric policies to weaken and divide labor, thus facilitating its exploitation. Stability in the economy and cheap labor promised larger entrepreneurial profits.[7] U.S. entrepreneurs sought to exploit external land, labor, and capital in order to achieve the pre-crisis expectations of accumulation.

The southern states, in a colonial relationship to the Northeast, faced devastating losses in the economic downturn. The South used jim crowism, the exclusion of blacks from labor unions, the sharpening of tenant farming and sharecropping practices, and Booker T. Washington's accommodation through economic submission to preserve the exploitation of blacks. The increased exploitation of blacks raised the level of social conflict. Joel Williamson, in describing the period from 1889 to 1915 as one of the two "hot times" in southern race relations, has affirmed C. Vann Woodward's focus upon the racial turmoil of the 1890s. In this period society redefined the place of blacks in order to hinder their capacity to defend their political and economic rights and thus to facilitate their exploitation.[8]

Blacks were often the targets of manipulation to satisfy white objectives. In the decades after the Civil War, white politicians in both parties manipulated black desires to escape bad memories of the South in order to serve the objectives of white-dominated political factions. North American domestic policies increasingly persuaded alienated southern blacks to seek escape. Black dreams of escaping the exploitation included the back-to-Africa movements, a colonization scheme planned for Mexico, and "black towns" in Oklahoma and elsewhere. Around 1900, some white entrepreneurs offered southern blacks the opportunity to dig a canal in Panama, to build railroads in Guatemala, or to work elsewhere in Central America.[9]

The U.S. government's desire for better treatment of North Americans abroad was sharpened by the rapid entrepreneurial penetration of Guatemala. Around the turn of the century, U.S. entrepreneurs dominated Guatemala's railroad system, the United Fruit Company monopolized fruit exportation, and a variety of investment syndicates—the Windsor Trust, the Young syndicate, the Seligman-Keith group, and the "American" syndicate—were struggling to obtain financial, mining, and business opportunities in Guatemala. Among the interested parties listed in these various syndicates were a score of individuals and firms of considerable reputation: August Belmont, Cornelius Vanderbilt, Adolph Stahl, Minor Keith, Schwartz and Co., Seligman and Co., United Fruit, Speyer and Company, and executive officers from Brown Brothers and Co., Germania Life Insurance, U.S. Steel Corporation, Vermont Copper, Maitland, Coppel and Co., Lee, Higginson and Co., International Metals Co., Commercial National Bank of Washington, D.C., and Consolidated Coal. U.S. investment in Guatemala increased from 6 million dollars in 1897 to 36.5 million in 1914.[10] To encourage such imposing individuals and firms to pursue investment and financial projects in Guatemala, the State Department had to maintain a climate of respect for entrepreneurs and capitalists.

Although U.S. economic interests in Guatemala dated from 1823, the entrance of U.S. capital in appreciable quantities did not occur until after liberal revolutions of 1861 in the United States and 1871 in Guatemala. Earlier, Guatemala had attracted only modest amounts of foreign capital, mostly in merchant ventures led by the British with some Spanish, French, German, and Belgian participation. After the 1871 revolution, Guatemalan liberals stressed communications development to give its coffee producers access to the world market and to facilitate what they hoped would be Guatemala's avenue to wealth and prosperity. The cumbersome market route by sailing out of Pacific ports and around Cape Horn hindered the expansion of Guatemalan coffee. Several Atlantic coast railroad projects in the 1870s and 1880s had failed for lack of funds. The 1885–1897 upswing in world coffee prices stimulated the demand for an Atlantic coast railroad, and in the mid-1890s a determined Guatemalan president used forced loans to draft national capital for the project. The railroad and other development projects attracted foreign capital to Guatemala, most evidently from U.S. and German investors. The State Department, aware that Guatemala had traditionally not attracted U.S. businessmen, sought to create conditions that would encourage North American capitalists to dominate the eastern area of Guatemala.[11]

Both U.S. and Guatemalan elites had long histories of racial bias linked to labor exploitation. Guatemalans had always assumed that the Atlantic railroad would open up the vast eastern lowlands to economic development. Although Guatemalan officials resorted to forced Indian labor to implement the developmental schemes aimed at exploiting the lowlands, the Indians were neither willing nor skilled workers. When the Indian population alone proved inadequate, railroad entrepreneurs turned to Irish, Jamaicans, Chinese, and U.S. blacks to supply the labor. U.S. officials encouraged the projects. Many U.S. entrepreneurs and charlatans entered Central America to investigate economic opportunities. The wish of these capitalists for reliable and culturally acceptable workers, and the U.S. economy's persistent high unemployment, encouraged some laborers to seek employment in Central America. Both U.S. and Guatemalan officials and businesses were prepared to use blacks in the Caribbean area in almost any way that seemed to offer profit.[12]

In the years after 1900, some of these black workers became involved in incidents that produced special cases for consuls and diplomats. The State Department employed individuals whose values and perspectives were shaped by elite attitudes, customs, and education which encompassed race and class hierarchies. Thus State Department responses to incidents involving North American citizens revealed the same perspectives on race and class found in domestic progressivism. Complaints of U.S. blacks against abuses by Guatemalan officials posed a dilemma for white diplomats:

though racially prejudiced, they had to extend some protection to black Americans because they did not want Central Americans to become accustomed to pushing North Americans around.[13]

The prospect of black immigrants settling in Central America had long enticed some Central Americans with visions of agricultural development and material progress, yet it also troubled them with fears of racial and cultural decline and even loss of independence, since the work of U.S. economic intervention was being done by blacks. In the 1880s, U.S. Consul D. W. Herring suggested that North America's colored population, as laborers and settlers, would help capture "the trade, the profits, and the advantages arising from the development" of Honduras; he was especially sanguine about the railroad investment, which he said promoted immigration, peace, and well-being. In 1904, French Consul Emile Joré worried that the United States might export "their black population which ought to be for the [Central American states] a veritable danger" to their independence. Central American societies needed agricultural labor for development, but they feared great power intervention.[14]

As the United States aggressively expanded in the last half of the nineteenth century, the U.S. government redefined its duties abroad to promoting, not merely protecting, U.S. penetration abroad. Rising numbers of businessmen and investments abroad increased the number of financial claims that were potentially valuable weapons against host countries. The State Department linked the U.S. economic role, visible in part in claims, to its political objectives.[15] Thus U.S. economic penetration generated tensions that required a constant redefinition of U.S. objectives and policies. In general, protection of U.S. citizens and property—especially in smaller, peripheral states—was expanding in a manner that limited the host country's sovereignty. U.S. officials were often involved in complicated citizenship cases in which claims to U.S. citizenship were possibly fraudulent. Not infrequently, Latin Americans obtained U.S. citizenship papers without ever setting foot in the United States; they bribed officials or resorted to some form of deceit. When a naturalized U.S. citizen, returning to his native Guatemala, complained of efforts to collect forced loans and to restrict his movements, U.S. Minister Leslie Combs saw "a principle of the greatest importance involved in this case which should be settled at once." The principle was extensive protection for anyone carrying a U.S. passport.[16] In the early twentieth century, the argument for providing more protection for U.S. citizens abroad would confront the culturally uncomfortable reality that many of those citizens were black.

Despite their rhetorical claims of fair treatment and encouragement of self-government, U.S. officials frequently challenged the authority of Central American states because allowing them full sovereignty jeopardized U.S. penetration. After two Guatemalan servants of the U.S. legation, who did not have diplomatic immunity, were arrested in June 1905, one escaped and returned to the legation. Disregarding international law, Combs chastised the Guatemalan government without investigating the facts of the incident. Relying upon the power imbalance, he informed Guatemalan authorities: "I could not recognize the right of the Government to arrest servants of the Legation, without due notification and consent of the Legation."[17] He considered protection to Guatemalans in the official service of the United States vital in principle because businessmen and promoters were entering Guatemala in rapidly increasing numbers around 1900, and they and their Guatemalan employees had to be placed beyond disturbing interference from Guatemalan officials.

Combs's concern about infringement upon the rights of even lowly U.S. citizens, like blacks and naturalized Hispanics, persuaded him to advocate policies that restricted Guatemalan sovereignty. Although the Guatemalan constitution clashed with "our views," Combs said, "we must insist peremptorily upon the recognition of the property and personal rights of every American citizen." He hoped to induce Guatemala to remove "the important conflict now existing between the constitution of that country and the principle we maintain." He was conscious that exerting strength "only to wound the susceptibilities of a weaker nation, either in the method or substance of our demands, would be degrading to ourselves, but a true service is rendered if we can lead them to a better appreciation of individual rights and their protection. I am sure a firm, frank insistence upon our views will secure the desired results without serious friction, but a failure to insist upon this position, when definitely taken, would injure our prestige." He argued that Americans arrested under Guatemalan law should be tried or released on bail within twenty-four hours. The U.S. government agreed in principle, but warned Combs that it would be "impossible to bring the accused to trial promptly with a due regard to the demands and interests of justice" in the United States. Combs was told not to make demands inconsistent with Guatemalan laws, its constitution, or "the actual interests of retributive justice."[18] But both Combs and the State Department assumed that U.S. standards should determine acceptable Guatemalan conduct and procedures.

In practice, U.S. assertions of authority in Guatemala observed certain flexible limitations. In 1905 Secretary of State John Hay informed U.S. officials that a corporation was considered a citizen of the state in which it was chartered, regardless of the nationality of the stockholders. In 1907 chargé William Sands was asked for help by John Thornton, an American with "an enviable reputation for business integrity" who had organized a corporation under Guatemalan law. When the Guatemalan government announced its intention to expropriate some of Thornton's property in Puerto Barrios, Thornton complained that since he could not obtain the price he wanted either from the government or from private interests, he faced a considerable loss unless the legation intervened on his behalf. Sands expressed regret that the State Department prohibited action on behalf of U.S. stockholders of foreign corporations. He himself wanted to exert U.S. power to hinder loss for a business venture.[19]

However, Hay's strictures did not prohibit the extension of good offices on behalf of U.S. enterprises. The U.S. government wanted an environment attractive to business interests. It welcomed "the exploitation in [Central America] of any legitimate beneficial American enterprises." In 1909 the State Department permitted Minister William Heimké's "personal unofficial good offices" on behalf of Speyer and Company and United Fruit when those firms planned jointly to exploit some financial and railroad opportunities in Guatemala.[20] The State Department's recognition of burgeoning U.S. trade and investment in Guatemala (and elsewhere in Central America) contributed to subtle shifts in the government's official role in the dealings of U.S. corporations with their host countries.

The State Department had to exercise vigilance to discover practices that would undermine the confidence of the growing numbers of U.S. businessmen abroad. During political unrest in 1907, so many Americans were called before the Guatemalan foreign minister and allegedly threatened that Sands requested Guatemala to issue future summonses in writing. In addition, he instructed the consul-general to attend the interrogation of each American summoned. These actions clearly infringed upon Guatemala's right to investigate. In 1908, he complained to Guatemalan President Manuel Estrada Cabrera about the lack of protection for U.S. citizens, citing "numerous instances in which Americans in Guatemala had been victims of assault, robbery, or murder" and "the perpetrators had been protected." He warned that, if Estrada Cabrera were not forced to make a drastic example, "these crimes against Americans would certainly multiply."[21] A shield against the undesirable characteristics of Guatemalan society and laws would place U.S. entrepreneurs in an advantageous position to compete in the exploitation of Guatemalan opportunities.

U.S. intervention in matters of "rights" may have produced short-term benefits, but in the long term it created costly problems on political and economic levels. It often earned U.S. citizens privileges that other foreign residents might not have had (thus increasing competition and tension between the metropole powers) and that natives certainly lacked (thus increasing anti-imperialism, nationalism, and anti-American feelings). The interventions also infringed upon sovereignty by producing a socioeconomic bias in the host society's political economy in favor of North Americans. The acquisition of special privileges produced an upward spiral effect since it magnified the value of preserving the "rights" of all U.S. citizens, even blacks.

As competition became more aggressive, North Americans became fond of promoting "progressive" good government in Central America—that is, in pressuring governments to create favorable conditions—order, stability, and efficiency—for U.S. business. The U.S. government considered Central America's value as a transit zone and market to be ample justification for increasing its economic, diplomatic, military, and cultural connections. U.S. officials hoped that weeding out undesirable aspects would encourage stability and order. The challenge of other metropole powers in Central America revitalized real and imaginary arguments to justify U.S. retention of a secure position in the Central American–Caribbean transit area.[22]

The intention to extend the scope of protection for North Americans abroad in order to facilitate expansion also extended U.S. racial prejudices into external relations. Expansion was sustained by racial arguments which claimed that backward, nonwhite societies would benefit from white rule. Theodore Roosevelt's administration emphasized the duty of superior "races" to uplift "backward" peoples. The superiority was ill-defined, but unmistakable. The confused, inconsistent use of the word *race* indicated cultural, ethnic, and (or) biological characteristics. For Roosevelt, "backward" societies were those without order, stability, and force, and only secondarily those judged to be deficient in cultural, political, and racial qualities. Whereas a mature Roosevelt publicly denied the widely held view that Darwinian competition selected the best societies, he in fact presumed that U.S. superiority and Central American backwardness justified expansion into the region.[23] It was the conventional wisdom in the Roosevelt era that U.S. entrepreneurial activity on the isthmus would produce prosperity and security for the United States and the Central American societies. The Central Americans, however, did not always see the benefits.

Not only were the Central Americans racially mixed peoples, but North Americans of various racial and ethnic stock were participating in expansion. In the early twentieth century, the United Fruit Company began to acquire domestic Guatemalan railroads, banana lands, and also Salvadoran railroads in search of a large interoceanic network. Jamaican and North American black labor was used on the largely U.S.-owned railroads and the banana plantations in Guatemala. Diplomats and enclave managers, often North Americans, expected to keep supervision of the labor force in their own hands, not those of the host states. United Fruit had transformed Puerto Barrios's hinterland into a banana plantation, using Indian and imported black laborers. About 1909, Secretary of Legation Hugh Wilson described United Fruit Company field manager Victor Cutter's "handling of negroes" as "remarkable":

> [Cutter] could fight the wildest of the [Jamaicans], he could outshoot them, his endurance was unlimited and his occasional flash of ferocious temper kept them cowed. . . . [They] were cheerful and reasonably industrious, but full of liquor they became dangerous. Cutter would face them down in their worst moments. . . . He kept the grin, the abrupt manner and, I suppose, the willingness to bash a buck negro should the latter become drunk and obstreperous.

United Fruit and other U.S. firms presumed that southern whites knew best how to manage blacks. The importation of numerous blacks, however, had upset many Guatemalans, who viewed this influx as corrupting their society.[24]

From late 1907 until 1910, a series of incidents involving Guatemalan officials—who allegedly injured, imprisoned, and otherwise violated the civil rights of U.S. blacks—placed the U.S. legation and consulates in Guatemala in a quandary over how far they should go to protect blacks. Their dilemma was eased somewhat because they generally considered Guatemalans to be a racially mixed population, and therefore also inferior; this made it easier to demand "justice" for blacks on grounds of their North American citizenship rather than their race.

The incidents involved North American blacks Simon Shine, George Milliken, Monroe Williams, George Fitzgerald, William Evans, George Davis, William Wright, Anthony Wallace, James Nelson, Joseph Little, Caleb Williams, John Woods, Walter Fields, and one Perry. Probably many had entered Guatemala from New Orleans around the turn of the century, originally attracted by railroad work and repelled by a society which was intensifying its violence toward blacks and narrowing its economic and social opportunities for them. For four of the blacks the date of immigration into Guatemala is given in the documents: three entered about 1895 (Simon Shine, Joseph Little, and Caleb Williams), the fourth entered about 1879 (George Fitzgerald).[25] The total number of U.S. blacks in Guatemala during the first decade of the twentieth century is unknown. They made up the bulk of the population of at least one village and resided also in other settlements, but no contemporary even ventured a guess at the total number. A few of them initiated small enterprises to service the black plantation and railroad workers.

The race of these laborers played an important role in their relations with Guatemalan and U.S. officials. The sudden flood of incidents beginning in 1907 may have been related to the approaching end of the construction of the Guatemalan Atlantic coast railroad. This railroad was completed in late 1908, but the need for foreign labor slackened in the final months of construction. Guatemala's elite had never liked the presence of large numbers of blacks, and the approaching completion of the railroad signaled the end of the need for toleration.

North American diplomats and residents in Guatemala commonly held racist views. The racism of Minister Combs and chargé Sands was exposed when some black citizens residing in Guatemala petitioned Sands for assistance in bringing to justice the Guatemalans who had lynched a black accused of murder. Sands instinctively presumed that the lynched black was guilty; while deploring "lynch law," he refused to demand justice for the accused (but dead) black, saying that "the victim in this case seems entitled to little sympathy." Combs noted that many complaints of mistreatment by Guatemalan officials came from blacks of the "criminal and vagabond class" of the American South, who were "both vicious and difficult to control." He advised caution in treating their complaints because they were no more reliable than Guatemalan natives.[26]

Of course, State Department officials regularly demanded protection for white citizens and businesses, even when their guilt was evident. The U.S. consul to Corinto, the black journalist James Weldon Johnson, had occasion to observe firsthand the racism of white North Americans in Central America, many of whom were soldiers of fortune, speculators, beachcombers, alcoholics, and transients of dubious character.[27] While Combs, Sands, and other white agents in Guatemala assumed the criminal nature of the blacks in Guatemala, Johnson saw evidence of the unsavory character of many white U.S. citizens in Central America.

The first major racial incident in Guatemala involving a U.S. black was brought to the legation's attention in the fall of 1907. The incident involved three blacks—Simon Shine, George Milliken, and Monroe Williams—who were part of a group led by a "General Jackson." Sands claimed that Jackson "was a genuine genius for statesmanship" who had "a notion that he would, like the great [Haitian leader Henri] Christophe, eventually create a Negro Kingdom of his own." According to Sands, "Jackson's colony of expatriates [near Zacapa in the Department of Izabal] was, curiously enough, comprised of southern Negroes—mostly Louisiana roustabouts or 'bad niggers' from the Mississippi levees and steamboat wharves." Sands considered the blacks residing on Guatemala's north coast inferior and criminally inclined, if not actually being sought by southern sheriffs and police.[28]

This incident occurred on September 16, 1907. The governor (Jefe Político) of the Department of Izabal, General Enrique Arias, was returning from a dinner party when he stopped his companions in front of Simon Shine's saloon and boarding house in the Guatemalan town of Zacapa. George Fitzgerald, a U.S. Negro who had catered the dinner that Arias had just attended, was in the Arias party; a resident of Guatemala since 1879, he spoke and wrote Spanish fluently and later described the incident in detail for the U.S. legation. Arias dismounted and bragged that he was going to give the Negroes a clubbing. He entered the saloon and accused Shine of being open without permission. Shine said he had the necessary papers and would get them, but Arias began beating Shine before he had moved more than a step or two. Arias and his aide pistol-whipped Shine, Milliken, and Monroe Williams severely enough that all required medical attention. No one explained why Arias and his followers had attacked Milliken, who had been outside the saloon. The local medical man and others advised Monroe Williams to leave the area to avoid other injuries, imprisonment, or even worse. Williams fled to Honduras and then returned to the United States, where several years later he attempted to reopen this matter. To obscure the nature of his brutal attack, Arias had the three blacks charged with various offenses, including not having the legal documents proving permission for the saloon to remain open. In fact, Shine possessed the required license and a receipt for fees paid for it. As a cover, Guatemalan officials planted a rumor that the incident was a conspiracy of Arias's enemies.[29]

The matter assumed larger proportions when Shine signed a letter addressed to President Theodore Roosevelt protesting his treatment and asking him to "protect us poor niggers from being beaten to death, we have no one to look to but you." Secretary of State Elihu Root forwarded the letter to Sands in late October 1907, and Sands ordered a thorough investigation by the consul-general and vice-consul. Meanwhile, Foreign Minister Juan Barrios promised prompt action, hinting at a severe sentence for the culprits and the removal of General Arias from office. Then an embarrassing twist stalled the resolution of the incident. Sands discovered that U.S. Vice-consul Edward Reed had drafted Shine's letter to Roosevelt and had put into it charges unrelated to the beating incident. The extraneous charges cast doubt on the veracity of Shine's complaint and probably made Guatemalan officials reluctant to settle the matter. When Sands tried to obtain redress for Shine and Milliken, both the Guatemalan foreign minister and president refused, playing upon North American prejudices with a general allegation about "coloreds, who unfortunately under the influence of alcohol, were accustomed to lose control over themselves."[30]

To assure himself of the truthfulness of the charges, Sands had Shine and Milliken brought to Guatemala City. After thoroughly investigating the affair, he assured Washington that there was no conspiracy aimed at General Arias, that Arias was known to be deceitful, and that Shine and Milliken were men "of good standing." He concluded that Shine's business had been ruined and that Milliken had been injured for life. Three months after the incident, Milliken was still under constant medical supervision for the injuries; both victims were so terror-stricken that Sands acknowledged that it would be difficult to persuade them to return to Zacapa.[31]

Sands's efforts to pursue the case met opposition from the Guatemalan government and from established U.S. business interests which feared a backlash against foreign enterprises. Since the Guatemalan government operated primarily on fear and loyalty, Sands doubted that anyone could obtain honest testimony. Arias, a favorite of Guatemala's dictatorial President Estrada Cabrera, had a record of cruelty. After Sands had called for action, the Zacapa court had compelled Milliken to sign a statement that he could neither read nor understand. Guatemalan officials did not limit their defense to the court case. Estrada Cabrera's agent in Washington persuaded the State Department to instruct Sands to drop the matter, but Sands warned the Department that the Guatemalan minister was misrepresenting the case on all important points.[32]

Despite instructions to drop the matter, Sands pursued the affair out of a desire to protect the growing number of whites entering business on the north coast who had also come under attack from Arias and other politicians of his stripe. But established U.S. firms often wanted to reach an accommodation with Guatemalan officials and certainly were not eager to encourage competitors to enter Guatemala. Foreign Minister Barrios had abandoned his initially conciliatory attitude, Sands cautioned, because of support "he seems to be receiving from certain Americans who fear that all Americans will be made to suffer by the Government if General Arias is punished." Sands was convinced that "the general interests of the United States in this country, as well as private interests of Americans would suffer seriously if the legation permitted a miscarriage or denial of justice in favour of, apparently, more important individual or corporate interests." If Shine's and Milliken's just complaints were not satisfied, he said, he wanted authorization to present a formal claim against Guatemala. If he were to secure protection for U.S. citizens and their property, he could "not distinguish between a prominent merchant or banker or railroad manager and a law-abiding Negro who has been unjustly treated."[33] Sands recognized that despite the short-sighted self-interest of some businessmen, the long-term U.S. interest in expansion required policies which would attract new entrepreneurial capital.

Facing compensation demands of $5,000 or $6,000 each for Shine and Milliken, Guatemala agreed to pay them $1,000 each and to remove General Arias. Sands accepted the settlement, but arranged for Shine and Milliken to leave the country before collecting their $1,000, "partly for their protection, partly to avoid any knowledge of this settlement reaching the rough and ignorant negro element [in Guatemala] to the prejudice of the local authority." In contrast, when white North Americans were abused, the U.S. diplomats commonly tried to keep them in the country to teach the Guatemalans a lesson. Root had instructed Sands not to insist upon removing Arias. Sands believed, however, that the State Department's generosity toward Arias, evident in its willingness not to insist upon his removal, was misplaced. He argued that "in many cases the agents of the Department are no more nor less than police agents whose duty it is to see that [the Department's] generosity is not abused." A Guatemalan court could not deliver justice against such a powerful figure as Arias for several reasons: because he used his authority to obtain false affidavits from real or pretended witnesses; because the Guatemalan foreign ministry might resort again to misrepresentation to persuade the State Department to issue inappropriate instructions for Sands; and "because American corporate interests [in Guatemala] have taken up the cause of the high military official to the detriment of the humbler American citizens, who were fully in their right." Despite Sands's best arguments in support of Arias's removal, Secretary of State Root remained unconvinced. He did not disturb the settlement that removed Arias, but he disapproved Sands's conduct in allowing the removal because he did not want to "humiliate" an important government official of a foreign country. Sands's insistence upon having Arias removed, however, received the special approval of U.S. agents in Central America for years after.[34] Arias's removal was commonly judged an innovative, convincing act to persuade Guatemalan (and Central American) officials of earnest U.S. intentions to protect personal and property rights, an essential step in promoting capital inflow into that region.

In another incident in 1908, the black American William Evans of New Orleans was publicly and brutally beaten for public drunkenness by a local Guatemalan military official in Las Quebradas, Department of Izabal. One American businessman labeled Evans a "very unruly member of any community, being nothing but a jail bird, capable of any atrocity." Consular agent Edward Reed, "an intelligent man of thirty years residence in Guatemala," uncovered similar judgments while conducting his investigation, but noted that the commandant was also drunk at the time of the fight that led to the arrest. Reed argued that "such an exhibition of brutality . . . even though the victim be a degraded American negro, should not be passed unnoticed, lest it weaken the respect of Guatemalan officials for American citizenship, and later bear fruit in beating of some worthy American." Consul-general Owen believed the existing undesirable conditions in Guatemala required that "the smallest case of injustice towards an American citizen should be vigorously taken up, and the offending officer be made to suffer." He maintained that extracting "justice" in the Negro cases would have "a most excellent effect."[35]

In December 1908 the State Department inquired about the promised Guatemalan investigation into the assault upon Evans and about "what steps have been taken towards the punishment of the officer and soldiers involved." Minister Heimké suspected that the Guatemalan foreign ministry was afraid to present President Estrada Cabrera with the U.S. demand to investigate the affair. Evans had been rearrested and placed incommunicado. To bolster Heimké's hand, Assistant Secretary of State Francis Mairs Huntington Wilson instructed him to inform Guatemala that the evidence indicated "Evans was the victim of an outrage on the part of the authorities." Only in early 1910 did the State Department learn that Guatemalan officials had finally jailed one of the culprits accused of beating Evans.[36] In effect, Reed and Owen persuaded the legation in Guatemala City and the State Department, which needed little convincing, to protect "unworthy" blacks in order to protect some "worthy" whites in the future.

Another incident occurred at Cayuga, Department of Izabal, in early 1909, when the local commandant at Livingston, Colonel Alberto García, who had a long record of assaults upon foreigners, was implicated in the murder of the black American William Wright. Heimké described García, who once ordered shots fired at the British vice-consul in Livingston, as "a very low type of man." García connived to suppress the investigation into Wright's death. Heimké rejected the Guatemalan offer to transfer García to another post, but this left García in place as the commandant at Livingston, in which capacity he would supervise any investigation into Wright's murder—a situation Heimké considered unacceptable. Presuming that the State Department would not allow him to demand García's removal, he sought to bolster his case for removal by invoking Consul-general Kent's judgment that "no demand upon [the Guatemalan] Government was so effective, far reaching and salutary" as Sands's action in effecting the removal of General Arias. The Wright murder incident remained pending until A. P. Willard, the white owner of a riverboat line serving the United Fruit plantations, complained that García's conduct was destroying his company. Race and class now had impact on the State Department, which quickly approved a demand for García's removal. In July 1909 Luis Estrada Monzón replaced García. In Heimké's view, the removal of García meant "pulling out by the roots an evil that is sapping the life out of every foreign industry" in his jurisdiction.[37]

The State Department's attitude toward local political and military officials changed when Secretary of State Philander Knox and Assistant Secretary Huntington Wilson replaced Elihu Root and Robert Bacon. Huntington Wilson not only approved the removal of García, but he also wanted the other culprits tracked down and brought to justice. Before the investigation was completed, he had officially referred to the killing of Wright as a "lynching." Sands repeated this word during subsequent negotiations with Guatemalan officials to underscore the U.S. position. The Department pushed for a continuation of the investigation into Wright's death. In early 1910 one of the culprits was sentenced to six years imprisonment, one was found innocent, two more were arrested, and Guatemala petitioned for the extradition of two others from Honduras.[38]

Other incidents involving U.S. blacks appeared to be minor affairs, but collectively they contributed to the record of the U.S. reaction to Guatemalan treatment of blacks. George Davis had been arrested in February 1908 and held for a year without trial on the charge of murder. In early 1909, he smuggled a note out of prison in which he claimed that he was denied food and that he had written several times to consular and legation officials without response. Heimké considered the treatment inhumane and a violation of Guatemalan and international law. The legation found Davis a competent Guatemalan lawyer, yet in August 1909 it learned that the Guatemalan Court of First Instance had found Davis guilty and sentenced him to ten years. The lawyer planned an appeal, but a year and a half later the matter was still not resolved. In another incident, James Nelson was sentenced to two years in jail at Zacapa for an unspecified crime. After completing his sentence, the authorities refused to release him, and Heimké undertook an investigation. In 1908 Walter Fields was assaulted and injured but did not file a complaint until he was threatened again in 1910; Sands expected he might have to act to protect Fields. The State Department records do not reveal the resolution of these incidents.[39]

By early 1910 the persistence of complaints like these prompted a change in policy of legation and State Department officials with regard to incidents involving blacks residing in Guatemala. In September 1909, Monroe Williams—one of the three blacks beaten in the original Shine, Milliken, and Williams affair at Zacapa—learned that Shine and Milliken had received $1,000 compensation for the beatings they suffered. He appealed first to chargé Sands and Vice-consul Reed who reported that there had been no money settled upon him. Undaunted, he wrote to the president and secretary of state seeking "his $1,000," convinced that it was "never too late for the United States . . . to straighten out business." The State Department inquired at the legation whether the earlier settlement encompassed all North Americans injured at the time, or merely the claims of Shine and Milliken. Sands did not respond to the question, but chose to make a different case: Williams was not an injured party but only a witness to the earlier affair, and he had later fled the country. In fact, Williams's affidavit, Shine's testimony, and other witnesses from 1907 agreed that Williams had been injured. In March 1910 Sands's new view of U.S.-Guatemalan relations so muddled his memory that he even denied having supported the removal of Arias in the earlier situation. He claimed the State Department had overruled him. In fact, Root had disapproved Sands's conduct in allowing the removal. Sands insisted that it "would be inadmissible to reopen this [Shine-Milliken] case, even if Monroe Williams' claim was meritorious."[40]

Sands was no longer willing to pursue such cases and hoped to persuade the State Department to follow his lead because he detected a spirit of accommodation in Guatemalan treatment of U.S. entrepreneurs. In April 1910 two other incidents involving blacks came to the legation's attention. The first, an assault on Joseph Little and Caleb Williams by the commanding officer of Panzós, carried the earmarks of the Shine-Milliken affair. The U.S. consul-general, the vice-consul, and the superintendent of the Verapaz Railroad attested to the upright character of the two blacks: Little and Williams, residents in the country since the mid-1890s, were hard-working men not given to quarrelsome or scandalous behavior. Nevertheless, Sands alleged that "the negroes in these places are men who have drifted here for work from our Southern states, ignorant, lazy, and often insolent, but not all vicious."[41] There was no determined call for justice from either the legation or from the State Department, merely a hope that some alternative form of satisfaction might be discovered.

The second case involved John Woods, who was arrested for theft, served eight days in jail, and was then released without the filing of charges, or any explanation. During his confinement Woods's property was plundered. Sands was at first interested in this incident, and Huntington Wilson urged pursuing the restoration of Woods's property if his story proved correct. On this occasion, it was the Guatemalans who resorted to a racial argument, hinting that Woods suffered from "the evil inclination of certain elements of the colored people of different nationalities to take things not belonging to them." In the end, Sands apparently decided that the Guatemalan officials had a point, and told the State Department that they had become more cooperative with U.S. business and "distinctly more careful in their treatment of Americans"—by which he could only have meant white Americans. Sands prevailed upon the State Department not to "press" any of the black cases, to drop the Monroe Williams appeal, and to begin to handle all such cases with caution. In fact, U.S. officials informally ceased pursuing all pending matters involving black residents of Guatemala.[42]

For several months in the spring and summer of 1910, Sands and Estrada Cabrera had disagreed whether U.S. protests on behalf of blacks were tantamount to interference in Guatemalan affairs and an impingement of Guatemalan good faith. In July 1910, Sands had received a flood of anonymous press clippings sent from Washington (he presumed from the Guatemalan legation) that illustrated "the violence in the United States against negroes." Sands excused U.S. conduct by observing that the incidents in the United States were part of the race question, while in Guatemala the incidents involved government officials, often men of high rank. Faced with this resumptive evidence that Guatemala would continue to resist U.S. pressure on behalf of its blacks citizens—and with the U.S. approval implied by the fact that Tulane University had granted Estrada Cabrera an honorary doctorate of law and New Orleans had given him the keys to the city—Sands told the State Department that he was in a weak position to alter the conduct of Estrada Cabrera's government. In late September he reported that Estrada Cabrera had made promises which indicated improvement in the handling of legal matters between North Americans and Guatemalan courts, and in adjusting some government practices in a manner favorable to U.S. interests. Guatemala, he said, had learned a lesson and was pursuing the course desired, at least with regard to white businesses. A few years later the French chargé assumed that a new Guatemalan law which required a $200 deposit before a Jamaican (or U.S.?) black could debark was aimed at the railroad company.[43]

Class, as well as race, was clearly an important factor in U.S. policy. U.S. workers, white as well as black, usually received inferior protection from the State Department in Central America. In August 1910, two white North Americans were discharged by the Costa Rican Northern Railroad for organizing a strike. They were deported according to U.S. Minister William Merry, "as disturbers of the public peace." Since the United States regularly deported immigrants who threatened to disturb domestic tranquillity, he doubted there could be any objection to Costa Rica's doing so. But in the case of Jacob H. Hollander, a businessman expelled from Guatemala for illegal business practices and misconduct, the State Department had persistently denied for over a decade that Guatemala had the right to expel a U.S. citizen "whose conduct became inconvenient."[44] The State Department's position on expulsion varied according to class and color. In the cases of black small businessmen in Guatemala (Shine and Milliken) or white workers in Costa Rica, the U.S. government encouraged expulsion of its citizens. In cases involving white businessmen linked to the corporate world (for example, Willard or Hollander), a presumption of truth was given the white complaint, often making independent investigation unnecessary.

The world economic crisis aggravated the competition among the industrial powers. These states competed for external factors of production and sources of wealth to facilitate the accumulation that their internal economies could no longer produce under politically and socially acceptable conditions of exploitation. Harsher internal exploitation was difficult in industrially advanced societies. The complicated production systems required workers to pursue considerable educational and technical training, which increased the systems' powers of accumulation, but limited the degree of worker exploitation compatible with sociopolitical order. It was easier to exploit a labor force that had its political or social voice muted, and so racism, ethnicity, and alien status were factors used to mute groups targeted for exploitation. In the South, tenant farming, debt-peonage, and Jim Crow laws continued to stunt black (and white) political and social protest. A migrant labor force, separated from its cultural and social base, also has a diminished capacity to protect its members. Prejudice—racial or cultural—furnished a convenient justification for dominance and exploitation. In the United States, the internal minority was subjected to conditions that made it seek flight internally (to Oklahoma or Kansas), externally (to Mexico or Central America), or in its imagination, as in the back-to-Africa movements.

The U.S. blacks who went to Guatemala enjoyed only minimal protection from "progressive" officials who were promoting expansion by assuring bearers of U.S. passports ample protection of person and property. In various incidents involving black U.S. citizens in Guatemala, State Department officials swallowed their pride and better judgment to insist upon arrangements favorable to the "bad niggers" from the Mississippi levees in order to protect the "worthy" white Americans who were entering Guatemala in larger numbers and with larger quantities of capital. North American diplomats, entering cultures that were alien and of only slight interest to them, needed to assure U.S. entrepreneurs of special rights and privileges. Any subtle, differentiated treatment of elements of U.S. society abroad—as in the case of the U.S. railroad employees in Costa Rica or the effective deportation of Shine and Milliken—was best reserved to a State Department decision or joint bargaining between the United States and the host state. Those blacks who fled the United States in the early twentieth century to seek opportunity in Guatemala, Panama, or other Central American states became tools for the expansion of U.S. power. Whether as victims or as observers, blacks suffered directly as the tools of expansion and indirectly from the ideological and moral degradation that accompanied the imperial mind-set.

8

An Isthmian Canal and the U.S. Overthrow

of Nicaraguan President José Santos Zelaya

Between 1897 and 1903 the U.S. government decided to build an isthmian canal at Panama. This decision crushed the expectations of many Nicaraguans that a canal on their territory would produce future well-being and security. The leaders of Nicaragua's political economy, and President José Santos Zelaya in particular, refused to accept the U.S. government's decision as binding upon the nation's destiny. Unable to convince the United States to reconsider the site for the canal or to agree to build a second canal at Nicaragua, Zelaya, from 1904 until he was overthrown in 1909, sought alternative sources of capital for a canal from investors in Japan or Europe (especially Germany and France).[1]

North American leaders were shocked when President Zelaya looked elsewhere for investment. They should not have been. In 1888, when the Nicaraguan government complained in vain that the U.S. government and U.S. canal entrepreneurs had not responded adequately to the French canal project at Panama, it sent former President Adán Cárdenas on a public mission to interest British, German, and Italian capitalists in its canal route. Fearful that Zelaya might secure a better economic position for Nicaragua outside the U.S. economic subsystem, the United States labeled him a tyrannical, self-serving, brutal, greedy disturber of Central American peace, an enemy of all U.S. businessmen, and an opponent of all reasonable diplomatic objectives. Behind this forest of labels stood mountains of mendacity. Latin Americanist Charles Stansifer has described how Zelaya furthered education, conducted a reasonable financial policy which U.S. intervention reduced to financial instability, got along satisfactorily with Costa Rica and Honduras (but not with Guatemala under Manuel Estrada Cabrera), was hard but fair toward defeated rebels and opposition leaders, and secularized Nicaraguan life. Estrada Cabrera, a butcher and despot, often resisted U.S. requests until convinced that the matter in dispute was important to the United States, at which point he would make a concession sufficient to retain U.S. approval; Zelaya, however, was capable of continued opposition to U.S. penetration, particularly after 1903.[2]

The U.S. political elite came to despise Zelaya as a threat to the spread of liberal democracy in the Central American–Caribbean area. Liberal theory assumes that the masses work best if they share, according to their ability to take advantage of equitable opportunities, in the economic rewards of the political economy. Bourgeois democratic theory insists that all men (in liberal systems) share in the political, social, and economic rewards. Thus when liberal states expand, all mankind shares in the social rewards. Such hypotheses (visible in the Open Door policy) encouraged the development of an international free market economy that tolerated massive exploitation, yet made it difficult to create a rationale for colonial subjugation. Since formal colonies were not possible, indirect means had to be established through comprador elites who could be co-opted, seduced, or hired by the promise of reward. Anyone who hindered liberal expansion, such as Zelaya was accused of doing, was acting against the best interests of mankind.[3]

Zelaya was fond of describing himself as a fighter, an organizer, and a civilizer, but he was also a real patriot who devoted his life to bettering his country's condition. The Zelaya regime enacted a constitution that provided for equal rights, property guarantees, habeas corpus, compulsory vote, compulsory education, the protection of arts and industry, minority representation, the separation of state powers, municipal independence, secularization of cemeteries, suppression of mort-main (land and other property which through will or testament is kept permanently from the economic marketplace), and civil marriage. Zelaya claimed responsibility for financial stability, improved communications, commerce, mail, telegraph, and parcel post services, and advances in agriculture and mining. Historian Gregorio Selser called Zelaya an enlightened despot who alienated many in and out of Nicaragua because of his constitutional reforms and his commitment to Central American union.[4]

Historian Benjamin Teplitz, a close student of Zelaya and his regime, called Zelaya and his allies "technicians in fields of political power and national development" who successfully modernized those areas of Nicaraguan society beneficial to the coffee and commercial elites. Teplitz and historian Jaime Biderman agreed that Zelaya was merely a spokesperson and front man for Managua's elite. According to Teplitz, the support of these powerful groups allowed Zelaya to be an "absolute caudillo." Teplitz admitted that "the [Nicaraguan] Liberals had a great reputation for physical violence, but on a regular basis they eschewed fury in order to share power and its rewards with their would-be rivals." He warned against the mistake of studying the Zelaya period as one of personal rule. Historian Whitney Perkins agreed that Zelaya used political power personally and was regarded by the State Department as a spoilsman and troublemaker, yet noted that most Central Americans thought more highly of him. Perkins did not believe that the elite deserted Zelaya because of internal factors. Teplitz and Biderman agreed that only when the United States threatened Nicaraguan economic and social stability did the Nicaraguan elite turn away from Zelaya. Biderman added that world economic factors helped to push the coffee barons into opposition.[5]

Other historians, several of them quite critical of Zelaya's rule, have implicitly rejected the State Department's assertion in the first decade of the twentieth century that internal turmoil and opposition to the government were central elements of Nicaraguan life at the turn of the century. Thus Charles Frazier accepted the State Department's image of Zelaya as a tyrannical and financially careless ruler, but he concluded that Nicaragua had experienced "marked progress . . . during his administration," and that "the succeeding administrations have not measured up to Zelaya's in their over-all progressiveness." He went so far as to say that even in 1958, Nicaragua had "not reached again the heights it attained during the Zelaya revolution," and he conceded that Zelaya "gave to a large portion of the Nicaraguans a feeling of nationalism." Similarly, Floyd Cramer pronounced Zelaya brutal and heartless, yet he also concluded that none of the succeeding administrations "measured up to Zelaya in general progressiveness."[6]

The memoirs and autobiographies of the conservative leaders who finally deposed Zelaya expressed ambivalent views regarding his alleged cruelty. José Joaquín Morales, one of the few prominent conservatives who cited specific acts of murder by the Zelaya regime, mentioned about a dozen cases of unjustified killing. In most instances, he conceded that the conservatives executed were implicated in acts of homicide, homicide by arson, or treason. In several instances, Morales noted the conservatives were killed after trial; on other occasions it is not clear if a trial occurred. Even Morales recorded that large numbers of captured conservative leaders were imprisoned and then released. He sharply criticized Zelaya's assault upon the property and wealth of the elite in Granada, the center of conservative power. Zelaya's chief opponent, Emiliano Chamorro, was arrested and deported several times. He condemned Zelaya for driving him into exile, but he never recalled suffering more than "great discomfort" in the sleeping and living arrangements, abysmal prison quarters, and unfriendly staff. Several conservative leaders—Chamorro, Carlos Cuadra Pasos, Carlos Selva, and Pedro J. Cuadra Chamorro—were captured and exiled. None mentioned being tortured or having companions tortured or killed. Thus evidence from the conservative leaders themselves refutes the charge of cruelty, at least in their cases. Teplitz has argued that Zelaya treated the conservative elite who opposed him quite well, but treated the poor followers of the conservatives harshly. Conservative Carlos Cuadra Pasos did not see Zelaya as characterized particularly by brutality, and in fact considered Theodore Roosevelt "a man of the same mien as Zelaya."[7] Even U.S. agents unsympathetic to Zelaya grudgingly conceded his ability. In sum, Zelaya's government had a mixed record, which suggests that its cruelty may have been class-influenced. Most scholars studying the Zelaya years acknowledge that there have been gross distortions of Zelaya's record.[8]

The charges against Zelaya were essentially constructed to justify removing him. Zelaya attempted to shift Nicaragua out of its status as a satellite, where it apparently had no future, into a relationship with other powers that would promise fulfillment of Nicaragua's dream of material advancement from a canal. Zelaya approached non-U.S. capitalists about a possible canal or other investments. Unfortunately, the U.S. government found Zelaya's policy at odds with its own well-being and security. One leading historian of Central America contended that the United States confronted a Zelaya who instituted a modest economic nationalism that drove U.S. business interests into alliance with Nicaraguan conservatives. Nicaraguan conservatives were amenable. Pedro J. Cuadra Chamorro claimed that Nicaragua's conservatives drew the proper lesson from Colombia's experience: when Colombian conservatives, "presuming to act out of pure patriotism," refused to cede the Panama canal right of way and territory, the United States simply seized what it wanted. Nicaraguan historian Adán Selva contended that because Zelaya was not absolutely subservient to U.S. interests, he had to be overthrown, not to liberate the Nicaraguan people, but to satisfy North American interests.[9]

The United States had sought access to the Pacific throughout the nineteenth century. The thrust toward Asia formed the background for the U.S. concern with the isthmian canal. The French Panama Canal project, begun in 1879, increased U.S. sensitivity to foreign presence in the Caribbean region. The U.S. government considered the poor servicing of the large foreign-held Caribbean–Central American debt an invitation to intervention. The Roosevelt Corollary to the Monroe Doctrine (1905), which sought to end the possibility of foreign intervention to resolve debt problems, was one manifestation of this paranoia about a loss of security in the greater canal region. Zelaya's search for foreign entrepreneurs to undertake a Nicaraguan canal in competition with the Panama Canal represented another type of threat. Since the United States was unable to alter Zelaya's perspective, unprepared to bear the costs of Nicaragua's lost prospects for material gain, and unwilling to allow Nicaragua to look elsewhere for fulfillment of its dreams, the United States and Nicaragua clashed with increasing ferocity in the years after 1903 until Zelaya was overthrown.[10]

In the late nineteenth century, a disjointed U.S. economy produced many investors, entrepreneurs, and charlatans who developed projects involving public and private ventures in the isthmus-Caribbean area. The increased activity placed larger demands on the diplomatic service. As competition became more aggressive, North Americans became involved in encouraging "progressive" good government in Central America, which meant creating conditions—order, stability, and efficiency—favorable for U.S. business. Plagued with "overproduction," the U.S. government did not want an open door in the New World, but it expected to find a favorable field in Latin America.[11]

Most North American observers of Central America, with the exception of U.S. residents of the Mosquito Coast, saw positive aspects in Zelaya's arrival to power in 1893. The focus of U.S.-Nicaraguan relations in the 1890s seldom wandered far from issues related to a canal. In the 1890s, Zelaya was reliable on the canal issue: he resisted every scheme in the Nicaraguan congress to take the canal project out of American hands, but he insisted that the Nicaraguan Canal Construction company was "rotten." From 1893 until 1897, a series of incidents on the Mosquito Coast reopened the question of whether Britain, Nicaragua, or the United States would exercise authority over that region. By the end of the 1890s, Zelaya controlled that region, which he expected U.S. entrepreneurs to develop as a prelude to building the canal. Construction and operation of a canal would line his pockets and those of his friends and bring development to all of Nicaragua.[12] So long as he expected a U.S.-built canal, Zelaya dangled Nicaragua's opportunities before North Americans, even when British, French, and German agents expressed interest.

The U.S. consul at San Juan del Norte, William Sorsby, and the U.S. minister to Costa Rica and Nicaragua, William Merry, continued to wail against perceived threats to "the vested and invested rights and capital of American citizens temporarily residing" in the Mosquito Reservation. Sorsby argued for special rights and privileges in the Mosquito area because of its relationship to a canal and because of the U.S. business activity in that region. Zelaya accommodated North Americans on the north coast as long as it seemed the United States would build the canal. His government became more selective in its treatment of U.S. entrepreneurs after the decision to build at Panama. Former Confederate General Edward Alexander, chosen to arbitrate a Nicaraguan–Costa Rican border dispute, laid most of the blame for the conflict on the Mosquito Coast on U.S. citizens and other foreigners, not Zelaya's administration. He found it "shameful" that U.S. residents of the Mosquito Coast could "get our State Dept. to bully poor little Nicaragua." Sorsby dismissed Alexander as "an old man . . . [who]

doesn't believe that a foreigner has many rights in this country." Sorsby insisted that North Americans should receive a privileged position on the Mosquito Coast, while Alexander expected equal, if not favored, treatment for Nicaraguans in Nicaraguan territory.[13]

In the years between 1897 and 1902, U.S. canal entrepreneurs and their allies often charged Nicaragua with sabotaging U.S. transit projects. Nicaraguan authorities repeatedly denied that they were seeking an alternative to a U.S.-constructed canal. They were, of course, seeking the best deal possible. They were encouraged in 1897 when the U.S. government appointed the first Admiral John G. Walker Canal Committee to reexamine the potential routes. The Walker Committee recommended the Nicaraguan route to Congress. While the Walker Committee deliberated, stories of Japanese interests surfaced. According to the New York *Herald*, Zelaya insisted that Japan was not "secretly negotiating with the Diet of the Greater Republic of Central America for permission to take the Nicaraguan Canal project out of the hands of the United States." To dispel any lingering misunderstanding, Zelaya and two ranking Greater Republic Diet officials publicly denied that the Japanese sought to control the interoceanic route. The Japanese *Weekly Times*, however, reported that the Japanese minister in Washington had turned down a canal treaty with Nicaragua because it would interfere with U.S. rights. Conceivably, Zelaya's government hoped to use rumors of Japanese interest to raise the U.S. price and increase the urgency for a Nicaragua canal. Zelaya repeatedly reaffirmed his desire for a U.S. firm to build the canal.[14]

Events between 1901 and 1903 strengthened Zelaya's growing distrust of U.S. intentions. In 1901 the second Walker Committee recommended the Panama route, provided that the New Interoceanic Canal Company could reduce its price from $109,141,500 to $40,000,000. Senators John T. Morgan and A. Barton Hepburn, longtime proponents of a Nicaraguan canal, warned Zelaya that U.S. officials perceived the Nicaraguan government as only modestly supportive of realistic canal concessions. Morgan, Hepburn, and State Department official Alvey A. Adee, a "good proven friend of Costa Rica," convinced Costa Rican diplomat Joaquín Bernardo Calvo that, if Nicaragua and Costa Rica made the concessions the United States had requested, the United States would build at Nicaragua. In 1902, Costa Rica and Nicaragua undertook a joint propaganda effort to neutralize the well-organized newspaper campaign in favor of a Panama canal, but their effort came too late. In November 1903 the United States facilitated Panama's revolt against Colombia, and then immediately extracted a favorable canal treaty as payment for its help.[15]

Nicaragua's loss of the transit route had a profound effect upon U.S.-

Nicaraguan relations. Prior to the acquisition of the Panama canal rights, U.S. officials in Central America judged Zelaya to be a competent, able leader. In October 1903 U.S. Minister to Costa Rica and Nicaragua William Merry, a veteran of thirty years of shipping, merchant, and diplomatic activity in Central America, confidentially praised Zelaya as Central America's ablest executive and a man of "great energy, industry and ability" who was friendlier to Americans than any other Central American president. Other U.S. officials agreed that Zelaya was competent and friendly toward the United States.[16]

The U.S. decision to build a canal at Panama eroded U.S.-Nicaraguan governmental relations, and initiated a bitter feud between Zelaya and the U.S. government, during which, as indicated earlier, U.S. officials thoroughly demonized Zelaya. Zelaya did not relieve his frustration chiefly upon U.S. businessmen, however. In various instances, he showed patience and goodwill toward them. For example, James Dietrick and his associates from Pittsburgh, whose extensive concessions and land grants dated from about 1890, continued to receive government favors after the 1903 Panama Canal concession.[17] Zelaya continued to offer certain concessions to North American individuals so long as they shared their bounty with him.

Beginning in 1903–1904, however, Zelaya's administration realized that if they were ever to benefit from the cornucopia of wealth linked to a transit route, they would have to find an alternative to U.S. financing and technical planning. The modernizing and industrializing nation of Japan needed outlets for surplus population and goods and wanted access to the North Atlantic's technological products and energy. And Nicaragua, under the right circumstances, might offer an attractive opportunity for a Japanese-controlled interoceanic transit route. Nicaraguan officials recognized that Japan, Germany, or a combination of European states were the only realistic alternatives to U.S. capital.[18]

Since Nicaragua had granted many concessions to U.S. entrepreneurs to attract U.S. support for a canal, Zelaya's government now had to reacquire some of them as bait to catch other foreign capitalists. For almost a decade the Nicaraguan government had tolerated nonfulfillment of the obligations of its U.S. concessionaires, hoping that this tolerance would encourage U.S. capitalists to build a canal. But about 1905, U.S. entrepreneurs, accustomed to skirting contract provisions, encountered a Nicaraguan government increasingly unwilling to ignore contractual violations. In the ensuing disputes over concessions Zelaya's government entered rough terrain because its policy envisioned conceding control over a canal route to nations outside the hemisphere.[19]

Even after Zelaya had initiated a policy of replacing unproductive U.S.

concessionaires with foreign interests, responsible U.S. officials in Central America gave him good marks as a leader. This praise continued long after Washington officials were condemning his leadership. While conceding that Zelaya was a military autocrat with prisons full of political prisoners, Merry contended that the Nicaraguans wanted peace and would "aid no revolutionary efforts in neighboring republics." In early 1906, Merry, subjected to persistent State Department condemnation of Zelaya, still presented a view of Zelaya that was on balance favorable.[20]

In 1907 Minister to Guatemala Philip Brown and various State Department officials charged Zelaya with gross misconduct. Brown blamed Zelaya's ambition for the 1907 Nicaraguan-Salvadoran war, despite the fact that U.S. agents in El Salvador were encouraging the faction allied with Zelaya. Only in early 1907 did Merry's view of Zelaya become negative on balance. In that year he decided that Zelaya's "defeat and departure from his unfortunate country will be a general relief and will tend to secure comparatively permanent peace," concluding that "with the exception of the [Guatemalan] Government of Estrada Cabrera . . . who is a more blood thirsty tyrant, the Zelaya Govt. is undoubtedly the worst in Spanish America." He charged Zelaya and his friends with draining the wealth of Nicaragua through special privileges. But even in mid-1907 Merry could still describe Zelaya (with condescension typical of the age) as "a man of extraordinary energy and industry for a son of the Tropics."[21]

At least one effort to condemn Zelaya contained information that undermined the case against him. In 1909 the U.S. chargé in Nicaragua, John H. Gregory, a bitter critic of Zelaya, took possession of a diary of a dead U.S. citizen which he said revealed "rampant graft"—a scandal involving many prominent Nicaraguans, including Zelaya and a New Orleans businessman named T. M. Solomon. The diary actually revealed that contrary to the State Department's charge of anti-Americanism, Zelaya was working well with U.S. business interests even as late as 1909, provided they shared the wealth.[22] Zelaya's anti-American sentiments were directed chiefly at the official policy of the U.S. government.

As the tension mounted between Nicaragua and the United States, foreign agents from Europe attempted to curry favor with Nicaragua's government. Germans were among the most active. German investment in Nicaragua, which had been 14 million marks ($3.5 million) in 1898, rose to either 24 million marks ($6 million) in 1905 or 250 million marks ($60 million) in 1906, depending upon the evaluation of conflicting reports in the German archives (see Table 8.1). A French report from 1907 estimated German investment at 50 million francs (about 40 million marks or $10 million). While they differ greatly, the sources all agree that the German capital invested in Nicaragua was two or three times larger than U.S. investments and larger than British investments in Nicaragua around 1905–1910.

Although the 1906 estimate of 250 million marks appears very high, there is no doubt that Germany's role in Nicaragua had grown markedly in the early years of the twentieth century. As early as 1899 U.S. agents had estimated German investment at over ten million dollars (about 44 million marks, or two and one-half times the U.S. investment). The number of German settlers in Nicaragua rose from about fifteen (only males residing near Managua) in 1891 to four hundred (males?) in 1905. The wife of the German consul claimed that during this period of Nicaraguan-German rapprochement, Zelaya had requested German engineers to evaluate the Nicaragua route. She claimed that the U.S. government overthrew Zelaya in 1910 when it learned of this step through an indiscretion. While her recollection may be inexact, the general argument that the United States was very upset with Zelaya's constant flirting with non-U.S. capital to build an alternative canal is correct. Emiliano Chamorro's recollections and U.S. intelligence reports supported the quantitative evidence of vastly increased German personal and material presence in Nicaragua.[23]

Germany also assumed a major role in Nicaragua's military establishment. Zelaya endured, German consul Dr. Friedrich August Heye pointed out, because "his weapon" was his army, which had been reorganized with German advisers and supported through a cadet school under German direction. "Germany had in any case no grounds to be unsatisfied with the continuation of [Zelaya's] rule," Heye observed, since Zelaya had been "generally friendly toward German interests, and, in any event, a strong government like his offered the best guarantee against American intervention."[24] The Germans, however, were not the only nation blocking U.S. objectives in Central America.

By 1907 the U.S. government expected Mexico to be a key actor in efforts to bring down Zelaya's government. Mexico, however, was unwilling to undermine Zelaya because such a step would strengthen Guatemala, Mexico's traditional nemesis in Central America. U.S. Minister Philip Brown was convinced that Mexico's attitude in Central American affairs was "not at heart of the same friendly, benevolent character as that of the United States." He was particularly upset when Mexico announced that it would condone any attempt to overthrow Estrada Cabrera in Guatemala. He was not upset, however, when the United States encouraged Costa Rica to join Honduras, El Salvador, and Guatemala in an assault upon Zelaya. Brown believed that Mexico was pursuing an independent policy aimed at

Table 8.1   Foreign Investment in Nicaragua, 1898–1918

	French	German	British	U.S.
1897				1m$
1898		14mM		
1899		10.47m$		4.04m$
1902	6.15mF			
1905		24mM		
1906		250mM	66mM	60mM
1907		50mF		
1908				3.4m$
1913	6mF	50mF	6.2m$	
1914				4.5m$
1918	25mF	2.5m$	10–15m$	20m$

Note: m = million; F = French francs (5F = $1); M = German marks (4.2M = $1); $ = U.S. dollars.

Sources: United Nations, *El financiamiento externo de América Latina* (New York, 1964); Organization of American States, *Foreign Investment in Latin America* (Washington, D.C., 1955); "La fortune française à l'étranger," *Bulletin de statistique et de législation comparée,* 26 (Oct. 1926), 476–77; J. Fred Rippy, "French Investments in Latin America," *Interamerican Economic Affairs* 2 (Autumn 1948), 52–71; Rafael Menjívar L., *Acumulación originaria y desarrollo del capitalismo en El Salvador* (San José, Costa Rica, 1980), 58–59; Sorsby to St. Dept., April 13, 1899, CD, San Juan del Norte: 16 (T348/1 16); P. Metternich to Burchard, June 12, 1899, Senatskommission für die Reichs- und auswärtigen Angelegenheiten, neu A III, C. 22, Staatsarchiv, Hamburg; U.S. Manufacturer's Bureau, *Monthly Consular and Trade Report* (Washington, D.C., 1900), 63:460–61, in José Francisco Guevara-Escudero, "Nineteenth Century Honduras: A Regional Approach to the Economic History of Central America, 1839–1914" (Ph.D. diss., New York University, Binghamton, 1983), 419; Paul Behneke to Emperor William, May 18, 1905, RM 5/v. 5401, von Ammon to Emperor William, Feb. 3, 1906, RM 5/v. 5402, Bundesarchiv, Militärarchiv, Freiburg, Germany; Désiré Pector, *Les richesses de l'Amérique centrale* (2nd ed,; Paris, [1980]), 298; Désiré Pector, *Régions isthmiques de l'Amérique tropicale* (Paris, 1925), 84; Chayet to MAE, Jan. 21, 1919, Amér. 1918–40, C. A., num. 68 (Nic.), AMAE, Paris.

avoiding exertions of U.S. power on both its northern and southern borders. He came to consider Mexico a hindrance to U.S. goals in Central America.[25]

As the U.S. government projected an increasingly negative image of Zelaya, he responded in ways that angered U.S. businessmen and agents. In 1907, T. M. Solomon, the manager of the New Orleans-based Central American Improvement Company, told Merry a story that he hoped would be recalled the next time Zelaya asked for U.S. good offices to restore peace in Nicaragua. During a business appointment, Solomon noticed dirt on the portrait of Theodore Roosevelt hanging in Zelaya's office. He remarked: "It has been dirtied and you should have it cleaned." Zelaya replied, "No, he has dirtied himself with the Weil case [Weil was a U.S. entrepreneur who filed a claim when Nicaragua sought to cancel his contract] and it does not deserve cleaning." By 1907 condemnation of the U.S. government was widespread in Nicaragua.[26]

In 1908 Zelaya's conservative opponents organized a parade to celebrate William Howard Taft's victory in the presidential elections. Hoping to attract U.S. support to their cause, they intended to criticize Zelaya under the guise of celebrating Taft. The parade began as a purely Nicaraguan event, but was later joined by three U.S. citizens. The inebriated conservatives shouted slogans calling for Nicaragua's annexation to the United States, the "liberty of Nicaragua," and seditious activity. It was rumored that they planned to attack the barracks in Managua, and Nicaraguan police eventually broke up the parade. Although Minister to Nicaragua John Gardner Coolidge maintained that the United States should stay out of Nicaragua's internal affairs, he desperately wanted to clip Zelaya's wings, so he seized upon the parade incident. He complained that North Americans in Nicaragua had been hindered in their celebration of Taft's victory. Zelaya's government denied that the parade was a North American celebration and insisted that it had simply acted to preserve order when the parade participants undertook illegal activities.[27]

The Managuan newspaper *La Tarde* lamented that Coolidge, probably influenced by chargé Gregory, had intervened to call for a public trial. The editorial condemned "Yankee Officials who . . . exceed their powers by treating these [Central American nations] as a conquered province." Nicaragua, *La Tarde* contended, must be allowed to maintain order and the "peace of the country without laying itself open thereby to the charge of unfriendliness to the United States."[28] When Nicaragua rebuffed this challenge to its sovereignty, U.S. officials charged anti-Americanism and condemned the Nicaraguan leadership.

When the parade incident backfired, Coolidge resigned and Gregory was recalled. Only a Nicaraguan native serving as vice-consul, José de Olivares, who was hostile to Zelaya, remained in Managua. Nicaraguan government assaults upon the United States became more vitriolic. Secretary of State Knox and Assistant Secretary of State Huntington Wilson lacked former Secretary of State Root's patience and sensitivity to Latin American attitudes, and his awareness of the trap of interventionist propensity. Zelaya was not willing to back down before the tougher Knox-Huntington Wilson position, so they tried to isolate him. Olivares described the "malicious resentment," "perverse misinterpretation," and "a general policy of incendiarism against our own and kindred influences which are striving for the redemption and future welfare of these countries." He warned that Zelaya's "press propaganda constitute[d] a more or less serious menace to our Government's influence" with the Central American people.[29]

Nicaragua was a disturbing factor in the region because it refused to concede Panama a monopoly on the economic benefits that would presumably gush from a canal route. Both the United States and Panama were concerned about the possibilities of competition from a Nicaraguan canal in foreign hands. Since U.S. capital was concentrated in the Panama Canal area, Nicaraguan developmental projects encountered increased difficulty attracting U.S. funds. Zelaya tested other areas for the capital necessary to develop Nicaragua. In 1909, his opponents, this time with more validity, accused him of shamelessly flirting with foreign governments and entrepreneurs. Zelaya's private secretary, Luis F. Corea, visited the European capitals and Japan, inquiring whether European or Japanese capitalists were interested in discussing a canal project. The Nicaraguan government claimed that the British were interested in a joint venture with Japan. A Nicaraguan conservative historian, however, claimed that the foreign powers refused a concession because of the disturbed state of Nicaragua. The Nicaraguan foreign minister warned Corea of the dangers of premature discovery by the United States. Consul Olivares expected Nicaraguan society to accept the rejection of its transit possibilities without objection. In an analysis that underscored the heart of the U.S.-Zelaya conflict, Olivares condemned Zelaya, who, "since the final selection of the Panama Canal route by our Government, has in more than one instance schemed to thwart the great enterprise by covertly exploiting the rejected Nicaraguan site." He considered Zelaya's negotiations with the Japanese to construct a canal near criminal. In mid-1909, a *Diario de Nicaragua* editorial suggested that a Nicaraguan-Japanese alliance would stymie U.S. imperialistic advances in Central America. There is no indication how seriously the Japanese took the Nicaraguan proposal, but U.S. officials suspected that Japan was looking for an opportunity to establish a foothold on the isthmus near a canal site.[30]

French interests were also willing to respond to Nicaraguan needs for capital, technology, and immigrants. The number of French settlers in Nicaragua had risen from fifty-four (males?) in 1893 to two hundred (males?) in 1904, and French investment in Nicaragua remained level at about six million francs in the first decade of the twentieth century. Despite this relatively modest presence, French financiers were eager to respond when the Nicaraguan government approached the French government in mid-1909 about floating a loan on the Paris stock exchange. A French government inquiry determined that Nicaragua was an acceptable financial risk.[31]

The French were not as certain about the political risk, however. Before responding, the French foreign minister inquired whether the U.S. government would interpret a loan as unfriendly. The U.S. secretary of state wanted the French government to inform the Nicaraguan agent that a loan would be conditional upon Nicaragua's settling its affairs with the United States. The French government accepted this proposal. France was unwilling to squeeze the United States, but found no objection to squeezing Nicaragua. Later, when the loan to Zelaya was about to be placed on the Paris stock exchange, the secretary of state changed his tune, claiming that any money Zelaya would get "would be without doubt spent to purchase munitions to oppress his neighbors" and in "hostility to peace and progress in Central America." The State Department also advised the French government that the Zelaya loan would not be advantageous for European creditors. The French minister in Washington concluded that the U.S. government intended to supervise the finances of the Central American countries in order to protect American and occasionally European interests. He warned that the U.S. government would not permit the direct intervention of Europe in Central America.[32] The Washington government had apparently decided that keeping Zelaya in financial difficulty was an important step in a program to remove him.

In the first decades of the twentieth century, Middle America from Mexico to Colombia experienced the heavy hand of U.S. policy which sought to compel acceptance of U.S. objectives aimed at security and well-being. As U.S.-Nicaraguan relations soured, the U.S. government sought a cat's paw for the overthrow of Zelaya in the form of a reliable Middle American comprador state (one led by citizens attached to and sustained by metropole firms, culture, or strategic interests). Guatemala was too distant, corrupt, and divided to function in this capacity; and besides, Estrada Cabrera had tried unsuccessfully for years to overturn Zelaya. U.S. agents dismissed Honduras because of the civil strife raging in that country. El Salvador was experiencing a wave of anti-Americanism. For a brief period, the State Department considered Mexico a likely candidate. When Mexico rejected the role, Costa Rica assumed a vital position.[33]

In early 1907, the U.S. government, fresh from a conference on peace and arbitration, voluntarily observed that "it would not feel at liberty to criticize the course of Costa Rica should that country deem it essential to her own protection to join with her sister Republics in Central America in an effort to end the [Zelaya] situation." But Costa Rica refused to join the anti-Zelaya campaign, and Costa Rican newspapers sharply criticized continued U.S. attacks upon Zelaya. Merry lamented the "considerable abuse of the United States Government and people being printed in the opposition Costa Rican papers." Many Costa Rican politicians resented the overbearing pressure to act against Zelaya, to leave the United Fruit Company untouched, and to conform to U.S. expectations.[34]

Despite repeated refusals, the U.S. government continued to pressure Costa Rica to act against the Nicaraguan leader. U.S. diplomats assigned Zelaya a nefarious role in Costa Rican politics; chargé Gregory, relying only on circumstantial evidence and rumor, reported that Zelaya had tried to influence the 1909 Costa Rican elections in favor of Ricardo Jiménez, who had "attained popularity by orating vs. foreigners, especially vs. Americans and the United Fruit Co. as the alleged oppressor of Costa Rica." If the Jiménez faction won the election, Gregory said, Zelaya would obtain great influence in Costa Rica. Merry inappropriately sermonized: "While *political liberty, free speech* and *press* are commendable, when granted to a people *unfit for them* the result is bad."[35]

U.S. Minister to Guatemala Heimké and Minister to Costa Rica Merry reacted differently to Costa Rican politics in 1909. Jiménez assured Merry that he was independent of Zelaya and that he was not anti-American. He admitted that some of his supporters, especially Máximo Fernández, were close to Zelaya; he said he hoped Zelaya would be deposed, because then Fernández's power would crumble in Costa Rica. Merry suspected that Jiménez's attitude toward the United States was ambivalent, but that his dissatisfaction with Fernández was real. Merry expected good rule from Jiménez if he avoided Fernández and selected honorable men. Heimké judged the situation differently. He deplored Zelaya's attempt "to impress his iniquitous, criminal and venal thumb-print upon such a clean and model republic as Costa Rica." He added: "While I deprecate armed hostility and further bloodshed, I think a perpetual peace could be obtained for these countries if the Governments of the United States and Mexico would raise no objections to giving El Salvador and Guatemala a chance to enter Nicaragua and wipe Zelaya off the rolls."[36] Heimké was merely reformulating a wish his government had communicated in other language to Central American governments since 1907.

The U.S. pressure on Costa Rica to adopt a hostile policy toward Zelaya was common knowledge in Central America. So was Costa Rica's resistance. After Jiménez was elected in 1909, German Minister Bonin questioned how long the new president could resist U.S. gold and preserve his neutral position between Zelaya and Estrada Cabrera. Jiménez had campaigned on neutrality in the squabble between Nicaragua, the United States, and Guatemala. His election was, in Bonin's words, "a blow as much for the Americans as for their pace-maker Estrada Cabrera."[37]

In late 1909 Zelaya's forces entered Costa Rica in the sparsely inhabited jungle area on the Atlantic coast to cut off support and supply areas that would be useful to U.S.-favored General Juan J. Estrada's revolutionary movement. U.S. officials seized the opportunity. They promised that if Costa Rica requested armed intervention to halt a Zelaya incursion, Guatemala and El Salvador would join the United States in cooperating with Costa Rica. Costa Rica replied that the minor border incursion was on the way to being satisfactorily resolved and that it considered itself "without motive to justify taking up arms against Zelaya." When Costa Rican Minister in the United States Joaquín Calvo warned that the United States was prepared to intervene in Nicaragua if the Central American states did not act first, the Costa Rican government contacted the other Central American states to oppose the incursion. Merry confirmed for Costa Rica that the United States would intervene if requested by Costa Rica, Guatemala, and El Salvador. Foreign Minister Ricardo Fernández Guardia assured Calvo that Costa Rica was determined "not to enter such dangerous actions as those proposed by Washington." It "considered the joint action proposed contrary to the Washington treaty and desired to maintain a neutral attitude."[38] Costa Rican officials considered the United States a more serious threat to Central American peace and harmony than Zelaya's Nicaragua.

The Costa Rican government expected to resolve its differences with Nicaragua through a satisfactory diplomatic arrangement rather than a resort to force. It insisted that it must "determine the time and form in which it ought to demand a reparation relative to the violation of territory." Huntington Wilson argued that Costa Rica's silence on Zelaya's invasion of its territory aided him to defeat Juan Estrada's revolutionary forces. Huntington Wilson, unconcerned with Estrada's violation of Costa Rican territory, considered the Costa Rican position counter to its "traditional and effective neutral posture." Costa Rica was not indifferent, Calvo replied; it was preparing a documented case, as prescribed by the 1907 Washington Treaties, which established a recognition policy, a Central American court, and other procedures to stabilize Central America. Considering the fact that the Washington Conference, inspired by the U.S. government, had labored to establish mechanisms of mediation and diplomacy to solidify peace and stability in Central America, Costa Rica would not make a hasty, unwarranted resort to force. When U.S. pressure to undertake armed action remained unrelenting, Foreign Minister Fernández Guardia blurted out in frustration:

> We do not understand here what interests can the Washington government have that Costa Rica assumes a resolutely aggressive position against Nicaragua, with the danger of compromising the observation of the . . . conventions of December 20, 1907. . . . It is in Central America's interest that U.S. action with respect to Nicaragua should assume the character of an international conflict and in no sense the character of an intervention tolerated and even less solicited or supported by the other signatory republics of the Washington Treaty.[39]

Costa Rica refused comprador status and resisted the anti-Zelaya campaign, insisting that the United States assume full responsibility for whatever action it chose to take in Nicaragua.

The repeated efforts of the U.S. government to prod Costa Rica into the lead in overthrowing Zelaya remained confidential until the Costa Rican election of 1923. During his presidential campaign in that year, Fernández Guardia publicly proclaimed that Knox had urged him to declare war on Nicaragua during the 1909 border dispute. In response, State Department official Dana Munro claimed that the only relevant item in the files was a published note of November 19, 1909, which indicated that the U.S. government would view intervention by the Central American states in a friendly light.[40] In fact, the U.S. and Costa Rican archives contained many documents for the years 1907–1909 attesting to official U.S. urging of various courses, including the use of force, intended to overthrow Zelaya, as well as documents proving that Costa Rica's government had always refused to serve as a surrogate in that project.

Until mid-1909, the United States used moral, financial, and material support to encourage dissidents in Nicaragua. As the winter approached with Zelaya still in power, the U.S. government used the execution of two U.S. soldiers of fortune as an excuse to undertake a large U.S. military build-up off the coast. Under threat of invasion, Zelaya turned over the presidency to José Madriz and left the country. Some Costa Rican newspapers vented popular dissatisfaction with U.S. policy, President Taft, and Secretary of State Knox. Although admitting that Costa Rica had the freest press in Latin America, Merry asked Costa Rican officials to exert "influence to procure from the management of [the] press in this Capital respectful treatment" of the U.S. president and other high officials. He professed to be amazed by the assault upon U.S. officials because the United States had rid Central America of "the worst enemy Costa Rica ever had: the President of Nicaragua." He was reading Costa Rican history through State Department glasses: most Costa Ricans considered the filibusterer William Walker their country's worst enemy and had serious reservations about Merry's list of the injuries that Zelaya had inflicted upon their country.[41] Merry's insistence that the Costa Rican government control its own press was a warning of the dangers ahead, as U.S. involvement in the internal affairs of Central America increased.

Fernández Guardia agreed with Merry's earlier admission "that the liberty of the press is real and effective in Costa Rica," and said that in providing for this freedom, Costa Rica had followed the U.S. example; but he added that all countries with a free press were bound to experience abuses of press freedom. Minister Calvo assured Assistant Secretary of State Adee and Huntington Wilson that the disparaging articles came from opposition newspapers that hoped to embarrass the government and said that since the same thing occasionally happened in the United States, there was no reason why the U.S. government should expect special treatment in Costa Rica. Nevertheless, Adee and Huntington Wilson expected that the Costa Rican government could influence the newspaper sentiments since "almost all the press of Latin American countries is [government] inspired." Despite Calvo's powerful reasoning, Knox remained adamant that Costa Rica should take action to curtail derogatory remarks against high ranking U.S. officials.[42] U.S. officials often disparaged Central American leaders, societies, and cultures; but in this case, they chastised Costa Rican leaders for not corrupting one of the freest presses in Latin America.

Spanish diplomat Manuel García Jove, a critic of Zelaya's regime, claimed that Latin American resentment over U.S. policy in overthrowing Zelaya was widespread and intense. He noted particularly the bitterness in El Salvador against the United States. Adee insisted that the U.S. position would not change because of Latin American propaganda charges that rested upon an erroneous interpretation of fair and impartial U.S. acts. Despite the unfavorable press in Latin America, Sands claimed to believe that the U.S. intervention in Nicaragua "has been received by the thinking element in Central America with satisfaction and hope." But the U.S. minister to Nicaragua, Thomas Dawson, discovered that the facts of Nicaraguan politics were very different from U.S. hypotheses. He estimated that the liberals comprised an overwhelming majority, perhaps as much as 85 percent of the voters.[43] U.S. officials commonly misread Latin American reactions to U.S. policies and conduct, while alleging that the Latin Americans were unappreciative and culturally unable to understand U.S. goals and objectives.

Costa Rica's disagreement with U.S. policy in Nicaragua continued after Zelaya had been ousted. Costa Rica accepted Madriz as Zelaya's constitutional successor. The United States, however, could not recognize Madriz precisely *because* he was constitutionally selected to succeed Zelaya. Under the Nicaraguan constitution, a successor served only during the absence of the president. If the United States recognized Madriz as constitutionally appropriate and Zelaya later returned to Nicaragua, Zelaya would become president again. The United States therefore insisted on completing the conservative revolution to make certain that Zelaya's removal was permanent.[44] There was to be no chance that Zelaya's independent policies could be reconstructed by Madriz or reinstituted by Zelaya.

In 1911 the German consul in San José reflected on the U.S. role in Nicaragua and its lingering resentment of Costa Rica's conduct. He argued that the U.S. government welcomed disorder, which it manipulated to subordinate the weak Latin American governments. The U.S. procedure was demonstrated in Nicaragua. After President Zelaya had raised Nicaragua's culture, honor, and justice above the norm for Central America, the U.S. government had labored to create disorder there. Nicaragua, the consul surmised, if allowed to continue under the course Zelaya had set, might have escaped the U.S. trap of subservience. A return to the old ways excused U.S. intervention. He offered no panacea, but cautioned that U.S. policy was detrimental to German interests.[45]

Zelaya's administration had no intention of accepting the economic backwardness that threatened Nicaragua as a consequence of the U.S. decision to build a canal at Panama. Zelaya looked diligently for capitalists who could finance an alternative canal and promote Nicaragua's development. U.S. officials presumed that a Nicaraguan canal financed by German, Japanese, French, and British sources would threaten U.S. dominance of the Caribbean–Central American region. Despite the fear and suspicion in Washington regarding foreign interests in Central America, there was little public support in the United States for an anti-Zelaya campaign until the administration charged Zelaya with anti-Americanism. Later, a U.S. puppet, President Adolfo Díaz, sold the United States an option on the route (incorporated in the William J. Bryan–Emiliano Chamorro Canal Treaty of 1914) to assure that no other metropole power would use a Nicaraguan canal as the basis for a challenge to U.S. preeminence in the Caribbean area.

The United States, without justification to deny Zelaya's authority under the rules it helped establish in the 1907 Washington treaties on Central America, covertly aided Nicaraguan dissidents (such as Juan Estrada and Adolfo Díaz) and hoped for overt action from a comprador satellite to overthrow Zelaya. Costa Rican officials resisted because they feared the precedent of a unilateral U.S. decision to destroy the political institutions and independence of a small state it had grown to dislike. Not just Costa

Ricans, but many Central Americans had reservations about U.S. efforts to organize a Central American armed intervention to overthrow Zelaya. Ultimately, and sadly, the United States acted alone to destroy Zelaya, perhaps the most competent ruler of independent Nicaragua in the pre-Sandinistas period.

9

A U.S. Dilemma: Economic Opportunity and

Anti-Americanism in El Salvador, 1901–1911

_____

In the early twentieth century, United States policies in El Salvador were inconsistent and at cross-purposes. An examination of the behavior of U.S. diplomats in El Salvador during the decade after the Spanish American War and the early stages of the Open Door policy reveals the contradictory nature of U.S. expansion. The United States expected the Salvadoran government to adopt political, financial, and commercial programs that would facilitate American penetration of that society. While U.S. political and economic influence was growing in El Salvador, that society was supposed to benefit materially through a transformation toward more liberal, democratic institutions. When U.S. material and ideological goals clashed, ideology gave way to economic and strategic objectives, which were accompanied by the persistent interference of U.S. businessmen and government officials in El Salvador's economic, political, and international affairs. The interference generated anti-Americanism among Salvadorans.[1]

U.S. involvement in El Salvador had been quite modest in the nineteenth century because the Central American country lacked size, population, and a Caribbean coastline. The U.S. role changed by the turn of the century following the rapid incorporation of the western United States into the national economy and the industrial growth of the Northeast and Midwest. With U.S. expansive energy directed into the trans-Mississippi West and beyond into the Pacific, El Salvador assumed a larger role in U.S. geopolitical thinking, evident by the establishment in 1897 and 1901 of two canal commissions, both chaired by Admiral John Walker, and the Hay-Pauncefote canal treaty of 1901. These developments revealed El Salvador as a likely terminal for a Nicaraguan interoceanic canal or railroad, as possessing a possible entrepôt–naval station in Fonseca Bay, and as an export center for its own and much of Guatemalan and Honduran production. It also boasted a supply of cheap labor. Its comparatively large and underemployed population (second only to Guatemala's in the isthmus area) meant that Salvadoran labor was exported to work on the Honduran and Guatemalan railroads, in Honduran mines, and on Caribbean fruit plantations.[2] In short, El Salvador assumed geopolitical importance in the great power competition for transit, communication, and market opportunities in the Pacific.

El Salvador's liberal political economy had achieved a modicum of political stability by the first decade of the twentieth century. The Salvadoran liberal elite had passed various land expropriation decrees between 1879 and 1882, and by the late 1890s the decrees had been largely implemented. Expropriation, however, stimulated civil disorders, six in fifteen years, which were crushed with the newly created and foreign-trained rural guard, militia, and army forces. Various foreign powers exercised influence on Salvador's armed forces. Chilean military advisers, trained by Germans, served in El Salvador in the late nineteenth century. The Chilean advisers were replaced in the late 1890s by a French military mission which remained into the 1920s. While the exploitation, repression, and maldistribution embedded in El Salvador's political economy would return to disturb that society periodically in the future, the immediate impact of foreign-trained troops was a brief period of comparative tranquillity. In the years from 1900 to 1914, the nation's economy and political stability offered some attractions to foreigners, especially to U.S. businessmen and government officials.[3] While the Salvadoran society was seeking internal stability from the domestic disorders of the 1880s and 1890s, U.S. society, also internally disarrayed in the 1873–1898 period, was searching for external sources to alleviate disorder there.

In the years from 1906 to 1913 U.S. diplomats and businessmen opposed Salvadoran presidents General Fernando Figueroa and Manuel Enrique Araujo because these leaders, selected and sustained by the traditional methods of Salvadoran politics, guided Salvadoran society in ways which upset the U.S. idealized dream for El Salvador. American dissatisfaction expressed itself in support for "democratic" opposition leader and perennial exile Prudencio Alfaro. Some of Alfaro's support came from individuals or factions (for example, the Moisant brothers [John, Alfred, George, and Edward], U.S. Consul John Jenkins, U.S. businessman P. P. Brownson, and Salvadoran General Potenciano Escalón and his supporters) which set a high priority on U.S. economic penetration of Salvadoran society. While Figueroa exhibited no great commitment to broad-based, popular participation in a fair, just society, Araujo represented some of the best sentiments for justice, fairness, and social improvement which Central America produced in that era of rampant liberalism and positivism. U.S. interference in El Salvador's internal power struggle demonstrated little sensitivity to the social, economic, or humanitarian qualities of the various Salvadoran leaders or factions. William A. Williams has described the tragedy that results from Americans wishing for humanitarian, democratic development in societies they have judged important for the expanding U.S. role in the world. The insistence that these societies adopt U.S. values and institutions negates the wish for self-government and democratic institutions, especially when comprador domestic elites, subservient to, dependent on, or co-opted by U.S. interests, tried to secure conditions essential to U.S. business, security, and ideology. The United States wanted Central America developed in a manner suitable for expanding U.S. economic and geopolitical interests, yet simultaneously it wished the Central American states to develop U.S. liberal institutions and democratic practices. The U.S. rhetoric called for constitutional democracies, according to historian John C. Chasteen, allowing only for "a decorative constitutional framework" that did not permit "political opposition."[4] To realign Salvadoran society, U.S. policy encouraged its destabilization. In part, U.S. officials acted aggressively in Salvadoran society in order to counteract influences by other foreign powers upon this society.

Besides the United States, Salvadoran political factions invited Guatemala, Nicaragua, and other foreign states to assume active roles in Salvadoran politics. The power struggle between Figueroa and Alfaro involved factions with support from Guatemalan President Manuel Estrada Cabrera and Nicaraguan President José Santos Zelaya. The support for factions by various Central American states in each other's political life had some logic and justification because these states shared the language, history, and some cultural characteristics. The Central American states also religiously proclaimed their intention to reestablish a Central American Union. The United States, however, was culturally and linguistically alien and demonstrated little interest in acquiring the knowledge or sensitivity which would have enlightened its relationship with El Salvador.[5] While the Central American states shared a dream of Central American union and remained within a Hispanic cultural tradition, U.S. interference ignored (perhaps even rejected) that tradition and sought to establish conditions favorable for U.S. economic activity. U.S. involvement which was culturally, economically, and politically insensitive lay at the foundation of the rising anti-Americanism.

In part, El Salvador was an alien battlefield for Central American strongmen and U.S. businessmen and diplomats who competed for wealth, power, prestige, and security. From the rise of Estrada Cabrera to the Guatemalan presidency in 1898 until the fall of Zelaya from the Nicaraguan presidency in 1909, these two strongmen struggled to dominate Central American society. Zelaya had worked well with the U.S. government until the decision to build a canal in Panama threatened to condemn Nicaragua to a dwarfed economic future. When Zelaya and his supporters searched for foreign capital to build a non-U.S.-controlled canal, the United States developed a tolerance for brutal dictator Estrada Cabrera and was willing to support him as a counterweight to Zelaya's prestige and power on the isthmus. El Salvador's political economy became one battleground for the power struggle between Zelaya and Estrada Cabrera. Zelaya generally supported the Alfaro faction because Figueroa opposed Central American union under Zelaya's leadership. Even Estrada Cabrera had originally negotiated with Alfaro and U.S. Consul Jenkins until the latter came to doubt his candor. Alfaro and Jenkins then opened talks with the Mexican diplomatic agent in Guatemala. Estrada Cabrera had no desire to help build a strong Salvadoran political faction under Alfaro which would owe political debts to the United States and to two political sources in Central America—Zelaya and Mexico—which the Guatemalan government considered hostile or unfriendly. At this point, Estrada Cabrera lost interest in the Alfaro faction. The Guatemalan president was hostile toward a Mexican-Salvadoran alliance because he charged that Mexico historically had seized Guatemalan northern territories. Mexican officials denied rumors of supporting the Salvadoran government, alleging Guatemala repeated such stories to justify new importation of arms.[6] As a counterweight to U.S., Mexican, and Zelayan intrigues in El Salvador, Estrada Cabrera reluctantly supported President Figueroa. The U.S. consular officials and business interests supported Alfaro because he held out promise for policies favorable to U.S. economic penetration.

Consul Jenkins and his allies believed a political transformation in El Salvador was the surest means to expand U.S. business and political opportunities in El Salvador. The Alfaro faction, the vehicle selected to perfect the political transformation, received material and moral support from various Americans, but chief among them were the Moisant family and Jenkins. The Moisant family apparently arrived in El Salvador from the U.S. west coast in the late nineteenth century, acquired several plantations, and entered banking, finance, and commerce. The brothers eventually became Salvadoran citizens, but in the first decade of the twentieth century they apparently retained U.S. citizenship. It is possible that they possessed dual citizenship. In the early twentieth century, the Moisants and Jenkins became disillusioned with the governing Salvadoran political faction because it refused to support their economic aspirations. To protect and expand their wealth, the Moisants entered Salvadoran politics, at times quite publicly, especially when they harbored the revolutionary chief General Escalón on their estate. The brothers were accused of numerous violations of

Salvadoran law and certainly were guilty of ill-considered activity. The ambivalent policies that Jenkins pursued were not signs of ignorance, but reflected the contradictions and tension inherent in the competitive nature of the U.S. political economy and ideological thinking. Jenkins's policy encouraged instability in El Salvador and strengthened Zelaya's influence in Central America. In these same years, the U.S. government sought to create order and stability by means of a Central American court and the overthrow of Zelaya. The more general goals for Central America were, however, subordinated to short-term, concrete economic gains in El Salvador. In 1911 the Spanish minister in El Salvador observed that the United States had supported Alfaro's revolutionary efforts for more than a dozen years in expectation of obtaining preponderant influence in El Salvador.[7] The Jenkins-Moisant group considered assurance of support for the Salvadoran political faction most sympathetic to U.S. penetration a vital step in obtaining the desired business opportunities. The size of the Moisant family and the variety of its activities revealed the breadth and depth of the private and public U.S. role in that country. The Moisants, however, represented only a fraction of U.S. involvement in El Salvador.

Although the United States publicly called for peace, order, and stability in Central America, U.S. support for such goals in El Salvador remained clouded. Rather than sustain the existing Salvadoran government, which the U.S. government recognized, Jenkins conducted public "covert" activity which encouraged a Salvadoran revolutionary faction and brought the mutual hostility between Mexico and Guatemala into El Salvador. In 1905 Jenkins took unauthorized leave to visit Guatemala, where he conspired with the revolutionary forces to overthrow the Salvadoran government. He met openly with President Estrada Cabrera and Salvadoran revolutionary leader Alfaro. Salvadoran President Figueroa complained confidentially to Costa Rican officials that Jenkins was distinctly partial toward Nicaraguans (Zelaya) and toward Salvadoran emigrants notorious for their opposition to the existing Salvadoran government. Jenkins was not pursuing a policy which promoted peace and stability in El Salvador, yet he received no reprimand from the State Department.[8]

The U.S. government continued to support its consul and the Moisants even after it learned that the brothers were linked to Zelaya and openly active in Salvadoran politics. Jenkins maintained close contact with Zelaya's consul, Felipe Nery Fernández, and with the Moisant brothers, who had hidden General Potenciano Escalón, an Alfaro supporter, on their estate. Jenkins had the audacity, President Figueroa told the Costa Rican government, to declare that Escalón was on the Moisant estate, but under his protection for humanitarian reasons.[9] Despite its announced objectives of stability and order, the U.S. government continued to tolerate the arrogant conduct of Jenkins, who looked to internal and external sources of support to unseat President Figueroa.

Jenkins missed no opportunity to irritate the Figueroa government and, once back in El Salvador, named Alfred J. Moisant his vice-consul without consulting his superior, Minister to Costa Rica William H. Merry, who was temporarily in charge of the legation in El Salvador. The Salvadoran government refused to accept Moisant's credentials because of his political activities, and Minister Merry, obviously with Jenkins in mind, warned all Americans to keep out of local politics. Merry acknowledged that the Moisant family was not quiet, peaceful, or businesslike (Merry apparently meant they were obstreperous, aggressive, argumentative, and frequently more attentive to political activity than to their business), but unfortunately involved extensively in Salvadoran politics. He noted that one Moisant brother, John, had already been expelled as a pernicious foreigner. The U.S. chargé in Guatemala, William Franklin Sands, supported Merry's charges, describing John Moisant as a well-known soldier of fortune with a reputation as a gun-slinger. Jenkins, P. P. Brownson, another American, and the Moisants, declared Sands, were aiding Zelaya and his ally Alfaro to gain influence in El Salvador, for which these Americans expected "fat contracts from Zelaya and Alfaro."[10]

Merry and Sands were not alone in condemning the conduct of members of the Moisant family. In 1906 and early 1907, most U.S. officials in Central America considered the Moisant clan a disturbing element in Salvadoran life, yet acted to protect them and their interests. In mid 1907 U.S. Consul-General George H. Murphy reported that George and Edward Moisant were in prison for aiding antigovernment revolutionaries, with losses on their estate mounting. Murphy hoped Merry and the arrival of the U.S. war vessel *Yorktown* (which he and Merry had requested) would secure the release of the two Moisant brothers, an adequate indemnity, and a guarantee against further molestation. Murphy did not mention an investigation to determine guilt or liability in regard to the imprisonment of the Moisants. He asserted that

> maintenance of American prestige and the right of protection claimed by American citizens for their persons and property in Central America require vigorous action. If these Governments can be taught that they are responsible, and responsible at once, for the acts of tyranny perpetrated upon American citizens, visitors to these countries like myself will hear less often from American residents the reproach that they are treated with less consideration . . . than are British subjects.[11]

Murphy did not condemn the conduct of the Moisant family, but he acknowledged that the Moisants were involved in matters which disturbed U.S.-Salvadoran relations.

Later, for reasons which are not clear, but which may be related to the U.S. government's desire to increase economic activities in Central America, Merry also decided that the Salvadoran government had badly treated the Moisants. He recognized that Figueroa's administration probably wished to punish the Moisants for having harbored on one of their plantations the dissatisfied presidential candidate, General Escalón, who was charged with organizing a revolt against the government. Merry unilaterally decided that evidence supporting the government's charge against the Moisants was mostly worthless and thus a weak basis for imprisonment without trial. Merry concluded that the Salvadoran officials had trespassed upon the Moisant property. He also believed he could obtain the release of George and Edward Moisant, but expected the government might insist upon sending George out of the country, an action that he thought would probably be in the brother's interest because of his criticism of the government. Both brothers, he admitted, "are open and avowed enemies of the Government and exercise no discretion in the protection of their interests. . . . Their intimacy with U.S. consul John Jenkins is a further mark against them," since El Salvador's government considered all close associates of Jenkins to be enemies of the state. Nevertheless, Merry intended to determine for himself what sum the Moisants might claim as damages and then cable for instructions to demand that sum.[12]

Merry continued to mix in the Moisant affair in ways which impinged on Salvadoran sovereignty. When he encountered local police about to arrest an American black employed on the Moisant estate, he cavalierly and without knowledge of the facts informed the officer in charge "to present my compliments to his superior and to say that they were arresting an innocent man without excuse." The records do not reveal whether Merry succeeded in intimidating the Salvadoran police into freeing the employee, but they explain his motivation. He recognized that the economic losses at the Moisant estate and other estates in El Salvador were due to laborers being conscripted to resist incursions of Nicaraguan armed rebels. The injury to the Moisant estates was, however, poetic justice, since John Moisant led one of the Nicaraguan revolutionary factions which had invaded El Salvador, seized Acajutla, and thus produced the need to conscript Salvadoran agricultural laborers for military service. Although the losses were related to the disturbances in El Salvador which the Moisant family was fostering with its political support for the revolutionary faction, Merry overlooked the obvious and decided the Salvadoran government was somehow responsible for the losses of the Moisant estate. His position on compensation for Moisant's losses was inconsistent with his repeated warnings to the Moisant family to stay out of Salvadoran politics "and [to] attend their profitable growing business." The Moisants "are militant Americans full of energy and industry and hard to protect," Merry informed the State Department, but he defended them because they were U.S. citizens involved in major economic enterprises. Merry rationalized to justify his defense of the Moisant family. While he insisted the other brothers were not responsible for John Moisant's actions, he admitted that family members were close and that all the brothers had sided with the invading Alfaro-Escalón faction to which John Moisant belonged.[13] While Merry infringed upon Salvadoran sovereignty (offering protection to John Moisant, who had taken up arms against El Salvador, and retaining rather than dismissing Jenkins) to protect the Moisant family, it was clear that the Moisants pursued objectives inconsistent with the announced U.S. policy of promoting tranquillity in Central America. The Moisants supported the revolutionary faction sympathetic to Zelaya, whom U.S. officials in Washington considered to be the chief source of disorder in Central America.

In 1909 Merry became concerned that the U.S. policy of support for the Jenkins-Moisant-Alfaro cabal in El Salvador might be spreading disorder to other areas in Central America. He suspected that the Moisant family, using funds supplied by Zelaya, might try to upset the Costa Rican election. One source of reliable information indicated to Merry that Zelaya had a large cache of arms—2,000 rifles, 200,000 rounds of ammunition, and four pieces of artillery—on the Nicaraguan–Costa Rican border at Salinas Bay. Merry learned that John Moisant, a Zelaya revolutionary agent who "is undoubtedly here on his business," was present in San José, Costa Rica, for several weeks during the presidential campaign. Since Merry knew John and his family well from the tumultuous 1907 and 1908 affairs involving Salvadoran politics, he became apprehensive when Moisant studiously avoided the U.S. legation. Although Merry had resisted the U.S. government's anti-Zelaya position in the years from 1903 to 1909, he nevertheless feared that the Moisant-Zelaya alliance could disrupt Costa Rica, which he considered to be the exemplary Central American society. He hoped to keep the Costa Rican election of 1909 free from Zelaya's influence. Ultimately, he concluded that the arms were presumably marshaled for another attempt to overthrow the Figueroa government in El Salvador and not to decide the Costa Rican election. He viewed the Moisant-Zelaya connection in Costa Rica as merely the consequence of the search for a safe place to organize a further excursion into Salvadoran affairs.[14]

Although revolutionary activity had subsided in El Salvador by 1909,

Alfred Moisant's charges of mistreatment kept the tension high. Merry presumed the Salvadoran mistreatment of the Moisants had occurred, in part, because Moisant controlled a bank which vigorously challenged and threatened the survival of three other banks in El Salvador that lent money to the government. In 1909 Moisant's Banco Nacional was condemned in El Salvador's *Diario Oficial* for activities contrary to national banking regulations. When a routine inspection established that the reserves of Moisant's bank had fallen below the legal minimum, Salvadoran law required a public warning about the danger of insolvency. The Salvadoran government and Moisant disagreed over whether the Banco Nacional had violated the banking law. Moisant claimed his banking business had suffered from the notification of insufficient reserves published in the *Diario Oficial*. The U.S. government, without conducting an independent investigation and relying solely upon Moisant's assertions, urged the Salvadoran government to publish a retraction. El Salvador's foreign minister complained to the U.S. minister about the role of the United States in the affair. The U.S. government, he noted, had taken a strong stand on an issue it little understood and, without evidence, had labeled the legal actions of El Salvador's president "incorrect and misleading." Salvadoran officials refused to publish the retraction in the precise wording that Moisant and the U.S. government demanded. The Salvadoran government insisted upon an explanatory introduction because they judged their actions correct, and because the Moisant-U.S. rectification statement would have publicly humiliated the government. The resolution, requiring an interpretation of El Salvador's constitution and various Salvadoran laws, should have been less a diplomatic and political battle and more a search for legal and constitutional precedents and interpretation. Neither Moisant nor the U.S. government ever suggested resolving the matter in the courts. Conscious of El Salvador's need for capital, Figueroa had always acted favorably toward banks and Moisant's bank in particular. For example, in 1905 (before the Moisant family had allied itself with Alfaro), when Moisant's bank had been threatened with bankruptcy, Figueroa had compelled the other Salvadoran banks to assist it. In March 1910 the matter was resolved quietly and confidentially on an amicable basis between El Salvador and Moisant. This agreement, U.S. Minister Heimké admitted, left the U.S. government to suffer a loss of prestige and respect because it had officially urged an uncompromising hard line while the Salvadoran government and Alfred Moisant had been willing to compromise.[15]

U.S. diplomats not only intruded into Salvadoran political and economic life, but also intervened in El Salvador in an ill-conceived effort to compel the Salvadoran government to adopt more humane policies. In 1908

U.S. chargé John H. Gregory indicated that the Salvadoran government caused suffering and discontent among Salvadoran citizens because it was months, even years, behind in paying civil officials. After visiting a middle-level official, he "insisted that the [Salvadoran] Government make some effort to ameliorate the situation and destroy the causes of discontent." When he learned that El Salvador would begin paying back wages, his victory prompted him to make further demands. He told the Salvadoran president to "surround himself with more representative men" and to initiate "other minor reforms . . . such as releasing political prisoners." Gregory realized he might have overstepped his diplomatic authority, yet he judged he was "doing about what the Department at Washington would like to see brought about and was willing to take the risk for the benefit of the people here." The State Department mildly chastised him for his actions, but took no stronger step because the arrival of U.S. Minister Henry Percival Dodge terminated Gregory's authority as chargé.[16] Despite public statements in favor of humanitarian and democratic progress in Central America, the U.S. government seldom instructed its officials to endorse such goals.

More commonly, U.S. official activity was evident in political and economic spheres to produce the order and stability presumed essential for U.S. dominance in Central America. The desire for order had been one of the reasons for the Central American Conference which met in Washington in 1907. The 1907 Central American agreements included a court which was expected to eliminate the inter–Central American intrigues and revolutionary support evident in Guatemalan and Nicaraguan roles in El Salvador around 1906–1907. The first case presented to the Central American Court involved Honduran charges against El Salvador and Guatemala for interference in its internal affairs during a 1907 dispute. The U.S. government had strongly urged El Salvador and Guatemala to submit the matter to the Central American Court of Justice. At first, the Salvadoran leadership and populace had been reluctant to do so because they considered the Guatemalan position to be without foundation and insulting. Moreover, the Salvadoran government believed its support for Manuel Bonilla had been consistent with U.S. policy in Central America because Bonilla led the Honduran faction opposed to Zelaya. Most Salvadorans believed their government finally agreed to go before the court only under U.S. pressure. Even in the preliminary stages of the case, Salvadorans expressed strong anti-American sentiments through a deluge of literature and slogans. U.S. Minister Dodge voiced concern to the Salvadoran foreign ministry about the widespread anti-American campaign. If the Central American court rendered a judgment against El Salvador, he warned, there would likely be an even greater outpouring of anti-American sentiment. The court's decision in early 1909 absolved both El Salvador and Guatemala, but it hardly reduced anti-American sentiment in El Salvador, because, in the meantime, U.S. intervention to overthrow Zelaya in Nicaragua had generated widespread anti-American sentiment in El Salvador.[17]

The anti-Americanism in El Salvador in the early twentieth century was chiefly derived from policy clashes and public activity related to the Moisant-Jenkins-Alfaro turmoil and from the U.S. government's pursuit of its vision of a more stable and humanitarian social order as reflected in the 1907 Central American Conference in Washington. Over the decades, U.S. officials had been dissatisfied with their inability to obtain a satisfactory revision of the Salvadoran tariff. One of the attractions of the Alfaro faction was its implied willingness to cooperate with the United States on tariff reform, if it ever obtained the executive office. The Figueroa government did not pursue policies which the State Department considered fair to U.S. businessmen. U.S. officials were shocked to learn in 1908 that a new Salvadoran-French commercial treaty gave French goods tariff advantages over U.S. products. Upon learning that the United States did not receive most-favored-nation treatment and that there was "a differential treatment to the advantage of France and the detriment of our trade in a country which is under no small obligations to the United States," State Department official Robert Bacon ordered an official inquiry. In response to the inquiry, El Salvador offered a defense of its policy which did not impress U.S. officials. Minister Dodge could not understand El Salvador's contention that the United States "ought to extend similar [preferences granted by the French] to Salvadoran products" in order to receive the benefits extended to the French. In a further effort to blunt U.S. criticism, Salvadoran officials claimed they were considering denouncing the French agreement; hence they were reluctant to extend its benefits to other countries. After cabinet consultations, El Salvador's president insisted that extending the tariff benefits to the United States would greatly shrink the revenues and endanger repayment of Salvador's foreign debt. Dodge, convinced by the arguments of the Salvadoran president and cabinet, presumed that El Salvador would offer the United States at least some duty reductions consistent with its financial situation and obligations.[18]

U.S. chargé Arthur Hugh Frazier observed that the method required to obtain Salvadoran tariff concessions was patient, persistent negotiating for specific, limited reductions. He wanted tariff reductions on key U.S. exports to El Salvador, such as cotton goods, flour, drugs, perfumery, leather goods, and hardware. Despite Frazier's warning, Secretary of State Knox wanted El Salvador to initiate a liberal trade policy toward the United States. The State Department considered El Salvador's discrimination against U.S. products so objectionable that it was "almost unique in this hemisphere." Rather than granting such concessions to the United States, El Salvador extended the preferential duties given the French to Italian products, which "still further aggravate[d] the present discrimination against the United States by Salvador." Knox and State Department official Adee wanted El Salvador warned of the forthcoming U.S. double tariff—maximum and minimum tariff rates would allow the U.S. government quick means to chastise nations which pursued trade policies considered inimical to the United States—with the implication that Salvadoran products might suffer the maximum U.S. tariff allowed. Knox and Adee could not comprehend why El Salvador offered the United States less favorable commercial terms than it did France and Germany. Despite Knox's and Adee's complaints, Frazier observed that the actual value of U.S. imported products on the Salvadoran free list was larger than the combined value of all other states.[19] Precisely because U.S. trade with El Salvador was so extensive, it became much easier for the Salvadoran government to make tariff concessions to other nations. With the national revenue heavily dependent upon tariff income, concessions to weaker trading partners had minor impact upon state income. Although U.S. trade with El Salvador was growing in the early twentieth century, Knox believed Salvadoran tariff concessions would have produced even more dramatic trade expansion.

The State Department confronted the contradictions arising when varied interest groups—investment and commercial sectors—aggressively pushed the U.S. system upon peripheral countries. U.S. political figures discovered that support for investment or commerce required different policies. Those firms or sectors of the economy not effectively supported cried out in protest; those aided often discovered their goals undermined by other State Department objectives. The U.S. government learned that increasing investment in and commerce with El Salvador were not necessarily compatible objectives. Chargé Frazier had difficulty in persuading El Salvador to facilitate the construction of a Salvadoran railroad line to connect with the Guatemalan railroad owned by Minor Cooper Keith of United Fruit Company. Keith hoped to extend the Guatemalan railroad through El Salvador to complete an interoceanic transit line. El Salvador's president appeared "to be a little afraid of the domination of the United Fruit Company." The Salvadoran government resisted United Fruit's penetration until U.S. diplomatic intervention overcame the resistance. United Fruit benefited from the fact that the American-owned El Salvador Railway Company charged inflated internal monopoly rates and planned to monopolize El Salvador's steamship traffic. The predatory activity of the El Salvador Railroad Company created a hostile reaction in El Salvador which opened up the possibility for the Keith railroad project. The State Department welcomed El Salvador's determination to create competition via a contract with the Keith–United Fruit interests.[20]

Simultaneously with the El Salvador–Keith railroad agreement, Frazier had succeeded, after decades of struggle by various State Department officials, in obtaining a draft commercial treaty to reduce duties on the entrance of California and midwestern products into the Salvadoran market. A short time later, the tariff reductions acquired after the long struggle were lost. To raise the funds to finance the construction of the Keith railroad, El Salvador had levied a surtax on all imports and exports. The surtax (a byproduct of State Department intervention in Keith's railroad scheme) undermined the hard-earned reduction in duties. On one hand, the State Department labored diligently to reduce duties on U.S. products entering El Salvador. On the other hand, U.S. officials urged a railroad investment scheme which, by requiring a surcharge, effectively canceled the tariff concessions. Perplexed, Knox had Minister Heimké "express to the United Fruit Company the hope of the Department that the Keith concession will not turn out to be an implement to increase the burdens upon American trade with Salvador."[21] The State Department was confronting the limitations of its capacity to serve conflicting U.S. interests abroad. Even when officials in the State Department tried to serve general rather than specific interests, they were in fact creating conditions more favorable to particular sectors of the U.S. economy, rather than the economy as a whole. In this instance, Keith obtained a railroad concession under favorable terms, but U.S. commercial interests saw their hard-won commercial treaty undermined by the Salvadoran government's need to raise funds for the railroad construction. Neither of these State Department actions—involving the tariff or the railroad—revealed much concern for El Salvador's people. Most Salvadorans lacked the income to ride the railroad or purchase U.S. consumer goods. The State Department's presumptions that U.S. perspectives should shape El Salvador's political economy generated suspicion and distrust of U.S. policies among Salvadorans which often surfaced as anti-Americanism.

The surtax on imports to fund United Fruit's railroad had repercussions for El Salvador's trading partners. The French threatened to denounce their commercial treaty with El Salvador unless their products were exempted from the surtax. Since France was the largest importer of Salvadoran coffee, its threat carried considerable weight. Heimké warned that a Salvadoran policy which exempted French imports from the surtax while leaving U.S. goods subject to the tax "would constitute a new discrimination against American commerce." He reminded the Salvadoran government that the United States also imported considerable coffee. In addition, Heimké hinted that his government could exert influence on Salvadoran legislators.[22] Despite U.S. diplomatic efforts, France obtained some modest relief from the 1909 surtax, remaining in a commercially privileged position.

The continuing dispute between U.S. and Salvadoran officials over the tariff was related to the question of economic and political dependency. The United States was El Salvador's chief trading partner (although France purchased most of the coffee), but desired to further strengthen its commercial ties with that country. El Salvador's President Manuel Enrique Araujo was leary of excessive reliance upon any single foreign trade partner or political master. He strove to maintain balanced relations with the major powers. In 1911 Heimké hoped that Araujo's administration might grant the United States the commercial privileges "now enjoyed by France, Germany, and Belgium." Dodge, former U.S. minister to El Salvador who had moved to the State Department, seconded Heimké's view that the United States might "obtain some specific advantages for American commerce, beyond those now enjoyed by other powers." U.S. economic links to El Salvador were also dependent upon an extradition treaty which would allow U.S. firms to bring any agents who misused their authority back to domestic courts for punishment. While El Salvador agreed in principle to an extradition treaty, the specific negotiations were slow and difficult. Heimké and Dodge were disappointed that more progress was not being made on an extradition treaty. Despite Salvadoran reluctance, Dodge recommended pressing the matter. Unmoved by U.S. pressure on commercial and extradition affairs, Araujo remained wary of dependence upon major powers and labored to build an independent El Salvador and hoped for a strong Central American union.[23]

Araujo sought to develop El Salvador's economy, but in a manner that promoted social responsibility and was not abusive of the poorer elements of the population, even if his policies created temporary disturbances. U.S. officials, however, drew upon the domestic progressive ideology and rhetoric to explain and justify the need for order and stability in those areas judged vital to U.S. well-being and security. A first step would entail terminating the civil wars and inter–Central American struggles. Earlier, U.S. leadership at the Central American Conference of 1907 had underscored its desire to mediate and arbitrate for peace and stability in Central America if the conditions were favorable to its objectives. The Central American political, economic, and military leaders did not uniformly welcome the U.S. intervention expressed at the 1907 meeting. El Salvador's political elite had revealed its reluctance to follow U.S. direction. Araujo continued this tradition of suspicion of U.S. objectives. In 1911, French Minister Auguste Jean Marc Fabre believed Araujo was acknowledged as "champion" of Central America "in the resistance to U.S. encroachment." Fabre recognized that the United States would have welcomed a mediator's role in the disputes involving El Salvador, but he observed:

> If the opportunities to fulfill [a mediator's role] are multiplied and if they [the United States] are successful in it, that would allow them to rule here in a manner of 'pax americana' providing them almost all the advantages of a takeover of Central America, without presenting the many inconveniences that a protectorate would bring with it, since it would be disguised. . . . The mediator's role would be difficult to maintain. The Central Americans are suspicious and, if the governments sometimes look for external assistance, as El Salvador just did in making use of the United States, they are nevertheless roundly detested by everybody for appealing to a foreign power.[24]

Araujo's experience with U.S. officials in the early twentieth century convinced him that the small Central American states needed to cooperate if they wished to protect their sovereignty and independence.

Araujo's strong stand for Salvadoran independence and his healthy suspicion of U.S. power made the president the object of rumors that his public image covered a reality of collusion with the "colossus of the North." Fabre mistakenly lent credence to the rumor that the State Department had welcomed Araujo's overtures for U.S. support in the 1912 presidential election campaign. According to the rumor, the State Department agreed to support Araujo if the Salvadoran would place his request in writing. In return for its support, the State Department wanted a commercial treaty advantageous to the United States and a commitment to create in El Salvador "a large bank of emission the direction of which would remain in the hands of New York financiers." In fact, Araujo never considered himself an opponent of the United States nor did he change direction. He had always presumed that his policy would best serve Salvadoran interests and those of foreign powers wishing to conduct business with an independent El Salvador over the long term.[25]

Araujo's concern with underscoring Salvadoran sovereignty, especially with regard to the United States, was related to the view of many Salvadorans that the United States presumed special prerogatives in Central America. The imperial manner in which the United States implemented its metropole role generated ill will and distrust. Since about 1900, U.S. government and businesses often sought to mold El Salvador's political economy to serve their penetration of that country. The Central American republics often objected when the United States resorted to force because, individually or collectively, they could scarcely expect to be victorious if force governed U.S.–Central American relations. For example, the U.S. military intervention in Nicaragua in 1912 found little sympathy in El Salvador. Araujo announced that the U.S. intervention would provoke "a great scandal on the whole continent" and produce "consequences which are difficult to perceive." The U.S. minister in El Salvador had no sooner stated that no more troops would land, when 3,500 additional marines arrived in Nicaragua. In 1912 El Salvador tried unsuccessfully to organize its sister Central American states for collective opposition to U.S. intervention in Nicaragua. When the other states agreed privately, but proved reluctant to oppose publicly a determined U.S. intervention in Nicaragua, little El Salvador, in the words of a French diplomat, "attempted a collective action of El Salvador." The Salvadoran president telegraphed the U.S. authorities his government's conviction that U.S. military intervention in Nicaragua was in discordance with the 1907 Central American agreement which condemned intervention.[26] Salvadorans considered the precedent of arbitrary U.S. intervention in Nicaragua as a threat to their independence and self-government.

Upon the eve of opening the Panama Canal, President William Howard Taft sent Knox on a goodwill mission to ameliorate the residual distrust of U.S. policy on the isthmus. Taft's administration recognized that the Central American and Caribbean area had become a vital point in U.S. trade with the world. Antagonism and anti-Americanism because of the U.S. role in El Salvador and Nicaragua prompted the Salvadoran military to take extraordinary measures to protect Knox during his visit in early 1912. The Salvadoran chief-of-staff assigned the danger to Knox to dissident, disgruntled Americans, not to Salvadorans: "There is nothing to fear from Salvadorans, we have under surveillance 25 or 30 strangers, but they are all Americans."[27] While there was good reason for many Salvadorans to wish Knox harm, the Salvadoran military chief did not explain why Americans posed a threat to him. Salvadorans were unhappy with U.S. tariff policy, support for Keith's railroad project, the undermining of El Salvador's independence, the U.S. threat to Salvadoran security in Fonseca Bay (a Salvadoran and Honduran interpretation of the terms of the U.S.-Nicaraguan canal treaty), and U.S. military interference in Nicaragua. There were also fresh memories of the U.S. support for Escalón, Alfaro, Jenkins, the Moisants, the Zelaya-revolutionaries who invaded El Salvador in 1907, and the U.S. insistence that El Salvador face Honduran charges before the Central American Court in 1908–1909. Knox's mission was expected to erase, or at least blur, the "colossus of the North" image.

Salvadorans, like many other Latin Americans, viewed U.S. expansion and intervention as a threat to their culture as well as to their independence and economic well-being. Araujo intended to undermine U.S. cultural, ideological, and political influence by supporting the Hispano-American University, founded in Bogatá, Colombia, in the early twentieth century. This university, aiming at a transnational, Hispanic response to increased U.S. involvement in Latin American societies, had attracted considerable support from intellectuals, but little funding. Araujo agreed to transfer the university to El Salvador in 1911. The U.S. minister in El Salvador distrusted the institution's purpose. In 1912, under U.S. pressure, Araujo allowed the paper institution (it had a small staff, but no buildings) to move further north to Mexico.[28] U.S. officials were sensitive to the importance of cultural institutions and symbols. The formation of a university, aimed at strengthening Latin culture and by extension undermining Anglo-Saxon cultural influences in Latin America, became a matter of concern and quiet opposition.

The U.S. government's decision to interfere in Salvadoran internal affairs to create a political climate best suited to shortterm U.S. economic, political, and security interests was ill-advised. With little understanding of either El Salvador or Central America, the U.S. government could scarcely coordinate its own competitive economic demands—trade, investment, and security—into a coherent foreign economic policy. Jenkins labored to destabilize El Salvador and to aid Zelaya, while Washington called for stability, order, and the overthrow of Zelaya. The United States struggled for a new tariff arrangement with El Salvador which a U.S. entrepreneur then undermined in order to obtain control over El Salvador's railroad system. U.S. officials treaded upon Salvadoran sovereignty and sought to mold its foreign economic ties in a form inimical to Salvadoran economic and cultural well-being. The ambivalent, self-serving nature of these U.S. efforts generated anti-Americanism. El Salvador's elite remained suspicious and distrustful of U.S. actions well into the future. With this legacy for guidance, El Salvador's government opposed the 1912 Nicaraguan intervention, as well as the 1914 Bryan-Chamorro Treaty, and remained neutral in World War I.

Conclusion

The foregoing essays, in describing various aspects of the rivalry that grew out of the internationalization of laissez-faire competition, suggest some of the problems this competition created for peripheral states like those in Central America. International competition had been common in the mercantilist age, but most nation states had attempted to regulate it through imperial monopolies and other laws and customs. The decline of mercantilism and the rise of laissez-faire societies in the eighteenth and early nineteenth centuries, after brief periods of national internal development, shifted more competition into the international sphere. In the late nineteenth and early twentieth centuries, the inability of laissez-faire systems to deal with grave internal and external economic crises (such as the world depression of 1873–1898) and the strong pattern of interactions between metropole and peripheral regions in the world system magnified world economic problems. The political units in this disturbed world economy sought to alleviate their internal social and economic problems through social imperialism—the use of external relations to solve internal problems. The international devices used by nation-states—diplomacy, military power, financial institutions, technology, marketing facilities, multinational corporations—are essential elements in the story of expansionism. The objectives of social imperialism guided these devices to mold the modern world system.

U.S. society pursued policies to bolster its living standard and achieve an elevated rate of capital accumulation. In the nineteenth and early twentieth centuries the United States experienced several major adjustments of its social order: (1) it used liberal ideology (commonly in some social Darwinian variation) to explain and justify the social and economic changes of the industrial revolution; (2) it adopted corporate, or organized, capitalism when liberal capitalism proved unable to establish the order and stability needed to protect the capital accumulated under the brief experiment with the free market system (roughly 1861–1890); and (3) it pursued social imperialism (or Open Door imperialism) in an effort to allow continued rapid capital accumulation while blunting internal social protest against the maldistribution of wealth under the liberal economic system. Social imperialism sought to increase the living standard of the domestic working class (it made them an imperial labor class, which profited from the labor of peripheral workers) in order to achieve the stability and order required for a smoother, more predictable domestic economy.

In the 1860s the leadership of the rising industrial system in the United States would not permit Southern secession because the liberal ideology espoused by Adam Smith and his adherents linked a nation's material well-being and security to an expanding market (commonly equated with "growth"). Security and well-being required preserving the national territory and transforming peripheral regions into units that "fit" the metropole's social, economic, and political realities and dreams. The political leadership in the South, only vaguely aware of the forces of the world system, misjudged the power of King Cotton. Textile materials were indeed vital to the nineteenth-century world system; but the textile did not have to be cotton and, if cotton, it did not have to come from the South. Southern leaders saw the value of the Central American isthmus more as a source of booty than as the world trade link of the industrial North Atlantic communities with the Pacific basin. Ultimately, the Confederacy tried to disrupt Union commercial activity around the isthmus. In short, the South began to recognize the functioning of a world system, but excluded itself from its operation. This was the essence of American exceptionalism.

U.S. trade expansion—the potential savior of the crisis-plagued U.S. economy—was never seen as dependent upon the penetration of Central America, or even Latin America, but rather as requiring use of the isthmus to incorporate the market of the Pacific basin into the North Atlantic industrial community. Thus the Central American isthmus acquired a key role in U.S. expansionism because of its unique capacity to give U.S. merchants access to the Pacific basin.

From the 1860s to the 1890s, U.S. liberals implemented a national development program which included a national currency, a national banking system, a protective tariff, aid for communication and transportation networks, encouragement of aid for immigration, and aid for agricultural and mining education. The search for markets expanded beyond the national borders and called for new perspectives from U.S. diplomats. In 1869 Louisianan George McWillie Williamson, appointed minister to Central America, struggled to redirect Central American trade toward Louisiana and the Gulf Coast area. He recognized that this required not merely establishing isthmian internal communications, growth in Central America's agriculture and commerce, and steamship lines between Guatemala (Central America) and New Orleans, but also a reformed consular corps to serve U.S. businesses more adequately. He believed that dealing with the periodic "overproduction" problem in the United States called for U.S. agents abroad to be active in promoting U.S. interests instead of merely protecting them. An increasing number of U.S. officials and businessmen began to reach a similar conclusion.

In the depression-filled last quarter of the nineteenth century, the private sector searched for a device to pool capital, limit competition, stabilize market activity, and yet allow profits to remain large. After its experiments with pools and trusts (entrepreneurial inventions to limit costs, share markets, and restore order and profitability to businesses) proved unsuccessful in limiting competition, it settled ultimately upon the holding company (a corporation that owns other corporations). The domestic ideologies that accompanied the transformation were social Darwinism (an explanation for social change which held that natural, evolutionary laws governed societies) and the gospel of wealth (the idea from Andrew Carnegie that the acquisition of wealth entailed Christian stewardship of what was, in fact, God's wealth). Both these perspectives muted protest: with Natural Law or God guiding the production and distribution of wealth, who could protest? Since the domestic economy developed unevenly, the markets for certain sectors of production became "saturated" earlier than others. When faced with saturation of their domestic market, producers, distributors, and speculators increasingly looked abroad to alleviate their problems. Holding companies, commonly called multinational corporations on the international level, relied upon ideology (Nature, God, Manifest Destiny, or a civilizing mission) to lend moral justification to their vigorous search for markets to absorb the glut of production or capital.

In the late nineteenth century, the communications network serving the U.S. economy—the railroads and shipping lines—spread beyond national borders into Mexico, the Caribbean, and Central America. Despite a domestic market plagued with rapid cyclical changes, the ability of U.S. firms to extract profit from the domestic economy remained consistently high due to a friendly federal political environment which used subsidies, tax laws, or generous access to national resources to aid the enterprises. Capital accumulation occurred at a furious pace. Gradually pressure rose to create more opportunity for capital export. Not only confidence artists like John C. Frémont—who developed railroad schemes in the United States, Mexico, and Costa Rica that envisioned immense profits—but hard-nosed entrepreneurs looked abroad for opportunities to invest accumulated capital in economic activity which they believed they had mastered. When Charles Crocker, Leland Stanford, and William Huntington (the entrepreneurs of the Central Pacific railroad) found no more attractive investment opportunities in western U.S. railroads, they built or purchased Guatemalan railroads in the 1870s and 1880s. In those decades the liberal regimes in Central America encouraged the influx of metropole capital and entrepreneurs, seeing it as a potent stimulus to the growth of their own national economies.

The study of Central America's foreign relations in the nineteenth and early twentieth centuries has usually focused on Britain and the United States, but this perspective has overlooked significant Central American relationships with other metropole powers. For example, when Frémont discovered that he could not easily profit from the Costa Rican railroad venture, he authorized an agent to entice Prussian Chancellor Otto von Bismarck with the prospect of creating a German naval base at Puerto Limón, Costa Rica. After a news leak exposed Prussian interests, Bismarck withdrew from this diplomatically risky venture, but this was only a minor tactical retreat. During the Bismarck years, the Germans upgraded their diplomatic representation in Central America in response to large increases in German trade and investment. In the 1870s, when German residents encountered difficulties with the Nicaraguan government, Bismarck's government startled U.S. officials by gathering a six-ship squadron on Nicaragua's coasts to extract an indemnity and symbolic salute. After initially supporting the German position in the Eisenstück affair, U.S. officials realized that such support hampered their efforts to secure a dominant position in Latin America under the Monroe Doctrine and its latter-day expression, panamericanism. In the early 1880s, German-U.S. relations were shaken when German Minister Werner von Bergen publicly accused the United States of imperial ambitions in Central America. Increased German activity also provoked warning signals from British and French diplomats in the late nineteenth century.

The political doctrine of panamericanism was used to justify efforts by the United States to ameliorate the cyclical crises of its own industrial economy and to expand its economic and political authority in Latin America while simultaneously undermining European competitors. The recurring depressions of 1873–1898 increased the numbers of businessmen, politicians, and intellectuals who believed that the United States needed to expand its external markets. In these years, the Panama Canal project of French engineer Ferdinand de Lesseps and German penetration of the Caribbean–Central American area greatly disturbed them. Because they expected to be able to export surplus production freely into the world economy, Americans were appalled by the idea that a European metropole competitor might gain control of the vital isthmian link between the Atlantic and Pacific trade areas. International economic competition therefore joined domestic need in leading the U.S. government to revitalize older policies aimed at limiting competition in the New World. The Monroe Doctrine was revived, European incursions into the hemisphere were judged hypersensitively, and panamericanism was rekindled in the 1870s and 1880s.

Beginning in the 1890s, U.S. foreign policy relied on political, military, and diplomatic maneuvering to obtain economic and financial penetration. From about 1890 until World War I, the U.S. political economy increasingly used multinational corporations to transfer abroad the exploitation of the domestic labor force and the consequent problems of social unrest and the discontentment of the working force. To facilitate discussion of the role of these transnational entities in the world economy, we need some new terms. The term *home country* designates the nation-state in which the corporation is headquartered or where its trademarks, logos, patents, licenses, blueprints, and technology are controlled. The term *host country* refers to the nation-state where the corporation operates through affiliated firms, daughter corporations, or other licensed enterprises. The recurring social crises in the United States and other metropole home countries revealed that the laissez-faire system could not function without refinement because it produced uncertainty, chaos, and dangerous social crises, not to speak of threats to profits, to capital accumulation, and to the preservation of class, status, prestige, and power.

In host countries, these multinational corporations often built isolated centers of extraction, exploitation, and production, which are commonly called "enclaves." These enclaves in Central America encompassed banana plantations, mining, railroad construction, and port services (wharves, insurance, lighters, import-export firms, shipping, and so forth), all of which distributed the host country production into the world economy. Enclave development facilitated the crafting of a "comprador" elite, whose function was to welcome and support metropole enterprises. The comprador group, consisting of representatives of the indigenous middle class or elite in the Central American societies, allowed foreign interests to maximize their production of wealth. After the 1870s, metropole influence spread into all areas of Central American life—educational, professional, military, administrative, and public service.

A major U.S. goal during the Spanish-American War of 1898 was to obtain access to Asia. The early military encounters in that war occurred in the Philippines, Wake Island, and Guam, and only near the end were Cuba and Puerto Rico involved. But U.S. cooperation with revolutionary forces in Panama was closely related to U.S. expansion in Asia, because a canal was essential to tie the Pacific to the industrial base in the northeastern and north central states. Repeated U.S. pronouncements on New World affairs called for order, stability, and the peaceful transfer of political power. U.S. officials, including President Theodore Roosevelt, encouraged revolt, however, when they learned that the new Panamanian government would immediately agree to a favorable canal treaty. While undermining regional order to advance its own interests, the U.S. government preached inter-American harmony to Latin American states. Panamericanism, aimed at strengthening U.S. influence and undermining possible foreign penetration, took permanent form around 1903 with the decision to hold regular meetings of the Pan American Union, which functioned chiefly as a device for U.S. penetration of Latin America.

When the U.S. political economy rejected blacks socially, culturally, and economically in the late nineteenth century, some blacks fled the country to seek employment with Guatemala's Atlantic coast railroad project. Around 1908 State Department officials protected these U.S. blacks from physical assaults by Guatemalan officials. This decision was not easily reached, but U.S. officials decided that all U.S. citizens, even blacks, had to receive the utmost protection and respect if U.S. capitalists were to be induced to enter Central America. The established capitalists, however, found that protecting the rights and property of U.S. citizens often alienated local officials so thoroughly that they turned sour on the requests of these entrepreneurs to extend the time or to expand the scope of their concessions. Thus the efforts to protect the rights of U.S. citizens and to induce new investment frequently clashed with the aspirations of established U.S. enterprises. For this reason, when the Guatemalan government agreed to accommodate (white) entrepreneurs and enterprises, the State Department dropped further action on the behalf of the black complainants.

Social imperialism intensified metropole competition because it encrusted the points of contact in peripheral areas with the issues of metropole well-being and prosperity: the competing metropole states generally looked inward to home country issues rather than outward to host country needs. This slighting of local conditions stimulated the resistance of Central American peripheral societies to their exploitation. Although the Central American states repeatedly tried to play one metropole state off against another in the nineteenth century, this strategy was seldom successful and became increasingly less useful in the twentieth century. The persistent (and frequently increasing) opposition in the Central American societies promoted the use of force or threats of force by metropole states. The greater the resistance, the greater was the need to restrict the sovereignty and independence of Central American states. When the metropole states began to realize that the use of force reduced their ability to create and extract accumulation in a host country, they turned to comprador groups.

The metropoles encouraged dependency. By definition, the restriction of the sovereignty of a peripheral state designates the extent of its dependence on a metropole. Dependency was also nurtured because the peripheral areas were seen as essential to the well-being and security of the metropole. The Roosevelt corollary to the Monroe Doctrine is an illuminating example of the process. When the Roosevelt administration decided that the risk of unwanted foreign intervention required U.S. supervision of the international debt financing of the Caribbean–Central American states, the "logic" of dependency took over.

Thus in the twentieth century the United States shared the sovereignty of the peripheral states in the Caribbean region. For example, it often exercised the sovereign powers involved in collecting revenue to repay debt: it supplied customs commissioners, finance supervisors, and other revenue and disbursement agents—along with the military personnel to enforce revenue collection and to preserve the order necessary to permit business activity without which there could be no collection of revenue. Restricted sovereignty establishes a chain of dependency. The same result follows from the supervision of "democracy" or "freedom" in another state. If a metropole denies that a peripheral state has these characteristics and interferes in its internal social processes, the metropole serves as the arbiter of "democracy" and "freedom" in that state; the peripheral state depends upon the metropole to define, and possibly implement, "freedom," "democracy," or "financial responsibility." William A. Williams has described the recurring tragedy of U.S. international relations that results from a struggle between two tendencies within its Open Door liberal order: one of these defines the periphery as essential for the material well-being and security of the United States so that it must necessarily be subjected to U.S. supervision and control; the other sees it ideologically, as deserving self-government and freedom. The tragedy is that most often the materialism of the liberal order triumphs over its social and ideological goals.

By the early twentieth century, the Central American states, swamped with metropole agents pushing development schemes, had surrendered to metropole interests control of the major elements of their internal communications, public utilities, national debt, currency, state revenue, and other economic activities that produced the national wealth. The Central American societies struggled to find a secure role in the revised world order, but the huge power imbalances between the metropoles and themselves largely determined who succeeded. These peripheral governments—influenced in significant ways by the comprador elite—had a modest share of control over their political economies, but they were frequently held solely responsible for any failures that touched metropole enterprises or banks, or for any assertions of sovereignty that seemed to threaten metropole security.

U.S. policies in Central America were often at cross-purposes in other ways. For example, between 1906 and 1913, while officially denouncing violence and revolution, U.S. officials covertly supported a revolutionary faction in El Salvador because this faction advocated trade and investment positions advantageous to U.S. interests. At the same time, this Salvadoran faction was allied with Nicaraguan President José Santos Zelaya, whom the United States was trying to overthrow because it distrusted his links with German and Japanese capitalists. Between 1907 and 1909, despite its appeal for peace, order, and stability on the isthmus, the United States repeatedly urged Costa Rica to assault Zelaya's government. The United States sought to stabilize the political economies of Central America through political and judicial pacts signed in Washington in 1907 and 1923, yet in order to preserve its own freedom of action, it refused to become a party to either agreement. The U.S. leadership assumed that progressive law, order, and stability would further U.S. penetration of Central America, but when a particular situation revealed that law, order, and stability might not further this objective, it readily changed its "principles."

One early metropole response to domestic economic crisis had been to heal the malfunctioning laissez-faire system by extending it worldwide, a strategy evident in British free trade policies, the U.S. Open Door, and President Woodrow Wilson's Fourteen Points (points two through six of which described a world free trade system). The Open Door—a special version of free trade—offered supposedly equal opportunity in trade, investment, and communications instead of the complete removal of trade barriers. Unleashing laissez-faire in the world system, where the mechanisms of political, judicial, and social control were weaker than within the metropole nation states, brought opportunities to the metropole entrepreneurs and instability and loss of sovereignty to the peripheral states. In order to alleviate problems at home and to strengthen national security and well-being, the metropole leadership intended to exercise only modest control over the entrepreneurs who went abroad in search of personal wealth.

In the early twentieth century European competition with the United States sharpened. German entrepreneurs were scurrying to enter Central American public utilities as a means of introducing the technological products of Siemens, Allgemeine Elektrizitäts-Gesellschaft (AEG), and other firms. German banks financed coffee trade and utilities investments. France also interacted in important ways with other metropole powers and with the Central American societies. In the early part of the century French capital, trade, culture, and residents had resumed a major and dynamic role in Central America. U.S. policy in the early twentieth century urged the replacement of non-U.S. interests from the transit area.

World War I and its aftermath disrupted and decimated the European presence in Central America. The war underscored the maturing of the U.S. political economy, which had incorporated its western territory and thirty million European immigrants into its expanding production system between 1860 and 1914. Essentially isolated from the European war, the U.S. political economy secured dominance in the whole Caribbean and Central American area. The United States had initiated its active interventionism in the decades before World War I and would continue this aggressive policy throughout the 1920s. The weakened European powers wanted to reenter the vital isthmian area, but since they lacked the material or political capacity to force equal opportunity in the region, they had to settle for whatever crumbs the United States allowed to fall from the table.

From the outbreak of World War I to the 1940s, the United States sought to secure its hegemony and to incorporate large elements of Central America into its economic and cultural orbit. U.S. hegemony in Central America seemed secure in the 1930s, but the contradictory and unstable nature of organized capitalism (a hybrid of laissez-faire ideology and bureaucratic-corporatist structures) allowed little room for self-confidence in a competitive world system. Through the Central American treaty system of 1923, the Import-Export Bank, the Rio Pact, and a revitalized Organization of American States, and by expanding the multinationalization of economic activity, achieving informal colonization through enclaves and retirement areas, and engaging in cultural and scientific exchange, the United States acted to preserve its hegemonic position.

Since World War II the United States has experienced decolonization just as the European powers had in the interwar years and again in the 1940s and 1950s. U.S. leaders misunderstood the Guatemalan problems in the 1950s, the Guatemalan and Nicaraguan guerrilla conflicts in the 1960s, the Nicaraguan opposition to the Anastasio Somoza regime and legacy in the 1970s and 1980s, and the civil war in El Salvador in the 1970s and 1980s. All these phenomena are best understood as part of a worldwide anti-imperialism phase. Unfortunately, North America's populace and political elite have difficulty acknowledging their imperial past and present. In what is often proclaimed to be an age of well-being and democracy, the U.S. government and the bulk of the society have commonly sided with the few wealthy and the conservative regimes. As the major imperial power of the twentieth century, the United States has been the last to confront the deimperialization process, just as in the nineteenth century it managed, along with Cuba and Brazil, to be among the last of the slave societies in the Western World.

Appendix: Historiographical Excursion into
Southern International History

_____

The leadership of the South was similar in composition and outlook throughout the mid-nineteenth century. The Southern leadership did recognize, on a practical level, that the Caribbean and Middle America (Mexico, Central America, and Panama) were important to the Northern and Southern economies. Since the early nineteenth century, Yankee labor and capital had increased production of certain items faster than a liberal economic system could find suitable markets in the New World or Europe, so distribution had to expand into the Pacific basin. Southern leaders had long recognized certain fundamental ties between cotton and the world economy, but Southern businessmen would normally have said "England," "France," or "Europe" instead of the world economy because they perceived economic forces narrowly. This Southern leadership badly misread that system when it acted upon the belief that cotton was king.[1]

King cotton assumptions rested upon the belief that Europe needed Southern cotton, when all it needed was fibers for use in textile production. European textile mills and consumers could have developed alternative cotton supplies, switched to alternative fibers, or developed alternative consumption patterns to mitigate the cotton shortage. The Confederacy learned that as a peripheral area it had difficulty even influencing the terms of exchange with metropole areas. Recognizing its dependency, the South rebelled to become an independent state in the mistaken view that independent political authority would alter its economic relationship to the world, and that effective political independence was readily achievable without economic self-reliance.[2]

Historians of the middle period of the nineteenth century have not isolated and analyzed this faulty comprehension adequately. Concern with the primacy of cotton, southern exceptionalism, and failed southern nationalism has limited their capacity to analyze southern history in the nineteenth century. Studies of the Civil War often grasp at the military events of the Civil War, the internal political and economic problems, or personalities—distributing the blame to key figures for the inability to obtain recognition, to break the blockade, and to sell cotton—rather than in broader theoretical considerations.[3]

To break the poverty of this interpretation, historians need to consider the links of the basic structure of Southern and Northern societies to the world system described by the sociologist Immanuel Wallerstein. The focus should be Confederate thought and strategy in regard to the relationship of its and the Union's political economies to the world. Antebellum cotton producers had acknowledged that web of relationships when they presumed that increased consumption of cotton textiles in Asia meant a rising price for their raw cotton. Only by understanding the relationship of the political economies of the sections to the rest of the world can the role of international relations and the sectional perspectives in interaction with the world be evaluated in regard to the policy and leadership of the Civil War adversaries.[4] Cotton had limited value outside the world system. Over the long term, it was immaterial which merchants purchased Southern cotton. In the short run, Confederate cotton policy distorted the role of Britain, France, and Belgium in the world cotton system.

A number of historians have peeked behind the confines of an event-filled parochial history of the Confederacy. Various historians have recognized fundamental relationships between the sectional conflict and the world. Charles Beard, Raimundo Luraghi, and William A. Williams have linked the Civil War to an altered political economy in the United States, viewing the Civil War as part of a clash of agrarian mercantilism with industrial capitalism. In 1959 Avery Craven countered provincial approaches to the Civil War by describing a shift from local political and economic power to a national perspective, a preliminary version of Robert Wiebe's "search for order." He argued that the South did not adjust well to the transformations jolting U.S. society and hence the Civil War and Southern defeat followed. By focusing upon the relationship of local or regional to national, he overlooked the world aspects of mercantilism, Southern cotton, and Northern fleets and industries. The Italian historian Luraghi described a similar process and carried it into a broader international setting. He, unfortunately, became so enamored of Southern aristocracy that, after placing the North-South conflict in a comparative world perspective, he insisted the South was different. Some historians have also argued for the continuity of the nineteenth-century southern political economy, which they see as operating within a world economic order. They have recognized that the South supplied raw cotton to European (or Northern) manufacturers, financiers, distributors, and consumers in exchange for industrial products.[5]

Emory Thomas, though he misread the structural nature of the Confederate-European relationship, did observe the subordinate role of the Confederacy in the world cotton trade: "To the Southerners' chagrin, 'King Cotton' proved to be a puppet monarch whose strings the Confederacy did not control." The lack of control was common in the relations of periphery to core. Peter Parish recognized the incongruence in the South's belief that the Confederacy could function better without the world than the world could function without the South. Gavin Wright has argued that world cotton prices were in decline in the mid- and late nineteenth century, so that even without the Civil War, Southern society faced traumatic changes which the planters and cotton merchants only poorly perceived.[6] These historians have brought us closer to a broader view of the South in the mid-nineteenth century. We need to go the rest of the way and recognize that, within the world economy, the South occupied a dependent, peripheral relationship which used coerced labor, imported industrial and consumer goods, and borrowed foreign capital, technology, and cultural models.

Stanley Lebergott has recently called attention to the overlooked impact of commercial policy upon the fate of the Confederacy, arguing that the planters' individualistic insistence upon producing cotton for personal gain, thereby diverting land and labor from the tasks of producing food and attending to military needs, hampered the war effort. He undermines his argument, however, when he points out that the common wisdom of the planter elite was that wealth came from selling cotton for the world market: "Six decades of expanding cotton markets had convinced the South that it possessed a near monopoly on cotton and that Great Britain and France would writhe in revolution if denied the South's supply." Sixty years' experience had indeed taught the planter elite to increase revenue by increasing production. The cotton planter believed that his experiences verified cyclical, supply-demand theory. The disruptive element was distribution, not production. Moreover, many planters did increase food production. The cotton planters were not alone in such presumptions. In the nineteenth and twentieth centuries, midwestern corn and wheat farmers, automotive and steel manufacturers, and most other sectors of laissez-faire capitalism have followed a theory and an interpretation of historical experience that dictates increasing production to overcome financial shortfall.[7] Some planters attempted to solve their economic problems and those of the Confederacy by producing more cotton, which could be sold for pounds sterling, to purchase military supplies and consumer goods. Many Southerners passingly recognized aspects of the world textile market and particularly the world cotton textile market, but in the crisis of 1860–65, they overlooked the systemic forces of the world economy.

Modern Civil War historians have had some difficulty understanding the Confederate relationship to industrialization and industrial production. The authors of *Why the South Lost* insisted that the Confederate leaders paid little attention to the blockade. Other historians contend that the blockade, though disruptive, was not the cause of the Confederate defeat. These historians have failed to recognize that the blockade severed the ties of the peripheral South to its industrial base in Europe. The Confederate industrial revolution, they argue, "helps explain this almost blasé attitude toward the blockade."[8] But the world economy, though specialized, was not segmented; it functioned as a whole. The South could not import because it could not export well. The Confederacy had difficulty acquiring foreign loans because its political and economic conditions were not reassuring to foreign financiers. Its political economy was weak because the mechanisms for distributing its production were disrupted. And, most emphatically, Confederate society was not undergoing an industrial revolution, as many claim; it was simply struggling to meet ad hoc demands for industrial products. Industrialization requires widespread changes in capital, labor, and land use, in education and technology, and in the interchange of men, ideas, capital, and machines with other advanced societies. Not until after World War II were such signs of an industrial civilization widely evident in the former Confederacy. It is a conceptual error to argue that the South experienced four years of an industrial revolution during the Civil War and then marked time for a hundred years to finish that revolution. Despite some notable improvisations, the Southern economy made little progress toward becoming an industrial society during the Civil War.[9]

The narrow vision of much Civil War scholarship has not only misapplied the concept of industrialization, but also that of nationalism. Nationalism accompanied most states which industrialized under a liberal economic order. Nationalism helped define the market and served to persuade the laborers to accept altered forms of education, discipline, and production for the consumption of an invisible consumer. The authors of *Why the South Lost* argued that the South failed to achieve independence because, while it had a national government and symbols, songs, flag, officials, and army, it lacked the second form of nationalism—the "emotional bond." Nationalism does not divide analytically between institutions and emotions, but between emotional and rational varieties. During the War of 1812, John Quincy Adams recognized the difference between the rational form he advocated and naval officer Stephen Decatur's emotional nationalism. Reportedly Decatur had declared: "Our country! In her intercourse with foreign nations, may she always be in the right; but our country, right or wrong." Adams declared his toast would be: "May our country be always successful, but whether successful or otherwise, always right. I disclaim as unsound all patriotism incompatible with the principles of eternal justice." Adams's nationalism required a rational and moral man, not the possibly immoral and certainly thoughtless man Decatur appealed to. Rather than an emotional high, an intelligent and moral appeal generated persistent nationalism. Adams's nationalism offered that hope.[10] The Southern population had enjoyed a recurring "emotional bond"—over slavery and states' rights—since the 1820s. It should be more fruitful to examine the extent to which Confederate laborers, businessmen, military officers, and government officials evaluated the cost of continued resistance, the likelihood of success, and the objectives one might achieve through further resistance.

Currently, Civil War historians use the determined nationalism of the Vietnam conflict to explain the defeat of the South. The argument, accepting some version of Leninist, Maoist, Guevarist, or Giapian thought, claims that will and commitment would allow "materially" weak societies (Confederacy or Vietnam) to defeat a stronger power (Abraham Lincoln's Federal Union or Lyndon Johnson's "Great Society"), provided the national will of the materially weaker is much stronger than the will of the materially stronger. Many recent writers on the Confederate defeat conclude that the superior will of the North contributed more to defeat the South than industrial power or material wealth. These historians have renovated Richmond newspaperman Edward Pollard's argument from the 1860s. Pollard and these historians claim the Confederate leadership failed to bolster the will to sacrifice. This perspective ignores the heavy foreign intervention in Vietnam which quickly transformed that conflict into one of U.S. wealth and manpower behind some Vietnamese versus a Vietnamese nationalism supported with extensive material aid from China and the Soviet Union. The Vietnamese war had more structural similarity with the American revolution, a war with extensive foreign involvement and part of a world conflict, than the Civil War, an essentially internal conflict.[11] There are, however, important differences between a war between metropole powers in the international sphere and a national crisis in a semi-peripheral area within the world system.

Abbreviations

Adam	Archive de l'armée de la mer
AMAE, Madrid	Archivo del ministerio de asuntos extranjeros, Madrid
AMAE, Paris	Archive du ministère des affaires étrangères, Paris
Amef	Archive du ministère de l'économie et finance
AmLeg	National Archives, Record Group 84, Post Records, American Legation
AMRE	Archivo del ministerio de relaciones exteriores, Tegucigalpa, Honduras
AN, CR	Archivos Nacionales, San José, Costa Rica
CD	National Archives, Record Group 59, Consular Dispatches
CP	Correspondence politique (AMAE, Paris)
DD, CA	National Archives, Record Group 59, Diplomatic Dispatches, Central America
DI	National Archives, Record Group 59, Diplomatic Instructions
FRUS	U.S. Department of State, *Papers Relating to the Foreign Relations of the United States*
LC	Library of Congress
MAE	Ministro de asuntos extranjeros or Ministre des affaires étrangères
MRE	Ministro de relaciones exteriores
Notes to CA	National Archives, Record Group 59, Records of the Department of State, Notes to Central America
ORN	*Official Records of the Union and Confederate Navies in the War of the Rebellion*
PAAA	Politisches Archiv des Auswärtigen Amts, Bonn
PRO FO	Public Records, Office, Foreign Office series, London
RCSA	Records of the Confederate States of America, Library of Congress

Notes

Introduction

1 Immanuel Wallerstein, "The Rise and Future Demise of the World Capitalist System: Concepts for Comparative Analysis," *Comparative Studies in Society and History* 16 (Sept. 1974), 387–415; essays by Nicole Bousquet, James C. Cronin, Albert Bergesen, Cynthia H. Enloe, and Suzanne Jonas and Marlene Dixon in Terence K. Hopkins and Immanuel Wallerstein, eds., *Processes of the World-System* (Beverly Hills, 1980); Christopher Chase-Dunn, "Core-Periphery Relations: The Effects of Core Competition," in Barbara Hockey Kaplan, ed., *Social Change in the Capitalist World Economy* (Beverly Hills, 1978), 159–76; Peter B. Evans, Dietrich Rueschemeyer, and Theda Skocpol, eds., *Bringing the State Back In* (Cambridge, Eng., 1985); Immanuel Wallerstein, *The Politics of the World-Economy* (Cambridge, Eng., 1984).

2 On the world system or world economy theories of international relations, see Fernand Braudel, *Civilisation matérielle, économie et capitalisme, xve–xviiie siècles* (3 vols.; Paris, 1979), translated as *The Structures of Everyday Life, The Wheels of Commerce,* and *The Perspective of the World* (New York, 1984); Fernand Braudel, *Afterthoughts on Material Civilization and Capitalism* (Baltimore, 1977); Immanuel Wallerstein, *The Modern World System* (3 vols.; Orlando, 1974–1988); Immanuel Wallerstein, *Historical Capitalism* (London, 1983); Terence K. Hopkins and Immanuel Wallerstein, eds., *World-Systems Analysis: Theory and Methodology* (Beverly Hills, 1982); Andre Gunder Frank, "A Plea for World System History," *Journal of World History* 2:1 (Spring 1991), 1–28; Theda Skocpol, ed., *Vision and Method in Historical Sociology* (Cambridge, Eng., 1984), esp. chaps. 1, 5, 9, 10, and 11; Charles Tilly, *Big Structures, Large Processes, Huge Comparisons* (New York, 1984).

3 Thomas McCormick, *China Market: America's Quest for Informal Empire, 1893–1901* (Chicago, 1967); Bernard Semmel, *Imperialism and Social Reform, 1885–1914* (Cambridge, Eng., 1960); Hans-Ulrich Wehler, *Der Aufstieg des amerikanischen Imperialismus* (Göttingen, 1974).

4 Fernando H. Cardoso and Enzo Faletto, *Dependency and Development in Latin America* (Berkeley, 1979); Andre Gunder Frank, *Capitalism and Underdevelopment in Latin America* (New York, 1967); Samir Amin, *Unequal Development* (New York, 1976).

5 Immanuel Wallerstein, "Antisystemic Movements: History and Dilemmas," and Samir Amin, "The Social Movements in the Periphery: An End to National Liberation?" in Samir Amin, Giovanni Arrighi, Andre Gunder Frank, and Immanuel Wallerstein, *Transforming the Revolution: Social Movements and the World-System* (New York: Monthly Review, 1990), 13–53, 96–138.

6   Ciro Cardoso and Héctor Pérez Brignoli, *Centro América y la economía occidental (1520–1930)* (San José, Costa Rica, 1977); Ralph Lee Woodward, "Central America from Independence to c. 1870," in Leslie Bethell, ed., *The Cambridge History of Latin America* (5 vols.; Cambridge, Eng., 1982–1988), 3:471–506; Ralph Lee Woodward, *Central America: A Nation Divided* (2nd ed.; New York, 1985); Héctor Pérez Brignoli, *Breve Historia de Centro América* (Madrid, 1985).

7   Cardoso and Pérez Brignoli, *Centro América y la economía occidental (1520–1930)*; R. L. Woodward, "Central America from Independence to c. 1870"; R. L. Woodward, *Central America: A Nation Divided*; Thomas Schoonover, "Prussia and the Protection of German Transit through Middle America and Trade with the Pacific Basin, 1848–1851," *Jahrbuch für Geschichte von Staat, Wirtschaft und Gesellschaft Lateinamerikas,* 22 (1985), 393–422; Pérez Brignoli, *Breve Historia de Centro América;* Thomas Schoonover, "Costa Rican Trade and Navigation Ties with the United States, Germany, and Europe, 1840–1885," *Jahrbuch für Geschichte von Staat, Wirtschaft und Gesellschaft Lateinamerikas* 14 (1977), 269–309.

8   Thomas Schoonover, "Metropole Rivalry in Central America, 1820s to 1929: An Overview," in R. L. Woodward, ed., *Central America: Historical Perspective on the Contemporary Crisis* (Westport, 1988), 21–46; Thomas Schoonover, "Imperialism in Middle America: United States Competition with Britain, Germany, and France in Middle America, 1820s–1920s," in Rhodri Jeffreys-Jones, ed., *Eagle against Empire: American Opposition to European Imperialism, 1914–1982* (Aix-en-Provence, 1983), 41–58.

9   Ciro Cardoso, "Central America: The Liberal Era, ca. 1870–1930," in Leslie Bethell, ed., *The Cambridge History of Latin America* (5 vols.; Cambridge, Eng., 1982–1988), 5:197–227; Pérez Brignoli, *Breve Historia de Centro América;* Cardoso and Pérez Brignoli, *Centro América y la economía occidental (1520–1930);* Walter LaFeber, *Inevitable Revolutions: The United States in Central America* (New York, 1983).

10 Schoonover, "Metropole Rivalry in Central America, 1820s to 1929"; Lester D. Langley, *Struggle for the American Mediterranean: United States–European Rivalry in the Gulf-Caribbean, 1776–1904* (Athens, Ga., 1976); LaFeber, *Inevitable Revolutions;* Thomas Schoonover, "Germany in Central America, 1820s to 1929: An Overview," *Jahrbuch für Geschichte von Staat, Wirtschaft und Gesellschaft Lateinamerikas* 25 (1988), 33–59.

11 R. L. Woodward, *Central America: A Nation Divided;* Cardoso, "Central America: The Liberal Era, ca. 1870–1930"; Pérez Brignoli, *Breve Historia de Centro América;* Cardoso and Pérez Brignoli, *Centro América y la economía occidental (1520–1930);* R. L. Woodward, "Central America from Independence to c. 1870."

12 LaFeber, *Inevitable Revolutions;* Langley, *Struggle for the American Mediterranean;* Schoonover, "Metropole Rivalry"; Paul Kennedy, *The Rise and Fall of the Great Powers* (New York, 1987).

13 Richard van Alstyne, *The Rising American Empire* (Chicago, 1965); Robert May, *The Southern Dream of a Caribbean Empire, 1854–1861* (Baton Rouge, 1973); Charles Vevier, "American Continentalism: An Idea of Expansionism, 1845–1910," *American Historical Review* 65 (Jan. 1960), 323–35; Eric Foner, *Free Soil, Free Labor, Free Men* (London, 1970); Thomas Schoonover, "Misconstrued Mission: Black Colonization in Mexico and Central America during the Civil War," *Pacific Historical Review* 49 (Nov. 1980), 607–20.

14 Norman Graebner, *Empire on the Pacific: A Study of American Continental Empire* (New York, 1955); van Alstyne, *The Rising American Empire.*

15 Leonard P. Curry, *Blueprint for Modern America* (Nashville, 1968); Wehler, *Der Aufstieg des amerikanischen Imperialismus;* William Appleman Williams, *The Contours of American History* (Chicago, 1966), 225–343.

16 Walter LaFeber, *The New Empire: An Interpretation of American Expansion, 1860–1898* (Ithaca, 1963); Kenneth Hagan, *American Gunboat Diplomacy and the Old Navy, 1877–1889* (Westport, 1973).

17 On the U.S. economy during the late nineteenth century, see Gabriel Kolko, *Main Currents in Modern American History* (New York, 1976); Robert Wiebe, *The Search for Order, 1877–1920* (New York, 1967); Samuel P. Hays, *The Response to Industrialism, 1885–1914* (Chicago, 1957); Walter Edward Lowrie, "France, the United States, and the Lesseps Panama Canal: Renewed Rivalry in the Western Hemisphere, 1879–1889" (Ph.D. diss., Syracuse University, 1976); David McCullough, *The Path between the Seas: The Creation of the Panama Canal, 1870–1914* (New York, 1977); William Appleman Williams, *The Tragedy of American Diplomacy* (2d ed.; New York, 1972).

18 Schoonover, "Germany in Central America, 1820s to 1929"; Schoonover, "Metropole Rivalry"; McCormick, *China Market;* Semmel, *Imperialism and Social Reform;* Hans-Ulrich Wehler, *Grundzüge der amerikanischen Aussenpolitik: 1750–1900* (Frankfurt, 1983); William Appleman Williams, *The Roots of the Modern American Empire: A Study of the Growth and Shaping of Social Consciousness in a Marketplace Society* (New York, 1969); Richard Rubinson, "Political Transformation in Germany and the United States," in Barbara Hockey Kaplan, ed., *Social Change in the Capitalist World Economy* (Beverly Hills, 1978), 39–73; Tony Smith, *The Pattern of Imperialism: The United States, Great Britain, and the Late-industrializing World since 1815* (Cambridge, Eng., 1981).

19 Amin, Arrighi, Frank, and Wallerstein, *Transforming the Revolution.*

1 The Confederates in Central America: Coming to Grips with the World System

1 Frank L. Owsley, *King Cotton Diplomacy: Foreign Relations of the Confederate States of America* (Chicago, 1931); Gordon H. Warren, "The King Cotton Theory," in Alexander Deconde, ed., *Encyclopedia of American Foreign Policy* (3 vols.; New York, 1978), 2:515–20. On the world system, see Wallerstein, *The Modern World System;* Braudel, *Civilization and Capitalism;* William Woodruff, *The Struggle for World Power, 1500–1980* (London, 1981). Frank Vandiver, "Jefferson Davis and Confederate Strategy," in Bernard Mayo, ed., *The American Tragedy* (Hampden-Sydney, Va., 1959), 19–32, is an example of passive acknowledgment of world forces that are subordinated to Confederate history, especially its military history.

2 May, *The Southern Dream of Caribbean Empire;* Gavin Wright, *The Political Economy of the Cotton South* (New York, 1978), xii, 7–8, 92–98.

3 Wallerstein, "The Rise and Future Demise of the World Capitalist System"; Hopkins and Wallerstein, eds., *World-Systems Analysis;* Chase-Dunn, "Core-Periphery Relations: The Effects of Core Competition"; May, *The Southern Dream of Caribbean Empire;* Robert May, *John A. Quitman: Old South Crusader* (Baton Rouge, 1985); Vevier, "American Continentalism."

4 James G. Randall and David Donald, *The Civil War and Reconstruction* (2nd ed.; Lexington, Mass., 1969), 357–58; van Alstyne, *The Rising American Empire,* 147–

69; Vevier, "American Continentalism"; May, *The Southern Dream of Caribbean Empire*, esp. 217–49; Thomas Schoonover, *Dollars over Dominion: The Triumph of Liberalism in Mexican–United States Relations, 1861–1867* (Baton Rouge, 1978), 27, 31–35, 81–82; José Augustín Quintero to Robert M. T. Hunter, August 20, 1861, Hugh McLeod, "Memorandum [addressed to Quintero] on the true route of the Pacific Rail Road for the Confederate States," n. d., Records of the Confederate States of America, Library of Congress (hereafter RCSA), vol. 8; Richard E. Beringer, Herman Hattaway, Archer Jones, and William N. Still, *Why the South Lost the Civil War* (Athens, Ga., 1986); Archer Jones, *Confederate Strategy from Shiloh to Vicksburg* (Baton Rouge, 1961), 16–32; E. Merton Coulter, *The Confederate States of America* (Baton Rouge, 1950).

5 Emory Thomas, *The Confederate Nation, 1861–1865* (New York, 1979), 167–89; Peter Parrish, *The American Civil War* (New York, 1975), 398–401; Stanley Lebergott, "Why the South Lost: Commercial Purpose in the Confederacy, 1861–1865," *Journal of American History* 70 (June 1983), 58–74.

6 Charles Beard, *The Industrial Revolution* (London, 1901); Williams, *The Contours of American History*; Chase-Dunn, "Core-Periphery Relations," 159–76; Avery O. Craven, "Background Forces and the Civil War," in Bernard Mayo, ed., *The American Tragedy*, 17–18; Raimundo Luraghi, *The Rise and Fall of the Plantation South* (New York, 1978), 146–52; Harold D. Woodman, *King Cotton and His Retainers: Financing and Marketing the Cotton Crop of the South, 1800–1925* (Lexington, Ky., 1968), 141–95; Bob Sutcliffe, "Imperialism and Industrialization in the Third World," in Roger Owen and Bob Sutcliffe, eds., *Studies in the Theory of Imperialism* (London, 1972), 171–92; Wiebe, *The Search for Order*.

7 George W. Dalzell, *The Flight from the Flag: The Continuing Effect of the Civil War upon the American Carrying Trade* (Chapel Hill, 1940), 3–4; James Callahan, *The Diplomatic History of the Southern Confederacy* (rpt. ed.; Springfield, Mass., 1957), 71–80, 145; Ray C. Colton, *The Civil War in the Western Territories* (Norman, Okla., 1959), v–vi, 207; David Potter and Don Fehrenbacher, *The Impending Crisis: 1848–1861* (New York, 1976), 145–76.

8 John Belohlavek, "A Philadelphian and the Canal: The Charles Biddle Mission to Panama, 1835–1836," *Pennsylvania Magazine of History and Biography* 104 (Oct. 1980), 450–61; Karl Bermann, *Under the Big Stick: Nicaragua and the United States since 1848* (Boston, 1986), 39–102.

9 Gabriel G. Tassara to Premier (Spain), Oct. 9, 1860, legajo 2566, Archivo del ministerio de asuntos extranjeros (hereafter AMAE, Madrid); Antonio José de Irisarri to Pedro Aycinena, Nov. 21, 1860, April 21, 1861, in Enrique del Cid Fernández, ed., *Epistolario inédito de Antonio José de Irisarri* (Guatemala, 1966), 57–58, 69–70; Lewis Cass to Luis Molina, Nov. 26, 1860, Record Group 59, Records of the Department of State, Notes to Central America: vol. 1 (Microcopy 99/reel 10), National Archives, hereafter Notes to CA: 1 (M 99/r 10); Ephraim George Squier to J. Wortley, Jan. 20, 1861, E. George Squier papers, cont. 2, Library of Congress (hereafter LC).

10 LaFeber, *Inevitable Revolutions*, 28–31; R. L. Woodward, *Central America: A Nation Divided*, 131, 134, 136–46.

11 Ralph Lee Woodward, "Guatemalan Cotton and the American Civil War," *Inter-american Economic Affairs* 18 (1965), 87–94; Thomas Schoonover, "Mexican Cotton and the American Civil War," *The Americas* 30 (April 1974), 429–47; Jim Handy, *Gift of the Devil: A History of Guatemala* (Boston, 1985), 58–61; William A. Beck,

"American Policy in Guatemala, 1839–1900" (Ph.D. diss., Ohio State University, 1954), 29–43.

12 R. L. Woodward, "Guatemalan Cotton"; Cardoso and Pérez Brignoli, *Centro América y la economía occidental*, 149–80.

13 Thomas Schoonover, "Misconstrued Mission"; Irisarri to Aycinena, Dec. 31, 1861 (two letters), in del Cid Fernández, ed., *Epistolario de Irisarri*, 101–2.

14 Robert Toombs to Jefferson Davis, April 29, 1861, RCSA, vol. 60; McLeod to Quintero, n. d., "Memorandum on the true route of the Pacific Rail Road," RCSA, vol. 8, reel 8, LC; Colton, *Western Territories*, 4, 207; Martin Hardwick Hall, *Sibley's New Mexico Campaign* (Austin, 1960), xiii–xiv, 122–23, 225–26; James A. Howard, "New Mexico and Arizona Territories," in LeRoy H. Fischer, ed., *The Western Territories in the Civil War* (Manhattan, Kan., 1977), 88.

15 Clement Eaton, *A History of the Southern Confederacy* (New York, 1954), 85–86; Howard Nash, Jr., *A Naval History of the Civil War* (New York, 1972), 300.

16 May, *Southern Dream of Empire*, 248; Thomas Schoonover, "Foreign Relations and Kansas in 1858," *Kansas Historical Quarterly* 42 (Winter 1976), 345–52.

17 Andrew B. Dickinson to William H. Seward, July 11, Aug. 29, 1861, Record Group 59, Diplomatic Despatches, Central America (Nicaragua): volume 7 (Microcopy, 219/reel 13), National Archives, hereafter DD, CA (Nic.): 7 (M 219/r 13); Charles N. Riotte to Seward, June 15, 1863, DD, CA (CR): 1 (M 219/r 18).

18 Elisha Oscar Crosby to Seward, July 21, 1862, July 21, 1863, DD, CA (Guat.): 4 (M 219/r 7); Crosby to John M. Dow, May 20, 1861, John M. Dow papers, box 1, Cornell University.

19 Irisarri to Aycinena, May 15, 1865, in del Cid Fernández, ed., *Epistolario de Irisarri*, 202–4.

20 Irisarri to Seward, Oct. 28, 1861, Notes from CA: 4 (T 34/r 6); Irisarri to Aycinena, April 21, May 21, 1861, Molina to Irisarri, Sept. 25, 1863, in del Cid Fernández, *Epistolario de Irisarri*, 69–70, 73, 143.

21 David Hoadley to Dow, June 18, 1861, Dow papers, box 1; Crosby to Seward, July 6, 1861, DD, CA (Guat.): 4 (M 219/r 7); Dickinson to Seward, Sept. 14, 1861, March 10, 1862, DD, CA (Nic.): 7 (M 219/r 13); Ebba Schoonover and Thomas Schoonover, "Bleeding Kansas and Spanish Cuba in 1857: A Postscript," *Kansas History* 11 (Winter 1988/89), 240–42; Kinley J. Brauer, "Gabriel García y Tassara and the American Civil War: A Spanish Perspective," *Civil War History* 21 (1975), 5–27.

22 James R. Partridge to Seward, April 22, 1865, DD, CA (Salv.): 1 (M 219/r 23); Graebner, *Empire on the Pacific*; van Alstyne, *Rising American Empire*, 147–69.

23 Schoonover, *Dollars over Dominion*, 140–44, 166–67, 191–92; unsigned report, Feb. 24, 1863, Affaires divers politiques, carton 2, folder: Affaires coloniales Belgiques, Archive du ministère des affaires étrangères, Paris, hereafter AMAE, Paris.

24 George Raymond to Frederick W. Seward, Nov. 14, 1861, Aug. 25, 26, Oct. 11 (2 items), Nov. 13 (2 items), 1862, Charles Leas to F. Seward, Jan. 24, March 17 (3 items), April 10, 17, 25 and 28, 1863, record group 59, Consular Despatches, National Archives, hereafter CD, Belize: 1 (T 334/r 1); Leas to F. Seward, May 15, 24, June 16, July 22, 1863, CD, Belize: 2 (T 334/r 2); Leas to F. Seward, March 10, April 1, 1864, Feb. 3, 1865, CD, Belize: 3 (T 334/r 3).

25 Dickinson to Zepada, Nov. 8, 1861, in Dickinson to Seward, Nov. 12, 1861, Dickinson to Zepada, Dec. 26, 1861, in Dickinson to Seward, Jan. 14, 1862, Dickinson to Seward, Feb. 13, June 12, 1862 (2 letters), DD, CA (Nic.): 7 (M 219/r 13); Crosby to

Seward, July 21, 1861, March 6, 1862, DD, CA (Guat.): 4 (M 219/r 7); Partridge to Seward, May 19, June 3, 1862, and enclosures, DD, CA (Hond.): 1 (M 219/r 22); Roy F. Nichols and Eugene H. Berwanger, *The Stakes of Powers, 1845–1877* (2nd ed.; New York, 1982), 109–10.

26   Brainerd Dyer, "Confederate Naval and Privateering Activities in the Pacific," *Pacific Historical Review* 3 (1934), 433–43; Dalzell, *The Flight from the Flag*, 142–43.

27   Gideon Welles to John B. Montgomery, June 10, 1861, Captain Richie to David Porter, July 8, 1861, G. T. Ruston to Edward Middleton, Dec. 24, 1864, A. Bell to Middleton, Feb. 4, Nov. 1, 1862, and other correspondence in folders 2 and 3, Edward Middleton papers, Southern Historical Collection, University of North Carolina; Amos Corwine to Seward, June 14, Aug. 12, 1861, CD, Pan.: 8 (M 139/r 8); J. P. Rankin to Alexander R. McKee, Dec. 19, 1861, McKee to Abraham Lincoln, Feb. 4, 1862, CD, Pan.: 9 (M 139/r 9); Dickinson to Seward, June 14, 1861, DD, CA (Nic.): 7 (M 219/r 13); McKee to Seward, June 7, Nov. 14, 16, 1864, with enclosures, CD, Pan.: 10 (M 139/r 10).

28   Dyer, "Confederate Naval and Privateering Activities," 438–40.

29   James M. Tindel to Judah Benjamin, July 1, 1863, U.S. Department of the Navy, *Official Records of the Union and Confederate Navies in the War of the Rebellion* (30 vols.; Washington, D.C., 1894–1927), series II, vol. 1, 418–20, hereafter *ORN*, series, vol., pages (also in RCSA, vol. 25, reel 15, LC); William Morrison Robinson, *The Confederate Privateers* (New Haven, 1928), 271–72.

30   A. J. Grayson to Jefferson Davis, Aug. 21, 1863, Benjamin to Grayson, Dec. 11, 1863, *ORN*, II, vol. 1, 421–23 (also in RCSA, vol. 17, reel 10, LC); Robinson, *Confederate Privateers*, 270.

31   Thomas E. Hogg to Benjamin, May 3, 1864, and enclosure, James M. Mason to Benjamin, April 12, 1864, Benjamin to Henry Hotze, May 5, 1864, *ORN*, II, vol. 3, 1082–84, 1111–13; Stephen R. Mallory to Hogg, May 7, 1864, with McKee to Seward, Nov. 14, 1864, CD, Pan.: 10 (M 139/r 10); Robinson, *Confederate Privateers*, 206–7, 272–75; Dyer, "Confederate Naval and Privateering Activities," 440–42. Owsley, *King Cotton Diplomacy*, does not mention Hogg's project nor any other on the Pacific side of Central America.

32   Hogg to Benjamin, May 3, 1864, and enclosure, Mason to Benjamin, April 12, 1864, Benjamin to Hotze, May 5, 1864, *ORN*, II, vol. 3, 1082–84, 1111–13; Mallory to Hogg, May 7, 1864, with McKee to Seward, Nov. 14, 1864, CD, Pan.: 10 (M 139/r 10); Robinson, *Confederate Privateers*, 206–7, 272–75; Dyer, "Confederate Naval and Privateering Activities," 440–42.

33   Thomas Savage to McKee, Oct. 3, 1864, in McKee to Seward, Oct. 25, 1864, McKee to Seward, Nov. 5, 16, 1864, Jan. 4, 1865, and enclosures, CD, Pan.: 10 (M 139/r 10); Charles Follin to Sec. St., June 21, 1864, CD, Omoa, Truxillo, and Ruatan: 3 (T 477/r 3); F. W. Rice to Seward, Nov. 4, 16, 1864, CD, Colon: 4 (T 193/r 4); Leas to F. Seward, Dec. 19, 1863, CD, Belize: 2 (T 334/r 2); Gary G. Kuhn, "United States Maritime Influence in Central America, 1863–1865," *American Neptune* 32 (1972), 284–85; Dyer, "Confederate Naval and Privateering Activities," 442. Also Partridge to Seward, Jan. 7, March 20, 1865, DD, CA (Salv.): 1 (M 219/r 23).

34   Leas to F. Seward, Dec. 1, 16, 1864, Jan. 10, 16, Feb. 3, 1865, CD, Belize: 3 (T 334/r 3); correspondence of Rear-Admiral G. F. Pearson, Commander H. K. Davenport, John M. Dow, Nov. 6, 15, 17, 1864, *ORN*, I, vol. 3, 359–64; Robinson, *Confederate Privateers*, 275.

35 Allan McLane to Welles, Dec. 16, 1864, Jan. 17, 1865, McKee to Seward, Jan. 4, 1865,
    William H. Allen to Seward, Jan. 3, 1865, and responses, *ORN*, I, vol. 3, 396–97, 409–
    11.

36 Benjamin to William Preston, Jan. 7, 1864, RCSA, container 17, reel 10, LC.

37 William T. Minor to Seward, March 11, 1865, Welles to Pearson, March 29, 1865,
    Welles to John Guest, May 5, 1865, Pearson to Welles, May 6, 1865, *ORN*, I, vol. 3,
    484–85, 510–11.

38 Robinson, *Confederate Privateers*, 276–77; Owen M. Long to Hamilton Fish, Sept.
    12, 1870, Alfred T. A. Torbert to Fish, Oct. 6, 1870, U.S. Department of State, *Papers
    Relating to the Foreign Relations of the United States, 1870* (Washington, D.C.,
    1871), 261–63, 280–82.

2 · Speculators and Schemers: Frémont, Bismarck, and the Costa Rican Railroad

1   On world system theory, see Braudel, *Civilisation matérielle*, and Wallerstein, *The
    World System*. William H. McNeill, *The Rise of the West* (New York, 1963), divided
    the industrial era from 1850 to 1950 into a first, or British phase, and a second, or
    German and American phase.

2   Otto Graf zu Stolberg-Wernigerode, *Germany and the United States of America
    during the Era of Bismarck* (Philadelphia, 1937), 86–131, 211–12; Manfred Jonas,
    The United States and Germany: A Diplomatic History (Ithaca, 1984), 23–26;
    Hans W. Gatzke, *Germany and the United States: A "Special Relationship?"* (Cam-
    bridge, Mass., 1980), 33–38; Schoonover, "Germany in Central America, 1820s to
    1929"; Schoonover, "Prussia and the Protection of German Transit through Middle
    America and Trade with the Pacific Basin, 1848–1851"; Hendrik Dane, *Die wirt-
    schaftlichen Beziehungen Deutschlands zu Mexiko und Mittelamerika im 19. Jahr-
    hundert* (Cologne, 1971); Julio Castellanos Chambranes, *El imperialismo alemán en
    Guatemala* (Guatemala, 1977); Schoonover, "Imperialism in Middle America."

3   Helmuth Stoecker, "Preussisch-deutsche Chinapolitik in den 1860/70er Jahren," in
    Hans-Ulrich Wehler, ed., *Imperialismus* (Cologne, 1976), 243–58; Otto Pflanze, *Bis-
    marck and the Development of Germany* (3 vols.; Princeton, N.J., 1963–1990),
    3:113–14; Herbert Schottelius, *Mittelamerika als Schauplatz deutscher Kolonisa-
    tionsversuche, 1840–1865* (Hamburg, 1939); Alfred Vagts, "Hopes and Fears of an
    American-German War, 1870–1915, I," *Political Science Quarterly* 54:4 (Dec. 1939),
    515–16. Holger Herwig, *Politics of Frustration: The United States in German Naval
    Planning, 1889–1941* (Boston, 1976), 43, 68–72, 95–96, and *Germany's Vision of
    Empire in Venezuela, 1871–1918* (Princeton, 1986), 141–42, describe continued Ger-
    man naval interest in the Caribbean.

4   Dr. Carl Bernhard to [Franz Hugo Hesse?], Aug. 20, 1866 (A. A. II Rep. 6, Nr. 3520), 2.
    4. 1., Abt. II, Nr. 639, Bundesarchiv, Merseburg, (formerly Deutsches Zentralarchiv);
    Eduard Delius to the Foreign Ministry, Aug. 6, 1866, Rep. 77, Tit. 226, Nr. 118, Band
    2, Bundesarchiv, Merseburg.

5   Delius to Ulysses S. Grant, Jan. 1881, HM 20343, U.S. Grant papers, Huntington
    Library, San Marino, Calif.

6   Watt Stewart, *Keith and Costa Rica: A Biographical Study of Minor Cooper Keith*
    (Albuquerque, 1964), 4–6; W. Rodney Long, *Railways of Central America and the
    West Indies* (Washington, D.C., 1925), 98; Richard J. Houk, "The Development of

Foreign Trade and Communication in Costa Rica to the Construction of the First Railway," *The Americas* 10 (Oct. 1953), 197–209; J. Fred Rippy, "Relations of the United States and Costa Rica during the Guardia Era," *Bulletin of the Pan American Union* 77:2 (Feb. 1943), 61–66. Delmer G. Ross, "Emergent Costa Rican Nationalism: Financing Railway Construction," *SECOLAS Annals* 8 (1977), 84–93, mentions the various early steam railroad and animal power railways, but focuses upon the financing of Keith's project.

7 Addison M. Bailey to Seward, Jan. 10, 1869, CD, CA (CR): 2 (T 35/r 2); Bailey to Fish, Sept. 10, 1869, Jan. 25, March 9, 1870, DD, CA (CR): 3 (M 219/r 20); Stewart, *Keith and Costa Rica,* 4–6.

8 Edmund Pougin, *L'état de Costa Rica* (Anvers, Belg., 1863); David Hoadley to John M. Dow, Aug. 28, 1861, John M. Dow papers, box 1; Charles N. Riotte to Seward, Aug. 29, Sept. 13, 27, 1861, Jan. 24, Sept. 11, Oct. 12, 1862, DD, CA (CR): 1 (M 219/r 18); Charles Stansifer, "E. George Squier and the Honduran Interoceanic Railroad Project," *Hispanic American Historical Review* 46 (1968), 1–27.

9 Riotte to Seward, Sept. 13, 27, 1861, Jan. 24, Oct. 12, 1862, DD, CA (CR): 1 (M 219/r 18).

10 J. T. Meagher, "Costa Rica and Its Railroad," *Overland Monthly* 10 (1873), 160–73; Francisco Parraga to Ambrose W. Thompson, Jan. 30, 1861, and Thompson to A. T. Brett, May 23, 1865, Richard W. Thompson papers, box 5, Rutherford B. Hayes Library, Fremont, Ohio; Allan Wallis to Sec. St., May 30, 1861, Foreign Office series 21, vol. 15, reel 5, Public Records Office (Great Britain), hereafter FO 21/15, r. 5, PRO; [A. W. Thompson], *Contract for Coal &c. at the isthmus of Chiriqui* (Washington, D.C. [1861?]); Abraham Lincoln to Herrán, June 11, 1862, and Herrán to Lincoln, June 14, 1862, both with Luis Molina to MRE (CR), June 14, 1862, Ministro de Relaciones Exteriores, caja 39, Archivos Nacionales, Costa Rica, hereafter MRE, caja 39, AN, CR.

11 Riotte to Seward, Jan. 10, April 25, 1866, DD, CA (CR): 2 (M 219/r 19); Seward to Riotte, June 12, July 9, 1866, Record Group 59, Diplomatic Instructions, National Archives, hereafter DI, CA: 17 (M 77/r 29); Frederick W. Seward, *Reminiscences of a War-time Statesman and Diplomat, 1830–1915* (New York, 1916), 300–302, 327, 343–44, 346.

12 Allan Nevins's biographies, *Frémont: The West's Greatest Adventurer* (2 vols.; New York, 1928), 668–87, and *Frémont: Pathmarker of the West* (New York, 1939), 583–601 (quotation from page 599), discuss John C. Frémont's business ethics and character; Julius Grodinsky, *Transcontinental Railroad Strategy, 1869–1893: A Study of Businessmen* (Philadelphia, 1962), 8, considers Frémont's Memphis, El Paso, and Pacific railroad was mismanaged.

13 Schoonover, *Dollars over Dominion,* 261–62; Robert W. Frazer, "The Ochoa Bond Negotiations of 1865–1867," *Pacific Historical Review* 11 (Dec. 1942), 397–414; Gutiérrez correspondence in cajas 48, 49, and 51, AN, CR; and Matías Romero, *Correspondencia de la legación mexicana en Washington durante la intervención extranjera* (10 vols.; Mexico, 1870–1892), vols. 8, 9, and 10, describe Frémont's shady operations in Mexico and Costa Rica. Neither M. Z. Froneck, "Diplomatic Relations between the United States and Costa Rica, 1823–1882," (Ph.D. diss., Fordham University, 1959), 190–203, nor Jeffery Casey Gaspar, "El ferrocarril al Atlántico en Costa Rica, 1871–1874," *Anuario de Estudios Centroamericanos* 2 (1976), 291–344, even mentions Frémont's negotiations or his railroad concession.

14 Werner F. Leopold, "Der Deutsche in Costa Rica," *Hamburger Wirtschaftschronik* 3
    (Oct. 1966), 147–51; Henry F. W. "Guillermo" Nanne, "Dictation concerning con-
    struction of railroads, etc. in Central America, 1885," n. d., H. H. Bancroft Collec-
    tion, Bancroft Library, University of California, Berkeley; Rippy, "Guardia Era," 64–
    65.

15 Riotte to Seward, March 10, June 9, 10, 1866, DD, CA (CR): 2 (M 219/r 19); Seward to
    Riotte, June 12, July 9, 1866, DI, CA: 17 (M 77/r 29).

16 Gutiérrez to MRE, Sept. 29, 1866, MRE, caja 48, AN, CR.

17 Gutiérrez to MRE, Nov. 30, 1866, MRE, caja 48, Gutiérrez to MRE, Feb. 9, July 31,
    Aug. 9, 1867, MRE, caja 49, AN, CR; Wallis to Lord Stanley, Sept. 7, 1866, Jan. 9,
    Feb. 6, 1867, FO 21/23 (r 7), PRO; Albert G. Lawrence to Seward, Feb. 10, 1867, DD,
    CA (CR): 3 (M 219/r 20).

18 Wallis to Lord Stanley, Sept. 7, 1866, Jan. 9, Feb. 6, 1867, FO 21/23 (r 7) PRO; Riotte to
    Seward, Sept. 8, 1866, DD, CA (CR): 3 (M 219/r 20).

19 Gutiérrez to MRE, Feb. 27, 1867 and enclosures, Frémont to Gutiérrez, Aug. 6, 1867,
    MRE, caja 49, AN, CR.

20 Gutiérrez to MRE, April 10, July 31, Aug. 9, 30, 1867, MRE, caja 49, AN, CR;
    B. Squier Cotrell to Seward, Aug. 23, 1867, CD, San Juan del Norte: 4 (T 348/r 4).

21 Gutiérrez to MRE, April 10, July 31, Aug. 9, 30, 1867, MRE, caja 49, AN, CR.

22 Gutiérrez to MRE, July 31, Aug. 9, 30, Oct. 10, 1867, MRE, caja 49, AN, CR.

23 Arthur Morrell to Seward, Oct. 10, 1867, in U.S. Department of State, *Papers Relating
    to the Foreign Relations of the United States, 1867* (Washington, D.C., 1868), hereaf-
    ter *FRUS, 1867,* pt. 2, 280–81; Morrell to Seward, Aug. 23, Dec. 24, 1867, DD, CA
    (CR): 3 (M 219/r 20).

24 Gutiérrez to MRE, Jan. 10, 1868, MRE, caja 51, AN, CR.

25 Edmund C. Pechin, et al., to A. Esquivel, Jan. 31, 1868, Ministerio de Fomento, legajo
    275, AN, CR; Helmuth Polakowsky, "Estación naval alemana en Costa Rica," *Re-
    vista de los Archivos Nacionales* [Costa Rica] 7 (1943), 56–65; Tulio von Bülow,
    "Sobre el proyecto de base naval alemana en 1868," *Revista de los Archivos Na-
    cionales* [Costa Rica] 7 (1943), 147–49.

26 Morrell to Seward, Feb. 8, 1868, DD, CA (CR): 3 (M 219/r 20).

27 Gutiérrez to MRE, July 15, 1868, William Aufermann to Julio Volio, July 15, 1868,
    MRE, caja 51, AN, CR.

28 Undated extract of E. E. Verebelij letter [1867?], Bundesarchiv, Potsdam, (formerly
    Deutsches Zentralarchiv) 09.01, Nr. 52602; Polakowsky, "Estación naval alemana en
    Costa Rica," 56–65; Rippy, "Guardia Era," 64; Stolberg-Wernigerode, *The Era of
    Bismarck,* 211, 222.

29 Morrell to Seward, May 8, 25, 1868, enclosing Friedrich Wilhelm Franz Kinderling to
    J. Friedrich Lahmann, April 20, 1868, Lahmann to Volio, May 1, 1868, and Volio to
    Lahmann, May 6, 1868, DD, CA (CR): 3 (M 219/r 20), also in *FRUS, 1868,* pt. 2, 327–
    34; Polakowsky, "Estación naval alemana en Costa Rica," 56–65; von Bülow, "Pro-
    yecto de base naval alemana," 147–49.

30 Morrell to Seward, May 8, 25, 1868, enclosing Kinderling to Lahmann, April 20, 1868,
    Lahmann to Volio, May 1, 1868, and Volio to Lahmann, May 6, 1868, DD, CA (CR): 3
    (M 219/r 20); Kinderling to Royal High Command of the Navy, May 22, 1868, 2.4.1
    Abt. II, Nr. 644 (A.A. II Rep. 6, Nr. 3573), Bundesarchiv, Merseburg; E. Corbett to Lord
    Stanley, May 25, 1868, FO to Corbett, July 21, 1868, FO 15/134, r. 50, PRO.

31 Gutiérrez to MRE, Aug. 31, 1868, MRE, caja 51, AN, CR; circular, Rudolf Delbrück to

missions in London, Paris, St. Petersburg, Vienna, Florence, and Washington, July 3, 1868, Carl Schurz to Friedrich von Gerolt, June 20, July 9, 1868, in *Die auswärtige Politik Preussens, 1858–1871*, vol. 10, 106–9.

32 von Gerolt to Bismarck, Oct. 28, 1868, Riotte to von Gerolt, Oct. 4, 1868, Auswärtiges Amt (09.01), No. 52613, Bundesarchiv, Potsdam; Polakowsky, "Estación naval alemana en Costa Rica," 56–65; von Bülow, "Proyecto de base naval alemana," 147–49.

33 Kinderling to Royal High Command of the Navy, May 22, 1868, 2.4.1 Abt. II, Nr. 644 (A.A. II Rep. 6, Nr. 3573), Bundesarchiv, Merseburg; Delius to Grant, Jan. 1881, HM 20343, Grant papers.

34 Rudolf Lahmann to Foreign Ministry, July 10, 1868, Rep. 77, Tit. 226, Nr. 118, Band 2, Bundesarchiv, Merseburg; von Gerolt to Otto von Bismarck, Oct. 20, 1868, enclosing an extract of Riotte to von Gerolt, Oct. 4, 1868, Auswärtiges Amt (09.01), Nr. 52613, Bundesarchiv, Potsdam; "Franz Kinderling," MSg 1/1101, p. 185, Bundesarchiv, Militärarchiv, Freiburg; Morrell to Seward, May 8, 25, 1868, DD, CA (CR): 3 (M 219/r 20); certification of Morrell, U.S. Consul, June 8, 1868, Nr. 52613, Das Bundesconsulat in San José (Costa Rica), 1868–1886, Bundesarchiv, Potsdam.

35 *Informe . . . 1868* (San José, Costa Rica, [1868]), 1–3; Gutiérrez to MRE, Aug. 31, 1868, Volio to Ezquivel, Oct. 27, 1868, MRE, caja 51, AN, CR.

36 Bailey to Seward, Jan. 10, 1869, CD, San José: 2 (T 35/r 2); Jacob Blair to Seward, Jan. 9, 1869, DD, CA (CR): 3 (M 219/r 20); Juan B. Mata to Ministro de Fomento, April 22, 1869, C. H. Billings to Ministro de Fomento, July 9, 1869, Fomento, folders 124 and 276, AN, CR; Julien O. de Cabarrus to Ministère des affaires etrangères (hereafter MAE), Feb. 19, 1869, Feb. 28, 1870, Correspondence consulaire et commerciale, Guat., v. 8, AMAE; Blair to Fish, May 25, 31, 1869, Bailey to Fish, Sept. 10, 1869, Jan. 25, March 9, 1870, DD, CA (CR): 3 (M 219/r 20); Fish to Blair, Jan. 21, 1871, Blair to Fish, March 10, 1871, *FRUS, 1871*, 249–50; Long, *Railways of Central America and the West Indies*, 98.

37 Delius to Grant, Jan. 1881, HM 20343, Grant papers; Polakowsky, "Estación naval alemana en Costa Rica," 56–65.

38 Blair to Fish, Sept. 13, 1871, DD, CA (CR): 4 (M 219/r 21), or *FRUS, 1871*, 252–53; J. R. Gill to Daniel Strobel Martin, Feb. 1, 1872, Daniel Strobel Martin Collection, South Caroliniana Library, University of South Carolina; Morrell to Fish, June 15, 1872, CD, San José: 3 (T 35/r 3); Blair to Fish, June 23, 1872, *FRUS, 1873*, pt. 1, 210–12; Stewart, *Keith and Costa Rica*, 4–6.

39 Manuel María Peralta to Director of the Pacific Mail Steamship Line, March 31, 1876, Peralta to Herrera, April 14, 1876, MRE, libro copiador 1876–1877, AN, CR; entries March 23, June 20, 29, 1879, Hamilton Fish diaries, cont. 320, Hamilton Fish papers, LC.

3 George M. Williamson and Postbellum
Southern Expansionism

1 Curry, *Blueprint for Modern America*; Williams, *The Contours of American History*, esp. 225–342; Richard Rubinson, "Political Transformation in Germany and the United States"; van Alstyne, *The Rising American Empire*, 147–69; Milton Plesur, *America's Outward Thrust: Approaches to Foreign Affairs, 1865–1890* (DeKalb, Ill., 1971), esp. 14–34, 157–81; Schoonover, *Dollars over Dominion*; Edward Chase Kirk-

land, *Industry Comes of Age: Business, Labor and Public Policy, 1860–1897* (Chicago, 1967), 291–93. On free trade or social imperialism, Semmel, *The Rise of Free Trade Imperialism;* Hans-Ulrich Wehler, *Bismarck und der Imperialismus* (Cologne, 1969), 112–26, 454–502. Historians have challenged the market expansion perspective. See Paul Holbo, "Economics, Emotion, and Expansion: An Emerging Foreign Policy," in H. Wayne Morgan, ed., *The Gilded Age* (Syracuse, 1970), 199–221; J. A. Thompson, "William Appleman Williams and the 'American Empire,'" *Journal of American Studies* 7 (April 1973), 91–103; William H. Becker, "American Manufacturers and Foreign Markets, 1870–1900: Business Historians and the 'New Economic Determinists'," *Business History Review* 47 (Winter 1973), 466–81; David M. Pletcher, "Rhetoric and Results: A Pragmatic View of American Economic Expansionism, 1865–98," *Diplomatic History* 5 (Spring 1981), 93–105.

2 George M. Williamson to Fish, Oct. 16, 1873, DD, CA: 4 (M 219/r 27); E. Merton Coulter, *The South during Reconstruction, 1865–1877* (Baton Rouge, 1947), 245–51, 265ff; Tom E. Terrill, *The Tariff, Politics, and American Foreign Policy, 1874–1901* (Westport, 1973), 14–36; Joe Gray Taylor, *Louisiana Reconstructed, 1863–1877* (Baton Rouge, 1974), 350–62; Peter George, *The Emergence of Industrial America: Strategic Factors in American Economic Growth since 1870* (Albany, 1982), 1–8, 131–34.

3 Robert E. May, "Lobbyists for Commercial Empire: Jane Cazneau, William Cazneau, and U.S. Caribbean Policy, 1846–1878," *Pacific Historical Review* 48 (August 1979), 383–412; Tennant S. McWilliams, "The Lure of Empire: Southern Interest in the Caribbean, 1877–1900," *Mississippi Quarterly* 29 (Winter 1975–76), 43–63; Joseph A. Fry, "John Tyler Morgan's Southern Expansionism," *Diplomatic History* 9 (Fall 1985), 329–46; O. Lawrence Burnette, Jr., "John Tyler Morgan and Expansionist Sentiment in the New South," *Alabama Review* 18 (July 1965), 163–82; James B. Murphy, *L. Q. C. Lamar: Pragmatic Patriot* (Baton Rouge, 1973), 140–41; David M. Pletcher, "Inter-American Trade in the Early 1870s—A State Department Survey," *The Americas* 33 (April 1977), 593–612. Tennant S. McWilliams's recent book sees little expansionism in the postbellum south: *The New South Faces the World: Foreign Affairs and the Southern Sense of Self, 1877–1950* (Baton Rouge, 1988), 16. On continuity and discontinuity in southern leadership, see Carl Degler, *Place over Time: The Continuity of Southern Distinctiveness* (Baton Rouge, 1977), 110–24; Laurence Shore, *Southern Capitalists: The Ideological Leadership of an Elite, 1832–1885* (Chapel Hill, 1986), 168, 188–90; Steven Hahn, *The Roots of Southern Populism* (New York, 1983), 1–11. For a brief, insightful discussion of the continuity-discontinuity debate, see Michael Wayne, *The Reshaping of Plantation Society: The Natchez District, 1860–1880* (Baton Rouge, 1983), 197–204.

4 In addition to the essays by May, Fry, Burnette, and McWilliams noted in note 3, see Gavin Wright, *Old South, New South: Revolutions in the Southern Economy since the Civil War* (New York, 1986), vi–vii; James C. Cobb, "Beyond Planters and Industrialists: A New Perspective on the New South," *Journal of Southern History* 54 (Feb. 1988), 46. On southern expansionism, see Eugene D. Genovese, *The Political Economy of Slavery* (New York, 1967), 243–74; van Alstyne, *The Rising American Empire*, 147–69; May, *The Southern Dream of a Caribbean Empire*.

5 Traces of George M. Williamson's life are found in *National Cyclopedia of American Biography* (New York, 1893—), 12:52; Alcée Fortier, *Louisiana: Comprising Sketches* (3 vols.; n. p., 1914), 3:681–82; Henry Edward Chambers, *A History of*

Louisiana (3 vols.; New York, 1925), 3:15; "In Memoriam of George Williamson [the son]," *Proceedings of the Louisiana Academy of Sciences* 10 (1945–46), 15–17; Fredricha Doll Gute and Katherine B. Jeter, *Historical Profile: Shreveport, 1850* (Shreveport, 1982), 38, 47, 84, 89; Taylor, *Louisiana Reconstructed*, 232–36.

6   May, "Lobbyists for Commercial Empire," 409–12; Taylor, *Louisiana Reconstructed*, 314–63; Charles S. Campbell, *The Transformation of American Foreign Relations, 1865–1900* (New York, 1976), 50–66; LaFeber, *The New Empire*, 36–39.

7   David A. Wells, "How Shall the Nation Regain Prosperity?" *North American Review* 125 (1877), 110–32, 283–308; Hans Rosenberg, *Grosse Depression und Bismarckzeit* (Berlin, 1967); Williams, *The Roots of the Modern American Empire*, 4–46; Wehler, *Der Aufstieg des amerikanischen Imperialismus*, 7–73; LaFeber, *The New Empire*, 1–3, 62–63, 102–12, 150–53, 407–17; Williamson to Fish, Sept. 28, 1873, Aug. 17, 1874, *FRUS, 1874*, 99–101, 180–81. Ragnhild Fiebig-von Hase, *Lateinamerika als Konfliktherd der deutsch-amerikanischen Beziehungen, 1890–1903* (2 vols., Göttingen, 1986), 2:587–611, 643–63, develops many of these points for the period 1889–1910.

8   R. L. Woodward, *Central America: A Nation Divided*, 149–202; Cardozo and Pérez Brignoli, *Centro América y la economía occidental*, 149–80, 185–92, 199–208, 270–75, 289–320; Jorge Mario García LaGuardia, *La reforma liberal en Guatemala* (Guatemala, 1972); Handy, *Gift of the Devil*, 57–75; James A. Morris, *Honduras: Caudillo Politics and Military Rulers* (Boulder, Colo., 1984), 1–7.

9   Joy Jackson, *New Orleans in the Gilded Age: Politics and Urban Progress, 1880–1896* (Baton Rouge, 1969), 204–14; James P. Baughman, "Gateway to the Americas," in Hodding Carter, ed., *The Past as Prelude: New Orleans, 1718–1968* (New Orleans, 1968), 280–87; *The City of New Orleans: The Book of the Chamber of Commerce and Industry of Louisiana* (New Orleans: George W. Engelhardt, 1894), 4; D. Clive Hardy, *The World's Industrial and Cotton Centennial Exposition* (New Orleans, 1978).

10 Hamilton Fish to Williamson, June 17, 1873, DI, CA: 17 (M 77/r 29); Williamson to Fish, April 3, 1874, DD, CA: 5 (M 219/r 27); U.S. Congress, House of Representatives, *Letter from the Secretary of State, Transmitting an Annual Report upon the Commercial Relations of the United States with Foreign Nations During the Year 1876*, 44th Cong., 2nd sess., House Executive Document 45, pp. 7, 271, 284; Hagan, *American Gunboat Diplomacy and the Old Navy*, 7–10.

11 Williamson to Fish, Oct. 16, 1873, DD, CA: 4 (M 219/r 27); Henry Houben to Williamson, Nov. 14, 1873, with Houben to William Hunter, Feb. 20, 1874, Houben to John Chandler Bancroft Davis, June 6, 1874, CD, Guat.: 3 (T 337/r 3); A. C. Prindle to J. S. Cadwalader, Sept. 20, 1876, Prindle to F. Seward, Sept. 15, Dec. 10, 1877, Earl D. Braden to F. Seward, Aug. 18, 1879, Braden to John Hay, March 10, 1880, CD, Belize: 5 (T 334/r 5).

12 Williamson to Fish, June 19, 1873, DD, CA: 4 (M 219/r 27); "Intereses económicos," *El bien público* (Guat.), Oct. 3, 1880, p. 1; Williamson to Fish, Sept. 28, 1873, *FRUS, 1874*, 99–101.

13 Williamson to Fish, June 19, 1873, DD, CA: 4 (M 219/r 27); "Intereses económicos," *El bien público* (Guat.), Oct. 3, 1880, p. 1; Williamson to Fish, Sept. 28, 1873, *FRUS, 1874*, 99–101; Handy, *Gift of the Devil*, 60–69; Woodward, *Central America*, 152–56; Delmer G. Ross, "The Construction of the Interoceanic Railroad of Guatemala," *The Americas* 33 (Jan. 1977), 430–56; Delmer G. Ross, *Visionaries and Swindlers:*

The Development of the Railways of Honduras (Mobile, 1975); Williamson to William M. Evarts, Sept. 24, 1877, DD, CA: 14 (M 219/r 33); John Graham to Hunter, Oct. 1874, CD, Guat.: 3 (T 337/r 3).

14 Williamson to Fish, Oct. 16, 1873, DD, CA: 4 (M 219/r 27); Williamson to Fish, March 27, 1874, DD, CA: 5 (M 219/r 27); Kenneth E. Davison, The Presidency of Rutherford B. Hayes (Westport, 1972), 198–99.

15 Seward to Allan A. Burton, Jan. 16, 1862, DI (Col.): 16 (M 77/r 45); Williamson to Fish, Oct. 16, 1873, DD, CA: 4 (M 219/r 27); Williamson to Fish, March 27, 1874, DD, CA: 5 (M 219/r 27).

16 Williamson to Fish, Dec. 30, 1873, DD, CA: 4 (M 219/r 27); Williamson to Fish, March 27, 1874, DD, CA: 5 (M 219/r 27); Houben to Williamson, Nov. 14, 1873, with Houben to Hunter, Feb. 20, 1874, Houben to Davis, June 6, 1874, CD, Guat.: 3 (T 337/r 3).

17 Davison, The Presidency of Hayes, 202–4; Bermann, Under the Big Stick, chap. 7; Stolberg-Wernigerode, Germany and the United States of America during the Era of Bismarck, 170.

18 Williamson to Fish, Nov. 2, 1873, DD, CA: 4 (M 219/r 27); Vicente Herrera to Fish, Nov. 21, 1873, Notes from CA Leg.: 5 (T 34/r 7); MRE (Nic.) to MRE (Hond.), March 23, 1874, in El Nacional (Hond.), April 23, 1874, p. 2; Vicente Quadra, "Mensaje del señor Presidente de la República don Vicente Quadra, al Congreso de 1875," Jan. 13, 1875, Gaceta de Nicaragua, Jan. 16, 1875, pp. 25–27; Williamson to Fish, Nov. 18, 1874, DD, CA: 7 (M 219/r 29); Williamson to Fish, June 15, 1876, DD, CA: 11 (M 219/r 31); Williamson to Evarts, Oct. 22, 1878, DD, CA: 15 (M 219/r 34); F. Seward to Williamson, Nov. 27, 1878, DI, CA: 17 (M 77/r 29); Cornelius A. Logan to Evarts, April 5, 1880, DD, CA: 16 (M 219/r 35).

19 José de Marcoleta to Derby, Aug. 27, 1877, FO 56/27 (r 7), PRO; Promemoria betreffend unsere Reklamation gegen Nicaragua in der Angelegenheit des Kaiserlichen Konsulats in Leon (Berlin, 1877), including Bernhard Ernst von Bülow to Dr. Merck, Dec. 21, 1877, Senat CI VI, No. 16ᵈ, vol. 1, Fasc. 9, Staatsarchiv Hamburg; Williamson to Evarts, April 8, May 19, 1877, DD, CA: 12 (M 219/r 32); Williamson to Evarts, June 16, July 12, 25, Aug. 18, 1877, DD, CA: 13 (M 219/r 32); Locock to Earl of Derby, Feb. 22, June 19, 1877, FO 15/175 (r 66), PRO; Locock to Marques of Salisbury, April 27, 1878, Bayerisches Hauptstaatsarchiv, Abt. II, MA 76002, Geheimes Staatsarchiv, Munich; B. von Werner, Ein deutsches Kriegsschiff in der Südsee (Leipzig, 1889), 46–53; A. Tesdorf, Geschichte der kaiserlich deutschen Kriegsmarine in Denkwürdigkeiten von allgemeinem Interesse (Kiel, 1889), 199–202; Karl Paschen, Aus der Werdezeit zweier Marinen (Berlin, 1908), 186–87, 192–97; Paul Koch, "Aus der Zeit von Admiral v. Stosch," Marine-Rundschau 14 (1903), 694–96; Schoonover, "Germany in Central America"; Williamson to Evarts, Jan. 25, 1878, DD, CA: 14 (M 219/r 33).

20 Williamson to Evarts, Sept. 24, 1877, Jan. 25, 1878, RG 59, DD, CA: 14 (M 219/r 33) (also in FRUS, 1877, pp. 18–30); Williamson to Fish, Feb. 12, 1877, DD, CA: 11 (M 219/r 31); Williamson to Fish, Feb. 28, 1877, DD, CA: 12 (M 219/r 32); Locock to Derby, July 16, 1877, FO 15/176 (r 66), PRO; Evarts to Max von Thielmann, July 21, 1877, F. Seward to Thielmann, Aug. 17, 1877, Notes to For. Leg., Germany: (M 99/r 30); Anselmo H. Rivas to Sec. St., April 4, 1878, J. E. Hollenbeck to Evarts, May 21, 1878, Notes from Nic. Leg.: 2 (T 797/r 2); Bernhard Ernst von Bülow, Deutsche Politik (Berlin, 1916), 18–19; Rivas circular to all Latin American governments,

May 15, 1878, *Revista del Archivo General de la Nación* (Nicaragua) 2 (1967), 83–89; Schoonover, "Metropole Rivalry in Central America." U.S. officials in Central America constantly warned of increasing German influence and activity.

21 Williamson to Fish, Feb. 2, 1875, *FRUS, 1875*, pt. 1, 149; Williamson to Fish, Jan. 14, 1875, DD, CA: 7 (M 219/r 29).

22 Williamson to Fish, July 22, 1874, DD, CA: 6 (M 219/r 28); Williamson to Fish, Jan. 4, 1874, DD, CA: 7 (M 219/r 29); Locock to Derby, June 30, 1875, FO 15/165 (r 62), PRO; Locock to Derby, May 6, 1876, FO 15/170 (r 64), PRO.

23 Williamson to Fish, Jan. 29, 1875, DD, CA: 7 (M 219/r 29).

24 Circulars, July 13, Aug. 7, 1877, *FRUS, 1877*, 2–7; LaFeber, *The New American Empire*; Williams, *The Modern American Empire*; Wehler, *Der Aufstieg des amerikanischen Imperialismus.*

25 Williamson to Fish, Aug. 17, 1874, *FRUS, 1874*, 180–81.

26 Williamson to Evarts, Sept. 24, 1877, DD, CA: 14 (M 219/r 33) (also in *FRUS, 1877*, 18–30).

27 Williamson to Evarts, Sept. 24, 1877, DD, CA: 14 (M 219/r 33).

28 Memorandum for John W. Foster, [1876], Edward Lee Plumb papers, box 3, folder 37, Special Collections, Stanford University; Long to Hunter, Sept. 30, 1878, CD, Pan.: 14 (T 139/r 14); M. Graham to Salisbury, Oct. 22, 1878, FO 15/183 (r 68), PRO. On German views regarding overproduction and expansion, see Wehler, *Bismarck und der Imperialismus*; on British response to economic depression, social disorder, and expansion, see Semmel, *The Rise of Free Trade Imperialism*; on European competitiveness in Central America, see Schoonover, "Imperialism in Middle America: United States Competition with Britain, Germany, and France in Middle America, 1820s–1920s," and Schoonover, "Metropole Rivalry in Central America." On British, German, and U.S. commercial competition, see Houben to Williamson, Nov. 14, 1873, with Houben to Hunter, Feb. 20, 1874, John Graham to Hunter, Oct. 1874, CD, Guat.: 3 (T 337/r 3); Reichskanzler to Werner von Bergen, Sept. 12, 1878, von Bergen to B. E. von Bülow, Nov. 2, 1878, 09.01 (Auswärtiges Amt), Nr. 52602, Bundesarchiv, Potsdam; Locock to Derby, Sept. 24, 1875 (2 dispatches), FO 15/164 (r 62), PRO; Logan to Evarts, Oct. 10, 1879, DD, CA: 15 (M 219/r 34); Locock to Derby, May 25, 1877, FO 39/42 (r 14), PRO; decree, April 25, 1878, Poder Ejecutivo, libro copiador 1876–1885, Archivos Nacionales, Tegucigalpa, Honduras, hereafter AMRE, Hond.; Vagts, "Hopes and Fears of an American-German War, 1870–1915, I," 515–16; George M. Fisk, "German-American Diplomatic and Commercial Relations, Historically Considered," *American Monthly Review of Reviews* 25:3 (March 1902), 326.

29 Williamson to Fish, March 5, 1877, DD, CA: 12 (M 219/r 32); Williamson to Fish, April 30, and enclosures, May 10, 1874, DD, CA: 5 (M 219/r 27).

30 William Hair, *Bourbonism and Agrarian Protest: Louisiana Politics, 1877–1900* (Baton Rouge, 1969), 93; clipping *La sociedad económica*, [1877], p. 7; *Informe de la sociedad de inmigración* (Guatemala, [1878]); *La sociedad de inmigración*, nos. 1–5 (Jan. 15 to July 31, 1879), in Guatemala, Sociedad de Inmigración (1877–1889) collection, box 1, Manuscript and Archives, New York Public Library; "Sociedad de Inmigración," *La Sociedad Económica*, Dec. 7, 1877, pp. 1–2; "Sociedad de Inmigración," *La Sociedad Económica*, Dec. 18, 1877, pp. 2–4; editorial and article, *La Sociedad Económica*, Feb. 8, 1878, pp. 1–2; "Inmigración a la Alta Verapaz," *El Quetzal* (Guat.), Oct. 15, 1879, p. 3; D. P. Fenner to Hunter, March 26, 1878, CD, Guat.: 4 (T 337/r 4); R. L. Woodward, *Central America*, chap. 6.

31 Williamson to Evarts, Oct. 23, Dec. 28, 1878, Jan. 31, 1879, DD, CA: 15 (M 219/r 34);

Evarts to Williamson, Feb. 8, 1879, Lerellon A. Brown to Logan, April 3, 1879, DI, CA: 18 (M 77/r 30); Locock to Derby, Feb. 20, 1878, FO 15/181 (r 68), PRO.

4 The Eisenstück Affair: German and U.S. Rivalry in Central America, 1877–1890

1 On German interest in Central America, see Castellanos Chambranes, El imperi-alismo alemán en Guatemala, esp. 1–38; Julio Castellanos Chambranes, "Aspectos del desarrollo socio-económico y político de Guatemala 1868–1885, en base de materiales de archivos alemanes," Política y Sociedad 3 (Jan.–June 1977), 7–14; Gerhard Sandner, Zentralamerika und der ferne karibische Westen: Konjunkturen, Krisen und Konflikte, 1503–1984 (Stuttgart, 1985), 141–80; Schoonover, "Germany in Central America, 1820s–1929"; Dane, Die wirtschaftlichen Beziehungen Deutschlands zu Mexiko und Mittelamerika im 19. Jahrhundert, 91–153. On deteriorating official and public U.S.-German relations, see Jonas, The United States and Germany: A Diplomatic History, 35–64; Gatzke, Germany and the United States, 39–44; Fisk, "German-American Diplomatic and Commercial Relations, Historically Considered," 326; Vagts, "Hopes and Fears of an American-German War, 1870–1915, I," 515–16; Schoonover, "Imperialism in Middle America," 41–57; Rubinson, "Political Transformation in Germany and the United States," 39–73.

2 On the domestic origins of German expansionism, see Imanuel Geiss, "Sozialstruk-tur und imperialistische Dispositionen im zweiten deutschen Kaiserreich," in Karl Holl and Günther List, eds., Liberalismus und imperialistischer Staat: Der Imperi-alismus als Problem liberaler Parteien in Deutschland, 1890–1914 (Göttingen, 1975), 40–61; Hans-Ulrich Wehler, "Industrial Growth and Early German Imperial-ism," in Owens and Sutcliffe, eds., Studies in the Theory of Imperialism, 71–92; Rosenberg, Grosse Depression und Bismarckzeit; Michael Stürmer, Die Reichsgrün-dung: Deutscher Nationalstaat und europäisches Gleichgewicht im Zeitalter Bis-marcks (Munich, 1984).

3 Hartmut Pogge von Strandmann, "Domestic Origins of Germany's Colonial Expan-sion under Bismarck," Past and Present 42 (Feb. 1969), 140–59; Wehler, Bismarck und der Imperialismus, 42–135, 454–502; Stolberg-Wernigerode, Germany and the United States of America during the Era of Bismarck, 169–70, 307–9; Horst Müller-Link, Industrialisierung und Aussenpolitik: Preussen-Deutschland und das Zaren-reich von 1860 bis 1890 (Göttingen, 1977); Jonas, The United States and Germany, 25; Gatzke, Germany and the United States, 41. Jonas and Gatzke overlook the rising suspicion which U.S. diplomats and businessmen in Central America noted of German activity. On social imperialism, see Bernard Semmel, The Rise of Free Trade Imperialism (Cambridge, Eng., 1970).

4 Detlef Albers, Reichstag und Aussenpolitik von 1871–1879 (Berlin, 1927), 98–101; Konstantin Bulle, Geschichte der Jahre 1871 bis 1877 (2 vols.; Leipzig, 1878), 1:420–21. On Prussian-German expansion into Asia, see Stoecker, "Preussisch-deutsche Chinapolitik in den 1860/70er Jahren." On German penetration of the Caribbean, Herwig, Politics of Frustration; Herwig, Germany's Vision of Empire in Venezuela, 1871–1918, 141–74; Brenda Gayle Plummer, Black and White in the Caribbean: The Great Powers and Haiti, 1902–1915 (Baton Rouge, 1988).

5 von Gerolt to Otto von Bismarck, Jan. 11, 1869, Vereinigte Staaten I C 59, vol. 1, Politisches Archiv des Auswärtigen Amts, Bonn, West Germany, hereafter PAAA; Logan to James G. Blaine, June 15, 1881, DD, CA: 17 (M 219/r 37); Schoonover,

"Metropole Rivalry in Central America," 21–46; Bermann, *Under the Big Stick*, 103–22; McCullough, *The Path between the Seas*; LaFeber, *The New Empire*, 36–39, 50–51; Wehler, *Der Aufstieg des amerikanischen Imperialismus*, 24–73; Schoonover, "Imperialism in Middle America," 46–48.

6 Riotte to Fish, Dec. 21, 1870, DD, CA (Nic.): 11 (M 219/r 16); LaFeber, *Inevitable Revolutions*, 28–34.

7 German diplomatic and consular officials active in Nicaragua are listed in Appendice D of Göetz von Houwald, *Los Alemanes en Nicaragua* (Managua, 1975), 415–20.

8 Evarts to Max von Thielmann, July 21, 1877, F. Seward to Thielmann, Aug. 17, 1877, Notes to For. Leg., Germany: (M 99/r 30); Rivas to Sec. St., July 3, 11, 1877, Notes from For. Leg., CA: 5 (T 34/r 7); *Promemoria betreffend unsere Reklamation gegen Nicaragua in der Angelegenheit des Kaiserlichen Konsulats in Leon*, including B. E. von Bülow to Merck, Dec. 21, 1877, Senat C1 VI, No. 16ᵈ vol. 1, Fasc. 9, Staatsarchiv Hamburg; Williamson to Evarts, June 16, July 12, 25, Aug. 18, 1877, DD, CA: 13 (M 219/r 32); Kurt von Schloezer to Evarts, April 24, Aug. 22, 1877, Thielmann to Evarts, July 18, 19, 1877, Thielmann to Seward, July 18, 1877, Notes from Prussian Leg.: 14 (M 58/r 14). For Nicaraguan printed documents on the Eisenstück affair, see *Revista del Archivo General de la Nación* (Nicaragua) 2 (1967), 3–120. Other documents are in Charles Samver and Jules Hopf (eds.), *Nouveau recueil général de traités et autres actes relatifs aux rapports de droit international*, 2nd series (Göttingen, 1878), 2:337–43; Ludwig Hahn, *Fürst Bismarck: Sein politisches Leben und Wirken* (5 vols.; Berlin, 1881), 3:509–19.

9 Anselmo H. Rivas, *Memoria de Relaciones Exteriores, Justicia, Comercio i Agricultura . . . 1877* (Granada, Nic., 1877); Marcoleta to Derby, Aug. 27, 1877, FO 56 (Nicaragua)/27 (r 7), PRO; Enrique Guzmán, *Editoriales de la Prensa 1878* (Managua, 1977), 355–402; Enrique Guzmán, *Las gacetillas, 1878–1894* (Managua, 1975), 175–77; Francisco Ortega Arancibia, *Cuarenta años (1838–1878) de historia de Nicaragua* (3rd ed.; Managua, 1974), 491–93.

10 Marcoleta to Derby, Aug. 27, 1877, FO 56 (Nicaragua)/27 (r 7), PRO; Thielmann to Evarts, July 10, 1877, Schloezer to Evarts, April 24, 1878, Notes from Prussian Leg.: 14 (M 58/r 14); Schloezer to Evarts, April 17, 1878, Thielmann to Evarts, June 3, 1878, Notes from Prussian Leg.: 15 (M 58/r 15); B. E. von Bülow to Count von Flemming, Dec. 5, 1877, Faszikels 233/11569, Generallandesarchiv Karlsruhe; Locock to Derby, Feb. 22, June 19, 1877, FO 15 (Costa Rica)/175 (r 66), PRO.

11 Marcoleta to Derby, Aug. 27, 1877, FO 56 (Nicaragua)/27 (r 7), PRO; Rivas to Sec. St., April 4, 1878, J. E. Hollenbeck to Evarts, May 21, 1878, Notes from Nic. Leg.: 2 (T 797/r 2); Williamson to Evarts, Jan. 25, 1878, DD, CA: 14 (M 219/r 33); B. E. von Bülow to Merck, Dec. 21, 1877, in *Promemoria betreffend unsere Reklamation gegen Nicaragua*, Senat, C1 VI, No. 16ᵈ vol. 1, Fasc. 9, Staatsarchiv Hamburg. The exchange between Nicaraguan, German, and U.S. agents in late June 1877 is found in *Revista del Archivo de la Nación* 2 (1967), 67–72.

12 Locock to Earl of Derby, July 16, 1877, FO 15/176 (r 66), PRO.

13 Evarts to Thielmann, July 21, 1877, F. Seward to Thielmann, Aug. 17, 1877, Notes to For. Leg., Germany: (M 99/r 30); Williamson to Fish, Feb. 12, 1877, DD, CA: 11 (M 219/r 31); Williamson to Fish, Feb. 6, 1877, Williamson to Evarts, April 8, May 19, 1877, DD, CA: 12 (M 219/r 32); Williamson to Evarts, June 16, July 12, 1877, DD, CA: 13 (M 219/r 32); Thielmann to F. Seward, July 1877, Thielmann to Evarts, July 18, 1877, Notes from Prussian Leg.: 14 (M 58/r 14).

14 Evarts to Thielmann, July 21, 1877, F. Seward to Thielmann, Aug. 17, 1877, Notes to

For. Leg., Germany: (M 99/r 30); Rivas to Sec. St., April 4, 1878, Hollenbeck to Evarts, May 21, 1878, Notes from Nic. Leg.: 2 (T 797/r 2); Williamson to Evarts, Jan. 25, 1878, DD, CA: 14 (M 219/r 33); Rivas to Sec. St., July 3, 11, 1877, Notes from For. Leg., CA: 5 (T 34/r 7); Rivas circular to all Latin American governments, May 15, 1878, and *La Tertulia* (Masaya), April 15, 1878, p. 232, in *Revista del Archivo General de la Nación* (Nicaragua) 2 (1967), 6–7, 83–89.

15 Williamson to Evarts, Sept. 24, 1877, DD, CA: 14 (M 219/r 33), also found in *FRUS, 1877*, 18–30; Locock to Derby, Feb. 22, June 19, 1877, FO 15 (Costa Rica)/175 (r 66), PRO.

16 Derby to Marcoleta, Dec. 15, 1877, Marcoleta to Derby, Oct. 6, Dec. 28, 1877, H. J. Elliott memorandum, Dec. 25–28, 1877, Law Officers to Derby, Nov. 24, 1877, FO 56/27 (r8) PRO.

17 Williamson to Evarts, Aug. 18, 1877, DD, CA: 13 (M 219/r 32); Locock to Derby, Jan. 19, 1878, FO 15/181 (r 68), PRO.

18 Maudes to Min. Marine, Feb. 26, 1878, BB⁴ 1090 Archive de l'armée de la mer, hereafter, Adam; A. d'Oncien de la Batie to du Seignlay, March 7, 1878, du Seignlay to Min. Marine, June 8, 1878, BB⁴ 1093, Adam.

19 B. E. von Bülow, *Deutsche Politik*, 18–19; Pflanze, *Bismarck and the Development of Germany*, 2:372; Wilhelm von Massow, ed., *Fürst von Bülows Reden* (5 vols.; Leipzig, 1910–15), 2:235–38, 3:80–81, 4:144–46; Josef März, "Aus der Vorgeschichte der deutschen Kolonialpolitik," *Koloniale Rundschau* 26 (April–June 1934), 86–93; B. E. von Bülow to von Bergen, March 8, 1879, Rep. I, Nr. 40, vol. 1 (1876–1883), Bundesarchiv, Potsdam; Paul Koch, *Vierzig Jahre Schwarz-Weiss-Rot* (Berlin, 1908), 3–11; Tesdorpf, *Geschichte der kaiserlich deutschen Kriegsmarine*, 177–202; Paschen, *Aus der Werdezeit zweier Marinen*, 170–97; Maximilian von Hagen, *Bismarck's Kolonialpolitik* (Stuttgart, 1923), 1–41, 55–57.

20 B. E. von Bülow to von Bergen, March 14, 1879, B99-5-1, 4289/93194 Legación de Alemania, 1876–1888, Archivo General de Centro América, Guatemala City, Guatemala; Tesdorpf, *Geschichte der kaiserlich deutschen Kriegsmarine*, 199–202; Koch, "Aus der Zeit von Admiral v. Stosch," 694–96; Paschen, *Aus der Werdezeit zweier Marinen*, 186–87, 192–97; von Werner, *Ein deutsches Kriegsschiff in der Südsee*, 46–53; B. E. von Bülow to von Flemming, May 14, 1878, Faszikels 233/ 11569, Generallandesarchiv Karlsruhe; B. E. von Bülow to von Bergen, March 8, 1879, Rep. I, Nr. 40, vol. 1 (1876–1883), Bundesarchiv, Potsdam; B. E. von Bülow's remarks before the Reichstag, in Germany, Reichstag, *Stenographische Berichte über die Verhandlungen des Deutschen Reichs*, 3. Legislaturperiode, Feb. 25, 1878, 206–8; *La Tertulia* (Masaya, Nicaragua), April 15, 1878, p. 232, in the *Revista del Archivo de la Nación* (Nicaragua) 2 (1967), 6–7.

21 Locock to Salisburg, April 27, 1878, Bayerisches Hauptstaatsarchiv, Abt. II, MA 76002, Geheimes Staatsarchiv, Munich; Schloezer to Evarts, April 17, 1878, Thielmann to Evarts, June 3, 1878, Notes from Prussian Leg.: 15 (M 58/r 15); C. Heyden to Otto Peyer, May 24, 1892, 09.01, Nr. 52608, Bundesarchiv, Potsdam; von Bergen to von Bismarck, Feb. 4, 26, Nov. 6, 1866, Feb. 28, 1887, Abt. IA, Amerika Generalia 5, vol. 3, PAAA.

22 Williamson to Evarts, Sept. 24, 1877, DD, CA: 14 (M 219/r 33); David Strother to Hunter, Oct. 4, 1879, *FRUS, 1879*, 838–40; H. H. Leavitt to Asst. Sec. St., April 4, 1885, CD, Managua: 1 (T 634/r 1); Dupre to James D. Porter, April 13, 1887, CD, San Salv.: 2 (T 237/r 2); Victor Vifquain to William Wharton, Aug. 10, 1890, CD, Colon (Aspinwall): 14 (T 193/r 14); Herwig, *Germany in Venezuela*, 44–48.

23 Logan to Evarts, June 14, 1880, DD, CA: 16 (M 219/r 35); various correspondence in
    09.01, Nr. 52614, Das Kaiserliche Deutsche Konsulat in San José (Costa Rica), Bun-
    desarchiv, Potsdam; von Bergen to Bismarck, Jan. 27, 1885, 09.01, Nr. 52604, Bun-
    desarchiv, Potsdam; Lorenzo Monfúfar to German Foreign Minister, May 20, June 7,
    Aug. 13, 1880, B99-7-2-1, 4654/93690, Archivo General de Centroamérica, Guate-
    mala City, Guatemala.
24 B. E. von Bülow to von Bergen, Sept. 12, 1878, A.A. I C, Nr. 1, Central America, vol. 1,
    Bundesarchiv, Potsdam; Wehler, *Bismarck*, 39–111, 230–31, 423–45, 454–502.
25 von Bergen to B. E. von Bülow, Nov. 2, 1878, A.A. I C, Nr. 1, Central America, vol. 1,
    Bundesarchiv, Potsdam.
26 Hofmann to Chambers of Commerce and businessmen's associations, June 3, 1880,
    Rep. 120 C. XIII 16ª, Nr. 8, Bundesarchiv, Merseburg.
27 Justice Minister to Emperor, July 7, 1879, 2.2.1., Nr. 23571, Bundesarchiv, Merseburg;
    von Houwald, *Los Alemanes en Nicaragua*; Harmut Froeschle, *Die Deutschen in
    Lateinamerika: Schicksal und Leistung* (Tübingen, 1979), has a chapter on German
    social and cultural impact on each Central American country.
28 Evarts to Andrew D. White, Aug. 6, 1880, DI, Germany: 16 (M 77/r 67); Logan to
    Evarts, Oct. 14, 1880, Jan. 7 (enclosing Gallegos to Logan, Oct. 24, 1880), Feb. 1, 1881,
    DD, CA: 17 (M 219/r 37); Titus to Hunter, Sept. 20, 1881, CD, Guatemala: 4 (T 337/r
    4); von Bergen to Bismarck, Feb. 26, 1886, Abt. 1A, Amerika Generalia 5, vol. 3,
    PAAA; Leyden to Bismarck, Sept. 11, 1885, IA, Amerika Generalia 5, Band 2, PAAA;
    Wolfram von Rotenhan to Bismarck, July 16, 1885, Abt. 1A, Columbien 1, vol. 4,
    PAAA.
29 Logan to Evarts, April 14, 1879, May 14, 1880, DD, CA: 16 (M 219/r 35); Logan to
    Evarts, Jan. 9, 1881, DD, CA: 17 (M 219/r 37); Logan to Frederick Frelinghuysen,
    Feb. 10 and 13, 1882, DD, CA: 18 (M 219/r 38).
30 Logan to Evarts, April 14, 1879, May 14, 1880, DD, CA: 16 (M 219/r 35); Logan to
    Evarts, Jan. 9, 1881, DD, CA: 17 (M 219/r 37); Logan to Frelinghuysen, Feb. 10 and 13,
    1882, DD, CA: 18 (M 219/r 38).
31 The German-U.S. competition, rising distrust, and hostility is so well known that a
    footnote almost seems out of order. Consult Richard Dean Burns, ed., *Guide to
    American Foreign Relations since 1700* (Santa Barbara, 1982), chaps. 12, 13, and 14.
32 For insight into the Zelaya years in U.S.-Nicaraguan relations, see Bermann, *Under
    the Big Stick*, 123–50; R. L. Woodward, *Central America*, chap. 7; Benjamin Teplitz,
    "The Political and Economic Foundations of Modernization in Nicaragua: The Ad-
    ministration of José Santos Zelaya, 1893–1909" (Ph.D. diss., Howard University,
    1973); Jaime Biderman, "The Development of Capitalism in Nicaragua: A Political
    Economic History," *Latin American Perspectives* 10 (Winter 1983), 7–32; Emiliano
    Chamorro, *El Último Caudillo: Autobiografía* (Managua, 1983), 248.

5 *Conflicting U.S. and Central American
   Economic Priorities*

 1 LaFeber, *The New Empire*, esp. 102–21; Williams, *The Roots of the Modern Ameri-
    can Empire*; Wehler, *Der Aufstieg des amerikanischen Imperialismus*, 74–91.
 2 Williams, *The Contours of American History*, 225–343; Kolko, *Main Currents in
    Modern American History*; Wiebe, *The Search for Order, 1877–1920*.
 3 Curry, *Blueprint for Modern America*; Williams, *The Contours of American History*,
    225–343; Wehler, *Der Aufstieg des amerikanischen Imperialismus*, 74–91; John P.

Harrison, "Science and Politics: Origins and Objectives of Mid-Nineteenth Century Government Expeditions to Latin America," *Hispanic American Historical Review* 35 (May 1955), 175–202; Plesur, *America's Outward Thrust*, 22–23, 103–25.

4   Langley, *Struggle for the American Mediterranean*; Lowrie, "France, the United States, and the Lesseps Panama Canal." On U.S.–Central American relations, see LaFeber, *Inevitable Revolutions*, 31–34.

5   Davison, *The Presidency of Rutherford B. Hayes*, 198–99, and Kolko, *Main Currents in Modern American History*, describe the transformation of the U.S. economy during the last half of the nineteenth century; Lowrie, "France, the United States, and the Lesseps Panama Canal, 1879–1889."

6   Achille Viallate, "Les États-Unis et le Pan-Américanisme," *Revue des deux mondes* 51 (1909), 420–21; LaFeber, *The New Empire*, esp. 102–21; Hagan, *American Gunboat Diplomacy and the Old Navy*, 7–10, 188–92; Williams, *The Roots of the Modern American Empire*, 246–50, 293–316, 327–28; Wehler, *Der Aufstieg des amerikanischen Imperialismus*, 74–91; Jens Jessen, "Die ökonomische Grundlage der panamerikanischen Idee," *Schmollers Jahrbuch* 52 (1928), 79–111; Richard Carlyle Winchester, "James G. Blaine and the Ideology of American Expansionism" (Ph.D. diss., University of Rochester, 1966); Alice Felt Tyler, *The Foreign Policy of James G. Blaine* (Minneapolis, 1937); Thomas Karnes, "Pan-Americanism," in Alexander DeConde, ed., *Encyclopedia of American Foreign Policy* (3 vols.; New York, 1978), 2:730–41. J. Lloyd Mecham, *A Survey of United States–Latin American Relations* (Boston, 1965), 89–96, argued that Blaine's policy sought investment and market opportunities and presumed a broad range of common interests among New World states. Winchester has convincingly rejected the idea that Blaine sought investment opportunities. Becker, "American Manufacturers and Foreign Markets, 1870–1900," rejects the Williams-LaFeber thesis of a push for markets to absorb overproduction. He ignores, however, the relevant business–State Department correspondence, State Department internal correspondence, and records of conferences and fairs.

7   LaFeber, *The New Empire*, 1–61, 102–21; Wehler, *Der Aufstieg des amerikanischen Imperialismus*, 19–109; Plesur, *America's Outward Thrust*; Robert Beisner, *From the Old Diplomacy to the New, 1865–1900* (2nd ed.; Arlington Heights, Ill., 1986); Campbell, *The Transformation of American Foreign Relations, 1865–1900*.

8   Russell H. Bastert, "A New Approach to the Origins of Blaine's Pan American Policy," *Hispanic American Historical Review* 39 (Aug. 1959), 375–76, 412; Russell H. Bastert, "Diplomatic Reversal: Frelinghuysen's Opposition to Blaine's Pan American Policy in 1882," *Mississippi Valley Historical Review* 42 (March 1956), 662–71; Georg Herbert zu Münster to Bismarck, Dec. 21, 1881, Benert to Bismarck, Jan. 19, 1882, Vereinigte Staaten von Nord-Amerika 1, vol. 2, PAAA.

9   Ricaurte Soler, *Idea y cuestión nacional latinoamericana* (Mexico, 1980), 201–16; Williamson to Fish, Oct. 16, 1873, DD, CA: 4 (M 219/r 27).

10 Winchester, "Blaine and the Ideology of American Expansionism," 2–5, 38–39, 87, 110–14, 117, 137–43, 248–53; Bastert, "A New Approach to the Origins of Blaine's Pan American Policy," 375–76, 412; Vevier, "American Continentalism," 323–35.

11 Circular to U.S. diplomats accredited to independent American states, July 13, 1888, *FRUS, 1888*, pt. 2, 1658–59.

12 Riotte to Fish, Dec. 21, 1870, DD, Nic.: 11 (M 219/r 16); Francis Mairs Huntington Wilson, *Memoirs of an Ex-Diplomat* (Boston, 1945), 170–76.

13 MRE to Hinton Helper, Jan. 22, 1883, copiador 2, AMRE, Hond.; Cleto González

Víquez to John Arthur Lynch, July 8, 1885, MRE, libro copiador 1885, AN, CR; MRE to Helper, Sept. 17, 1885, MRE, libro copiador 1885–1905, AN, CR.

14 Joseph Smith, "The Latin American Trade Commission of 1884–85," *Inter-American Economic Affairs* 24 (Spring 1971), 3–10, 24; James Floyd Vivian, "The South American Commission to the Three Americas Movement: The Politics of Pan Americanism, 1884–1890" (Ph.D. diss., American University, 1971), 44–47.

15 Frelinghuysen to Sharpe, July 23, Nov. 8, 1884, DI, Special Missions: 3 (M 77/r 153); William E. Curtis to Sec. St., Oct. 17, 24, 29, Nov. 24, 1884, Despatches from the U.S. Commission to Central and South America: 1 (T 908/r 1).

16 John Schroeder to Hunter, Nov. 14, 25, Dec. 26, 1884, CD, San José: 3 (T 35/r 3).

17 Ibid.

18 Ibid.

19 Ibid.

20 Curtis to Sec. St., Feb. 21, 27, 1885, enclosing Castro's statement on mutual trade benefits, Desp. from the U.S. Commission to C. and So. Amer.: 1 (T 908/r 1); Smith, "Latin American Trade Commission," 13–14.

21 "Costa Rica—Fifth Report of the Commission to the Central and South American States," March 3, 1885, Curtis to Sec. St., Feb. 21, 27, 1885, Desp. from the U.S. Commission to C. and So. Amer.: 1 (T 908/r 1); J. P. H. Gastrell to Earl Granville, May 30, 1885, FO 15/220 (r 82), PRO.

22 Curtis to Sec. St., March 18, 1885, Curtis, "Abstract of the Report . . . upon the trade relations with the Republic of Guatemala . . . ," n. d., Desp. from the U.S. Commission to C. and So. Amer.: 1 (T 908/r 1); Smith, "Latin American Trade Commission," 14; Vivian, "The South American Commission," 107–9.

23 Thomas C. Reynolds to the President, June 3, 27, 1885, Desp. from the U.S. Commission to C. and So. Amer.: 1 (T 908/r 1); Vivian, "The South American Commission," 202–11.

24 Williams, *Contours of American History*; Semmel, *Imperialism and Social Reform*; Gallagher and Robinson, "The Imperialism of Free Trade," 1–15; Wehler, *Der Aufstieg des amerikanischen Imperialismus*; Resumen de la entrevista confidencial . . . , [March 11, 1889], MRE, caja 97, AN, CR.

25 D. W. Herring to George L. Rives, Nov. 25, 1888, CD, Teguc.: (T 352/r 2); Vivian, "The South American Commission," 353–55.

26 Pérez Zeledón to MRE, April 6, 1889, MRE, caja 97, AN, CR; LaFeber, *The New Empire*, 102–21; Wehler, *Der Aufstieg des amerikanischen Imperialismus*, 74–91.

27 Manuel Aragón to Ricardo Jiménez, Dec. 20, 1889, MRE, libro copiador 59, AN, CR.

28 McCormick, *China Market*; LaFeber, *The New Empire*, 62–101, 112–20, 136–49; Wehler, *Der Aufstieg des amerikanischen Imperialismus*, 24–91; Vevier, "American Continentalism," 323–35; van Alstyne, *The Rising American Empire*, 124–94; Thomas F. Bayard to Henry Hall, Feb. 1, 1887, DI, CA: (M 77/r 30).

29 Emmerich Arco-Valley to Bismarck, June 26, 1888, IA, Vereinigte Staaten von Nord-Amerika 20, Band 1, PAAA (copy of above and note dated Oct. 10, 1888 in III Hauptabteilung, Nr. 1111, Geheimes Staatsarchiv Preussischer Kulturbesitz, Berlin).

30 von Bergen to Bismarck, Aug. 3, 1888, IA, Mexiko 2, Band 2, PAAA; MAE to Ministère du Commerce, July 7, 1888, Commerce, F¹² 6543, Archive National, Paris.

31 Los Angeles Board of Trade to Blaine, Sept. 25, 1889, RG 43, Records of International Conferences, Commissions, and Expositions, entry 21, box 19, NA.

32 Correspondence from the National Board of Trade, Omaha Board of Trade, Chicago

Chamber of Commerce, Richmond Chamber of Commerce, American Short-Horn Breeders Association, New Haven Chamber of Commerce, Produce Exchange of Chicago, and Commercial Exchange of Philadelphia, Sept.–Nov. 1889, RG 43, entry 21, box 19, NA.

33 Walter T. Hagar and C. Ross Smith (Commercial Exchange of Philadelphia) to St. Dept., [1889], RG 43, entry 21, box 19, NA.

34 William Henry Trescott to Blaine, May 4, 1889, William Henry Trescott papers, University of South Carolina.

35 Trescott to Blaine, May 4, 1889, Trescott papers.

36 J. M. Muñoz to Curtis, "Report on Central American trade with the United States," Aug. 1889, RG 43, entry 18, box 19, NA.

37 Robert W. Rydell, *All the World's a Fair: Visions of Empire at American International Expositions, 1876–1916* (Chicago, 1984); Hardy, *The World's Industrial and Cotton Centennial Exposition*; Edwin F. Uhl to Luther F. McKinney, Sept. 7, 1894, DI, Col.: 18 (M 77/r 47); Clifford B. Casey, "The Creation and Development of the Pan American Union," *Hispanic American Historical Review* 13 (Nov. 1933), 437–56; Harold F. Peterson, *Diplomat of the Americas: A Biography of William I. Buchanan, 1852–1909* (Albany, 1977).

38 Aragón to MRE, Feb. 26, 1890, MRE, caja 99, AN, CR; Lanzing B. Mizner to Blaine, Dec. 2, 11, 22, 1890, DD, CA: 33 (M 219/r 53); R. L. Woodward, *Central America: A Nation Divided*, 154; LaFeber, *Inevitable Revolutions*, 33–34.

39 William Wharton to John T. Abbott, Sept. 16, 1891, DI, Col.: 18 (M 77/r 47); D. H. Hodgsdon to Thomas H. Hubbard, Feb. 1, 1908, Hubbard to A. D. Sheppard, Feb. 19, 1908, Pacific Improvement Company records, box 14, folder 1, William Huntington Library, San Marino, California; Robert Neal Seidel, "Progressive Pan Americanism: Development and United States Policy toward South America, 1906–1931" (Ph.D. diss., Cornell University, 1973).

40 Joaquín Bernardo Calvo to Pacheco, Jan. 25, 1898, MRE, caja 133, AN, CR; Aragón to Calvo, Feb. 16, 1898, MRE, libro copiador 176, AN, CR; Emile Joré to MAE, June 25, 1898, Correspondence politique to 1918, Costa Rica, Finances I, N. S. 3, AMAE, Paris.

41 John Blackburn to Curtis, Feb. 22, 1893, Curtis to Calvo, Feb. 23, 1893, MRE, caja 111, AN, CR.

42 "Propaganda americanista en España," and "El egoísmo Norte-americano," *La República*, Nov. 22, 1884, p. 1; Francis A. Stout to Daniel Ammen, April 19, 1887, Daniel Ammen papers, box 3, folder 12, University of California, Los Angeles; Frederick B. Pike, *Hispanismo, 1898–1936: Spanish Conservatives and Liberals and Their Relations with Spanish America* (Notre Dame, 1971); Alcide Ebray, "Une réconciliation: L'Espagne et l'Amérique Latine," *Revue des deux mondes* (Nov. 15, 1901), 427–53; Hans von Eyb to Bernhard von Bülow, March 22, 1901, R 2/1453, Bundesarchiv, Koblenz; Rafael Iglesias to president of the Hispanic-American Social and Economic Congress, Jan. 4, 1902, MRE, libro copiador 93, AN, CR.

6 *Morality and Political Purpose in Theodore Roosevelt's Actions in Panama in 1903*

1 Frederick W. Marks, III, "Morality as a Drive Wheel in the Diplomacy of Theodore Roosevelt," *Diplomatic History* 2 (Winter 1978), 43–62; Frederick W. Marks, *Velvet*

on Iron: The Diplomacy of Theodore Roosevelt (Lincoln, 1979); James F. Vivian, "The 'Taking' of the Panama Canal Zone: Myth and Reality," *Diplomatic History* 4 (Winter 1980), 95–100; Richard H. Collin, *Theodore Roosevelt's Caribbean: The Panama Canal, the Monroe Doctrine, and the Latin American Context* (Baton Rouge, 1990), 127–338; Robert A. Friedlander, "Reassessment of Roosevelt's Role in the Panamanian Revolution of 1903," *Western Political Quarterly* 14 (June 1961), 535–43; Theodore Roosevelt, *An Autobiography* (New York, 1929), 521–27; Theodore Roosevelt to Albert Shaw, Oct. 10, 1903, in Joseph B. Bishop, *Theodore Roosevelt and His Times* (2 vols.; New York, 1920), I:279.

2 Walter LaFeber, *The Panama Canal: The Crisis in Historical Perspective* (rev. ed.; New York, 1989), 29–57; McCullough, *The Path between the Seas*; Dana G. Munro, *Intervention and Dollar Diplomacy in the Caribbean, 1900–1921* (Princeton, 1964), 41, 59–60; Dwight Carroll Miner, *The Fight for the Panama Route* (New York, 1940), 143–45; Schoonover, "Imperialism in Middle America," 41–58; Thomas G. Dyer, *Theodore Roosevelt and the Idea of Race* (Baton Rouge, 1980), esp. 89–170; Richard H. Collin, *Theodore Roosevelt, Culture, Diplomacy, and Expansion: A New View of American Expansion* (Baton Rouge, 1985); William C. Widener, *Henry Cabot Lodge and the Search for an American Foreign Policy* (Berkeley, 1980). James M. Skinner describes the role of the French canal interests and the French government in *France and Panama: The Unknown Years, 1894–1908* (New York, 1989).

3 Roosevelt, *An Autobiography*, 521–27; Munro, *Intervention and Dollar Diplomacy*, 49–51, 56–57, 60; Philip C. Jessup, *Elihu Root* (2 vols.; New York, 1938), 1:402–5; Huntington Wilson, *Memoirs of an Ex-Diplomat*, 296–97; Michael H. Hunt, *Ideology and U.S. Foreign Policy* (New Haven, 1987), chap. 3; Wilfrid H. Callcott, *The Caribbean Policy of the United States, 1910–1920* (Baltimore, 1942), 150–57; Howard K. Beale, *Theodore Roosevelt and the Rise of America to World Power* (New York, 1956), 101–6; David H. Burton, *Theodore Roosevelt: Confident Imperialist* (Philadelphia, 1968), 102; William Harbaugh, *Power and Responsibility: The Life and Times of Theodore Roosevelt* (New York, 1961), 199–200.

4 Roosevelt, *An Autobiography*, 521–27; Munro, *Intervention and Dollar Diplomacy*, 49–51, 56–57, 60; Grunau to Auswärtiges Amt, July 29, 1903, Abt. IA, Columbien 5, vol. 1, PAAA. For strong condemnations of U.S. conduct, see Gordon Connell-Smith, *The United States and Latin America* (New York, 1974), 104–5; Alonso Aguilar, *Pan-Americanism from Monroe to the Present* (New York, 1965), 47–49.

5 Bunau-Varilla to José Marroquín, June 13, 1903, John Bigelow papers, box 24, Manuscript and Archives, New York Public Library.

6 Theodore Roosevelt, speech, April 2, 1903, Bigelow papers. Francis B. Loomis, "The position of the United States on the American continent—some phases of the Monroe Doctrine," *Annals of the American Academy of Political and Social Sciences* 22 (July 1903), 1–19, copy in Francis B. Loomis papers, reel 7, folder 44, Department of Special Collections, Stanford University. Phillip Darby, *Three Faces of Imperialism: British and American Approaches to Asia and Africa, 1870–1970* (New Haven, 1987), 142–224; Gérard Pierre-Charles, *El Caribe contemporáneo* (Mexico, 1981), 71–84.

7 Loomis to John Bassett Moore, Aug. 12, 1903, Moore, "Considerations on the present situation with respect to the canal treaty with Colombia," [August 14, 1903], John Bassett Moore papers, box 134, folder "Latin America–Panama Affair," LC; Moore, "1903," Moore papers, box 207, folder "Panama Canal," LC.

8   Moore, "Considerations on the present situation," Moore papers.

9   Ibid.

10 Miner, *The Fight for the Panama Route*, reproduces and discusses the Moore memorandum, 427–32, although not very critically, 341–45; Burton, *Roosevelt: Confident Imperialist*, 125–27; Miles P. DuVal, *Cadiz to Cathay: The Story of the Long Diplomatic Struggle for the Panama Canal* (Stanford, 1947), 259–68, 279–81. Only historians Miner and Burton have recognized the importance of Moore's August 1903 memorandum, but neither paid particular attention to later Moore memoranda and correspondence. Nor did Miner or Burton discuss the ties between Moore's ideas and the views of Loomis and Bunau-Varilla.

11 Bunau-Varilla to Moore, Oct. 3, 1903, Moore papers, box 134, folder "Latin America–Panama Affair," LC; Miner, *The Fight for the Panama Route*, 355–56, 361; McCullough, *The Path between the Seas*, 349–51, 359–60; Gustavo Adolfo Mellander, *The United States in Panamanian Politics* (Danville, Ill., 1971), 15–16.

12 Bunau-Varilla to Moore, Oct. 3, 1903, Moore papers.

13 John B. Moore, "1903," Moore papers, box 207, folder "Panama Canal," LC; Miner, *Fight for the Panama Route*, 356–60; McCullough, *Path between the Seas*, 349–60; Mellander, *The United States in Panamanian Politics*, 22.

14 Felix Ehrman to Hay, Nov. 3 (two telegrams), Nov. 6, 1903, Amador to Hay, Nov. 3, 1903, Loomis papers, reel 1; Bureau of Navigation to *Nashville*, Nov. 4, 1903, Loomis papers, reel 2.

15 Hay to Charlemagne Tower, Nov. 5, 20, 1903, DI, Germany: 21 (Microcopy 77/reel 72); Bunau-Varilla to de la Esprilla, Nov. 25, 1903, Bigelow papers, box 24.

16 Moore, "1903" and "Professor Moore on Panama," *New York Evening Post*, Nov. 11, 1903, Moore papers, box 207, folder "Panama Canal," LC; Roosevelt, *Autobiography*, 525–27; Miner, *Fight for the Panama Route*, 355–56, 359, 380; Jessup, *Elihu Root*, 1:404; Munro, *Intervention and Dollar Diplomacy*, 50; DuVal, *Cadiz to Cathay*, 255–340, esp. 279–321.

17 Moore, "1903" and "Professor Moore on Panama," *New York Evening Post*, Nov. 11, 1903, Moore papers.

18 Ibid.

19 Burton, *Roosevelt: Confident Imperialist*, 127; David H. Burton, *Theodore Roosevelt* (New York, 1972), 121; McCullough, *Path between the Seas*, 349–52, 359; Miner, *Fight for the Panama Route*, 356, 361; Friedlander, "Roosevelt's Role in the Panamanian Revolution," 536–40. Archibald Cary Coolidge, *The United States as a World Power* (New York, 1909), 276–79, speculated that the United States knew about the coming revolt, did nothing to interfere, and acted inappropriately toward a friendly nation.

20 Max Farrand to Frederick J. Turner, Jan. 29, 1913, and Turner's notes on Farrand's memorandum, Frederick J. Turner collection, box 19 (9), Huntington Library, San Marino, California. For the full text of the Turner-Farrand notes, see Thomas Schoonover, "Max Farrand's Memorandum on the U.S. Role in the Panamanian Revolution of 1903," *Diplomatic History* 12 (Fall 1988), 501–6.

21 Turner's notes on Farrand's memorandum, Turner collection, box 19 (9).

22 Ibid.

23 Ibid.

24 Ibid. See also John Major, "Who Wrote the Hay–Bunau-Varilla Convention?" *Diplomatic History* 8:2 (Spring 1984), 115–24.

25 Turner's notes on Farrand's memorandum, Turner collection, box 19 (9).

26 Ibid.

27 Frank Ninkovitch, "Theodore Roosevelt: Civilization as Ideology," *Diplomatic History* 10 (Summer 1986), 221–45; Beale, *Theodore Roosevelt and the Rise of America to World Power*, 101–9; Ali Mazrui, "From Social Darwinism to Current Theories of Modernization: A Tradition of Analysis," *World Politics* 21 (Oct. 1968), 69–83; David H. Burton, "Theodore Roosevelt: Confident Imperialist," *Review of Politics* 23 (April 1961), 358–63; David H. Burton, "Theodore Roosevelt's Social Darwinism and View on Imperialism," *Journal of the History of Ideas* 26 (Jan. 1965), 103–18; Walter LaFeber, *The American Age: United States Foreign Policy Abroad since 1750* (New York, 1989), 203–6, 211–17.

28 George E. Mowry, *The Era of Theodore Roosevelt and the Birth of Modern America* (New York, 1958), 112; Howard C. Hill, *Roosevelt and the Caribbean* (Chicago, 1927), 198, 211–13; Richard D. Challener, *Admirals, Generals, and American Foreign Policy, 1898–1914* (Princeton, 1973), 177, 406–7; Warren F. Kimball, *Mission, Money, and Manifest Destiny: U.S. Foreign Policy, 1901–1913* (St. Louis, 1979), 2–4; Marks, "Morality in the Diplomacy of Theodore Roosevelt," 43–62; Marks, *Velvet on Iron*.

29 Loomis to Moore, Moore papers, box 134, folder "Latin America–Panama Affair," LC; Memorandum, Loomis papers, reel 6, folder 34, "Panama Canal."

30 Loomis to Moore, Moore papers, box 134, folder "Latin America–Panama Affair," LC; Hay to Arthur M. Beaupre, Nov. 6, 11, 1903, DI, Colombia: 19 (Microcopy 77/reel 48); Memorandum, Loomis papers, reel 6, folder 34 "Panama Canal"; G. Wallace Chessman, *Theodore Roosevelt and the Politics of Power* (Boston, 1969), 99.

31 Loomis, "Some Phases of the Panama Question," Dec. 15, 1903, Loomis papers, reel 7, folder 44. The French government never gave any indication of the least desire to involve itself in isthmian affairs in opposition to U.S. policy. See Skinner, *France and Panama*.

32 Wiebe, *The Search for Order*, chap. 9; Hays, *The Response to Industrialism*, chap. 8; Williams, *The Tragedy of American Diplomacy*; Lloyd Gardner, "A Progressive Foreign Policy, 1900–1921," in William A. Williams, ed., *From Colony to Empire: Essays in the History of American Foreign Traditions* (New York, 1972), 203–51; William Leuchtenberg, "The Progressive Movement and American Foreign Policy, 1898–1916," *Mississippi Valley Historical Review* 39 (1952), 453–504; Mazrui, "From Social Darwinism to Modernization."

7 *The World Economic Crisis, Racism, and U.S.*
Relations to Central America, 1893–1910

1 Rosenberg, *Grosse Depression und Bismarckzeit*; Wehler, *Der Aufstieg des amerikanischen Imperialismus*, 24–73; McCormick, *The China Market*, 17–52; Williams, *The Contours of American History*; Lester Langley, *The United States and the Caribbean in the Twentieth Century* (Athens, Ga., 1980), 3–62.

2 I find the structural-functional approach to immigration theory is more convincing and has more explanatory power, although I realize that equilibrium theory supplies a major contrary approach. See Charles H. Wood, "Equilibrium and Historical-Structural Perspectives on Migration," *International Migration Review* 16 (Summer 1982), 298–319; Robert L. Bach and Lisa A. Schraml, "Migration, Crisis, and Theoretical Conflict," *International Migration Review* 16 (Summer 1982), 320–41; Peter

Marschalck, *Bevölkerungsgeschichte Deutschlands im 19. und 20. Jahrhundert* (Frankfurt, 1984), 7–52; Magnus Mörner, *Adventurers and Proletarians: The Story of Migrants in Latin America* (Pittsburgh, 1985), 124–29; Alejandro Portes and John Walton, *Labor, Class, and the International System* (New York, 1981), 7–34, 41–49; Giovanni Arrighi, "Marxist Century–American Century: The Making and Remaking of the World Labor Movement," in Amir, Arrighi, Frank, and Wallerstein, *Transforming the Revolution*, 54–95.

3   Semmel, *Imperialism and Social Reform*; McCormick, *The China Market*, 17–52; Wehler, *Der Aufstieg des amerikanischen Imperialismus*, 37–73.

4   R. L. Woodward, *Central America*, chap. 7; Semmel, *Imperialism and Social Reform*.

5   John Hope Franklin, *From Slavery to Freedom* (5th ed.; New York, 1980), 295–308; Willard B. Gatewood, *Black Americans and the White Man's Burden, 1898–1903* (Urbana, 1975), 6–21, 322–25; Philip W. Kennedy, "The Racial Overtones of Imperialism as a Campaign Issue, 1900," *Mid-America* 48 (July 1966), 196–205; Joel Williamson, *The Crucible of Race: Black-White Relations in the American South since Emancipation* (New York, 1984), ix–xii, 50–61, 511–13; Seth M. Scheiner, "President Theodore Roosevelt and the Negro, 1901–1908," *Journal of Negro History* 47 (July 1962), 169–82.

6   Mörner, *Adventurers and Proletarians*, 26–30, 35–41, 108–10; Hobart A. Spalding, Jr., *Organized Labor in Latin America* (New York, 1977), xii–xv, 1–15; Michael L. Conniff, *Black Labor on a White Canal: Panama, 1904–1981* (Pittsburgh, 1985), 16–18; Eric R. Wolf, *Europe and the People without History* (Berkeley, 1982), 361–83; Mazrui, "From Social Darwinism to Current Theories of Modernization"; Philip W. Kennedy, "Race and American Expansion in Cuba and Puerto Rico, 1895–1905," *Journal of Black Studies* 1 (March 1971), 306–15; LaFeber, *Inevitable Revolutions*, 31–49; R. L. Woodward, *Central America: A Nation Divided*, 177–202; Kolko, *Main Currents of Modern American History*, 1–33, 67–99; Williams, *The Tragedy of American Diplomacy*, 1–89.

7   Wiebe, *The Search for Order, 1877–1921*; Kolko, *Main Currents of Modern American History*; Gabriel Kolko, *Triumph of Conservatism: A Reinterpretation of American History, 1900–1916* (Chicago, 1963); Hays, *The Response to Industrialism*.

8   On the rejection of blacks in the southern labor force and their plight at the turn of the century, see C. Vann Woodward, *The Strange Career of Jim Crow* (New York, 1957); C. Vann Woodward, *The Burden of Southern History* (New York, 1961), 154–63; C. Vann Woodward, *American Counterpoint: Slavery and Racism in the North-South Dialogue* (Boston, 1976), 212–33, 256–59; C. Vann Woodward, *Origins of the New South, 1877–1913* (Baton Rouge, 1971), 228–34, 266–67, 360–65; Franklin, *From Slavery to Freedom*, 282–87; Williamson, *The Crucible of Race*, ix–xii, 59–69, 511–13; Lerone Bennett, Jr., *The Shaping of Black America* (Chicago, 1975), 248–75; Benjamin Brawley, *A Social History of the American Negro* (New York, 1970), 320–25; August Meier and Eliott Rudwick, *From Plantation to Ghetto* (New York, 1970), 189–93; Ray Marshall, "The Negro in Southern Unions," in Julius Jacobson, ed., *The Negro and the American Labor Movement* (Garden City, 1968), 128–54; Hair, *Bourbonism and Agrarian Protest*, 170–97, 222–23, 245–46; Dale Somers, "Black and White in New Orleans: A Study of Urban Race Relations, 1865–1900," *Journal of Southern History* 40 (Feb. 1974), 35–42.

9   Conniff, *Black Labor on a White Canal*, 6–8, 22, 25, 34–35; Lancelot S. Lewis, *The West Indian in Panama: Black Labor in Panama, 1850–1914* (Washington, D.C.,

1980), 43; Nell Irvin Painter, *Exodusters: Black Migration to Kansas after Recon-struction* (New York, 1977), 3–16, 256–61; J. Fred Rippy, "A Negro Colonization Project in Mexico, 1895," *Journal of Negro History* 6 (Jan. 1921), 66–73.

10 Sands to Sec. St., Oct. 16, 1909, Jan. 3, 1910, Record Group 84, Post Records, American Legation, Guatemala, Despatches 1909–10, National Archives, hereafter AmLeg. Guat., Desp. 1909–10; Knox to George W. Young, Jr., Jan. 22, 1910, Knox to J. W. Seligman and Company, Feb. 24, 1910 (same to Bradley W. Palmer, to Speyer, and to Windsor Trust Company), Palmer to Knox, Nov. 16, 1909, AmLeg. Guat., Instr. 1909–10; R. L. Woodward, *Central America,* chap. 7; LaFeber, *Inevitable Revolutions,* chap. 1; Handy, *Gift of the Devil,* 60–75; United Nations, *El financiamiento externo de América Latina* (New York: United Nations, 1964).

11 R. L. Woodward, *Central America,* 149–202; Cardoso and Pérez Brignoli, *Centro América y la economía occidental,* 199–310; LaFeber, *Inevitable Revolutions,* 34–39; Castellanos Chambranes, *El imperialismo alemán en Guatemala;* Schoonover, "Germany in Central America, 1820s to 1929: An Overview," 33–59; Schoonover, "Imperialism in Middle America," 44–49; Schoonover, "Metropole Rivalry in Central America, 1820s to 1930," 21–46.

12 R. L. Woodward, *Central America,* 153–66, 175–76, 186–94; Carol A. Smith, *Labor and International Capital in the Making of a Peripheral Social Formation: Economic Transformation of Guatemala, 1850–1980* (Washington, D.C., 1984); David McCreery, *Development and the State in Reforma Guatemala, 1871–1885* (Athens, Ohio, 1983); David McCreery, "Debt Servitude in Rural Guatemala, 1876–1936," *Hispanic American Historical Review* 63 (Nov. 1983), 735–59, esp. 750–53; Handy, *Gift of the Devil,* 75–82; Christopher Lasch, "The Anti-imperialists, the Philippines, and the Inequality of Man," *Journal of Southern History* 24 (Aug. 1958), 319–31; Beale, *Theodore Roosevelt and the Rise of America to World Power,* 41–47; Rubin Francis Weston, *Racism in U.S. Imperialism* (Columbia, S.C., 1972), 7–30; David Healy, *U.S. Expansion: The Imperialist Urge in the 1890s* (Madison, 1970), 39–41, 240–47; James P. Shenton, "Imperialism and Racism," in Donald Sheehan and Harold C. Syrett, eds., *Essays in American Historiography: Papers Presented in Honor of Allan Nevins* (New York, 1960), 231–50; Poultney Bigelow to Sec. of Political Science Association, Dec. 27, 1905, Paul S. Reinsch papers, box 1, Wisconsin State Historical Society, Madison. El Salvador permitted René Keilhauer to import railroad laborers, but not Asiatics or blacks. See Delmer G. Ross, *Visionaries and Swindlers* (Mobile, 1975), 108.

13 Gardner, "A Progressive Foreign Policy, 1900–1921," 203–51; Wiebe, *The Search for Order,* esp. chap. 9; Hays, *Response to Industrialism,* esp. chap. 8; Jerry Israel, *Progressivism and the Open Door: America and China, 1905–1921* (Pittsburgh, 1971); Hans-Jürgen Schröder, "Ökonomische Aspekte der amerikanischen Aussen-politik, 1900–1923," *Neue Politische Literatur* (July–Sept. 1972), 298–321; William E. Gibbs, "James Weldon Johnson: A Black Perspective on 'Big Stick' Diplomacy," *Diplomatic History* 8 (Fall 1984), 329–34; Bennett H. Wall, Joe Gray Taylor, et al., *Louisiana: A History* (Arlington Heights, Ill., 1984), 228–38.

14 Fitz Henry Warren to Fish, May 30, 1869, DD, CA (Guat.): 5 (M 219/r 8); D. W. Herring to James D. Porter, Oct. 14, 1886, CD, Tegucigalpa: 1 (T 352/r 1); Emile Joré to MAE, March 27, 1904, Correspondence politique to 1918, Costa Rica, Travaux publiques, N. S. 5, AMAE, Paris; Lester James Schmid, "The Role of Migratory Labor in the Economic Development of Guatemala" (Ph.D. diss., University of Wisconsin,

1967), 64–69. On the early impact of racial bias upon U.S. relations with Latin America, see John Johnson, "The Racial Composition of Latin American Port Cities at Independence as Seen by Foreign Travelers," *Jahrbuch für Geschichte von Staat Wirtschaft und Gesellschaft Lateinamerikas* 23 (1986), 247–66; Schoonover, "Misconstrued Mission"; R. L. Woodward, *Central America,* 129–30, 146–48, 156–65; Handy, *Gift of the Devil,* 65–75.

15 Plesur, *America's Outward Thrust,* 3–34, 157–81; Williams, *The Roots of the Modern American Empire;* LaFeber, *The New Empire.*

16 Leslie Combs to Hay, March 25, 1903, DD, CA: 47 (M 219/r 67); Combs to Hay, Oct. 25, 1904, attached note W. L. Penfield to Diplomatic Bureau, Nov. 25, 1904, DD, CA: 51 (M 219/r 70).

17 Combs to Hay, June 26, 1905, DD, CA: 51 (M 219/r 70).

18 Combs to Hay, March 25, 1903, DD, CA: 47 (M 219/r 67); Combs to Hay, Oct. 25, 1904, attached note Penfield to Diplomatic Bureau, Nov. 25, 1904, DD, CA: 51 (M 219/r 70); Beck, "American Policy in Guatemala, 1839–1900," 84–86.

19 William F. Sands to Robert Bacon, Oct. 28, 1907, AmLeg., Guat., Desp. 1907–08.

20 William Heimké to Philander Knox, April 6, 1909, AmLeg. Guat., Desp. 1909, pt. 2.

21 Sands to Elihu Root, Nov. 8, 1907, AmLeg. Guat., Desp. 1907–08; William Franklin Sands, *Our Jungle Diplomacy* (Chapel Hill, 1944), 110, 113.

22 Wiebe, *The Search for Order,* 224–255; Leuchtenberg, "The Progressive Movement and American Foreign Policy"; Gerald W. Markowitz, "Progressives and Imperialism: A Return to First Principles," *Historian* 37 (1975), 257–75; Gardner, "A Progressive Foreign Policy, 1900–1921," 203–51.

23 Burton, "Theodore Roosevelt: Confident Imperialist," 360–77; Walter LaFeber, "The Constitution and United States Foreign Policy: An Interpretation," *Journal of American History* 74 (Dec. 1987), 705; Harbaugh, *Power and Responsibility,* 140–41; Beale, *Theodore Roosevelt,* 41–47, 74–81, 348–49; Mowry, *The Era of Theodore Roosevelt and the Birth of Modern America,* 92–94; LaFeber, *The American Age,* 203–13.

24 Stanford A. Mosk, "The Coffee Economy of Guatemala, 1850–1918: Development and Signs of Instability," *Interamerican Economic Affairs* 9 (Winter 1955), 6–20; Handy, *Gift of the Devil,* 57–75; Julio Castellanos Chambranes, *Coffee and Peasants in Guatemala* (South Woodstock, Vt., 1985); Wilson, *The Education of a Diplomat,* 36–37; General Charles Mangin to MAE, July 20, 1921, Amérique 1918–40, Centrale Amérique, num. 21, AMAE, Paris (also in 7N3378, Mission Mangin, dossier 3, Archive de l'armée de la terre, Paris).

25 Sands to Root, Nov. 21, 1907, RG 84, AmLeg. Guat., Desp. 1907–08; Benjamin Kidd, *The Control of the Tropics* (New York, 1898), 38–45, 72–77, offers a subtle description of the racial inferiority of Central American societies; Alfred P. Schultz, *Race or Mongrel* (Boston, 1908), 152, 340–43, 350–51, offers a callous, blunt description of Central American racial inferiority. Beck, "American Policy in Guatemala," 86–90, described only the Shine and Milliken cases, which he considered minor matters.

26 Sands to Root, April 3, 1906, DD, CA: 52 (M 219/r 71); Combs to Root, May 1, 1906, DD, CA: 53 (M 219/r 72); James Weldon Johnson, *Along This Way: The Autobiography of James Weldon Johnson* (New York, 1943), 257–60, 267, 270; Gibbs, "James Weldon Johnson," 330, 333–34, 347; "Twenty-one Years in Central America," *Central American Bulletin* 18:1 (Jan. 15, 1912), 7–13. An examination of New Orleans Police Records from about 1873 to 1915, including the Colored Index, 1900–1915, located in the New Orleans Public Library, produced no indication that the thirteen

blacks involved in diplomatic incidents in Guatemala had ever had trouble in New Orleans.

27 Sands to Root, April 3, 1906, DD, CA: 52 (M 219/r 71); Combs to Root, May 1, 1906, DD, CA: 53 (M 219/r 72).

28 Sands, *Our Jungle Diplomacy*, 99–101, 108–12.

29 Sands to Root, Oct. 14, 21, 29, Nov. 14, 14, 20, Dec. 6, 18, 21, 1907, Jan. 2, Feb. 13, 1908, AmLeg. Guat., Desp. 1907–08; Sands to Sec. St., March 27, 1910, enclosing affidavit of Monroe Williams, Oct. 9, 1907, AmLeg. Guat., Desp. Oct. 1909–March 1910.

30 Sands to Root, Oct. 14, 21, 29, Nov. 14, 14, 20, Dec. 6, 18, 21, 1907, Jan. 2, Feb. 13, 1908, AmLeg. Guat., Desp. 1907–08; Root to Sands, Oct. 26, 1907, enclosing William P. Kent to Asst. Sec. of State, Oct. 2, 1907, Simon Shine to Theodore Roosevelt, Sept. 23, 1907, AmLeg. Guat., Instructions, 1907–08. A copy of the Shine to Roosevelt letter was published in the *Literary Digest* 37 (June 12, 1909), 1000.

31 Sands to Root, Jan. 2, Feb. 13, 1908, AmLeg. Guat., Desp. 1907–08.

32 Sands, *Our Jungle Diplomacy*, 99–101, 108–12; Sands to Root, Jan. 13, Feb. 13, 1908, AmLeg. Guat., Desp. 1907–08; affidavit of Monroe Williams, Oct. 9, 1907, AmLeg. Guat., Desp. Oct. 1909–March 1910.

33 Ibid.

34 Sands, *Our Jungle Diplomacy*, 99–101, 108–12; Sands to Root, Nov. 20, 1907, Jan. 2, 10, Feb. 13, 1908, AmLeg. Guat., Desp. 1907–08; Heimké to Knox, June 17, 1909, AmLeg. Guat., Desp. 1909, pt. 2; "Our Citizens Mistreated in Central America," 999–1000; Root to Sands, Jan. 20, March 17, 1908, AmLeg. Guat., Instr. 1907–1908.

35 Evans to Edward Reed, May 20, 1908, V. A. Knight to Reed, June 7, 1908, William Owen to Heimké, June 20, 1908, Heimké to Root, Sept. 30, 1908, AmLeg. Guat., Desp. July–Dec. 1908; Heimké to Knox, Sept. 21, 1909, AmLeg. Guat., Desp. 1909, pt. 2; Sands to Sec. of State, Dec. 1, 1909, Jan. 6, March 1, 1910, AmLeg. Guat., Desp. Oct. 1909–March 1910; Alvey A. Adee to Heimké, Dec. 7, 1908, AmLeg. Guat., Instr. March–Dec. 1908; Francis Huntington Wilson to Sands, Oct. 20, 1909, AmLeg. Guat., Instr. 1909–10.

36 Sands to Sec. of State, Dec. 1, 1909, Jan. 6, March 1, 1910, AmLeg. Guat., Desp. Oct. 1909–March 1910; Adee to Heimké, Dec. 7, 1908, AmLeg. Guat., Instr. March–Dec. 1908; Huntington Wilson to Sands, Oct. 20, 1909, AmLeg. Guat., Instr. 1909–10.

37 Heimké to Knox, March 30, June 17, July 6, Sept. 21, 1909, AmLeg. Guat., Desp. 1909, pt. 2; Sands to Sec. of State, Jan. 6, 13, March 1, 10, 16, 1910, AmLeg. Guat., Desp. Oct. 1909–March 1910.

38 Sands to Sec. of State, Jan. 6, 13, March 1, 10, 16, 1910, AmLeg. Guat., Desp. Oct. 1909–March 1910; Knox to Heimké, June 30, 1909, Huntington Wilson to Heimké, May 13, Aug. 6, 1909, AmLeg. Guat., Instr. 1909.

39 George Davis to William Kent, Jan. 6, 1909, enclosed with Heimké to Root, Jan. 13, 1909, Heimké to Guillermo Aguirre, April 22, 1909, Heimké to Knox, July 20, Aug. 23, 1909, AmLeg. Guat., Desp. 1909, pt. 2; Bacon to Heimké, Feb. 24, 1909, AmLeg. Guat., Instr. 1909.

40 St. Dept. to Sands, Dec. 14, 1909, Monroe Williams to William H. Taft, Nov. 17, 1909, Williams to Philander Knox, Dec. 14, 1909, AmLeg. Guat., Instr. Oct. 1909–March 1910; "Our Citizens Mistreated in Central America," 1000; Sands to Sec. St., March 27, 1910, AmLeg. Guat., Desp. Oct. 1909–March 1910.

41 Sands to Sec. St., April 20, June 14, 1910, AmLeg. Guat., Desp. 1910, vol. 2.

42   Sands to Sec. St., April 20, 28, 1910, AmLeg. Guat., Desp. 1910, vol. 2; Sands to Sec.
     St., July 2, Sept. 21, 1910, AmLeg. Guat., Desp. 1910, vol. 3; Huntington Wilson to
     Sands, May 6, Sept. 1, 1910, AmLeg. Guat., Instr. Oct. 1909–March 1910; Adee to
     R. S. Reynolds Hitt, Nov. 9, 1910, AmLeg. Guat., Instr. Oct. 1910–Jan. 1911.

43   Sands to Manuel Estrada Cabrera, April 1, 13, 1910, Estrada Cabrera to Sands, April 4,
     1910, Sands to Sec. St., June 14, 23, 1910, enclosing Aguirre to Sands, June 13, 1910,
     Sands to Aguirre, June 17, 1910, AmLeg. Guat., Desp. 1910, vol. 2; Sands to Knox,
     July 27, Sept. 21, 24, 1910, AmLeg. Guat., Desp. 1910, vol. 3; Adee to Reynolds Hitt,
     Nov. 9, 1910, AmLeg. Guat., Instr. Oct. 1910–Jan. 1911; Albert Antoine Revelli to
     MAE, Oct. 31, 1921, F³⁰ 1956: Guatemala, Archive du ministère de l'économie et des
     finances, Paris.

44   William Merry to Castro Quesada, Aug. 4, 1910, MRE, caja 197, AN, CR; Beck,
     "American Policy in Guatemala," 73–80; George W. Crichfield, *American Suprem-
     acy: The Rise and Progress of the Latin American Republics and Their Relations to
     the United States* (2 vols.; New York, 1908), 2:12–13.

*8   An Isthmian Canal and the U.S. Overthrow
of Nicaraguan President José Santos Zelaya*

 1   On U.S.-Nicaraguan relations, see Bermann, *Under the Big Stick;* Richard L. Millett,
     Guardians of the Dynasty (Maryknoll, N.Y., 1977), 20–24; Richard L. Millett, "His-
     torical Setting," in James D. Rudolph, ed., *Nicaragua: A Country Study* (Washington,
     D.C., 1982), 15–19; LaFeber, *Inevitable Revolutions,* esp. 34–39; William Roger
     Adams, "Strategy, Diplomacy, and Isthmian Canal Security, 1880–1917" (Ph.D. diss.,
     Florida State University, 1974), 251–52, 257–60.

 2   Cardoso and Pérez Brignoli, *Centro América y la economía occidental,* 181–92, 205–
     8, 275–78; Woodward, *Central America,* 157–202. For the State Department position
     on Zelaya, see Isaac Joslin Cox, *Nicaragua and the United States, 1909–1927* (Bos-
     ton, 1927), 705–7; U.S. Department of State, *A Brief History of the Relations be-
     tween the United States and Nicaragua 1909–1928* (Washington, D.C., 1928), 3–5;
     U.S. Department of State, *The United States and Nicaragua: A Survey of the Rela-
     tions from 1909 to 1932* (Washington, D.C., 1932), 6–9; Huntington Wilson, *Mem-
     oirs of an Ex-Diplomat,* 209–10; Jessup, *Elihu Root,* 1:507–11; Munro, *Intervention
     and Dollar Diplomacy in the Caribbean, 1900–1921,* 140; "Zelaya: The Menace of
     Central America," *Review of Reviews* 37 (June 1908), 496–97. For refutation of the
     U.S. position, see Charles L. Stansifer, "José Santos Zelaya: A New Look at Nic-
     aragua's 'Liberal' Dictator," *Revista/Review Interamericana* 7 (Fall 1977), 469–71;
     José Mata Gavida, *Anotaciones de historia pátria centroamericana* (2nd ed.; Guate-
     mala, 1969), 365; Manuel Vidal, *Nociones de historia de Centro América* (8th ed.;
     San Salvador, 1969), 330–32; *José Santos Zelaya: President of Nicaragua* (New York,
     1906); José Santos Zelaya, *La revolución de Nicaragua y los Estados Unidos* (Madrid,
     [1910]); José Santos Zelaya, *Refutation of the Statements of President Taft* (Paris,
     [1911]). On Estrada Cabrera, see Sands to Sec. St., Jan. 3, 1910, AmLeg. Guat., Desp.
     1909–1910; Pablo de Benito to MAE, Oct. 24, 1910, H1609, AMAE, Madrid; Sands,
     Our Jungle Diplomacy, 72, 83, 85–87; Floyd Cramer, *Our Neighbor Nicaragua* (New
     York, 1929), 130–35; Rafael Arévalo Martínez, *¡Ecce Pericles!* (San José, 1983). See
     also the novel of Nobel Prize winner Miguel Angel Asturias, *El Señor Presidente.*

 3   Williams, *The Tragedy of American Foreign Policy,* chap. 1; McCormick, *The China*

Market, 105–6; Charles E. Frazier, "The Dawn of Nationalism and Its Consequences in Nicaragua" (Ph.D. diss., University of Texas, 1958), 27–28. On compradors, see Dale L. Johnson, "Dependence and the International System," and "On Oppressed Classes," in James D. Cockcroft, Andre Gunder Frank, and Dale L. Johnson, eds., *Dependence and Underdevelopment: Latin America's Political Economy* (Garden City, 1972). On free trade imperialism, John Gallagher and Ronald Robinson, "The Imperialism of Free Trade," *Economic History Review*, 2nd series, 6 (1953), 1–15. On world system theory, Braudel, *Capitalism and Material Life*; Wallerstein, *The Modern World System*.

4 *José Santos Zelaya: President of Nicaragua*, 5–18; Adán Selva, *Lodo y ceniza de una política que ha podrido las raíces de la nacionalidad nicaragüense* (Managua, 1960), 48–49; Gregorio Selser, *Nicaragua de Walker a Somoza* (Mexico, 1984), 82.

5 Teplitz, "The Political and Economic Foundations of Modernization in Nicaragua, 393, 401–3, 413–20; Frazier, "Nationalism in Nicaragua," 24–25; Whitney T. Perkins, *Constraints of Empire: The United States and Caribbean Intervention* (Westport, 1981), 22; Jaime Biderman, "The Development of Capitalism in Nicaragua: A Political Economic History," *Latin American Perspectives* 10 (Winter 1983), 10–12.

6 Frazier, "Nationalism in Nicaragua," 11–15, 24–28; Cramer, *Our Neighbor Nicaragua*, 130–35.

7 Chamorro, *El último caudillo: Autobiografía*, 43–44, 73–74; Carlos Cuadra Pasos, *Obras* (2 vols.; Managua, 1976), 1:217, 2:277; José Joaquín Morales, *De la historia de Nicaragua de 1889–1913* (Granada, Nicaragua, 1963), 52, 57–58, 63, 67–68, 74, 99–178, 231; Teplitz, "Modernization in Nicaragua," 417; Carlos Selva, *Un poco de historia* (Guatemala, 1948), 28, 58–59, 146–51.

8 Sands, *Our Jungle Diplomacy*, 79; Frazier, "Nationalism in Nicaragua," 11–15, 24–28; Challener, *Admirals, Generals, and American Foreign Policy, 1898–1914*, 72–73, 289–99; Stansifer, "José Santos Zelaya," 468–85; Richard V. Salisbury, *Costa Rica y el istmo, 1900–1934* (San José, 1984), 16–18, 27, 73–76, 109; Francisco Gamboa G., *Costa Rica: Ensayo histórico* (San José, 1971), 68–75.

9 A. Selva, *Lodo y ceniza*, 48–49; Pedro J. Cuadra Chamorro, *Motivos sobre el Tratado Chamorro-Bryan* (Managua, 1950), 6; Cardoso, "Central America: The Liberal Era," 5:222, 225.

10 Van Alstyne, *The Rising American Empire*, 147–94; William L. Neumann, *America Encounters Japan: From Perry to MacArthur* (Baltimore, 1963), 107–34; Selser, *Nicaragua de Walker a Somoza*, 75–79, 87; Claribel Alegría and D. J. Flakoll, *Nicaragua: La revolución sandinista* (Mexico, 1982), 29–31; Cuadra Chamorro, *Motivos sobre el Tratado Chamorro-Bryan*, 23; A. Selva, *Lodo y ceniza*, 48–49; Schoonover, "Metropole Rivalry in Central America, 1820s–1930," 21–46; Schoonover, "Imperialism in Middle America," 41–58; Langley, *The United States and the Caribbean in the Twentieth Century*, 46–52; Lester Langley, *The Banana Wars: An Inner History of American Empire* (Lexington, Ky., 1983), 55–61.

11 Williams, *The Tragedy of American Diplomacy*; Wiebe, *A Search for Order*, chap. 9; Gardner, "A Progressive Foreign Policy," 203–51; Leuchtenberg, "The Progressive Movement and American Foreign Policy," 483–504; Markowitz, "Progressivism and Imperialism: A Return to First Principles," 257–75; Salvatore Prisco III, *John Barrett, Progressive Era Diplomat: A Study of a Commercial Expansionist, 1887–1920* (University, Ala., 1973); Sands, *Our Jungle Diplomacy*, 106–7.

12 "Nicaraguan Troubles," *San Francisco Chronicle*, Feb. 28, 1896, p. 6; Lewis Baker to

Walter Gresham, May 25, 1894, DD, CA: 58 (M 219/r 78); William Sorsby to William R. Day, May 5, 1898, Sorsby to John B. Moore, June 13, 1898, CD, San Juan del Norte: 15 (T 348/r 15); memorandum of Luis F. Corea conversation with Asst. Sec. of State, May 25, 1898, National Archives, Record Group 59, Notes from Nic. Leg.: 3 (T 797/r 3); Rudolph Wiesike to Day, Feb. 4, 1898, CD, Managua: 4 (T 634/r 4); William Merry to Day, May 9, 1898, DD, CA: 63 (M 219/r 83); Jules Cambon to Theophile Delcasse, April 13, 1900, Correspondence politique à 1918, Amérique centrale I, Nouveau série, AMAE, Paris, hereafter CP 1918, Amér. cent. I, N. S. 1, AMAE, Paris; LaFeber, *The New Empire*, 219–28; Wehler, *Der Aufstieg des amerikanischen Imperialismus*, 143–54; David Healy, "A Hinterland in Search of a Metropolis: The Mosquito Coast, 1894–1910," *International History Review* 3 (Jan. 1981), 20–43; Lawrence A. Clayton, "The Nicaraguan Canal in the Nineteenth Century: Prelude to American Empire in the Caribbean," *Journal of Latin American Studies* 19 (Nov. 1987), 323–52; Craig Dozier, *Nicaragua's Mosquito Coast: The Years of British and American Presence* (University, Ala., 1985), 141–59; John Fielding, "La diplomacía norteamericana y la reincorporación de la Mosquitia," *Boletín nicaragüense de bibliografía y documentación* 26 (Nov.–Dec. 1978), 15–23; Rising Lake Morrow, "A Conflict between the Commercial Interests of the United States and Its Foreign Policy," *Hispanic American Historical Review* 10 (Feb. 1930), 2–13.

13   Sorsby to Asst. Sec. St., April 13, 1899, CD, San Juan del Norte: 16 (T 348/r 16); Chester Donaldson to David J. Hill, Feb. 15, 1899, CD, Teguc.: 6 (T 352/r 6); Sorsby to Hill, June 30, 1899, CD, San Juan del Norte: 17 (T 348/r 17); Hay to Merry, June 3, 1899, DI, CA: 21 (M 77/r 33); Edward P. Alexander to wife, April 23, July 13, 1899, Hay to Alexander, April 5, June 25, 1900, Edward P. Alexander papers, box 3, folder 46, Southern Historical Collection, University of North Carolina; Sorsby to Thomas W. Cridler, April 11, 1900, CD, San Juan del Norte: 18 (T 348/r 18); Lloyd Gardner, Walter LaFeber, Thomas J. McCormick, *Creation of the American Empire: U.S. Diplomatic History* (Chicago, 1973), 281–82.

14   "No Deal with Japan," *New York Herald*, Sept. 3, 1897, clipping in RM 5/vol. 5425, Bundesarchiv, Militärarchiv, Freiburg, Germany; Baker to Sherman, Sept. 6, 1897, DD, CA: 62 (M 219/r 82); Baker to Sherman, Oct. 14, 1897, Merry to Sherman, Nov. 1, 1897, DD, CA: 63 (M 219/r 83); Hay to Merry, Aug. 23, 1901, DI, CA: 22 (M 77/r 34); Clayton, "The Nicaragua Canal in the Nineteenth Century," 323–52.

15   Calvo to Pacheco, July 31, Nov. 11, 1902, MRE, caja 154, AN, CR; LaFeber, *The Panama Canal*; Schoonover, "Max Farrand's Memorandum," 501–6.

16   Merry to Hay, Oct. 25, 1903, DD, CA: 72 (M 219/r 92); Paul Schieps, "United States Commercial Pressures for a Nicaragua Canal in the 1890s," *The Americas* 20 (April 1964), 333–58; Dozier, *Nicaragua's Mosquito Shore*, 172–76, 181; A. L. M. Gottschalk to Hill, July 7, 1903, CD, San Juan del Norte: 20 (T 348/r 20).

17   Albert Beveridge to Root, Nov. 30, 1908, AmLeg. Nic., Inst. 1908–09; Altamirano to Nic. Leg., Aug. 12, 1905, memorandum of interview, Aug. 31, 1905, Notes from Nic. Leg.: 4 (T 797/r 4); Hans Ernst Schlieben to B. von Bülow, April 24, 1903, 09.01, Nr. 12493, Bundesarchiv (former Deutsches Zentralarchiv), Potsdam, Germany; William Penn Henley to Loomis, March 18, 1904, CD, Cape Gracias a Dios: 1 (T 538/r 1); Merry to Hay, Sept. 30, Oct. 28, 1904, DD, CA: 72 (M 219/r 92); Stansifer, "José Santos Zelaya," 477–78.

18   Cuadra Pasos, *Obras*, 1:437–38, 584; Huntington Wilson, *Memoirs of an Ex-Diplomat*, 196–97; Schoonover, "Imperialism in Middle America," 41–57; J. Fred

Rippy, "The Japanese in Latin America," *Inter-American Economic Affairs* 3 (Summer 1949), 50–60; Yoshinori Ohara, *Japan and Latin America* (Santa Monica, 1967), vii–viii, 1–4; Joseph O. Baylen, "American Intervention in Nicaragua, 1909–1933," *Southwestern Social Science Quarterly* 35 (Sept. 1954), 150; Langley, *The Banana Wars*, 56, 65; Ernst Daenell, *Das Ringen der Weltmächte um Mittel- und Südamerika* (Berlin, 1919), 25–27.

19   Millett, *Guardians of the Dynasty*, 20–24; Millett, "Historical Setting," 15–19.

20   Merry to Root, April 17, 1906, DD, CA: 74 (M 219/r 94) .

21   Merry to Root, Feb. 28, 1907, AmLeg. CR, Desp. 1905–07; Fernando Figueroa to Luis Anderson, April 27, 1907, MRE, caja 171, AN, CR; Merry to Root, June 18, 1907, AmLeg. CR, Desp. 1907–10; Stansifer, "José Santos Zelaya," 478.

22   Merry to Root, Dec. 20, 1907, AmLeg. CR, Desp. 1905–07; John H. Gregory to Sec. St., Feb. 6, 1909, AmLeg. Nic., Desp. 1908–09.

23   Alfred Vagts, *Deutschland und die Vereinigten Staaten in der Weltpolitik* (2 vols.; New York, 1935); Herwig, *Politics of Frustration*, 67–109; Robert Freeman Smith, "Latin America, the United States, and the European Powers, 1830–1930," in Leslie Bethell, ed., *The Cambridge History of Latin America* (5 vols.; Cambridge, 1982–86), 5:98–99; Cuadra Pasos, *Obras*, 1:217, 437–38, 584; Thomas A. Bailey, "Interest in a Nicaragua Canal, 1903–1931," *Hispanic American Historical Review* 16 (Feb. 1936), 2–10; Schoonover, "Germany in Central America," 33–59; Challet to MAE, Feb. 4, 1896, CP 1918, Nic., Politique intérieure, N.S. 1, AMAE, Paris; Paul Poncelet to Alvensleben, June 21, 1898, 09.01, Nr. 12489, Bundesarchiv, Potsdam; Pourtalès-Gorgier to MAE, March 24, 1920, CP 1918, Guat., Politique extérieure, N.S. 5, AMAE, Paris; Behneke to Emperor William, May 18, 1905, RM5/v. 5402, May 18, 1905, RM5/v. 5412, Bundesarchiv, Militärarchiv, Freiburg; J. Fabres to MAE, Jan. 21, 1912, CP 1918, Pan., Canal de Panama VI, AMAE, Paris; Chamorro, *El Último Caudillo*, 248. See also RG 165, Military Intelligence Department, file 1766-R-3/6.

24   Friedrich August to von Bülow, Dec. 22, 1905, A. 3. C. 1., Nr. 104, Staatsarchiv, Bremen; Langley, *Banana Wars*, 20–22; Huntington Wilson, *Memoirs of an Ex-Diplomat*, 196–97.

25   Philip Brown to Root, Oct. 3, 1906, May 15, 1907, AmLeg. Guat., Desp. 1907–08; Calvo to Luis Anderson, Sept. 1, 5, 11, 1907, MRE, caja 174, AN, CR; Manuel García Jove to MAE, July 14, 1908, April 17, 1909, H1609, AMAE, Madrid; Walter V. and Marie V. Scholes, *The Foreign Policies of the Taft Administration* (Columbia, Mo., 1970), 38, 48.

26   Merry to Root, Feb. 2, 1907, AmLeg. CR, Desp. 1905–07. The Weil case involved a North American businessman who collected Nicaraguan government revenues under license. He collected in silver, but insisted in paying the Nicaraguan government in depreciated paper.

27   John Gardner Coolidge to Sec. St., Nov. 10, 12, 15, 1908, AmLeg. Nic., Desp., 1908–09.

28   R. Lulio, "The Granada Conspiracy," *La Tarde* (Managua, Nic.), Dec. 1908, translated copy in AmLeg. Hond., Desp. 1908.

29   Coolidge to Sec. St., Nov. 19, 1908, José de Olivares to Asst. Sec. St., April 1, 1909, AmLeg. Nic., Desp., 1908–09; Henry Percival Dodge to Sec. St., Dec. 19, 1908, AmLeg. Hond., Desp. 1908; Knox to Nicaraguan chargé, Dec. 4, 1909, enclosed with Sands to AmLeg. Hond., Dec. 5, 1909, AmLeg. Hond., Instr. 1908–10; Munro, *Intervention and Dollar Diplomacy*, 160–61; Dozier, *Nicaragua's Mosquito Shore*, 181–86; Perkins, *Constraints of Empire*, 24–25.

30 Morales, *Historia de Nicaragua*, 278–79; Olivares to Asst. Sec. St., April 6, 1909, AmLeg. Nic., Desp. 1908–1909; García Jove to MAE, April 17, 1909, H1609, AMAE, Madrid; Scholes, *Foreign Policies of Taft*, 49–50; Cuadra Chamorro, *Tratado Chamorro-Bryan*, 23; Harold Norman Denny, *Dollars for Bullets* (New York, 1929), 34–37; A. Selva, *Lodo y ceniza*, 66–68; Daenell, *Das Ringen um Mittel- und Südamerika*, 25–27; Bailey, "Interest in a Nicaragua Canal, 1903–1931," 2–3, but note Bailey's reservation, 12. A. Selva quoted from Zelaya's instructions to Corea, which he found in the Nicaraguan Archivo Nacional. Denny quotes the same document, quite possibly a translation of Selva's version rather than the original. Unfortunately that archive was destroyed in the 1931 fire and earthquake. See also Johann Heinrich Bernsdorff to B. von Bülow, Jan. 7, 1909, IA, Columbien I, vol. 23, Rabe to von Bülow, April 28, 1909, Panama I, vol. 7, photocopies, ca. 1910, Botschaft Madrid (Panama), Pol. Nr lg, PAAA.

31 MAE to Min. Finances, May 3, July 2, 17, Aug. 3, 1909, enclosing U.S. min. in CR to Huntington Wilson, June 19, 1909, Stephen Pichon to Min. Finances, June 3, 1909, F30 3932: folder Nic., Archive du ministère de l'économie et finance, hereafter Amef.

32 MAE to Jean Jules Jusserand, May 17, 24, June 4, 1909, Jusserand to MAE, May 22, July 1, 1909, Henry White to Pichon, May 28, 1909, Min. Finances to MAE, May 29, 1909, MAE to Min. Finances, July 2, 1909, CP 1918, Nic., Finances, Emprunts, N. S. 3, AMAE, Paris (copies in F30 3931: folder Nic., Amef); Tony Chauvin to MAE, July 28, 1909, Pierre Lefèvre-Pontalis to MAE, July 30, Aug. 26, 1909, CP 1918, Hond., Finances, N. S. 3, AMAE, Paris (copies in F30 3931: folder Hond., Amef); Chauvin to Morgan, Harjes and Company, July 31, 1909, Chauvin to Min. Finances, Aug. 3, 1909, MAE to Min. Finances, Sept. 14, 1909, F30 3931: folder Hond., Amef.

33 Robert Bacon to Merry, March 6, 1907, AmLeg. CR, Instr. 1907; Munro, *Intervention and Dollar Diplomacy*, 47–48, implied reversed roles in the exchange between the United States and Costa Rica; Hugh G. Campbell, "Mexico and Central America: The Continuity of Policy," in R. L. Woodward, ed., *Central America: Historical Perspective on the Contemporary Crisis*, 229–31; Bermann, *Under the Big Stick*, 123–50.

34 Merry to Root, Feb. 29, 1908, AmLeg. CR, Desp. 1907–10.

35 Gregory to Sec. St., Feb. 6, 1909, AmLeg. Nic., Desp. 1908–09; Merry to Heimké, June 16, 1909, AmLeg. Guat., Desp. 1909, pt. 2.

36 Merry to Sec. St., Nov. 26, 1909, AmLeg. CR, Desp. 1907–10; Merry to Sec. St., March 26, 1909, AmLeg. CR, Desp. 1910–11; Heimké to Merry, July 26, 1909, AmLeg. Guat., Desp. 1909, pt. 2.

37 Bonin to Theobold Bethmann-Hollweg, Sept. 18, 1909, IA, Costa Rica 1, Bd. 3, PAAA.

38 Ricardo Fernández Guardia to Calvo, Nov. 23, 1909, MRE, libro copiador 170, AN, CR; Fernández Guardia to Calvo, Nov. 25, 1909, MRE, libro copiador 157, AN, CR; Munro, *Intervention and Dollar Diplomacy*, 173–74, presents the case for no U.S. involvement in the Estrada revolt; Challener, *Admirals, Generals, and American Foreign Policy*, 289–99, Healy, "The Mosquito Coast, 1894–1910," present the case for U.S. assistance to Estrada; Lewis Einstein to Sec. St., Nov. 9, 1911, RG 59, Decimal files, 711.18/4, U.S. & CR (M 670/r 1). See also de Benito to MAE, Oct. 10, 1910, H1609, AMAE, Madrid.

39 Fernández Guardia to Calvo, Nov. 27, 1909, MRE, libro copiador 170, AN, CR; Calvo to Fernández Guardia, Nov. 28, 1909, MRE, caja 188, AN, CR; Munro, *Intervention and Dollar Diplomacy*, 206; Bailey, "Nicaragua Canal, 1903–1931," 6, 10.

40 Roy T. Davis to Sec. St., Oct. 31, 1924, Dana G. Munro to Andrew D. White, Nov. 19,

1924, National Archives, Record Group 59, Decimal files, 717.24 and 26, Nic. & other states (M 634/r 1).

41 Merry to Fernández Guardia, Jan. 5, 1910, MRE, caja 197, AN, CR; Benito to MAE, Oct. 10, 1910, H1609, AMAE, Madrid.

42 Fernández Guardia to Merry, Jan. 8, 1910, Calvo to Fernández Guardia, Jan. 22, Feb. 5, March 2, 1910, MRE, caja 193, AN, CR; Knox to Merry, Jan. 29, 1910, AmLeg. CR, Instr. 1910.

43 Calvo to Manuel Castro Quesada, July 8, Aug. 17, 1910, MRE, caja 193, AN, CR; Sands to Sec. St., Jan. 3, 1910, AmLeg. Guat., Desp. 1909–10; Huntington Wilson, *Memoirs of an Ex-Diplomat*, 265–66; Scholes, *Foreign Policies of Taft*, 60; García Jove to MAE, March 20, 1909, June 29, 1910, legajo H1609, AMAE, Madrid.

44 Fernández Guardia to Calvo, Jan. 22, 1910, MRE, libro copiador 157, AN, CR; Calvo to Fernández Guardia, April 8, 1910, Calvo to Castro Quesada, July 8, Aug. 17, 1910, MRE, caja 193, AN, CR.

45 German consul to von Bethmann-Hollweg, Aug. 17, 1911, IA, Costarica 1, Band 4, PAAA.

9 A U.S. Dilemma: Economic Opportunity and Anti-Americanism in El Salvador, 1901–1911

1 John C. Chasteen, "Manuel Enrique Araujo and the Failure of Reform in El Salvador, 1911–1913," *South Eastern Latin Americanist*, 27 (Sept. 1984), 1–16; LaFeber, *Inevitable Revolutions*, 31–39.

2 Curry, *Blueprint for Modern America*; van Alstyne, *The Rising American Empire*, 147–94; Prisco, *John Bartlett, Progressive Era Diplomat*, 31–62; Peterson, *Diplomat of the Americas: A Biography of William I. Buchanan*, 140–325. On the U.S. foreign policy outlook at this time, see McCormick, *China Market*; LaFeber, *The New Empire*; Wehler, *Der Aufstieg des amerikanischen Imperialismus*; R. Spottorno to MAE, Sept. 26, 1911, legajo H1729, AMAE, Madrid.

3 The best survey of El Salvador's history in the late nineteenth and early twentieth centuries is E. Bradford Burns, "The Modernization of Underdevelopment: El Salvador, 1858–1931," *Journal of Developing Areas*, 18 (1984), 293–316. A good introduction to the people and events of Salvadoran society in the 1890s and first decade of the twentieth century is Patricia A. Andrews, "Tomás Regalado and El Salvador, 1895–1906" (M.A. thesis, University of New Orleans, 1972). On Salvadoran economy, politics, and society, see Philip L. Russell, *El Salvador in Crisis* (Austin, 1984), 22–28; Liisa North, *Bitter Grounds: Roots of Revolt in El Salvador* (Toronto, 1981), 17–24; Knut Walter, "Trade and Development in an Export Economy: The Case of El Salvador, 1870–1914" (M.A. thesis, University of North Carolina, 1977), esp. 1–5, 35–37, 56–57, 95–96; R. L. Woodward, *Central America: A Nation Divided*, 171. On the ideological, political, and socioeconomic roots of El Salvador's coffee economy from 1870 to 1920, see Derek N. Kerr, "La edad de oro del café en El Salvador," *Mesoamérica*, 3 (June 1982), 1–25; Menjívar, *Acumulación originaria y desarrollo del capitalismo en El Salvador*, 25–81; Rafael Menjívar L., *Formación y lucha del proletariado industrial salvadoreño* (San Salvador, 1982), 25–48; Sonia Baires and Mario Lungo, "San Salvador (1880–1930): La lenta consolidación de la capital salvadoreña," *Anuario de estudios centroamericanos*, 7 (1981), 71–83; Eduardo Colindres, *Fundamentos económicos de la burguesía salvadoreña* (San Salvador, 1977),

24–30; Patricia A. Andrews, "El liberalismo en El Salvador a finales del siglo XIX," *Revista del pensamiento centroamericano*, 36 (July–Dec. 1981), 89–93; Mario Flores Macal, *Origen, desarrollo y crisis de las formas de dominación en El Salvador* (San José, Costa Rica, 1983), 58–75; David Browning, *El Salvador: Landscape and Society* (Oxford, Eng., 1971), 222–25.

4   William A. Williams, "The Frontier Thesis and American Foreign Policy," *Pacific Historical Review*, 24 (Nov. 1955), 379–95; Williams, *The Tragedy of American Diplomacy*, esp. 1–16; McCormick, *China Market*; LaFeber, *New Empire*; Wehler, *Der Aufstieg des amerikanischen Imperialismus*; R. L. Woodward, *Central America*.

5   Chasteen, "Araujo and Reform in El Salvador," 1–16; Tommy Sue Montgomery, *Revolution in El Salvador: Origins and Evolution* (Boulder, Colo., 1982), 42–48; Vidal, *Nociones de historia de Centro América*, 349–60; Alastair White, *El Salvador* (New York, 1973), 86–93; LaFeber, *Inevitable Revolutions*; R. L. Woodward, *Central America*.

6   Bermann, *Under the Big Stick*, chap. 9; Thomas Karnes, *The Failure of Union: Central America, 1824–1975* (Rev. ed.; Tempe, Ariz., 1975), 183–88; R. L. Woodward, *Central America*, 191–92; LaFeber, *Inevitable Revolutions*, 39–41; Salvador Mendienta, *La enfermedad de Centro América* (3 vols.; Barcelona, 1934), 3:318–19.

7   John H. Gregory to Sec. of St., March 10, 1908, AmLeg. Salv., Desp. 1908; David Alejandro Luna, *Manual de historia económica de El Salvador* (San Salvador, 1971), 217–18; R. Spottorno to MRE, Sept. 26, 1911, Jan. 3, 1912, Feb. 27, 1913, legajo H1729, AMRE, Madrid. The Moisant family remains influential in contemporary El Salvador's political economy.

8   John Jenkins to Ass. Sec. of St., Nov. 22, 1905, CD, San Salv.: 10 (T 237/r 10); Leslie Combs to Root, May 21, 1906, DD, CA: 53 (M 219/r 72); Fernando Figueroa to Luis Anderson, April 27, 1907, MRE, caja 171, AN, CR; Andrews, "Tomás Regalado and El Salvador," 61–69, 88–89; Luna, *Historia económica de El Salvador*, 217–18.

9   Figueroa to Anderson, April 27, 1907, MRE, caja 171, AN, CR.

10   Merry to Root, April 7, 1907, AmLeg. CR, Desp. 1907–10; Sands, *Our Jungle Diplomacy*, 79.

11   George H. Murphy to Sec. of St. May 16, 1907, AmLeg. CR, Desp. 1907–10.

12   Merry to Root, June 1, 1907, AmLeg. CR, Desp. 1907–10.

13   Merry to Root, June 18, 1907, AmLeg. CR, Desp. 1907–10.

14   Merry to Heimké, June 16, 1909, AmLeg. Guat., Desp. 1909, pt. 2; R. L. Woodward, *Central America*, 166–72.

15   Heimké to Sec. of St. Nov. 9, 1909, AmLeg. Salv., Desp. 1909; Heimké to Sec. of St., Jan. 21, 30, 31, April 7, 1910, AmLeg. Salv., Desp. 1910.

16   Gregory to Sec. of St., March 24, April 7, 1908, AmLeg. Salv., Desp. 1908; Root to Dodge, May 5, 1908, AmLeg. Salv., Instr. 1908.

17   Gregory to Sec. of St., April 7, 1908, Dodge to Sec. of St., Sept. 23 and 28, 1908, AmLeg. Salv., Desp. 1908; Root to Dodge, May 5, 1908, AmLeg. Salv., Instr. 1908; Chasteen, "Araujo and El Salvador"; Bermann, *Under the Big Stick*, 138–40; Cuadra Pasos, *Obras* 1:218–19; Morales, *De la historia de Nicaragua de 1889–1913*, 270–75; "The First Case before the Central American Court of Justice," *American Journal of International Law*, 2 (1908), 835–41; "The First Decision of the Central American Court of Justice," ibid., 3 (1909), 434–36; Juan del Castillo, *The People of the United States Not Liable for the Acts and Doings of President Taft and Secretary Knox* (N.p., [1913?]), 13–20.

18 Bacon to Dodge, May 1, 1908, AmLeg. Salv., Instr. 1908; Dodge to Sec. of St., Feb. 13, 1909, AmLeg. Salv., Desp. 1908; Walter, "Trade and Development in El Salvador," 72–86; Schoonover, "Imperialism in Middle America, 41–58.

19 Arthur Hugh Frazier to Sec. of St., March 31, 1909, AmLeg. Salv., Desp. 1909; Knox to Frazier, April 5, 1909, Adee to Frazier, Aug. 24, 1909, AmLeg. Salv., Instr. 1909; Luna, *Historia económica de El Salvador*, 226–27; Flores Macal, *Origen de dominación en El Salvador*, 68.

20 Frazier to Sec. of St. April 7, 1909, AmLeg. Salv., Desp. 1909; LaFeber, *Inevitable Revolutions*, 34–41; R. L. Woodward, *Central America*, 179–87.

21 Frazier to Sec. of St., April 7, 1909, AmLeg. Salv., Desp. 1909; Knox to Heimké, Nov. 12, 1909, AmLeg. Salv., Instr. 1909; Burns, "Modernization of El Salvador," 306; Chasteen, "Araujo and El Salvador," 7–8; Scholes, *The Foreign Policies of the Taft Administration*, 75.

22 Heimké to Sec. of St., March 23, 1910, AmLeg. Salv., Desp. 1910.

23 Heimké to Sec. of St., Jan. 12, 1911, Record Group 59, Decimal files, 711.16/4, U.S. & El Salv. (M 659/r 1), National Archives; Chasteen, "Araujo and El Salvador," 10–11; Flores Macal, *Origen de dominación en El Salvador*, 69.

24 Wiebe, *The Search for Order, 1877–1920*; Gardner, "A Progressive Foreign Policy, 1900–1921," 203–51; Leuchtenberg, "Progressivism and Imperialism," 483–504; Burns, "Modernization of El Salvador," 297–306; Auguste Jean Marc Fabre to MAE, Dec. 30, 1911, Feb. 4, 1912, Correspondence Politique to 1918, Salvador, Politique intérieure, Nouveau série 1, AMAE, Paris.

25 Fabre to MAE, Dec. 30, 1911, Feb. 4, 1912, CP to 1918, Salv., Pol. int., N. S. 1, AMAE, Paris; Chasteen, "Failure of Reform in El Salvador," 1–16.

26 García Jove to MAE, June 29, 1910, legajo H1609, AMAE, Madrid; Fabre to MAE, Dec. 29, 1912, CP to 1918, San Salv., Pol. extérieure, N. S. 3, AMAE, Paris; LaFeber, *Inevitable Revolutions*, 46–49; R. L. Woodward, *Central America*, 172, 186–87, 191–94.

27 Frank Gerome, "Secretary of State Philander C. Knox and His Good Will Tour of Central America, 1912," *SECOLAS Annals* 8 (1977), 72–83, quoting the Salvadoran chief-of-staff on page 78.

28 Spottorno to MAE, Jan. 3, 1912, legajo H1729, AMAE, Madrid.

Appendix: Historiographical Excursion into
Southern International History

1 Thomas, *The Confederate Nation*, 167–89, and Vandiver, "Jefferson Davis and Confederate Strategy," 19–32, are examples of passive acknowledgment of world forces which are subordinated to Confederate history, especially its military history.

2 Wallerstein, "The Rise and Future Demise of the World Capitalist System"; Hopkins and Wallerstein, eds., *World-Systems Analysis*; Chase-Dunn, "Core-Periphery Relations: The Effects of Core Competition"; Owsley, *King Cotton Diplomacy*; Warren, "The King Cotton Theory"; Steven Hahn, "Class and State in Postemancipation Societies: Southern Planters in Comparative Perspective," *American Historical Review* 95 (Feb. 1990), 75–98.

3 Beringer, Hattaway, Jones, and Still, *Why the South Lost the Civil War*; Jones, *Confederate Strategy from Shiloh to Vicksburg*, 16–32, and Coulter, *The Confederate States of America*, 19, argue that the Confederacy had no grand strategy other

than the defense of territory and ending the blockade. This is a fairly common perspective, often with minor variations. See also Charles W. Ramsdell, *Behind the Lines in the Southern Confederacy* (Baton Rouge, 1944), 83–122, Robert C. Black, III, "Thoughts on the Confederacy," in Donald Sheehan and Harold C. Syrett, eds., *Essays in American Historiography: Papers Presented in Honor of Allan Nevins* (New York, 1960), 20–36. The old argument that the Confederacy (and the southern states) defended race relations is without much merit. The blacks were brought to the New World as a labor force, to allow extensive social and personal accumulation; racial and social relations were and remained subordinate considerations.

4　Wallerstein, "The Rise and Future Demise of the World Capitalist System"; Hopkins and Wallerstein, eds., *World-Systems Analysis.*

5　Beard, *The Industrial Revolution*; Williams, *The Contours of American History*; Craven, "Background Forces and the Civil War," 17–18; Raimundo Luraghi, "The Civil War and the Modernization of American Society: Social Structure and Industrial Revolution in the Old South before and during the War," *Civil War History* 18 (Sept. 1972), 230–50; Luraghi, *The Rise and Fall of the Plantation South,* 146–52; Woodman, *King Cotton and His Retainers,* 141–95; Wiebe, *The Search for Order.*

6　Thomas, *Confederate Nation,* 176; Parrish, *The American Civil War,* 398–401; Wright, *The Political Economy of the Cotton South,* xii, 7–8, 92–98. See Jane Jacobs, *Cities and the Wealth of Nations* (New York, 1984), on the relationship of political and economic independence.

7　Lebergott, "Why the South Lost: Commercial Purpose in the Confederacy," 73. Wilfred Buck Yearns, *The Confederate Congress* (Athens, Ga., 1960), argues that there was an extensive shift in Confederate agriculture to food production.

8　Beringer, Hattaway, Jones, and Still, *Why the South Lost the Civil War,* x, 3, 59, 64–66, 425, 438–42.

9　Emory Thomas unconvincingly argues for Southern planters' creating an urban-industrial state, in "Reckoning with Rebels," in Harry P. Owens and James J. Cooke, eds., *The Old South in the Crucible of War* (Jackson, 1983), 9–12; Sutcliffe, "Imperialism and Industrialization in the Third World."

10　Beringer, Hattaway, Jones, and Still, *Why the South Lost the Civil War,* x, 3, 59, 64–66, 425, 438–42; Herman Hattaway and Archer Jones, *How the North Won: A Military History of the Civil War* (Urbana, 1983), ix–x, 701–2; John Quincy Adams to John Adams, August 1, 1816, in Walter LaFeber, ed., *John Quincy Adams and American Continental Empire* (Chicago, 1965), 140.

11　Lebergott, "Why the South Lost," 58–74; Paul D. Escott, *After Secession: Jefferson Davis and the Failure of Confederate Nationalism* (Baton Rouge, 1978), xii, 256–74; Paul Escott, "The Failure of Confederate Nationalism: The Old South's Class System in the Crucible of War," in Owens and Cooke, eds., *The Old South in the Crucible of War,* 15–28; Beringer, Hattaway, Jones, and Still, *Why the South Lost the Civil War*; Jack P. Maddex, Jr., "Pollard's *The Lost Cause Regained:* A Mask for Southern Accommodation," *Journal of Southern History* 40 (Nov. 1974), 595–612.

Sources

A. Archives and manuscript collections

COSTA RICA

Archivos Nacionales, San José
Congreso
Ministerio de Fomento
Relaciones Exteriores
cajas numbers 1–233
libros copiadores

FRANCE

Archive de l'armée de la mer, Paris
Séries: BB⁴, BB⁷, and BB⁸
Archive de l'armée de la terre, Paris
2eme Bureau, Attachés militaires
Archive du Ministère de l'économie et des finances, Paris
Séries: B and F³⁰
Archives Nationales, Paris
Fonds de la Marine, Séries moderne: BB³, BB⁴, GG²42
Fonds du Ministère de Commerce: F⁷, F¹², F²³
Archive du Ministère des affaires étrangères, Paris
Correspondence consulaire et commerciale (C. C. C.), 1793–1901: Colón; Guatemala; Panama; San José de Costa Rica; San Salvador
Correspondence politique (C. P.) à 1871: Amérique Centrale
Correspondence politique (C. P.), 1871 à 1896: Amérique Centrale; Amérique Latine; Costa Rica; Guatemala; Honduras; Nicaragua; Panama; San Salvador
Correspondence politique et commerciale (C. P.), 1897–1918 (Nouvelle série): Amérique Centrale; Amérique latine; Costa Rica; Guatemala; Honduras; Nicaragua; Panama; Salvador
Mémoires et Documents (M. D.): Amérique; Espagne; États-Unis; Mexique
Négotiations commerciales: Centre-Amérique

GERMAN FEDERAL REPUBLIC

Bayerisches Hauptstaatsarchiv, Abteilung II, Munich
Bayerische Gesandtschaft: London, Paris
Ministerium des Äussern

Bundesarchiv, Militärarchiv, Freiburg
  Reichsmarine: RM 3, RM 5, RM 6, RM 20, MSg
Bundesarchiv, Koblenz
  Deutsches Auslandsinstitut (R 57)
  Auswärtiges Amt (R 85)
  Reichskanzlerei (R 43)
Bundesarchiv, Merseburg (former Deutsches Zentralarchiv
  Abteilung I, Auswärtiges Amt
  Abteilung, II, Auswärtiges Amt
  Rep. 76, Ministerium für Wissenschaft, Kunst und Volksbildung
  Rep. 77, Ministerium des Innern
  Rep. 81, Zentral-Amerika
  Rep. 89, Geheimes Civilkabinett
  Rep. 120, Ministerium für Handel und Gewerbe
Bundesarchiv, Potsdam (former Deutsches Zentralarchiv)
  Auswärtiges Amt (09.01)
  Reichskanzleramt (14.01)
Geheimes Staatsarchiv Preussischer Kulturbesitz, Berlin
  I Hauptabteilung
    Preussisches Justizministerium (Rep. 84a)
    Preussisches Staatsministerium (Rep. 90)
  III Hauptabteilung
    Auswärtiges Amt
Generallandesarchiv, Karlsruhe
Handelskammerarchiv, Bremen
  Hp II: Costa Rica; Guatemala; Honduras; Nicaragua; Panama; San Salvador
Politisches Archiv des Auswärtigen Amts, Bonn
  Abteilung IA: Amerika Generalia; Columbien; Costarica; Guatemala; Handel; Honduras; Mexiko; Nicaragua; Panama; San Salvador; Spanien
  Abteilung IC: Vereinigte Staaten von Nord-Amerika 1
  Abteilung II: Wirtschaft—Frankreich/Costa Rica
  Politische Abteilung III: Costa Rica; Guatemala; Honduras; Mittel-Amerika; Nicaragua; Panama; San Salvador
Staatsarchiv, Bremen
  Gesandtschaften
  Handelskommission des Senats
  Senatsakten
  Senatskommission für Reichs- und auswärtige Angelegenheiten
Staatsarchiv, Hamburg
  Deputation für Handel, Schiffahrt und Gewerbe
  Hanseatische Gesandtschaften: Berlin; Washington
  Senatsakten
  Senatskommission für Reichs- und auswärtige Angelegenheiten
  Spezialakten

GREAT BRITAIN

Public Record Office, London
  Foreign Office (FO): FO 15 (Costa Rica); FO 21 (Central America–Guatemala); FO 39 (Honduras); FO 53 (Mosquito Coast); FO 56 (Nicaragua); FO 66 (San Salvador)

GUATEMALA

Archivo General de Centro América, Guatemala City
  Ministerio de Relaciones Exteriores

HONDURAS

Archivo del Ministerio de Relaciones Exteriores, Palacio Legislativo, Tegucigalpa
  unnumbered bound volumes of correspondence
  libros copiadores
  loose correspondence
Archivo Nacional, Tegucigalpa
  loose and bound material, all ministries, unmarked
  Ministerio de Relaciones Exteriores, 1880–1890

SPAIN

Archivo del ministerio de asuntos extranjeros, Madrid
  legajos: Costa Rica; El Salvador; Guatemala; Honduras; Nicaragua

UNITED STATES

Cornell University, Olin Library, Ithaca, N.Y.
  John M. Dow papers
Huntington Library, San Marino, California
  U.S. Grant papers
  Pacific Mail Steamship Company records
  Frederick J. Turner collection
Library of Congress, Washington, D.C.
  John Bassett Moore papers
  Ephraim George Squier papers
  Records of the Confederate States of America
National Archives, Washington, D.C.
  RG 43, International Conferences, Commissions, and Expositions
  RG 59, Department of State
    I. Country Series, 1776–1906
    Despatches from the U.S. Commission to Central and South America, 1884–1885
    (T-908)
    Despatches from U.S. Consuls: Amapala (T-589); Belize (T-334); Cape Gracias a
    Dios (T-538); La Ceiba (T-545); Colón (T-193); Guatemala (T-337); Managua
    (T-634); Omoa, Truxillo, and Roatán (T-477); Panamá (M-139); Port Limón (T-656);
    Puerto Cortés (T-661); San José (Costa Rica) (T-35); San José de Guatemala (T-35);
    San Juan del Norte (T-348); San Juan del Sur (T-152); San Salvador (T-237); Sonso-
    nate (T-440); Tegucigalpa (T-352); La Unión (T-395); Utila (T-701)
    Diplomatic Despatches, Central America (M-219)
    Diplomatic Despatches, Colombia (T-33)
    Diplomatic Despatches, Germany (M-44)
    Diplomatic Despatches, Panama (T-726)
    Diplomatic Instructions (M-77): All Countries; American States; Central Amer-
    ica; Panama
    Miscellaneous Documents Relating to Reciprocity Negotiations, 1848–1854,
    1884–1885; 1891–1892 (T-493)

Notes from Foreign Legations: Central America (T-34); Colombia (M-51); Costa Rica (T-799); El Salvador (T-798); Nicaragua (T-797); Panama (T-812)
Notes to Foreign Legations (M-99): Central America
II. Decimal File Series, 1910–1929
Central America and other states (M-674); Central America and the U.S. (M-673); Costa Rica and other states (M-671); Costa Rica and the U.S. (M-670); El Salvador and other states (M-660); El Salvador and the U.S. (M-659); Guatemala and other states (M-657); Guatemala and the U.S. (M-656); Honduras and the U.S. (M-648); Internal Affairs of Central America (M-672); Mexico and other states (M-315); Nicaragua and other states (M-634); Nicaragua and the U.S. (M-633); Panama and other states (M-609); Panama and the United States (M-608)
RG 84, Post Records
RG 165, War Department, General and Special Staffs
Military Intelligence Department
New Orleans Public Library, Special Collections, New Orleans
New Orleans Police Records, 1873 to 1915
Colored Index, 1900–1915
General Arrest indices
New York Public Library, Manuscripts and Archives, New York
John Bigelow papers
Guatemala Sociedad de Inmigración
Rutherford B. Hayes Library, Fremont, Ohio
Richard W. Thompson papers
Stanford University, Special Collections, Stanford, California
Francis B. Loomis papers
Pacific Improvement Company
Edward L. Plumb papers
University of California, Bancroft Collection, Berkeley
Ferrocarril de Salvador Letterbook
Guatemalan Biographical Sketches
Biography of William Lawrence Merry Typescript
Alfred K. Moe papers
Henry F. W. Nanne Memoir
University of California, Research Library, Los Angeles
Daniel Ammen papers
University of North Carolina, Southern Historical Collection, Chapel Hill
Edward P. Alexander papers
Edward Middleton papers
University of South Carolina, South Caroliniana Library, Columbia
Daniel Strobel Martin Collection
William Henry Trescott papers
Wisconsin State Historical Society, Madison
Paul S. Reinsch papers

B. Printed primary materials

I. MEMOIRS AND RECOLLECTIONS

Bülow, Bernhard Ernst von. *Deutsche Politik.* Berlin: Reimar Hobbing, 1916.

Chamorro, Emiliano. *El último caudillo: autobiografía.* Managua, Nicaragua: Union, 1983.

Cid Fernández, Enrique del, ed. *Epistolario inédito de Antonio José de Irisarri.* Guatemala: Ejército, 1966.

Cuadra Pasos, Carlos. *Obras.* 2 vols. Managua: Banco de América, 1976.

Ebray, Alcide. "Une réconciliation: L'Espagne et l'Amérique Latine." *Revue des deux mondes* (November 15, 1901), 427–53.

Fisk, George M. "German-American Diplomatic and Commercial Relations, Historically Considered." *American Monthly Review of Reviews* 25:3 (March 1902), 326.

Guzmán, Enrique. *Editoriales de la Prensa 1878.* Managua: Banco de América, 1977.

———. *Las gacetillas, 1878–1894.* Managua: Banco de América, 1975.

Hahn, Ludwig. *Fürst Bismarck: Sein politisches Leben und Wirken.* 5 vols. Berlin: Wilhelm Herz, 1881.

Huntington Wilson, Francis Mairs. *Memoirs of an Ex-Diplomat.* Boston: Bruce Humphries, 1945.

Johnson, James Weldon. *Along This Way: The Autobiography of James Weldon Johnson.* New York: Viking, 1943.

José Santos Zelaya: President of Nicaragua. New York: F. J. Dassori, 1906.

Kidd, Benjamin. *The Control of the Tropics.* New York: Macmillan, 1898.

Koch, Paul. "Aus der Zeit von Admiral v. Stosch." *Marine-Rundschau* 14 (1903), 694–96.

———. *Vierzig Jahre Schwarz-Weiss-Rot.* Berlin: E. S. Mittler und Sohn, 1908.

Loomis, Francis B. "The position of the United States on the American continent—some phases of the Monroe Doctrine." *Annals of the American Academy of Political and Social Sciences* 22 (July 1903), 1–19.

Massow, Wilhelm von, ed. *Fürst von Bülows Reden.* 5 vols. Leipzig: Philipp Reclam, 1910–15.

Meagher, J. T. "Costa Rica and Its Railroad." *Overland Monthly* 10 (1873), 160–73.

[Nicaraguan correspondence re: Eisenstück.] *Revista del Archivo General de la Nación* (Nicaragua), 2 (1967), 3–120.

Ortega Arancibia, Francisco. *Cuarenta años (1838–1878) de historia de Nicaragua.* 3rd ed.; Managua: Banco de América, 1974.

"Our Citizens Mistreated in Central America." *Literary Digest* 37 (June 12, 1909), 999–1000.

Paschen, Karl. *Aus der Werdezeit zweier Marinen.* Berlin: E. S. Mittler und Sohn, 1908.

Pougin, Edmund. *L'état de Costa Rica.* Anvers, Belgium: Kornicker, 1863.

Promemoria betreffend unsere Reklamation gegen Nicaragua in der Angelegenheit des Kaiserlichen Konsulats in Leon. Berlin: n.p., 1877.

Rivas, Anselmo H. *Memoria de Relaciones Exteriores, Justicia, Comercio i Agricultura ... 1877.* Granada, Nicaragua: Imprenta de "El Centro-Americano," 1877.

Roosevelt, Theodore. *An Autobiography.* New York: Charles Scribner's Sons, 1929.

Samver, Charles, and Jules Hopf, eds. *Nouveau recueil général de traités et autres actes relatifs aux rapports de droit international.* 2nd series. Göttingen: Dieterich, 1878.

Sands, William F. *Our Jungle Diplomacy.* Chapel Hill: University of North Carolina, 1944.

Schultz, Alfred P. *Race or Mongrel.* Boston: L. C. Page, 1908.

Selva, Adán. *Lodo y ceniza de una política que ha podrido las raíces de la nacionalidad nicaragüense.* Managua: ASEL, 1960.

Selva, Carlos. *Un poco de historia.* Guatemala: Gobierno de Guatemala, 1948.

Seward, Frederick W. *Reminiscences of a War-time Statesman and Diplomat, 1830–1915.* New York: G. P. Putnam's Sons, 1916.

Shine, William, to T. Roosevelt. *Literary Digest* 37 (June 12, 1909), 1000.

[Thompson, A. W.]. *Contract for Coal &c. at the isthmus of Chiriqui.* Washington: G. S. Gideon, [1861?].

"Twenty-one Years in Central America." *Central American Bulletin* 18:1 (January 15, 1912), 7–13.

Wells, David A. "How Shall the Nation Regain Prosperity?" *North American Review* 125 (1877), 110–32, 283–308.

Werner, B. von. *Ein deutsches Kriegsschiff in der Südsee.* Leipzig: F. A. Brockhaus, 1889.

Wilson, Hugh. *The Education of a Diplomat.* London: Longmans, Green, 1938.

Zelaya, José Santos. *La revolución de Nicaragua y los Estados Unidos.* Madrid: Bernardo Rodríguez, [1910].

———. *Refutation of the Statements of President Taft.* Paris: Waltener, [1911].

2. GOVERNMENT DOCUMENTS

The City of New Orleans. The Book of the Chamber of Commerce and Industry of Louisiana. New Orleans: George W. Engelhardt, 1894.

Germany. Reichstag. *Stenographische Berichte über die Verhandlungen des Deutschen Reichs,* 3. Legislaturperiode, 1878.

Informe . . . 1868. San José, Costa Rica: Imprenta Nacional, [1868].

Informe de la sociedad de inmigración. Guatemala: El Progreso, [1878].

Louisiana. *Official Journal of the Proceedings of the [Secession] Convention of the State of Louisiana [1861].* Baton Rouge: n. p., [1862].

Quadra, Vicente. "Mensaje de señor Presidente de la República don Vicente Quadra, al Congreso de 1875." *Gaceta de Nicaragua,* January 16, 1875, pp. 25–27.

Romero, Matías. *Correspondencia de la legación mexicana en Washington durante la intervención extranjera.* 10 vols. Mexico: Imprenta del Gobierno, 1870–1892.

United Nations. *El financiamiento externo de América Latina.* New York: United Nations, 1964.

U.S. Congress. House of Representatives. *Letter from the Secretary of State, Transmitting an Annual Report upon the Commercial Relations of the United States with Foreign Nations During the Year 1876,* 44th Cong., 2nd sess., House Executive Document 45.

U.S. Department of the Navy. *Official Records of the Union and Confederate Navies in the War of the Rebellion.* 30 vols. Washington: GPO, 1894–1927.

U.S. Department of State. *A Brief History of the Relations between the United States and Nicaragua 1909–1928.* Washington: GPO, 1928.

U.S. Department of State. *Papers Relating to the Foreign Relations of the United States.* Various vols. Washington: GPO, 1861– .

U.S. Department of State. *The United States and Nicaragua: A Survey of the Relations from 1909 to 1932.* Washington: GPO, 1932.

C. Newspapers

El Bien Público (Guatemala), 1880
El Nacional (Honduras), 1874
El Quetzal (Guatemala), 1879
La República (Madrid), November 22, 1884

Revista del Archivo de la Nación (Nicaragua), 1967
San Francisco Chronicle, February 28, 1896
La Sociedad Económica (Guatemala), 1877–78
La Sociedad de Inmigración (Guatemala), nos. 1–5 (January 15 to July 31, 1879)
La Tertulia (Masaya, Nicaragua), 1878

D. Dissertations and theses

Adams, William Roger. "Strategy, Diplomacy, and Isthmian Canal Security, 1880–1917." Ph.D. diss., Florida State University, 1974.

Andrews, Patricia A. "Tomás Regalado and El Salvador, 1895–1906." M.A. thesis, University of New Orleans, 1972.

Beck, William A. "American Policy in Guatemala, 1839–1900." Ph.D. diss., Ohio State University, 1954.

Frazier, Charles E. "The Dawn of Nationalism and Its Consequences in Nicaragua." Ph.D. diss., University of Texas, 1958.

Froneck, M. Z. "Diplomatic Relations between the United States and Costa Rica, 1823–1882." Ph.D. diss., Fordham University, 1959.

Guevara-Escudero, José Francisco. "Nineteenth Century Honduras: A Regional Approach to the Economic History of Central America, 1839–1914. Ph.D. diss., New York University, Binghamton, 1983.

Lowrie, Walter Edward. "France, the United States, and the Lesseps Panama Canal: Renewed Rivalry in the Western Hemisphere, 1879–1889." Ph.D. diss., Syracuse University, 1976.

Schmid, Lester James. "The Role of Migratory Labor in the Economic Development of Guatemala." Ph.D. diss., University of Wisconsin, 1967.

Seidel, Robert Neal. "Progressive Pan Americanism: Development and United States Policy toward South America, 1906–1931." Ph.D. diss., Cornell University, 1973.

Teplitz, Benjamin. "The Political and Economic Foundations of Modernization in Nicaragua: The Administration of José Santos Zelaya, 1893–1909." Ph.D. diss., Howard University, 1973.

Vivian, James Floyd. "The South American Commission to the Three Americas Movement: The Politics of Pan Americanism, 1884–1890." Ph.D. diss., American University, 1971.

Walter, Knut. "Trade and Development in an Export Economy: The Case of El Salvador, 1870–1914." M.A. thesis, University of North Carolina, 1977.

Winchester, Richard Carlyle. "James G. Blaine and the Ideology of American Expansionism." Ph.D. diss., University of Rochester, 1966.

E. Books and articles

Aguilar, Alonso. *Pan-Americanism from Monroe to the Present.* New York: Monthly Review, 1965.

Albers, Detlef. *Reichstag und Aussenpolitik von 1871–1879.* Berlin: Emil Ebering, 1927.

Alegría, Claribel, and D. J. Flakoll. *Nicaragua: La revolución sandinista.* Mexico: Era, 1982.

Allen, Cyril. *France in Central America: Felix Belly and the Nicaraguan Canal.* New York: Pageant, 1966.

Amin, Samir. *Unequal Development.* New York: Monthly Review, 1976.

Amin, Samir, Giovanni Arrighi, Andre Gunder Frank, and Immanuel Wallerstein. *Transforming the Revolution: Social Movements and the World-System.* New York: Monthly Review, 1990.

Andrews, Patricia A. "El liberalismo en El Salvador a finales del siglo XIX." *Revista del pensamiento centroamericano* 36 (July–December 1981), 89–93.

Arévalo Martínez, Rafael. ¡*Ecce Pericles!* San José, Costa Rica: EDUCA, 1983.

Asturias, Miguel Angel. *El Señor Presidente.* San José, Costa Rica: EDUCA, 1973.

Bach, Robert L., and Lisa A. Schraml. "Migration, Crisis and Theoretical Conflict." *International Migration Review* 16 (Summer 1982), 320–41.

Bailey, Thomas A. "Interest in a Nicaragua Canal, 1903–1931." *Hispanic American Historical Review* 16 (February 1936), 2–10.

Baires, Sonia, and Mario Lungo. "San Salvador (1880–1930): La lenta consolidación de la capital salvadoreña." *Anuario de estudios centroamericanos* 7 (1981), 71–83.

Barney, William L. "The Ambivalence of Change: From Old South to New in the Alabama Black Belt, 1850–1870." In *From the Old South to the New: Essays on the Transitional South,* edited by Walter J. Fraser, Jr., and Winfred B. Moore, Jr. Westport, Conn.: Greenwood, 1981.

———. *The Road to Secession: A New Perspective on the Old South.* New York: Praeger, 1972.

Bastert, Russell H. "Diplomatic Reversal: Frelinghuysen's Opposition to Blaine's Pan American Policy in 1882." *Mississippi Valley Historical Review* 42 (March 1956), 662–71.

———. "A New Approach to the Origins of Blaine's Pan American Policy." *Hispanic American Historical Review* 39 (August 1959), 375–412.

Baughman, James P. "Gateway to the Americas." In *The Past as Prelude: New Orleans, 1718–1968,* edited by Hodding Carter. New Orleans: Pelican House, 1968.

Baylen, Joseph O. "American Intervention in Nicaragua, 1909–1933." *Southwestern Social Science Quarterly* 35 (September 1954), 28–54.

Beale, Howard K. *Theodore Roosevelt and the Rise of America to World Power.* New York: Collier, 1956.

Beard, Charles. *The Industrial Revolution.* London: S. Sonnenschein, 1901.

Becker, William H. "American Manufacturers and Foreign Markets, 1870–1900: Business Historians and the 'New Economic Determinists.'" *Business History Review* 47 (Winter 1973), 466–81.

Beisner, Robert. *From the Old Diplomacy to the New, 1865–1900.* 2nd ed. Arlington Heights, Ill.: Harlan Davidson, 1986.

Belohlavek, John. "A Philadelphian and the Canal: The Charles Biddle Mission to Panama, 1835–1836." *Pennsylvania Magazine of History and Biography* 104 (October 1980), 450–61.

Bennett, Lerone, Jr. *The Shaping of Black America.* Chicago: Johnson, 1975.

Beringer, Richard E., Herman Hattaway, Archer Jones, and William N. Still. *Why the South Lost the Civil War.* Athens: University of Georgia Press, 1986.

Bermann, Karl. *Under the Big Stick: Nicaragua and the United States since 1848.* Boston: South End, 1986.

Biderman, Jaime. "The Development of Capitalism in Nicaragua: A Political Economic History." *Latin American Perspectives* 10 (Winter 1983), 7–32.

Bishop, Joseph B. *Theodore Roosevelt and His Times.* 2 vols. New York: Scribners, 1920.

Black, Robert C., III. "Thoughts on the Confederacy." In *Essays in American Historiography: Papers Presented in Honor of Allan Nevins*, edited by Donald Sheehan and Harold C. Syrett. New York: Columbia University Press, 1960.

Braudel, Fernand. *Civilisation matérielle, économie et capitalisme, xvᵉ–xviiiᵉ siècle.* 3 vols. Paris: Armand Colin, 1979. [Translated as *The Structures of Everyday Life, The Wheels of Commerce,* and *The Perspective of the World.* 3 vols. New York: Harper and Row, 1984.]

———. *Afterthoughts on Material Civilization and Capitalism.* Baltimore: Johns Hopkins University Press, 1977.

Brauer, Kinley J. "Gabriel García y Tassara and the American Civil War: A Spanish Perspective." *Civil War History* 21 (1975), 5–27.

Brawley, Benjamin. *A Social History of the American Negro.* New York: Macmillan, 1970.

Browning, David. *El Salvador: Landscape and Society.* Oxford: Clarendon, 1971.

Bülow, Tulio von. "Sobre el proyecto de base naval alemana en 1868." *Revista de los Archivos Nacionales* 7 (1943), 147–49.

Bulle, Konstantin. *Geschichte der Jahre 1871 bis 1877.* 2 vols. Leipzig: Duncker & Humboldt, 1878.

Burnette, O. Lawrence, Jr. "John Tyler Morgan and Expansionist Sentiment in the New South." *Alabama Review* 18 (July 1965), 163–82.

Burns, E. Bradford. "The Modernization of Underdevelopment: El Salvador, 1858–1931." *Journal of Developing Areas* 18 (April 1984), 293–316.

Burns, Richard Dean, ed. *Guide to American Foreign Relations since 1700.* Santa Barbara, Calif.: ABC-Clio, 1982.

Burton, David H. *Theodore Roosevelt.* New York: Twayne, 1972.

———. "Theodore Roosevelt: Confident Imperialist." *Review of Politics* 23 (April 1961), 358–77.

———. *Theodore Roosevelt: Confident Imperialist.* Philadelphia: University of Pennsylvania Press, 1968.

———. "Theodore Roosevelt's Social Darwinism and View on Imperialism." *Journal of the History of Ideas* 26 (January 1965), 103–18.

Callahan, James. *The Diplomatic History of the Southern Confederacy.* Springfield, Mass.: Walden, 1957.

Callcott, Wilfrid H. *The Caribbean Policy of the United States, 1910–1920.* Baltimore: Johns Hopkins University Press, 1942.

Campbell, Charles S. *The Transformation of American Foreign Relations, 1865–1900.* New York: Harper, 1976.

Campbell, Hugh G. "Mexico and Central America: The Continuity of Policy." In *Central America: Historical Perspective on the Contemporary Crisis,* edited by Ralph Lee Woodward, Jr. Westport, Conn.: Greenwood, 1988.

Cardoso, Ciro. "Central America: The Liberal Era, c. 1870–1930." In *The Cambridge History of Latin America,* edited by Leslie Bethell, 5:197–227. 5 vols. Cambridge: Cambridge University Press, 1982–1988.

Cardoso, Ciro, and Héctor Pérez Brignoli. *Centro América y la economía occidental (1520–1930).* San José: Editorial de la Universidad de Costa Rica, 1977.

Cardoso, Fernando H., and Enzo Faletto. *Dependency and Development in Latin America.* Berkeley: University of California Press, 1979.

Casey, Clifford B. "The Creation and Development of the Pan American Union." *Hispanic American Historical Review* 13 (November 1933), 437–56.

Casey Gaspar, Jeffery. "El ferrocarril al Atlántico en Costa Rica, 1871–1874." *Anuario de Estudios Centroamericanos* 2 (1976), 291–344.

Castellanos Chambranes, Julio. "Aspectos del desarrollo socio-económico y político de Guatemala 1868–1885, en base de materiales de archivos alemanes." *Política y Sociedad* 3 (January–June 1977), 7–14.

———. *Coffee and Peasants in Guatemala.* South Woodstock, Vt.: Plumsock, 1985.

———. *El imperialismo alemán en Guatemala.* Guatemala: Instituto de investigaciones económicas y sociales de la Universidad de San Carlos, 1977.

Castillo, Juan del. *The People of the United States Not Liable for the Acts and Doings of President Taft and Secretary Knox.* N. p.: n.p., [1913?].

Challener, Richard D. *Admirals, Generals, and American Foreign Policy, 1898–1914.* Princeton, N.J.: Princeton University Press, 1973.

Chambers, Henry Edward. *A History of Louisiana.* 3 vols. New York: American Historical Society, 1925.

Chase-Dunn, Christopher. "Core-Periphery Relations: The Effects of Core Competition." In *Social Change in the Capitalist World Economy,* edited by Barbara Hockey Kaplan. Beverly Hills, Calif.: Sage, 1978.

Chasteen, John C. "Manuel Enrique Araujo and the Failure of Reform in El Salvador, 1911–1913." *South Eastern Latin Americanist* 27 (September 1984), 1–16.

Chessman, G. Wallace. *Theodore Roosevelt and the Politics of Power.* Boston: Little, Brown, 1969.

Clayton, Lawrence A. "The Nicaraguan Canal in the Nineteenth Century: Prelude to American Empire in the Caribbean." *Journal of Latin American Studies* 19 (November 1987), 323–52.

Cobb, James C. "Beyond Planters and Industrialists: A New Perspective on the New South." *Journal of Southern History* 54 (February 1988), 44–68.

Colinres, Eduardo. *Fundamentos económicos de la burguesía salvadoreña.* San Salvador: Universidad Centroamericana José Simon Cañas, 1977.

Collin, Richard H. *Theodore Roosevelt, Culture, Diplomacy, and Expansion: A New View of American Expansion.* Baton Rouge: Louisiana State University Press, 1985.

———. *Theodore Roosevelt's Caribbean: The Panama Canal, the Monroe Doctrine, and the Latin American Context.* Baton Rouge: Louisiana State University Press, 1990.

Colton, Ray C. *The Civil War in the Western Territories.* Norman: University of Oklahoma Press, 1959.

Connell-Smith, Gordon. *The United States and Latin America.* New York: John Wiley, 1974.

Conniff, Michael L. *Black Labor on a White Canal: Panama, 1904–1981.* Pittsburgh: University of Pittsburgh Press, 1985.

Coolidge, Archibald Cary. *The United States as a World Power.* New York: Macmillan, 1909.

Coulter, E. Merton. *The Confederate States of America.* Baton Rouge: Louisiana State University Press, 1950.

———. *The South during Reconstruction, 1865–1877.* Baton Rouge: Louisiana State University Press, 1947.

Cox, Isaac Joslin. *Nicaragua and the United States, 1909–1927.* Boston: World Peace Foundation, 1927.

Cramer, Floyd. *Our Neighbor Nicaragua.* New York: Frederick A. Stokes, 1929.

Craven, Avery O. "Background Forces and the Civil War." In *The American Tragedy,* edited by Bernard Mayo. Hampden-Sydney, Va.: Hampden-Sydney, 1959.

Crichfield, George W. *American Supremacy: The Rise and Progress of the Latin American Republics and Their Relations to the United States*. 2 vols. New York: Bretano's, 1908.

Cuadra Chamorro, Pedro J. *Motivos sobre el Tratado Chamorro-Bryan*. Managua: Conservador Tradicionalista, 1950.

Curry, Leonard. *Blueprint for Modern America*. Nashville: Vanderbilt University Press, 1968.

Daenell, Ernst. *Das Ringen der Weltmächte um Mittel- und Südamerika*. Berlin: E. S. Mittler, 1919.

Dalzell, George W. *The Flight from the Flag: The Continuing Effect of the Civil War upon the American Carrying Trade*. Chapel Hill: University of North Carolina Press, 1940.

Dane, Hendrik. *Die wirtschaftlichen Beziehungen Deutschlands zu Mexiko und Mittelamerika im 19. Jahrhundert*. Cologne: Böhlau, 1971.

Darby, Phillip. *Three Faces of Imperialism: British and American Approaches to Asia and Africa, 1870–1970*. New Haven: Yale University Press, 1987.

Davison, Kenneth E. *The Presidency of Rutherford B. Hayes*. Westport, Conn.: Greenwood, 1972.

Degler, Carl. *Place over Time: The Continuity of Southern Distinctiveness*. Baton Rouge: Louisiana State University Press, 1977.

Denny, Harold Norman. *Dollars for Bullets*. New York: Dial, 1929.

Dobson, John M. *America's Ascent: The United States becomes a Great Power, 1880–1914*. DeKalb: Northern Illinois University Press, 1978.

Doll Gute, Fredricha, and Katherine B. Jeter. *Historical Profile: Shreveport, 1850*. Shreveport: National Society of the Colonial Dames, 1982.

Dozier, Craig. *Nicaragua's Mosquito Coast: The Years of British and American Presence*. University: University of Alabama Press, 1985.

DuVal, Miles P. *Cadiz to Cathay: The Story of the Long Diplomatic Struggle for the Panama Canal*. Stanford, Calif.: Stanford University Press, 1947.

Dyer, Brainerd. "Confederate Naval and Privateering Activities in the Pacific." *Pacific Historical Review* 3 (1934), 433–43.

Dyer, Thomas G. *Theodore Roosevelt and the Idea of Race*. Baton Rouge: Louisiana State University Press, 1980.

Eaton, Clement. *A History of the Southern Confederacy*. New York: Collier, 1954.

Escott, Paul D. *After Secession: Jefferson Davis and the Failure of Confederate Nationalism*. Baton Rouge: Louisiana State University Press, 1978.

———. "The Failure of Confederate Nationalism: The Old South's Class System in the Crucible of War." In *The Old South in the Crucible of War*, edited by Harry P. Owens and James J. Cooke. Jackson: University of Mississippi Press, 1983.

Evans, Peter B., Dietrich Rueschemeyer, and Theda Skocpol, eds. *Bringing the State Back In*. Cambridge: Cambridge University Press, 1985.

Fiebig-von Hase, Ragnhild. *Lateinamerika als Konfliktherd der deutsch-amerikanischen Beziehungen, 1890–1903*. 2 vols. Göttingen: Vandenhoeck and Ruprecht, 1986.

Fielding, John. "La diplomacía norteamericana y la reincorporación de la Mosquitia." *Boletín nicaragüense de bibliografía y documentación* 26 (November–December, 1978), 15–23.

"The First Case before the Central American Court of Justice." *American Journal of International Law* 2 (October 1908), 835–41.

"The First Decision of the Central American Court of Justice." *American Journal of International Law* 3 (April 1909), 434–36.

Fisk, George M. "German-American Diplomatic and Commercial Relations, Historically Considered." *American Monthly Review of Reviews* 25:3 (March 1902), 323–28.

Flores Macal, Mario. *Origen, desarrollo y crisis de las formas de dominación en El Salvador.* San José: Editorial de la Universidad de Costa Rica, 1983.

Foner, Eric. *Free Soil, Free Labor, Free Men.* London: Oxford, 1970.

Fortier, Alcée. *Louisiana: Comprising Sketches.* 3 vols. N.p.: Century Historical Association, 1914.

Frank, Andre Gunder. *Capitalism and Underdevelopment in Latin America.* New York: Monthly Review, 1967.

Franklin, John Hope. *From Slavery to Freedom.* 5th ed. New York: Knopf, 1980.

Frazer, Robert W. "The Ochoa Bond Negotiations of 1865–1867," *Pacific Historical Review* 11 (December 1942), 397–414.

Friedlander, Robert A. "Reassessment of Roosevelt's Role in the Panamanian Revolution of 1903." *Western Political Quarterly* 14 (June 1961), 535–43.

Froeschle, Harmut. *Die Deutschen in Lateinamerika: Schicksal und Leistung.* Tübingen: Horst Erdmann, 1979.

Fry, Joseph A. "John Tyler Morgan's Southern Expansionism." *Diplomatic History* 9 (Fall 1985), 329–46.

Gallagher, John, and Ronald Robinson. "The Imperialism of Free Trade." *Economic History Review*, 2nd series, 6 (1953), 1–15.

Gamboa G., Fransciso. *Costa Rica: Ensayo histórico.* San José, Costa Rica: Revolución, 1971.

García LaGuardia, Jorge Mario. *La reforma liberal en Guatemala.* Guatemala: EDUCA, 1972.

Gardner, Lloyd. "A Progressive Foreign Policy, 1900–1921." In *From Colony to Empire: Essays in the History of American Foreign Traditions*, edited by William A. Williams. New York: John Wiley, 1972.

Gardner, Lloyd, Walter LaFeber, and Thomas J. McCormick. *Creation of the American Empire: U.S. Diplomatic History.* Chicago: Rand McNally, 1973.

Gatewood, Willard B. *Black Americans and the White Man's Burden, 1898–1903.* Urbana: University of Illinois Press, 1975.

Gatzke, Hans W. *Germany and the United States: A "Special Relationship?"* Cambridge: Harvard University Press, 1980.

———. "The United States and Germany on the Eve of World War I." In *Deutschland in der Weltpolitik des 19. und 20. Jahrhunderts*, edited by Imanuel Geiss and Bernd Jürgen Wendt. Düsseldorf: Bertelsmann Universitätsverlag, 1974.

Geiss, Imanuel. "Sozialstruktur and imperialistische Dispositionen im zweiten deutschen Kaiserreich." In *Liberalismus und imperialistischer Staat: Der Imperialismus als Problem liberaler Parteien in Deutschland, 1890–1914*, edited by Karl Holl and Günther List. Göttingen: Vandenhoeck and Ruprecht, 1975.

Genovese, Eugene D. *The Political Economy of Slavery.* New York: Vintage, 1967.

George, Peter. *The Emergence of Industrial America: Strategic Factors in American Economic Growth since 1870.* Albany: State University of New York Press, 1982.

"George M. Williamson." *National Cyclopedia of American Biography*, 12:52. Many volumes. New York: J. T. White, 1893– .

Gerome, Frank. "Secretary of State Philander C. Knox and His Good Will Tour of Central America, 1912." *SECOLAS Annals* 8 (1977), 72–83.

Gibbs, William E. "James Weldon Johnson: A Black Perspective on 'Big Stick' Diplomacy." *Diplomatic History* 8 (Fall 1984), 329–34.

Graebner, Norman A. *Empire on the Pacific: A Study of American Continental Empire.* New York: Ronald, 1955.

Grodinsky, Julius. *Transcontinental Railroad Strategy, 1869–1893: A Study of Businessmen.* Philadelphia: University of Pennsylvania Press, 1962.

Hagan, Kenneth J. *American Gunboat Diplomacy and the Old Navy, 1877–1889.* Westport, Conn.: Greenwood, 1973.

Hahn, Steven. "Class and State in Postemancipation Societies: Southern Planters in Comparative Perspective," *American Historical Review* 95 (Feb. 1990), 75–98.

———. *The Roots of Southern Populism.* New York: Oxford University Press, 1983.

Hair, William I. *Bourbonism and Agrarian Protest: Louisiana Politics, 1877–1900.* Baton Rouge: Louisiana State University Press, 1969.

Hall, Martin Hardwick. *Sibley's New Mexico Campaign.* Austin: University of Texas Press, 1960.

Handy, Jim. *Gift of the Devil: A History of Guatemala.* Boston: South End, 1985.

Harbaugh, William H. *Power and Responsibility: The Life and Times of Theodore Roosevelt.* New York: Farrar, Straus, 1961.

Hardy, D. Clive. *The World's Industrial and Cotton Centennial Exposition.* New Orleans: Historic New Orleans Collection, 1978.

Harrison, John. "Science and Politics: Origins and Objectives of Mid-Nineteenth Century Government Expeditions to Latin America." *Hispanic American Historical Review* 35 (May 1955), 175–202.

Hattaway, Herman, and Archer Jones. *How the North Won: A Military History of the Civil War.* Urbana: University of Illinois Press, 1983.

Hays, Samuel P. *The Response to Industrialism, 1885–1914.* Chicago: University of Chicago Press, 1957.

Healy, David. "A Hinterland in Search of a Metropolis: The Mosquito Coast, 1894–1910." *International History Review* 3 (January 1981), 20–43.

———. *U.S. Expansion: The Imperialist Urge in the 1890s.* Madison: University of Wisconsin Press, 1970.

Hearden, Patrick J. *Independence and Empire: The New South's Cotton Mill Campaign, 1865–1901.* DeKalb: North Illinois University Press, 1982.

Herwig, Holger H. *Germany's Vision of Empire in Venezuela, 1871–1918.* Princeton, N.J.: Princeton University Press, 1986.

———. *Politics of Frustration: The United States in German Naval Planning, 1888–1941.* Boston: Little, Brown, 1976.

Hesseltine, William. *Confederate Leaders in the New South.* Baton Rouge: Louisiana State University Press, 1950.

Hill, Howard C. *Roosevelt and the Caribbean.* Chicago: University of Chicago Press, 1927.

Holbo, Paul. "Economics, Emotion, and Expansion: An Emerging Foreign Policy." In *The Gilded Age,* edited by H. Wayne Morgan. Syracuse, New York: Syracuse University Press, 1970.

Hopkins, Terence K., and Immanuel Wallerstein, eds. *World-Systems Analysis: Theory and Methodology.* Beverly Hills, Calif.: Sage, 1982.

Hopkins, Terence K., and Immanuel Wallerstein, eds. *Processes of the World-System.* Beverly Hills, Calif.: Sage, 1980.

Houk, Richard J. "The Development of Foreign Trade and Communication in Costa Rica to the Construction of the First Railway." *The Americas* 10 (October 1953), 197–209.

Houwald, Goëtz von. *Los alemanes en Nicaragua.* Managua: Banco de América, 1975.

Howard, James A. "New Mexico and Arizona Territories." In *The Western Territories in the Civil War*, edited by LeRoy H. Fischer. Manhattan, Kan.: Journal of the West, 1977.

Hunt, Michael H. *Ideology and U.S. Foreign Policy*. New Haven, Conn.: Yale University Press, 1987.

"In Memoriam of George Williamson [the son]." *Proceedings of the Louisiana Academy of Sciences*, 10 (1945–46), 15–17.

Israel, Jerry. *Progressivism and the Open Door: America and China, 1905–1921*. Pittsburgh: University of Pittsburgh Press, 1971.

Jackson, Joy. *New Orleans in the Gilded Age: Politics and Urban Progress, 1880–1896*. Baton Rouge: Louisiana State University Press, 1969.

Jacobs, Jane. *Cities and the Wealth of Nations*. New York: Vintage, 1984.

Jessen, Jens. "Die ökonomische Grundlage der panamerikanischen Idee." *Schmollers Jahrbuch* 52 (1928), 79–111.

Jessup, Philip C. *Elihu Root*. 2 vols. New York: Dodd, Mead, 1938.

Johnson, Dale L. "Dependence and the International System." In *Dependence and Underdevelopment: Latin America's Political Economy*, edited by James D. Cockcroft, Andre Gunder Frank, and Dale L. Johnson. Garden City, N.Y.: Anchor, 1972.

———. "On Oppressed Classes." In *Dependence and Underdevelopment: Latin America's Political Economy*, edited by James D. Cockcroft, Andre Gunder Frank, and Dale L. Johnson. Garden City, N.Y.: Anchor, 1972.

Johnson, John. "The Racial Composition of Latin American Port Cities at Independence as Seen by Foreign Travelers." *Jahrbuch für Geschichte von Staat, Wirtschaft und Gesellschaft Lateinamerikas* 23 (1986), 247–66.

Jonas, Manfred. *The United States and Germany: A Diplomatic History*. Ithaca, N.Y.: Cornell University Press, 1984.

Jones, Archer. *Confederate Strategy from Shiloh to Vicksburg*. Baton Rouge: Louisiana State University Press, 1961.

Karnes, Thomas. *The Failure of Union: Central America, 1824–1975*. Revised ed. Tempe: Arizona State University Press, 1975.

———. "Pan-Americanism." In *Encyclopedia of American Foreign Policy*, edited by Alexander DeConde, 2:730–41. 3 vols. New York: Scribner's, 1978.

Kaufmann, Burton. *Efficiency and Expansion: Foreign Trade Organization in the Wilson Administration, 1913–1921*. Westport, Conn.: Greenwood, 1974.

Kemp, Tom. *Economic Forces in French History*. London: Dennis Dobson, 1971.

Kennedy, Paul. *The Rise and Fall of the Great Powers*. New York: Random House, 1987.

Kennedy, Philip W. "Race and American Expansion in Cuba and Puerto Rico, 1895–1905." *Journal of Black Studies* 1 (March 1971), 306–15.

———. "The Racial Overtones of Imperialism as a Campaign Issue, 1900." *Mid-America* 48 (July 1966), 196–205.

Kerr, Derek N. "La edad de oro del café en El Salvador." *Mesoamérica* 3 (June 1982), 1–25.

Kimball, Warren F. *Mission, Money, and Manifest Destiny: U.S. Foreign Policy, 1901–1913*. St. Louis: Forum, 1979.

Kirkland, Edward Chase. *Industry Comes of Age: Business, Labor and Public Policy, 1860–1897*. Chicago: Quadrangle, 1967.

Kolko, Gabriel. *Main Currents in Modern American History*. New York: Harper and Row, 1976.

————. *Triumph of Conservatism: A Reinterpretation of American History, 1900–1916.* Chicago: Quadrangle, 1963.

Kuhn, Gary G. "United States Maritime Influence in Central America, 1863–1865." *American Neptune* 32 (1972), 277–86.

LaFeber, Walter. *The American Age: United States Foreign Policy Abroad since 1750.* New York: Norton, 1989.

————. "The Constitution and United States Foreign Policy: An Interpretation." *Journal of American History* 74 (December 1987), 695–717.

————. *Inevitable Revolutions: The United States in Central America.* New York: Norton, 1983.

————. *The New Empire: An Interpretation of American Expansion, 1860–1898.* Ithaca: Cornell University Press, 1963.

————. *The Panama Canal: The Crisis in Historical Perspective.* New York: Oxford University Press, 1978.

————, ed. *John Quincy Adams and American Continental Empire.* Chicago: Quadrangle, 1965.

Langley, Lester D. *The Banana Wars: An Inner History of American Empire.* Lexington: University of Kentucky Press, 1983.

————. *Struggle for the American Mediterranean: United States–European Rivalry in the Gulf-Caribbean, 1776–1904.* Athens: University of Georgia Press, 1976.

————. *The United States and the Caribbean in the Twentieth Century.* Athens: University of Georgia Press, 1980.

Lasch, Christopher. "The Anti-imperialists, the Philippines, and the Inequality of Man." *Journal of Southern History* 24 (August 1958), 319–31.

Lebergott, Stanley. "Why the South Lost: Commercial Purpose in the Confederacy, 1861–1865." *Journal of American History* 70 (June 1983), 58–74.

Leopold, Werner F. "Der Deutsche in Costa Rica." *Hamburger Wirtschaftschronik* 3 (October 1966) 147–51.

Leuchtenberg, William. "The Progressive Movement and American Foreign Policy, 1898–1916." *Mississippi Valley Historical Review* 39 (1952), 453–504.

Lévy-Leboyer, Maurice. "La croissance économique en France au xixᵉ siècle." *Annales: Economies, sociétés, civilisations* 23 (July–August 1978), 788–802.

Lewis, Lancelot S. *The West Indian in Panama: Black Labor in Panama, 1850–1914.* Washington, D.C.: University Press of America, 1980.

Long, W. Rodney. *Railways of Central America and the West Indies.* Washington, D.C.: GPO, 1925.

Luna, David Alejandro. *Manual de historia económica de El Salvador.* San Salvador: Editorial Universitaria, 1971.

Luraghi, Raimundo. "The Civil War and the Modernization of American Society: Social Structure and Industrial Revolution in the Old South before and during the War." *Civil War History* 18 (September 1972), 230–50.

————. *The Rise and Fall of the Plantation South.* New York: Franklin Watts, 1978.

McCormick, Thomas. *America's Half-Century.* Baltimore: Johns Hopkins University Press, 1990.

————. *The China Market: America's Quest for Informal Empire, 1893–1901.* Chicago: Quadrangle, 1967.

McCreery, David. "Coffee and Class: The Structure of Development in Liberal Guatemala, 1871–1885." *Hispanic American Historical Review* 61 (August 1976), 438–60.

———. *Development and the State in Reform Guatemala, 1871–1885.* Athens: Ohio State University Press, 1983.

———. "Debt Servitude in Rural Guatemala, 1876–1936." *Hispanic American Historical Review* 63 (November 1983), 735–59.

McCullough, David. *The Path between the Seas: The Creation of the Panama Canal, 1870–1914.* New York: Simon and Schuster, 1977.

NcNeill, William H. *The Rise of the West.* New York: Mentor, 1963.

McWilliams, Tennant S. "The Lure of Empire: Southern Interest in the Caribbean, 1877–1900." *Mississippi Quarterly* 29 (Winter 1975–76), 43–63.

———. *The New South Faces the World: Foreign Affairs and the Southern Sense of Self, 1877–1950.* Baton Rouge: Louisiana State University Press, 1988.

Maddex, Jack P., Jr. "Pollard's *The Lost Cause Regained:* A Mask for Southern Accommodation." *Journal of Southern History* 40 (November 1974), 595–612.

März, Josef. "Aus der Vorgeschichte der deutschen Kolonialpolitik." *Koloniale Rundschau* 26 (April–June 1934), 86–93.

Major, John. "Who Wrote the Hay–Bunau-Varilla Convention?" *Diplomatic History* 8:2 (Spring 1984), 115–24.

Marczewski, Jean. "Die 'Take-Off' Hypothese und die Erfahrung Frankreichs." In *Wirtschaft und Gesellschaft Frankreichs seit 1789,* edited by Gilbert Ziebura. Cologne: Kiepenheuer und Witsch, 1975.

Markowitz, Gerald W. "Progressives and Imperialism: A Return to First Principles." *Historian* 37 (1975), 257–75.

Marks, Frederick W., III. "Morality as a Drive Wheel in the Diplomacy of Theodore Roosevelt." *Diplomatic History* 2 (Winter 1978), 43–62.

———. *Velvet on Iron: The Diplomacy of Theodore Roosevelt.* Lincoln: University of Nebraska Press, 1979.

Marschalck, Peter. *Bevölkerungsgeschichte Deutschlands im 19. und 20. Jahrhundert.* Frankfurt: Suhrkamp, 1984.

Marshall, Ray. "The Negro in Southern Unions." In *The Negro and the American Labor Movement,* edited by Julius Jacobson. Garden City, N.Y.: Doubleday, 1968.

Mata Gavida, José. *Anotaciones de historia pátria centroamericana.* 2nd ed. Guatemala: Universidad de San Carlos, 1969.

May, Robert E. *John A. Quitman: Old South Crusader.* Baton Rouge: Louisiana State University Press, 1985.

———. "Lobbyists for Commercial Empire: Jane Cazneau, William Cazneau, and U.S. Caribbean Policy, 1846–1878." *Pacific Historical Review* 48 (August 1979), 383–412.

———. *The Southern Dream of Caribbean Empire, 1854–1861.* Baton Rouge: Louisiana State University Press, 1973.

Mazrui, Ali. "From Social Darwinism to Current Theories of Modernization: A Tradition of Analysis." *World Politics* 21 (October 1968), 69–83.

Mecham, J. Lloyd. *A Survey of United States–Latin American Relations.* Boston: Houghton Mifflin, 1965.

Meier, August, and Eliott Rudwick. *From Plantation to Ghetto.* New York: Hill and Wang, 1970.

Mellander, Gustavo Adolfo. *The United States in Panamanian Politics.* Danville, Ill.: Interstate, 1971.

Mendienta, Salvador. *La enfermedad de Centro América.* 3 vols. Barcelona: Maucci, 1934.

Menjívar L., Rafael. *Acumulación originaria y desarrollo del capitalismo en El Salvador.* San José, Costa Rica: EDUCA, 1980.

———. *Formación y lucha del proletariado industrial salvadoreño.* San Salvador: Universidad Centroamericana José Simón Cañas, 1982.

Millett, Richard L. *Guardians of the Dynasty.* Maryknoll, N.Y.: Orbis, 1977.

———. "Historical Setting." In *Nicaragua: A Country Study,* edited by James D. Rudolph. Washington, D.C.: GPO, 1982.

Miner, Dwight Carroll. *The Fight for the Panama Route.* New York: Columbia University Press, 1940.

Mörner, Magnus. *Adventurers and Proletarians: The Story of Migrants in Latin America.* Pittsburgh: University of Pittsburgh Press, 1985.

Montgomery, Tommy Sue. *Revolution in El Salvador: Origins and Evolution.* Boulder, Colo.: Westview, 1982.

Moore, James Tice. "Origins of the Solid South: Redeemer Democrats and the Popular Will, 1870–1900." *Southern Studies* 22:3 (Fall 1983), 285–301.

———. "Redeemers Reconsidered: Change and Continuity in the Democratic South, 1870–1900." *Journal of Southern History* 44 (August 1978), 357–78.

Morales, José Joaquín. *De la historia de Nicaragua de 1889–1913.* Granada, Nicaragua: Magys, 1963.

Morris, James A. *Honduras: Caudillo Politics and Military Rulers.* Boulder, Colo.: Westview, 1984.

Morrow, Rising Lake. "A Conflict between the Commercial Interests of the United States and Its Foreign Policy." *Hispanic American Historical Review* 10 (February 1930), 2–13.

Mosk, Stanford A. "The Coffee Economy of Guatemala, 1850–1918: Development and Signs of Instability." *Interamerican Economic Affairs* 9 (Winter 1955), 6–20.

Mowry, George E. *The Era of Theodore Roosevelt and the Birth of Modern America.* New York: Harper, 1958.

Müller-Link, Horst. *Industrialisierung und Aussenpolitik: Preussen-Deutschland und das Zarenreich von 1860 bis 1890.* Göttingen: Vandenhoeck und Ruprecht, 1977.

Munro, Dana G. *Intervention and Dollar Diplomacy in the Caribbean, 1900–1921.* Princeton, N.J.: Princeton University Press, 1964.

Murphy, James B. *L. Q. C. Lamar: Pragmatic Patriot.* Baton Rouge: Louisiana State University Press, 1973.

Nash, Howard, Jr. *A Naval History of the Civil War.* New York: A. S. Barnes, 1972.

Neumann, William L. *America Encounters Japan: From Perry to MacArthur.* Baltimore: Johns Hopkins University Press, 1963.

Nevins, Allan. *Frémont: Pathmarker of the West.* New York: Appleton, 1939.

———. *Frémont: The West's Greatest Adventurer.* 2 vols. New York: Appleton, 1928.

Nichols, Roy F., and Eugene H. Berwanger. *The Stakes of Power, 1845–1877.* 2nd ed. New York: Hill and Wang, 1982.

Ninkovich, Frank. "Theodore Roosevelt: Civilization as Ideology." *Diplomatic History* 10 (Summer 1986), 221–45.

North, Liisa. *Bitter Grounds: Roots of Revolt in El Salvador.* Toronto: Between the Lines, 1981.

Ohara, Yoshinori. *Japan and Latin America.* Santa Monica, Calif.: Rand, 1967.

Owsley, Frank L. *King Cotton Diplomacy: Foreign Relations of the Confederate States of America.* Chicago: University of Chicago Press, 1931.

Painter, Nell Irvin. *Exodusters: Black Migration to Kansas after Reconstruction.* New York: Knopf, 1977.

Parrish, Peter. *The American Civil War.* New York: Holmes and Meier, 1975.

Pector, Désiré. *Les richesses de l'Amérique centrale.* 2nd ed. Paris: E. Guilmoto, [1908].

———. *Regions Isthmiques de l'Amérique tropicale.* Paris: Société d'éditions géographiques, 1925.

Pérez Brignoli, Héctor. *Breve historia de Centro América.* Madrid: Alianza, 1985.

Perkins, Whitney T. *Constraints of Empire: The United States and Caribbean Intervention.* Westport, Conn.: Greenwood, 1981.

Peterson, Harold F. *Diplomat of the Americas: A Biography of William I. Buchanan (1852–1909).* Albany: State University of New York Press, 1977.

Pflanze, Otto. *Bismarck and the Development of Germany.* 3 vols. Princeton, N.J.: Princeton University Press, 1963–1990.

Pierre-Charles, Gérard. *El Caribe contemporáneo.* Mexico: Siglo XXI, 1981.

Pike, Frederick B. *Hispanismo, 1898–1936: Spanish Conservatives and Liberals and Their Relations with Spanish America.* Notre Dame, Ind.: University of Notre Dame Press, 1971.

Plesur, Milton. *America's Outward Thrust: Approaches to Foreign Affairs, 1865–1890.* DeKalb: Northern Illinois University Press, 1971.

Pletcher, David M. "Inter-American Trade in the Early 1870s—A State Department Survey." *The Americas* 33 (April 1977), 593–612.

———. "Rhetoric and Results: A Pragmatic View of American Economic Expansionism, 1865–98." *Diplomatic History* 5 (Spring 1981), 93–105.

Plummer, Brenda Gayle. *Black and White in the Caribbean: The Great Powers and Haiti, 1902–1915.* Baton Rouge: Louisiana State University Press, 1988.

Polakowsky, Helmuth. "Estación naval alemana en Costa Rica." *Revista de los Archivos Nacionales* 7 (1943), 56–65.

Portes, Alejandro, and John Walton. *Labor, Class, and the International System.* New York: Academic, 1981.

Potter, David, and Don Fehrenbacher. *The Impending Crisis: 1848–1861.* New York: Harper, 1976.

Prisco, Salvatore, III. *John Barrett, Progressive Era Diplomat: A Study of a Commercial Expansionist, 1857–1920.* University, Ala.: University of Alabama Press, 1973.

Rable, George C. "Bourbonism, Reconstruction, and the Persistence of Southern Distinctiveness." *Civil War History* 29 (June 1983), 135–53.

Ramsdell, Charles W. *Behind the Lines in the Southern Confederacy.* Baton Rouge: Louisiana State University Press, 1944.

Randall, James G., and David Donald. *The Civil War and Reconstruction.* 2nd ed. Lexington, Mass.: D. C. Heath, 1969.

Rippy, J. Fred. "French Investments in Latin America," *Interamerican Economic Affairs,* 2 (Autumn, 1948), 52–71.

———. "The Japanese in Latin America." *Inter-American Economic Affairs* 3 (Summer 1949), 50–60.

———. "A Negro Colonization Project in Mexico, 1895." *Journal of Negro History* 6 (January 1921), 66–73.

———. "Relations of the United States and Costa Rica during the Guardia Era." *Bulletin of the Pan American Union* 77:2 (February 1943), 61–66.

Roark, James L. *Masters without Slaves.* New York: Norton, 1977.

Robinson, William Morrison. *The Confederate Privateers.* New Haven: Yale University Press, 1928.

Rosenberg, Hans. *Grosse Depression und Bismarckzeit*. 2nd ed. Berlin: Walter de Gruyter, 1967.

Ross, Delmer G. "The Construction of the Interoceanic Railroad of Guatemala." *The Americas* 33 (January 1977), 430–56.

———. "Emergent Costa Rican Nationalism: Financing Railway Construction." *SECOLAS Annals* 8 (1977), 84–93.

———. *Visionaries and Swindlers: The Development of the Railways of Honduras*. Mobile: Institute for Research in Latin America, 1975.

Rubinson, Richard. "Political Transformation in Germany and the United States." In *Social Change in the Capitalist World Economy*, edited by Barbara Hockey Kaplan. Beverly Hills: Sage, 1978.

Russell, Philip L. *El Salvador in Crisis*. Austin, Tex.: Colorado River Press, 1984.

Rydell, Robert W. *All the World's a Fair: Visions of Empire at American International Expositions, 1876–1916*. Chicago: University of Chicago Press, 1984.

Salisbury, Richard V. *Costa Rica y el istmo, 1900–1934*. San José: Editorial Costa Rica, 1984.

Sandner, Gerhard. *Zentralamerika und der ferne karibische Westen: Konjunkturen, Krisen und Konflikte, 1503–1984*. Stuttgart: Franz Steiner, 1985.

Scheiner, Seth M. "President Theodore Roosevelt and the Negro, 1901–1908." *Journal of Negro History* 47 (July 1962), 169–82.

Schieps, Paul. "United States Commercial Pressures for a Nicaragua Canal in the 1890s." *The Americas* 20 (April 1964), 333–58.

Scholes, Walter V. and Marie V. *The Foreign Policies of the Taft Administration*. Columbia: University of Missouri Press, 1970.

Schoonover, Ebba, and Thomas Schoonover. "Bleeding Kansas and Spanish Cuba in 1857: A Postscript." *Kansas History* 11 (Winter 1988/89), 240–42.

Schoonover, Thomas. "Costa Rican Trade and Navigation Ties with the United States, Germany, and Europe, 1840–1885." *Jahrbuch für Geschichte von Staat, Wirtschaft und Gesellschaft Lateinamerikas* 14 (1977), 269–309.

———. *Dollars over Dominion: The Triumph of Liberalism in Mexican–United States Relations, 1861–1867*. Baton Rouge: Louisiana State University Press, 1978.

———. "Foreign Relations and Kansas in 1858." *Kansas Historical Quarterly* 42 (Winter 1976), 345–52.

———. "Germany in Central America, 1820s to 1929: An Overview." *Jahrbuch für Geschichte von Staat, Wirtschaft und Gesellschaft Lateinamerikas* 25 (1988), 33–59.

———. "Imperialism in Middle America: United States Competition with Britain, Germany, and France in Middle America, 1820s–1920s." In *Eagle against Empire: American Opposition to European Imperialism, 1914–1982*, edited by Rhodri Jeffreys-Jones. Aix-en-Provence: Université de Provence, 1983.

———. "Max Farrand's Memorandum on the U.S. Role in the Panamanian Revolution of 1903." *Diplomatic History* 12 (Fall 1988), 501–6.

———. "Metropole Rivalry in Central America, 1820s–1930: An Overview." In *Central America: Historical Perspective on the Contemporary Crisis*, edited by Ralph Lee Woodward, Jr. Westport, Conn.: Greenwood, 1988.

———. "Mexican Cotton and the American Civil War." *The Americas* 30 (April 1974), 429–47.

————. "Misconstrued Mission: Black Colonization in Mexico and Central America during the Civil War." *Pacific Historical Review* 49 (November 1980), 607–20.

————. "Prussia and the Protection of German Transit through Middle America and Trade with the Pacific Basin, 1848–1851." *Jahrbuch für Geschichte von Staat, Wirtschaft und Gesellschaft Lateinamerikas* 22 (1985), 393–422.

Schottelius, Herbert. *Mittelamerika als Schauplatz deutscher Kolonisationsversuche, 1840–1865.* Hamburg: Hans Christians, 1939.

Schröder, Hans-Jürgen. Ökonomische Aspekte der amerikanischen Aussenpolitik, 1900–1923." *Neue Politische Literatur* (July–September 1972), 298–321.

Selser, Gregorio. *Nicaragua de Walker a Somoza.* Mexico: Mex Sur, 1984.

Semmel, Bernard. *Imperialism and Social Reform, 1885–1914.* Cambridge: Cambridge University Press, 1960.

————. *The Rise of Free Trade Imperialism.* Cambridge: Cambridge University Press, 1970.

Shafer Jones, Robert. *A History of Latin America.* Lexington, Mass.: D. C. Heath, 1978.

Shenton, James P. "Imperialism and Racism." In *Essays in American Historiography: Papers Presented in Honor of Allan Nevins,* edited by Donald Sheehan and Harold C. Syrett. New York: Columbia University Press, 1960.

Shore, Laurence. *Southern Capitalists: The Ideological Leadership of an Elite, 1832–1885.* Chapel Hill: University of North Carolina Press, 1986.

Skinner, James M. *France and Panama: The Unknown Years, 1894–1908.* New York: Peter Lang, 1989.

Skocpol, Theda, ed. *Vision and Method in Historical Sociology.* Cambridge: Cambridge University Press, 1984.

Small, Melvin. "The United States and the German 'Threat' to the Hemisphere, 1905–1914." *The Americas* 28 (1972), 252–70.

Smith, Carol A. *Labor and International Capital in the Making of a Peripheral Social Formation: Economic Transformation of Guatemala, 1850–1980.* Washington, D.C.: Smithsonian Institute, 1984.

Smith, Joseph. "The Latin American Trade Commission of 1884–85." *Inter-American Economic Affairs* 24 (Spring 1971), 3–24.

Smith, Robert Freeman. "Latin America, the United States and the European Powers, 1830–1930." In *The Cambridge History of Latin America,* edited by Leslie Bethell, 5:83–119. 5 vols. Cambridge: Cambridge University Press, 1982–88.

Smith, Tony. *The Pattern of Imperialism: The United States, Great Britain, and the Late-industrializing World since 1815.* Cambridge: Cambridge University Press, 1981.

Soler, Ricaurte. *Idea y cuestión nacional latinoamericana.* Mexico: Siglo XXI, 1980.

Somers, Dale. "Black and White in New Orleans: A Study of Urban Race Relations, 1865–1900." *Journal of Southern History* 40 (February 1974), 35–42.

Spalding, Hobart A., Jr. *Organized Labor in Latin America.* New York: New York University Press, 1977.

Stansifer, Charles L. "E. George Squier and the Honduran Interoceanic Railroad Project." *Hispanic American Historical Review* 46 (1968), 1–27.

————. "José Santos Zelaya: A New Look at Nicaragua's 'Liberal' Dictator." *Revista/Review Interamericana* 7 (Fall 1977), 469–71.

Stewart, Watt. *Keith and Costa Rica: A Biographical Study of Minor Cooper Keith.* Albuquerque: University of New Mexico Press, 1964.

Stoecker, Helmuth. "Preussisch-deutsche Chinapolitik in den 1860/70er Jahren." In *Imperialismus,* edited by Hans-Ulrich Wehler. Cologne: Kiepenheuer und Witsch, 1976.

Stolberg-Wernigerode, Otto Graf zu. *Germany and the United States of America during the Era of Bismarck*. Philadelphia: Henry Janssen Foundation, 1937.

Strandmann, Hartmut Pogge von. "Domestic Origins of Germany's Colonial Expansion under Bismarck." *Past and Present* 42 (February 1969), 140–59.

Stürmer, Michael. *Die Reichsgründung: Deutscher Nationalstaat und europäisches Gleichgewicht im Zeitalter Bismarcks*. Munich: DTV, 1984.

Sutcliffe, Bob. "Imperialism and Industrialization in the Third World." In *Studies in the Theory of Imperialism*, edited by Roger Owen and Bob Sutcliffe. London: Longman, 1972.

Taylor, Joe Gray. *Louisiana Reconstructed, 1863–1877*. Baton Rouge: Louisiana State University Press, 1974.

Terrill, Tom E. *The Tariff, Politics, and American Foreign Policy, 1874–1901*. Westport, Conn.: Greenwood, 1973.

Tesdorpf, A. *Geschichte der kaiserlichen deutschen Kriegsmarine in Denkwürdigkeiten von allgemeinem Interesse*. Kiel: Lipsius und Tischer, 1889.

Thomas, Emory. *The Confederate Nation, 1861–1865*. New York: Harper, 1979.

———. "Reckoning with Rebels." In *The Old South in the Crucible of War*, edited by Harry P. Owens and James J. Cooke. Jackson: University Press of Mississippi, 1983.

Thompson, J. A. "William Appleman Williams and the 'American Empire'." *Journal of American Studies* 7 (April 1973), 91–103.

Tilly, Charles. *Big Structures, Large Processes, Huge Comparisons*. New York: Russell Sage Foundation, 1984.

Tyler, Alice Felt. *The Foreign Policy of James G. Blaine*. Minneapolis: University of Minnesota Press, 1937.

Vagts, Alfred. *Deutschland und die Vereinigten Staaten in der Weltpolitik*. 2 vols. New York: Macmillan, 1935.

———. "Hopes and Fears of an American-German War, 1870–1915, I." *Political Science Quarterly* 54:4 (December 1939), 514–35.

Van Alstyne, Richard W. *The Rising American Empire*. Chicago: Quadrangle, 1965.

Vandiver, Frank. *Basic History of the Confederacy*. New York: Nostrand, 1962.

———. "Jefferson Davis and Confederate Strategy." In *The American Tragedy*, edited by Bernard Mayo. Hampden-Sydney, Va.: Hampden-Sydney, 1959.

Vevier, Charles. "American Continentalism: An Idea of Expansion, 1845–1910." *American Historical Review* 65 (1960), 323–35.

Viallate, Achille. "Les États-Unis et le Pan-Américanisme." *Revue des deux mondes* 51 (1909), 419–45.

Vidal, Manuel. *Nociones de historia de Centro América*. 8th ed. San Salvador: Ministerio de Educación, 1969.

Vivian, James F. "The 'Taking' of the Panama Canal Zone: Myth and Reality." *Diplomatic History* 4 (Winter 1980), 95–100.

Wall, Bennett H., Joe Gray Taylor, et al. *Louisiana: A History*. Arlington Heights, Ill.: Forum, 1984.

Wallerstein, Immanuel. *Historical Capitalism*. London: Verso, 1983.

———. *The Modern World System*. 3 vols. New York: Academic Press, 1974–1988.

———. *The Politics of the World-Economy*. Cambridge: Cambridge University Press, 1984.

———. "The Rise and Future Demise of the World Capitalist System: Concepts for Comparative Analysis." *Comparative Studies in Society and History* 16 (September 1974), 387–415.

Warren, Gordon H. "The King Cotton Theory." In *Encyclopedia of American Foreign Policy*, edited by Alexander Deconde, 2:515–20. 3 vols. New York: Scribner's and Sons, 1978.

Wayne, Michael. *The Reshaping of Plantation Society: The Natchez District, 1860–1880*. Baton Rouge: Louisiana State University Press, 1983.

Wehler, Hans-Ulrich. *Der Aufstieg des amerikanischen Imperialismus: Studien zur Entwicklung des Imperium Americanum*. Göttingen: Vandenhoeck und Ruprecht, 1974.

———. *Bismarck und der Imperialismus*. Cologne: Kiepenheuer und Witsch, 1969.

———. *Grundzüge der amerikanischen Aussenpolitik: 1750–1900*. Frankfurt: Suhrkamp, 1983.

———. "Industrial Growth and Early German Imperialism." In *Studies in the Theory of Imperialism*, edited by Roger Owens and Bob Sutcliffe. London: Longman, 1972.

Weston, Rubin Francis. *Racism in U.S. Imperialism*. Columbia: University of South Carolina Press, 1972.

White, Alastair. *El Salvador*. New York: Praeger, 1973.

Widener, William C. *Henry Cabot Lodge and the Search for an American Foreign Policy*. Berkeley: University of California Press, 1980.

Wiebe, Robert. *The Search for Order, 1877–1920*. New York: Hill and Wang, 1967.

Wilkins, Mira. *The Emergence of Multinational Enterprise: American Business Abroad from the Colonial Era to 1914*. Cambridge: Harvard University Press, 1970.

Williams, William A. *The Contours of American History*. Chicago: Quadrangle, 1966.

———. "The Frontier Thesis and American Foreign Policy." *Pacific Historical Review* 24 (November 1955), 379–95.

———. *The Roots of the Modern American Empire: A Study of the Growth and Shaping of Social Consciousness in a Marketplace Society*. New York: Vintage, 1969.

———. *The Tragedy of American Diplomacy*. 2nd ed. New York: Delta, 1972.

Williamson, Joel. *The Crucible of Race: Black-White Relations in the American South since Emancipation*. New York: Oxford University Press, 1984.

Winckler, Martin. *Bismarcks Bündnispolitik und das europäische Gleichgewicht*. Stuttgart: Kohlhammer, 1964.

Wolf, Eric R. *Europe and the People without History*. Berkeley: University of California Press, 1982.

Wood, Charles H. "Equilibrium and Historical-Structural Perspectives on Migration." *International Migration Review* 16 (Summer 1982), 298–319.

Woodman, Harold D. *King Cotton and His Retainers: Financing and Marketing the Cotton Crop of the South, 1800–1925*. Lexington: University of Kentucky Press, 1968.

Woodruff, William. *The Struggle for World Power, 1500–1980*. London: Macmillan, 1981.

Woodward, C. Vann. *American Counterpoint: Slavery and Racism in the North-South Dialogue*. Boston: Little, Brown, 1976.

———. "Bourbonism in Georgia." In *Essays on the Age of Enterprise: 1870–1900*, edited by David Brody. Hinsdale, Ill.: Dryden, 1974.

———. *The Burden of Southern History*. New York: Vintage, 1961.

———. *Origins of the New South, 1877–1913*. Baton Rouge: Louisiana State University Press, 1971.

———. *The Strange Career of Jim Crow*. New York: Oxford University Press, 1957.

———. *Thinking Back: The Perils of Writing History.* Baton Rouge: Louisiana State University Press, 1986.

Woodward, Ralph Lee, Jr. *Central America: A Nation Divided.* 2nd ed. New York: Oxford University Press, 1985.

———. "Central America from Independence to c. 1870." In *The Cambridge History of Latin America,* edited by Leslie Bethell, 3:471–506. 5 vols. Cambridge: Cambridge University Press, 1982–1988.

———. "Guatemalan Cotton and the American Civil War." *Interamerican Economic Affairs* 18 (1965), 87–94.

Wright, Gavin. *Old South, New South: Revolutions in the Southern Economy since the Civil War.* New York: Basic, 1986.

———. *The Political Economy of the Cotton South.* New York: Norton, 1978.

Yearns, Wilfred Buck. *The Confederate Congress.* Athens: University of Georgia Press, 1960.

"Zelaya: The Menace of Central America." *Review of Reviews* 37 (June 1908), 496–97.

Index

Thomas Schoonover is Professor of History, University of Southwestern Louisiana and the author of *Dollars over Dominion: The Triumph of Liberalism in Mexican–United States Relations, 1861–1867.*

Library of Congress Cataloging-in-Publication Data
Schoonover, Thomas David, 1936–
The United States in Central America, 1860–1911 :
episodes of social imperialism and imperial rivalry
in the world system / Thomas Schoonover.
Includes bibliographical references and index.
ISBN 0-8223-1160-7
1. Central America—Foreign relations—United
States. 2. United States—Foreign relations—
Central America. 3. Central America—Economic
conditions. I. Title.
F1436.8.U6S36 1991
327.730728—dc20   91-12687 CIP